CHILDREN OF CAIN : VIO

DATE DUE

DE 18 '92			
MY 4'99			
MY 27'99			

CHILDREN OF CAIN

CHILDREN OF CAIN

VIOLENCE AND THE VIOLENT IN LATIN AMERICA

TINA ROSENBERG

WILLIAM MORROW AND COMPANY, INC.
New York

It is the policy of William Morrow and Company, Inc., and its imprints and affiliates, recognizing the importance of preserving what has been written, to print the books we publish on acid-free paper, and we exert our best efforts to that end.

Library of Congress Cataloging-in-Publication Data

Rosenberg, Tina.
    Children of Cain : violence and the violent in Latin America /
  Tina Rosenberg.
      p.   cm.
    ISBN 0-688-08465-6
    1. Medina, Alvaro, d. 1985. 2. Victims of terrorism—Colombia—
Medellín—Biography. 3. Judges—Colombia—Medellín—Biography.
4. Terrorism—Colombia—Medellín. 5. Narcotics dealers—Colombia—
Medellín. 6. Violence—Colombia—Medellín. I. Title.
HV6433.C6M437 1991
363.4'5'0922861—dc20
[B]   90-23863
                                              CIP

Printed in the United States of America

First Edition

1 2 3 4 5 6 7 8 9 10

BOOK DESIGN BY RUTH KOLBERT

TO
DIANA SANDLER
and the memory of
PHILIP SANDLER

ACKNOWLEDGMENTS

I must begin by thanking Michael Clark, who began it all for me. Without Michael I might have lived out my allotted years in blissful ignorance of the South's existence, more contented but infinitely poorer for it.

It was also my great good fortune to be hit by a bolt of lightning from the John D. and Catherine T. MacArthur Foundation. As it was designed to do, the phone call from Ken Hope changed my life, allowing me, among other things, to begin this book. Thanks also to the Carnegie Endowment for International Peace, especially Thomas Hughes's willingness to take a chance on me, Michael O'Hare's cheer and generosity, and Alicja Stevenson's secretarial help. Jeff Schoerner's intelligence and thoroughness as a fact-checker rescued me from several potentially embarrassing mistakes. At the Overseas Development Council I am grateful to Richard Feinberg, Ingeborg Bock, and Nani Makonnen.

Connie Roosevelt, my editor at William Morrow, single-handedly gives the lie to all the horror stories writers love to tell about their editors. I am grateful for her guiding vision of what this book should be, her toughness, her advocacy for the cause, and her uncanny ability to criticize and encourage in the same breath. Jim Landis at Morrow was a source of support and good cheer. Gail Ross, who took an interest in my work long before it seemed rational to do so, is a wonderful agent and friend.

Many friends and colleagues read drafts of chapters or the

whole book and gave me invaluable criticism. They are: Mick
Andersen, Anne-Marie Burley, Mario del Carril, Gregg
Easterbrook, Bill Finnegan, Larry Garber, José Gonzales,
Gillian Gunn, Michele Heisler, Cliff Krauss, Greg Moore,
Andy Moravcsik, Ritta Rosenberg, Paul Rosenberg, Michael
Smith, and Jon Swan.

In addition to many named in the text, I learned about
Latin America from conversations with the following people
and the book benefitted greatly as a result: Santiago Álvarez,
Steve Anderson, Humberto Burotto, Charlie Castaldi, Patti
Cohen, Tom Gjelten, Gustavo Gorriti, Chuck Lane, Doris
López, Michael Massing, Sandra Mejía, another Mike Smith,
Lucho Távara, and Alex Wilde. There are many, many people
throughout Latin America whom it would be imprudent to
thank here. Their courage in helping me makes it all the more
appreciated. This would have been a worse book without the
counsel of these friends; that it is not a better one is my fault
alone.

Finally, I am grateful for the wisdom, patience, generosity,
and love of two people: Mariela Vallejos and Rafael
Fuentealba. I will never think of Latin America without
thinking of them, and my five years there would have been
well spent even had I left with nothing more than their
friendship.

CONTENTS

INTRODUCTION
11

ONE
QUIJOTE
21

TWO
THE GOOD SAILOR
77

THREE
DIALECTIC
143

FOUR
THE LABORATORY
217

FIVE
THE TRIUMPH
271

SIX
THE PIG'S TAIL
331

SELECTED BIBLIOGRAPHY
389

INTRODUCTION

ANOTHER MASSACRE, reads the headline in *El Mundo* of Medellín, Colombia. "You can't finish reporting one massacre before another one takes place," a TV reporter says. Twenty murders a day are common in Medellín and fifty not unusual. Kidnapping has become an industry. You can rent a killer for ten dollars here; high school girls hire them to take care of romantic rivals.

I first arrived in Medellín in August 1988. It seemed to me a city from another galaxy; its inhabitants reacting in ways incomprehensible to the normal heart. How, I wondered, could people learn to live with such violence and chaos?

I learned. On my tenth day in Medellín I witnessed a murder being planned. The planning was done over coffee on the rooftop restaurant of my hotel, and sitting around the table, enjoying the breathtaking view, were two hired killers, the man buying their services (the object of the deal was his father), the ex-cop who arranged it—and I. The next day I realized that this meeting had been simply part of my reporting, part of my ordinary day. I had witnessed a murder being planned, and I had done nothing. This was exactly the type of behavior I was struggling to understand. Yet something in me had understood; after less than two weeks in the city, when put in a typical situation for many residents, I responded as they do.

To the average newspaper reader in the United States, Latin America seems overwhelmingly, numbingly violent, marked by political disappearances, repressive dictatorship, torture, death squads, and revolutions that invariably seem to bring more of the same. Before I went there, the images that I held of Latin America were of sobbing widows; bodies on the roadside; life lived to the music of gunfire. These are the pictures I formed from reading the newspaper—when I did not skip the stories on Latin America entirely. The events meant little to me because they had no human context. The names all sounded the same, the events never changed, and the people who acted in them seemed to be irrational monsters.

I moved to Latin America in 1985. I lived for two years in Managua, Nicaragua, and three in Santiago, Chile, and traveled in eleven other countries, writing articles for magazines. In most countries, I was haunted by one issue: violence. Not because all these places are like Medellín; indeed, the murder rate in Washington, D.C., where I live now, makes most of Latin America seem a sea of tranquility. ("What is it about your country?" asked Chilean friends after reading of yet another mass murder, this time a man shooting up a California McDonald's. "Is it something in your blood?")

But quantity is not the whole issue. Violence in Latin America is significant in part because so much of it is political: planned, deliberate, carried out by organized groups of society against members of other groups. It is used to make a point. It is committed by the institution entrusted with the protection of its citizens. And it is justified by large numbers of people. It is different from the purposeless, random, individual violence of the United States. It is more evil.

On my reporting trips I began to explore why people commit violence. I wanted to understand not just the details of the latest massacre or incident of torture, but the reality underlying the news: *why* there is always another massacre or incident of torture. The events by themselves explain nothing. Latins often comment that to tell the truth about Latin America, a writer must lie. The truest records of Latin American life are novels. It is only through fiction—or, second best, in true stories about people—that a writer can present not just an event but the world surrounding it that endows it with meaning.

This book attempts to illuminate violence through the true stories of people in six Latin American countries. It seeks to answer two questions: why people commit or participate in violence, and what it is about certain societies that encourages this activity. One or two main characters, each involved in a different type of political violence, serve as the anchor of each chapter. To help the reader understand their relationships to violence, I also draw on Latin American history, current events, and the stories of other people.

Much has been written about the victims of cruelty. This book, with a few exceptions, is not about the victims, but about those who make cruelty possible. Some are people who themselves have pulled a trigger; others are those who have not crossed that unsettlingly fine line and simply live in ways that allow violence to exist.

It is hard to imagine why an honest man would want to become a judge in Medellín. The forgone income opportunities are impressive. There is little chance of actually putting a criminal behind bars. It is usually a short career. But Alvaro Medina, an honest man, became a judge, and in 1984 he indicted Pablo Escobar, the head of the Medellín cocaine traffickers.

Medina, alone among the main characters in this book, is a hero. The villain in his story is his city, Medellín, which despite its glass skyscrapers and shopping malls is slipping back into the anarchy of medieval times. Medellín is the most violent city in the world not involved in an international war. Colombian society is dissolving. The state, which is large but not strong, lacks the authority to enforce its laws. One in a thousand crimes in Medellín is punished. There is no institution left to remind society of moral standards; violence becomes normal behavior.

If I don't take the case, Medina answered his wife's entreaties, "how can I ever expect a judge to be firm and honest?" Dying of Quijote, she called it. Medina felt so strongly what so many Colombians no longer can imagine: the idea—call it patriotism or naïveté—that they live in a civilized country.

This book begins with Medina's story: why so many in Colombia are willing to die of Quijote, and why Colombia, more so than any other Latin American country, demands this of its people.

In some societies, violence stems not from a lack of control but from too much: The state's reaction to breakdown is to strangle its people with order. The resulting silence is more sinister than the chaotic noise of Colombia, and it can be just as murderous. Alfredo Astiz is a captain in the Argentine navy, which prides itself on being the most civilized and gentlemanly branch of the armed services in the most cultured and European of Latin nations. Astiz is well educated, well traveled, intelligent, cultured, handsome, polite, and honest. And he is directly and personally responsible for the kidnapping of hundreds of unarmed people who then suffered unspeakable torture and vanished forever.

My first exposure to Astiz came when I saw his photo in a newspaper. He was laughing, his teeth flashing: he looked like a young President Kennedy. I set about tracking him down. En route I learned not just about Astiz but about the Dirty War that took place from 1976 to 1983, in which more than nine thousand Argentines disappeared. And I learned about the Argentine military. To them, their countrymen who were not allies in the fight against subversion were themselves subversives or their useful tools, which amounted to the same thing and merited the same punishment.

Astiz had a problem: He ran out of subversives. After the few real guerrillas were wiped out, the military had to invent them, and psychiatrists, journalists, and labor organizers disappeared into the bowels of the junta's concentration camps, never to come out.

In some places, however, the demons are quite real. Peru is home to the world's most vicious and enigmatic guerrilla group, the Shining Path, or Sendero Luminoso. Sendero breaks all the rules of guerrilla warfare: It commits brutal massacres of the very people whose hearts and minds it is trying to win over. It gets no outside support. It is radically Maoist in a time when not even Mao would be a Maoist anymore. "Only through the violence of class war will the people take power," Javier, a Senderista guerrilla, told me. "Fifty thousand people will have to die." Yet Sendero is the most successful guerrilla movement in the hemisphere; it is not just Javier and his friends who talk about Sendero taking over Peru.

I met Javier in jail in 1988; he was due for release, and he gave me his address and told me to look him up when I was again in Lima. When I returned two years later he agreed to spend a week giving me a tour of Sendero—in Lima—a closer look than any non-Peruvian journalist has ever had. I visited a Senderista "Shining Trench of Combat" inside Peru's maximum-security prison. I went to a Sendero square dance.

But the more I saw of the fanaticism of Javier and his compañeros, the less I understood how Sendero was able to grow. For that lesson I had a different teacher: Gladys, a twenty-four-year-old slum dweller with two children, dying of hunger and tuberculosis. She had never heard of Sendero Luminoso. But she was an expert on her own misery, and knew that Peru's government had never given her anything but trouble. In her situation, the idea of razing the state and starting over again would be eminently rational. She would have nothing to lose.

When I asked most Peruvians about how things were in their country, the answer was usually the same: "Terrible—a million percent inflation, garbage piling up, no jobs, no water, no electricity." At the square dance Javier introduced me to one of the compañeros, an engineering student. How are things? I said. "Great," he replied with enthusiasm. "A million percent inflation, garbage piling up, no jobs, no water, no electricity. The forces of history are really on our side."

The forces of history also have a sense of humor. How else to explain San Salvador's Fitness World, with its classes in English and walls lined with Garfield posters? The forces of history gave birth to Samuel Aguilar's beach house on the Salvadoran coast. I attended a pool party there; one of the guests had been indicted for directing a death squad and released, in the great Salvadoran legal tradition, for lack of evidence. Maids brought out tray after tray of seafood and we sat in the pool and ate. When our hands got sticky we dipped them in the water.

Roger Beltrán had brought me to the pool party. I had met Roger at another party, behind the fifteen-foot walls of a mansion in one of San Salvador's wealthiest neighborhoods. Beltrán and the rest of his friends conduct their lives behind those walls, which outline their world like the lines in a coloring book, shutting out their country's poverty and a war that has killed more than seventy thousand over the past twelve years. Their loyalty is to their class, not their country. The walls are a product of El Salvador's violence, but they are also its cause. The isolation of El Salvador's rich, their unwillingness to give up any of their privileges in exchange for social peace, has torn the country in two.

This arrangement—absolute privilege, absolute poverty—is what the Sandinista revolution tried to overturn. The revolution was an attempt to stop trying to unravel this Gordian knot and slice through it instead, replacing silence and repression with equality, dignity, freedom. Luis Carrión, scion of one of Nicaragua's wealthiest families, graduate of Phillips Exeter Academy in New Hampshire, returned to Nicaragua to fight as a Sandinista and become a Marxist Christian. He rebelled against repression of protesters, union organizers, and the political opposition, and the mistreatment of political prisoners. He was going to be a teacher in the New Nicaragua.

But when the New Nicaragua arrived, Carrión became not a teacher but a policeman, vice-minister of the interior. He watched as the revolution came under attack from the United States, as the rich sought to return to their old status of wealth and privilege, as the unenlightened, apolitical poor rejected the guidance of his sophisticated vanguard. Carrión responded to these events by repressing protesters, union organizers, and the political opposition, and by running jails in which political prisoners were mistreated. He turned, more and more, to the practices he had once fought against. The Sandinistas were more restrained than most, but Carrión's career mirrors the decay of the revolution—indeed, the decay of practically every revolution.

For 150 years, Chile was the exception to the endless circle. It was far from the wealthiest Latin country, but it had the largest middle class, highest education levels, and strongest political institutions and civic culture. It was a democracy. Everything Colombia was, Chile was not. Here, law and order ruled.

Then came General Pinochet's coup, his killing of roughly

two thousand and disappearance of another one thousand—in a country in which political killing had been unknown. Beginning in 1973, Chile became, for much of the world, the very symbol of state terror and repression.

For much of the world, that is, but not for Chileans. Jaime Pérez was a student leader and a socialist in 1973, a militant supporter of Salvador Allende, whom Pinochet overthrew. When I met him in 1986, he was once again leading protests against Pinochet. But for the first ten years of the Pinochet regime, when the human-rights violations were at their worst, Pérez slept.

When he thought about Pinochet at all in those early years, it was with gratitude. Chile was enjoying a wild economic boom. Pérez traded in his car for a new one every year. He bought three color TVs. "All I knew was that life was good," he said. "I suppose if I had allowed myself to think about it, it would have been obvious what was going on. I heard stories—but I didn't believe them."

Chileans woke up after an economic crash in 1982, and became the heroic protesters of the TV news clichés. Now that Pinochet is gone, Chile is once again in the community of successful democratic nations. But Chileans live with the disturbing reminder of their Faustian bargain with Pinochet. They glimpsed something dark within themselves. Pérez's is a cautionary tale, and one that reverberates all over the world.

These six stories illustrate for me the most important aspects of violence in Latin America. It is not my intention to present a caricature of Latin America as unrelievedly violent; obviously Latins do many things besides commit acts of cruelty. Neither, by choosing to write about a military officer in Argentina, for example, do I mean to imply that military repression is only an Argentine problem, nor that all Argentines are like Astiz. There are wonderful people in Argentina, and officers like Astiz exist all over Latin America and throughout the world. I chose to write about Astiz because he embodies the problem of military repression as well as anyone, and understanding how he thinks and why he acted as he did can help explain repression all over the world.

I chose my six countries after various reporting trips showed me that these countries were particularly symptomatic of different aspects of political violence. Some of my characters are people I met or heard about on reporting trips for magazines. Others I specifically sought out for this book. In most cases, people were eager to tell their stories, mainly because they are proud of what they have done. I repeatedly revisited the six countries over the course of two and a half years to interview more people, visit new places and collect information. Some people agreed to talk to me on the condition that I withhold their real names or details of their lives. Whenever I have changed names or details I have indicated so in the text.

Friends have asked me what it's like to spend time with torturers, guerrillas, and hit men. In truth, I found many of them likable. Javier, the Senderista guerrilla, is a funny, sarcastic kid who agonizes over the pain his choices in life have inflicted on his mother. In Argentina, while visiting an admiral who explained to me why the navy was correct to torture and kill, I noticed that the entrance hall to his elegant house was blocked by three low picnic tables covered with cheery plastic cloth. At noon each day, he explained, the children at a neighboring day-care center, which lacks a cafeteria, come to eat lunch prepared in the admiral's kitchen. Torturers are nice to their wives and children, goes an old cliché. The ones I met seemed to be.

I would have preferred them to be monsters. Coming to understand that this is not the case was disturbing—for what it taught me about these people, and ultimately, about myself. I did not want to think that many of the violent are "people like us": so civilized, so educated, so cultured, and because of that, so terrifying.

Some of those who commit or support heinous violence are functioning, successful, even admired members of their communities. One need not be pathological to do horrible things. The pathology, then, belongs to society. Interwoven throughout the stories is my attempt to answer the second question: What is it at the bottom of Latin America that allows political violence to thrive?

If I had to give just one answer, it would be: history. Most of Latin America was conquered and colonized through violence, setting up political and economic relationships based on power, not law. These relationships still exist today—indeed, in some countries they are stronger than ever.

The conquest was most brutal in the richest lands, especially those of the great Indian civilizations that offered the Spanish gold and slaves. These countries—Peru, Guatemala, Mexico—are the ones where society today is the most authoritarian and violent.

The countries that had the good fortune to be poor are today among Latin America's least violent societies; places such as Costa Rica, Uruguay, and—General Pinochet notwithstanding—Chile. These countries, like Canada, Japan, Barbados, France, and other liberal democracies, are citizenries. Their people are not merely inhabitants, but citizens. They feel part of the nation in which they live and feel bound by its rules. Law, not power, governs. The state is strong, not in the sense of being large but in that it enjoys popular legitimacy. People can bring about change by working within the system, without taking up arms.

The political culture that the conquest and colonization have bequeathed to each Latin nation has proved durable. It is very hard to change a country. Many good governments have tried. Also bad ones. Also foreign powers such as the United States and the Soviet Union. Peru, to give one example, has seen many different kinds of governments in the last twenty years: populist, a left-wing military dictatorship, conservative, social democrat. But none of them was able to impose the rule of law, or reduce Peru's political violence. These governments, and the societies they headed, were violent not because they were populist, or Marxist, or conservative, but because they were Peruvian.

As Pinochet shows, however, history is important, but it is not all-important. Current events matter. Chile before Pinochet was proud to be a society that respected law and human rights. And it is that once again, now that Pinochet is no longer president. But while he was there, he killed thousands of people. Peru, a nominal democracy, enjoys an elected civilian president, freedom of the press, a wide range of political parties, and an independent judiciary, and it is undoubtedly a much less violent place for it. Yet the Peruvian military has become the world's leader in making its own people disappear. One can only imagine what Peru would be like under dictatorship. Democracy is better. But it has not made Peru a citizenry. It is not enough.

Countries have, however, gradually changed their political culture. Every citizenry in the world was at one point not a citizenry, and contemporary Latin America is not very different from the ancient régime of Europe. History shows that countries make this transition when powerful groups recognize that their interests are served by the rule of law. Many different forms of pressure can help bring this about, both from inside and out. As I write this, for the first time in history, every country in Latin America except Cuba is currently governed by an elected civilian president. This is an important first step, and offers the possibility that Latin American nations will now press each other to move closer to citizenry.

How to accomplish this is beyond the scope of this book. I limit myself to trying to show why violence exists. The characters in this book speak Spanish, but their stories take place in all languages. It may be more common in the third world, but throughout history, seemingly civilized societies have turned to terror, often with the collaboration of otherwise good citizens— never on a larger scale than in one of the most civilized nations of Europe just fifty years ago. The people in this book can be found everywhere; *los violentos* are that way not because they are residents of Latin America, but because they are residents of this earth.

ONE

QUIJOTE

IN THE FORTY-SECOND AND LAST YEAR OF HIS LIFE, CHANCE handed Alvaro Medina, a justice of the Superior Court of Medellín, Colombia, a case that would eventually require him to indict Pablo Escobar, the most important cocaine trafficker in the world. Other judges in Medellín had faced this dilemma before. Doing nothing would make a judge rich and greatly improve his chances of living a long life. Issuing an indictment, on the other hand, would be a futile gesture, there being no chance, none at all, that there could be found police who would arrest Escobar, or witnesses who would testify, or jailers who would hold him. Since the late 1970s, when Escobar became the head of the Medellín traffickers, every judge confronted with this dilemma had made the only rational choice. Until Alvaro Medina indicted Pablo Escobar.

The case, which reached Medina in 1984, was part of a chain of events that started in 1976, cocaine's Stone Age, with the biggest cocaine bust in Medellín that year: thirty-nine pounds of the drug found in the spare tire of a truck driven by one Pablo Escobar, age twenty-seven. Escobar was a small-time hood who began his professional career by stealing gravestones, erasing the inscriptions, and reselling them at a discount. Later he became a car thief. Now he was trying something new, cocaine. Escobar went to jail for three months. In 1981, after Escobar was again at large, the two policemen who arrested him in 1976 were killed. The judge investigating the policemen's murders dropped the case after she received death threats, but it was reopened later.

After seven more judges had dropped the case, it reached Gustavo Zuluaga, a justice on Medina's court, who mounted a serious investigation. Zuluaga was repeatedly threatened, and on January 18, 1984, a man in a cab stopped Zuluaga's wife as she drove home one morning from bringing her husband to his office. He beat her with the butt of his revolver, stole her car, and pushed it off a cliff. It was this crime—the beating and intimidation of Zuluaga's wife and the destruction of her car—that Medina was investigating.

There was little unusual about the case. It was typical of the choice the judges of Colombia faced in almost all cases involving the cocaine traffickers, a choice that has become known as *plata o plomo* ("silver or lead," a bribe or a bullet). Because of *plata o plomo*, the traffickers have few concerns within the Colombian justice system. They need worry only about being extradited for trial in the United States, and their obsession with this prospect is so great that the Medellín traffickers call themselves the Extraditables. They make phone calls, send tapes, and write letters on Extraditables stationery, the letterhead of which reads, "Better a Grave in Colombia Than a Jail in the United States," with a little picture of a man in chains, his head bowed. The letters sometimes run to two or three pages, but their message is a simple one. In 1986, during one of the Colombian Supreme Court's periodic reexaminations of the extradition treaty, each justice received a letter that began, *"Hola, miserable."* The theme of the letter was that the extradition treaty was unjust, and the Extraditables would be forced to reply in kind. "Injustice breeds violence," the letter said. "We will finish off your family. We have no compassion of any kind." From 1980 to 1990 the Extraditables were presumed responsible for the murders of 300 judges and other employees of the judicial system, about 40 journalists, and more than 500 police.

The rise of the Mafia, as Colombians call the traffickers, was just the latest manifestation of several centuries' worth of violence that had incapacitated the Colombian justice system and, to a lesser extent, the whole government. It was a big circle: The Mafia took hold in Colombia because the justice system was incapable of fighting it, and that, of course, further undermined the justice system. The same situation could be seen on a larger scale in the country in general. The government was too weak to provide a way to solve problems through the legal system, so people turned to violence, which produced more breakdowns and yet more violence.

Medina hoped to break the vicious circle. His indictment of Escobar was an act of blind faith in his country's system of justice, which for all practical purposes had ceased to exist. Medina was an idealist, a man who took his children to the local army barracks to watch flag-raising ceremonies on Sunday mornings, who got misty-eyed singing the national anthem, who was putting his maid's children through school. His favorite book was *Don Quijote*. "He always said that if everyone did his duty, we would have a better world," said Luz Estela, his widow.

It was a maxim whose truth no one could doubt, but most people did not try to live by it. Why had Medina? The best explanation was that he had been reared that way. His mother, Eugenia—a small, trim, intelligent woman with short gray hair—invited me into the family home in the middle-class neighborhood of Los Laureles and seemed eager to talk about this son, who had been the second oldest of ten children. We sat in the living room. The usual pictures of Christ and the saints were noticeably absent; hard work was the religion of that household. Two of the children had gone into their father's business, a brick factory. Another was a lawyer, one an engineer, one a doctor; one had been a journalist, and one was in seminary. When the youngest brother became addicted to *basuco*—cocaine paste cigarettes—the whole family gathered to help him.

In a household of serious children Alvaro Medina had been the most serious. "When he was eight," said his mother, "I would see him falling asleep as he studied at night. I would tell him to go to sleep. He would say, 'I can't, Mom, I have to keep studying.' "

Alvaro grew up to be a stern young man. Newspaper photos showed a dark-haired man of middling height with a mustache, wearing tinted, black-rimmed glasses. Since childhood he had always wanted to be a lawyer. He became a judge at twenty-three and a Superior Court justice, one notch below the Supreme Court, at twenty-eight, one of the youngest justices in history. The following year he married Luz Estela Giraldo, a twenty-one-year-old law student who had worked as an intern in his office. When I met her, she was thirty-seven, a dignified beauty, her black hair pulled back into a bun, lipstick subdued, and finger-nails unpainted. The couple had bought a small house with a terra-cotta roof near the house in which Medina had grown up.

In Colombia it is the unusual lawyer who wants to become a judge. It was not a dangerous job in the days before cocaine, but it had other headaches. The Latin American legal system—based on the Napoleonic code—requires that judges themselves investigate crimes to determine guilt or innocence, but the state provides them with few resources. In theory they could ask the Judicial Police for help, but as Luz Estela explained, "The Judicial Police don't even have telephones." At night she and Medina drove around town to track down evidence or talk to witnesses. He, at least, had a car. Other judges take the bus.

Luz Estela is a lawyer in the luxurious new Municipal Building, administering budgets for the city of Medellín. Her office is large, with striking black furniture. "But I work for the city," she said. "Alvaro worked for a branch of the government the politicians didn't care about. They gave him basic furniture, a desk, simple chairs. The rest—bookshelves, curtains, an ash-tray—we had to bring from home."

Medina's office was in the Old National Palace. With its court-yards and layers of hallways with maroon arches and Spanish tile floors, the palace reminded me at first sight of the giant wedding-cake house etchings of Maurits Escher, in which the water always seems to flow downward yet ends up back where it starts. Garbage carpets the hallways. The walls in each office are lined with fat notebooks of handwritten case records. In faded ink they trace tortuous paths that almost always end in dismissals for lack of evidence. In each office six or eight men sit in front of manual Olivettis with keys missing, solemnly typing the judicial orders that circulate from judge to judge and produce nothing, justice flowing around and around, ending up back where it starts.

Colombia's judges have never been well paid, but with the rise of the Mafia and the cocaine dollars many have managed to find adequate compensation from other sources. If the couple's modest house and Luz Estela's current economic troubles were any indication, this was not Medina's way. His younger sister Clarita said that he had been offered millions of pesos but was proud never to have accepted a bribe. Indeed, he was shocked at the extent of the corruption around him. He often sent letters to the police, asking for new investigations and setting out details of cases he knew about. The police rarely did anything, and Medina explained their lack of response by saying that the letters must have gone astray on their way to the proper authorities. Then one day he personally handed a letter to a police official, and hours later he received an anonymous phone call; the caller read back selected parts and warned him that his efforts were earning him a death sentence. After that he stopped talking about letters getting lost in the mail.

Medina's heroes, Luz Estela said, were Rodrigo Lara Bonilla, the crusading thirty-six-year-old justice minister, and Alfonso Reyes Echandia, the president of the Supreme Court. Honest and brave men, they were leaders in Colombia's struggle to arrest and extradite the traffickers. By the end of 1985 they both would also be dead.

Reyes Echandia was killed with ten other Supreme Court justices when the army bombed the Justice Palace after the M-19 guerrillas stormed it in 1985. Many people believed the raid, which took place just before the court was due to vote on the extradition treaty, was financed by the drug traffickers.

Lara Bonilla had been killed the previous year. On April 30, 1984, two hired killers, known as *sicarios*—the word means "sycophants"—pulled up next to his car on a red motorcycle and shot him in the head with an Ingram machine pistol. The triggerman, who was sixteen, went to jail and awaited a trial. Six years later the case was still unresolved. The judge who indicted Pablo Escobar as the mastermind of the crime was killed shortly after when five *sicarios* shot him thirteen times as he sat in the back of a taxi in a traffic jam.

Medina received his Escobar case—the indictment for the intimidation of Zuluaga's wife—in the same month that Lara Bonilla was killed. If Medina had been wavering on whether to take it, the justice minister's death convinced him. "He was sick at heart about it," said Clarita, his sister. "He felt he had to do something."

Fifteen days after he took the case the threats started: letters, tape cassettes, and eight or nine phone calls a day—"Dr. Medina, we're calling from the Campo de Paz Cemetery, your grave is ready. . . . Dr. Medina, we're calling from your children's school. . . . Dr. Medina, we will send a bomb through the roof of your house." Respectful voices described, with creativity and gusto, the many possible ways that Dr. Medina could die. Some of the threats used judicial terms and were apparently written by lawyers, Luz Estela said. Others read back parts of legal opinions Medina had written over the years.

Fernando Gómez, president of the Superior Court, where Medina worked, had brought Medina onto the court and shared an office with him. He wept as he talked to me about Medina. "Every day we'd get calls with threats that his children would be kidnapped," he said. "We would change the phone number, and a few hours later the calls would start again."

Medina's family pleaded with him to quit. Juan David, a younger brother who ran the family brick factory in the green hills just outside the city, told me that he offered Medina a partnership in the prosperous business. Medina wouldn't listen.

He didn't listen to Luz Estela either. "You don't have to abandon your principles and make it a whitewash," she recalled having told him. "Just resign. Leave the country; go into private practice."

"A judge has to have a good legal reason for bowing out of a case," he said. "I don't have one. If I retire and become a lawyer, how can I ever expect a judge to be firm and honest?"

"I did all I could do to persuade him," Luz Estela told me. "Then, when he had decided, I had two choices: leave him or accept it. I accepted it."

Medina wrote to various branches of the police, requesting protection. He never received the bulletproof vest he wanted, but police intelligence assigned him a bodyguard, who came to pick him up in the morning and take him home from work. He stopped going out in the evenings. He had always been reserved, even to the point of curtness with family members; Luz Estela had often gone with the boys to family gatherings while Medina stayed home and read. Now he withdrew even more. He began to drink alone late at night in the house, listening to music.

Then, in November 1984, something changed. "It's final," he told Luz Estela. "I've been sentenced, and there's no pardon." She never knew why; but for some reason the uncertainty was suddenly gone, and this, in a strange way, lifted his spirits. "If they kill me tomorrow, at least in my last few months we'll have lived well," he told her. He began to laugh and joke with the family for the first time.

On March 8, 1985, his twenty-nine-year-old brother Diego, a journalist who worked at the Medellín newspaper *El Mundo*, was killed when his car ran off a cliff on a bad curve. The death could have been an accident, but Medina always suspected that it was a warning, his sister said. Later that month Medina, Luz Estela, and the boys went to Cartagena, a resort town on the Caribbean coast, for eight days of vacation. Medina was relaxed and happy. The family returned on a Saturday.

That Monday, for the first time since the bodyguard had been assigned, neither he nor his replacement showed up to take Medina to work. Luz Estela dropped him off downtown. At four he called her; the electricity was out in the building, and he was leaving. He went to a tailor's shop to try on two suits. Luz Estela picked him up there.

At seven o'clock two men parked a motorcycle down the street from the family's house. One walked into the front yard and stood under a tree, hidden from view from the street. Medina's son Rodrigo, nine, saw the man and opened the door. "Why are you standing there?" he asked him. The man shooed Rodrigo back into the house. A few minutes later, as Medina and Luz Estela got out of the car, the assassin shot Medina in the chest, arm, and leg. He died almost instantly. It was seven-twenty on April 8, 1985.

That night another of Medina's brothers, Carlos Hernán, a labor lawyer, received a call. "We've just killed your brother," a voice said. "If you start getting involved with that kind of case, we'll kill you, too." Luz Estela, who had seen the face of the killer—he was about twenty, she said, old for that kind of work—received the same call, along with others asking to speak to Pablo Escobar, a warning that she, too, was being watched.

Gustavo Zuluaga, the magistrate whose wife's car had been driven off the cliff, the crime Medina was investigating, was shot and killed on October 30, 1986. All charges have been dropped in the case of Zuluaga's wife. The first judge who investigated Medina's death dropped that case after his mother was beaten up. When I returned to Colombia in 1989, it was in the hands of another judge, Ricardo León Urrego, a short, bald man who laughed a lot. He showed me a stack of evidence two feet high. "I'm investigating," he said. He put his feet up on the desk and laughed some more.

"The case is making the rounds," said Luz Estela. "Nobody wants to touch it. It's too dangerous in a city where you can have someone killed for five thousand pesos." I had heard of *sicarios* who work for as little as three thousand pesos, about ten dollars. "Everyone knows who's behind the killings," said Fernando Gómez, Medina's officemate. "But to get the proof necessary for a court of law is difficult. You're lucky if the *sicarios* talk. But often they don't even know who hired them, and sometimes after a *sicario* does an important killing, he himself is killed."

Luz Estela was not angry with Medina; she had known all along what kind of man she married. She was angry at Colombia. "Nowadays most people just want to be judges if they can't do anything else—after they get fired from every other job," she said. She said that some students come out of the universities wanting to be honest judges. "In the universities people still have illusions," she said. "Everyone, at one point in his life, is a Don Quijote. Then gradually you lose your idealism and become Sancho Panza."

"Your husband never did," I said.

"Some people die of Quijote," she said.

She had been working for the city comptroller's office for a year. Before that she had worked as a lawyer administering the justice budget for Antioquia, the state whose capital is Medellín. The man who first hired her, Carlos Mauro Hoyos, had gone on to become attorney general of Colombia and a strong public backer of extradition. After her husband was killed, Luz Estela asked Mauro Hoyos for a job. "No, my child," Mauro Hoyos replied. "You've had enough troubles." On January 25, 1988, Mauro Hoyos was kidnapped on a Medellín highway; his body, punctured with multiple gunshot wounds, was found later that afternoon.

Luz Estela talked about leaving Colombia or moving to the countryside. Medellín, she said, was no place to bring up a family. "I want to raise my sons not to be such good people," she said. "I don't want them to be idealists. I want them to think of themselves more. I'm educating them to live."

But there was another possibility for Luz Estela. She was think-ing of becoming a judge. She had always wanted to become a labor judge but could not be named a judge while her husband was a justice. Labor judges in Medellín had to take cases from Urabá, a zone in which labor disputes had already produced hundreds of murders, and ruling in favor of a worker was not much safer than indicting a cocaine trafficker. She knew all about that, she said. "But the experience I have in administration would be useful. I know how common it is for workers to get cheated." She had a dreamy expression on her face. "You could do some-thing in that job," she said, "something really important."

WHEN I FIRST WENT TO MEDELLÍN IN 1988, I WAS MORE AFRAID than I had ever been in my life. The night before I arrived, I had dinner in Bogotá at the house of Tim Ross and Sarita Kendall, British journalists who had lived in Colombia for fourteen years. Tim had been covering "bang-bang," as the war correspondents call it, for a long time. Most correspondents burn out on trouble; Tim had just become addicted. I joked with Tim about my gruesome image of Medellín, fed by years of reading the headlines about drug violence and watching the evening news. There would be gunshots on the street, random knife fights, the man watching me from the shadows, phone calls warning me to mind my own business. I wanted Tim to say, "Don't worry, it's a piece of cake." Tim had seen everything. Instead, he laughed. "That sounds about right," he said. He told me with relish of the contract Pablo Escobar had put on his life. "They'll know about you the second you get to the airport in Medellín," he said.

Dinner was a slow process of getting drunk, looking at Tim's black-and-white photos of Bogotá's street children and boy pros-titutes in filthy jeans and delicate high heels, hearing stories of Tim's escape from a Bolivian prison with containers of film shoved up his rectum, and listening to his tapes of battle reports in El Salvador—"now there's machine-gun fire coming over my right shoulder . . ."—Jefferson Airplane's spooky "White Rabbit" and the Doors' dirge "The End." Under any other circumstances this would have been my idea of a good time. But I was going to Medellín the next day, and "The End" played in my head all night.

It was still buzzing "my only friend, the end" as I arrived in Medellín in a thunderstorm so violent that the plane could barely land. During the hourlong drive into the city the rain kept pushing us off the winding mountain road. Then my taxi got a flat tire. By that time I was so terrified I was certain that the Mafia had decided that shooting me in the airport was too merciful and had instead designed the flat tire, the rain, and the precarious state of the road to finish me off slowly. I reached my downtown hotel, checked in, and rushed upstairs. I shoved a chair and dresser against my door and lay down in the dark, listening to the rain, my head still full of Jim Morrison and "The End."

The next morning my fears vanished. The air was fresh from the rain. It was warm and dry, and the sun was shining. Medellín is beautiful, nestled in green mountains. I bought plastic bags filled with slices of pineapple, papaya, and mango from a sidewalk vendor and gave myself a tour of the city's center, with its mirrored skyscrapers and California-style brick shopping malls with atria.

Medellín, at least according to the people who live there, is known as Colombia's city of progress. Residents, Paisas, as they are called, sniff at Bogotá's bureaucracy and inefficiency. In the capital, according to the Paisas, people shuffle paper around. In Medellín people make things. The Paisas have long been considered the captains of Colombia's legal and illegal industries, dominating textiles, flowers, coffee, cattle, marijuana, and smuggling. Medellín's hospitals are the Latin American leaders in organ transplants. The work ethic here is almost Puritan. Paisas are considered efficient, punctual, friendly, and, as the world would note, effective businessmen.

Yet in this city of gardens and glass twenty murders a day have become commonplace, and fifty a day not unusual. The drug trade has crept like moss over Medellín, burrowing into each corner, covering the city's glittering surfaces with a layer of rot. Every part of the city—the government, the Catholic Church, the banks, the businessmen, the slums—has made its pact with cocaine. I came to Medellín to find out how a successful, modern city has led Colombia's breakdown into chaos and why, in the face of such overwhelming corruption and violence, people like Alvaro Medina are still willing to die of Quijote.

*   *   *

COCAINE CAME TO COLOMBIA IN THE MID-1970s. UNLIKE PERU or Bolivia, Colombia has neither land suitable for coca farming nor a history of coca use in its indigenous culture. Only about 15 percent of the coca leaf used in the business is grown in Colombia. The Colombians merely process the paste and export cocaine. When General Augusto Pinochet's crackdown drove cocaine traffic from Chile, the Paisas, who had the requisite business skills and proximity to the U.S. market, took it over.

Pablo Escobar and Jorge Ochoa, the most important of the Medellín drug lords, began as two of hundreds of small-time traffickers. What brought them to the top was their association with Carlos Lehder, a German-Colombian who, while serving a prison term in the United States for marijuana smuggling, met other smugglers and set up a U.S. cocaine distribution network. Escobar and Ochoa knew each other, but they did not pool their resources until 1981, when Ochoa's sister was kidnapped. The death squad they formed to kill the kidnappers was the first in a series of collaborations that knitted them together into the Medellín Mafia. Since the mid-1980s the Medellín traffickers have engaged in low-intensity warfare with the traffickers from the city of Cali. The casualties, notes pinned to their clothing stating, "I was killed for working for the Medellín traffickers," are often found along Colombia's highways, and the next day more bodies, "killed for working for the Cali traffickers," appear. But aside from the violence it uses against its Medellín rivals, the Cali group limits its activities to selling cocaine, eschewing the political action and death squads of the Paisas.

In Medellín violence became the trademark and primary business tool of the drug trade. The victims range from slum boys killed in petty turf wars to Cabinet ministers, politicians, journalists, and judges who get in the traffickers' way. The first cocaine magnicides, as the assassinations of the famous are called, were acts of terrorism designed to intimidate those who prosecuted the traffickers or supported extradition.

As the years passed, the violence spread to touch people who have nothing to do with drugs or politics. Most recently this was the result of the traffickers' deliberate policy. When the Mafia carried out its most important magnicide—that of Luis Carlos Galán, Colombia's leading presidential candidate, in August 1989—President Virgilio Barco declared war on the traffickers, decreeing the revival of the extradition treaty and initiating an intense manhunt for the drug lords. The Mafia, in response, began directing its terrorism against ordinary citizens. In nine months 259 people were killed by bombs blowing up in schools, shops, and public buildings. In April 1990 the Medellín traffickers offered to pay four thousand dollars to anyone killing a policeman; forty-two Medellín police were killed the next month.

But drug violence also took a more indirect route into the lives of ordinary people. The traffickers created a Frankenstein's monster that gradually slipped out of their control: the *sicarios*. In 1979 one of Escobar's men created the first school for *sicarios*; a reporter I met told me that police took her on a raid of one such school, with classrooms, blackboards, and diagrams of how to follow victims and how to shoot them in the head with a .38 from the back of a motorcycle. The schools sometimes also provide the weapon and the bike. Employing a hit man is not new in Colombia, but in the past it was a position with a certain grade of honor; a hit man of old worked for one boss and usually felt some sort of political allegiance. The new *sicarios* work for anyone who pays them, making it close to impossible to track the real author of a crime.

The *sicario* did for murder in Medellín what the transistor did for the radio. Killing is easy, cheap, and popular. Once the mark of the drug trade, the *sicarios* have now diversified. Hugo López, a professor of economics at the University of Antioquia, told me of a high school girl who was looking for a *sicario* to kill a romantic rival. López also knew of a man who was angry at his neighbor, whose new construction was causing water to flood the man's house. The neighbor was richer than he, and the man feared that if he sued, the neighbor would simply pay off the judge. His solution was to hire a *sicario* and have the neighbor killed.

The *sicarios* have become their own masters. They run their own death squads, with such names as Love for Medellín, Death to Homosexuals, or the Vampires. They kill leftists, public officials, police, vagrants, car thieves, drug addicts, and each other: *Sicarios* gather to rid their neighborhoods of *sicarios*. Groups of hooded men shoot up slum streets, bars, and dance halls at random, killing sometimes thirty people at a time.

Under its modern surface Medellín has become a medieval city. Citizens pay tribute to the drug lords who control the kingdom. The wealthy live in fortresses and hire private armies for protection. The slums are ruled by bands of assassins. "In the face of the overwhelming annual murder rate," wrote the Bogotá newsweekly *Semana*, "Colombians have forgotten that it is possible to die of old age, in bed."

By 1989 Colombia had almost as many men working in private security as in the seventy-thousand-man National Police. *Semana*'s advertisements offer readers bulletproof cars and supersecure apartments. There were 789 kidnappings in 1989; Colombians joke that to be truly accepted in high society, one has to be kidnapped at least twice.

Killing permeates the lives of people who have nothing to do with drugs or politics. The newspaper *El Mundo* one day carried the story of a woman who locked her doors after her baby was born and vowed not to go outside until the girl was grown. The woman's attempt to pull up the drawbridges did not succeed; her name reached the papers because someone broke into her house and began shooting, gravely wounding the infant with a stray bullet. The baby was undergoing a series of operations, and the prognosis was uncertain. If she was lucky, she could look forward to a life like that of her mother, who had renounced even going to the corner store to buy bread because of the overwhelming reality of violence.

No target is off limits. The most common reason children under twelve are brought to the emergency room in Medellín is not the normal sprains and breaks of childhood but gunshot wounds. Ricardo Aricapa, a reporter, told me that when he was assigned to cover the wake of Luís Fernando Vélez, a human rights leader, he wandered from Vélez's wake into the other salon of the funeral parlor, which contained the body of a priest. The priest had been driving his VW Beetle in El Poblado, Medellín's wealthiest neighborhood, when he refused to yield the right-of-way. The occupants of the other car shot him to death.

Soccer referees and beauty contest judges receive death threats. The newspaper *El Colombiano* carried a note on its crime pages about two gunmen who shot their way into Our Lady of Chi-quinquira Church during a wedding, killing the photographer and wounding the father of the bride. The archdiocese announced it would excommunicate the guilty parties.

The murder rate, which had been more or less steady for twenty years, began to rise in the late 1970s with the coming of cocaine and to skyrocket in 1986. The style of murder has changed as well: In 1979, 80 percent of the murders in Medellín were committed with knives, most of them occurring in the course of drunken fights. In 1988 guns were the weapon of choice in more than 80 percent of the killings. By the late 1980s Colombia had the highest homicide rate in the world for a country not at war: 68.1 murders per 100,000 people in 1989, eight times the rate in the United States, a country that is usually no laggard where violence is concerned. And Medellín has the highest murder rate in Colombia: an average of 15 a day in a metropolitan area of 2.2 million in early 1990, twelve times that of metropolitan Detroit. The murder rate is so high that the Medellín Metropolitan Health Department's report from 1986—a document that in most other cities would speak of diarrhea, tuberculosis, cancer, heart disease, and the like—begins with a quotation from Héctor Abad Gómez, who had been the president of the city's Human Rights Commission: "Why at this moment here, and in so many other corners of the earth, are the living things most dangerous to man not viruses, nor microbes, nor parasites, but human beings?" Abad Gómez's words acquired a personal twist when he himself was murdered in August 1987, shot in the street by two human beings. Medellín, Colombia's city of progress, has advanced to the point where the single leading cause of death is no longer disease, but multiple gunshot wounds.

At the emergency room of Medellín's Metropolitan Clinic on a weekend night, the families of victims stood outside, protected from a pouring rain by an overhang. A drunk man scolded himself loudly. In front of me stood an apparition, a man of about twenty whose head and hair were matted and caked with blood. He was smoking and talking with friends; apparently the blood was not his own.

Every few minutes a car, usually a taxi, drove up, and orderlies rushed out with a stretcher to fetch the wounded. Inside, a few dozen young men, many holding their own plasma bottles, lay on bare green metal tables. "We've become specialists in knife and gun traumas," said Jorge Gómez, a doctor who spoke to me hurriedly between patients.

Most of the patients I saw were bleeding from the chest. A man came in with knife wounds on his arms. "We can't see you," said the nurse. "Go around the corner to intermediate wounds."

I asked about head wounds, the mark of a *sicario*. "We get plenty of them," said Gómez. "But you won't see them waiting for attention here. All we can do for them is this," he said, making the sign of the cross.

I stayed four hours and saw two prostitutes who had overdosed, a middle-class woman with a troubled pregnancy, and about thirty victims of knife or gunshot wounds, four of them women. A man said he was here to look for his cousin, a seventeen-year-old girl who had disappeared the day before. She had gone shopping in the afternoon and never returned. A woman waiting outside told me that her twenty-three-year-old nephew had been knifed in a dispute over a gold chain. The nephew died. Another woman said she was waiting for her brother-in-law, who had yelled at a taxi driver for refusing to pick him up and been shot through the chest by the driver. After each patient came in, a heavy middle-aged woman mopped up the blood from the hallway. It was very hard work, and just before midnight she put her mop down, and sat in a chair, unable to keep up, while the tracks of blood gradually spread to cover the whole floor.

On my next trip to Medellín, *El Mundo* carried a report that two *sicarios* had forced their way into the emergency room to finish off a woman they had only managed to wound before. Evidently, this was not unusual. I talked to a man who said that he had seen a variation on this theme: *sicarios* approaching the families of victims waiting outside the hospital, offering their services to avenge the shooting of a loved one.

Two days after my visit to the hospital *El Mundo* reported that there had been an average of one violent death an hour over the weekend. An article giving an hour-by-hour description of the deaths from Saturday night to Sunday night was notable for, among other things, the author's skill in finding different ways to report a murder: "Someone took the life of Luís Alberto López at knifepoint. . . . Luís Alberto Patiño ceased to exist with a bullet in his head. . . . Mario Restrepo turned up dead with a bullet

in his head. . . . An unidentified person killed Néstor Alvarez
with three shots. . . . Sabino Piedrahita was found dead of knife
wounds. . . . Rubén Dario Jurado died when an unidentified
person shot him. . . . Eugenia Romero appeared assassinated."
In twenty-seven different murders the author repeated the phras-
ing only once.

THE QUESTION OF WHY AN ENTIRE NATION SEEMS BENT ON DYING
in the street has produced a new local science called vio-
lentology—as far as I can tell, a field of investigation found only
in Colombia. The first studies of the roots of Colombia's social
chaos were done about thirty years ago, and they have increased
dramatically in number, a product of the unfortunate need to
keep up with events. One recent publication on the subject comes
from a group of sociologists, anthropologists, military officers,
historians, and engineers. In March 1986 these violentologists
began meeting every week or two in Bogotá for four months to
study contemporary violence in Colombia.

The book the group wrote, *Colombia: Violencia y Democracia*,
argues that violence is caused by the breakdown of government
institutions, and its recommendations focus on strengthening
those institutions. "Medellín was poorer forty-five years ago, and
much less violent," said Santiago Peláez, the director of the
Center for Economic Research at the University of Antioquia
and one of the book's authors. "It's not just poverty that creates
violence. It's breakdown. The state does not have the power to
say that something is good or bad and impose a system of sanctions. We have 'big government' in Colombia, but that doesn't
mean we have strong government. A government is strong only
when the community reinforces it. If people in the community
don't feel part of the system and don't back it up, it can't work."

In a successfully functioning society, the group said, a
government—together with its institutions that create a sense of
community and shared values, such as courts and schools—is
an arbitrator. It teaches children that killing is wrong, for example, and punishes people who kill. In Colombia the government is too weak to play that role. Peláez used the trivial example
of litter. The same Latino who throws a cigarette wrapper onto

the street in Medellín would carefully put it in a trash bin if he were visiting Disney World, first, because he knows he will have to pay a five-hundred-dollar fine for littering in Florida, and second, because no one around him litters; there is a common accord that all will be better off if each puts his litter in a trash can. You need this social consensus to make the state work, Peláez said. The state can exist only if people believe in it.

It is hard to pinpoint exactly what in Colombian history set in motion the forces that created levels of violence approached nowhere else on the planet. Colombia's conquest and colonization were not very different from those of its neighbors—bloodier, perhaps, but the conquest was bloody all over Latin America.

Four hundred fifty years ago the legend of El Dorado began to circulate in Spain. El Dorado, the golden man, lived among so much gold that he covered his body with it. Explorers thought that El Dorado could be found in the mountains of South America in a place that became known as Colombia.

El Dorado was a myth, but there was gold, all right, and emeralds. Some of the worst criminals of Spain came to Colombia to find them. Spanish conquerers killed the whole tribe of the Muzo Indians to find out the location of an emerald mine rumored to be especially rich. Colombia was born of piracy, contraband, and desperate, feverish greed.

Colombia's geography—more diverse than that of most of its neighbors—also contributed to violence. It was not one country but many different countries: the hot, tropical coast of Cartagena; cool, high, green Bogotá; temperate Medellín; flat plains; jungle; mountains. Today half-hour-long flights link Bogotá and Medellín a dozen times a day, the local equivalent of the New York to Washington shuttle. Before the airplane, the trip was a perilous mountain journey that took weeks. Because of difficult communications, each landowner was effectively isolated, had his own army, and made up his own rules.

The establishment of a centralized government threatened the power of these landowners. The strife between them and the emerging urban merchants eventually became the Conservative-Liberal conflict. Between 1830 and 1903 Colombia had nine national civil wars, fourteen local civil wars, two international wars with Ecuador, two successful military coups, and one that failed. Between 1886 and 1900, 170,000 Colombians, 1 of every

20 citizens, died in wars. Although the conflicts concerned which set of elites would control Colombia, the people who died in them were not the landowners but their serfs.

There were some constants. Independence from Spain in the early nineteenth century brought Colombian-born rulers to power, but they still governed for the upper classes. The Liberals and the Conservatives (both parties were formed in the 1840s) preferred seeing 5 percent of the population killed to relinquishing power. To the vast majority of Colombians, however, which party was in office was irrelevant; their misery remained the same.

The other constant was the Catholic Church. In all Latin America only Colombia has a concordat, a treaty with the Vatican that makes the church a quasi-official body. The church has never been shy about its political role, and at times its identification with the Conservative party took on the overtone of a crusade. "Liberalism is a sin," wrote one bishop, "a veritable Jewish Sanhedrin against Christ and the Catholic Church." Priests flatly forbade Catholics to vote Liberal and warned Colombians that their choice was to vote Conservative or suffer the pains of hell.

In other countries with fossilized hierarchies and a reactionary church, large waves of immigration brought fresh blood and new ideas that opened up the political spectrum. The Italian and Jewish immigrants of the first part of this century who brought the trade union movement to Argentina, for example. There was no such immigration to Colombia.

Only one man in Colombian history threatened to break the oligarchy's stranglehold on the political system. It was the spark for the darkest age of Colombian history, one whose consequences are still in evidence today. Jorge Eliécer Gaitán, a small dark-skinned man from a lower-class family, was a lawyer, congressman, Cabinet minister, and mayor of Bogotá. In 1947 he took over the Liberal party, and he seemed destined to become Colombia's next president. The oligarchy's contempt for Gaitán was evident; both Conservatives and the traditional wing of his own Liberals called him El Negro. For them, Gaitán was a dangerous man, a speaker who could turn an anecdote about a high water bill into a spellbinding call to revolution. In February 1948 Gaitán organized a march to protest the government's repression of

the poor. Thousands of men and women holding candles walked
in haunting silence through Bogotá's streets.

Just before noon on April 9, 1948, a man in a gray suit walked
up to Gaitán on a Bogotá street and killed him with three shots.
Within minutes crowds had beaten Gaitán's assassin to death,
and three hours later Bogotá was in flames. Hordes burned the
houses of the rich, stores, government buildings, convents, and
even the cathedral. They broke the locks on the jail doors. Army
tanks rolled into the central plaza and began shooting into the
crowd. Probably more than three thousand people were killed
that day; over the next five years between two hundred thousand
and three hundred thousand died. Even by Colombian standards
those figures merited capital letters; the era became known as *La
Violencia*.

What was *La Violencia* about? It began with Gaitán's death,
but there was little class conflict involved. *La Violencia* soon
transformed itself into a supercharged version of what violence
in Colombia had always been: a power struggle between two
parties whose major difference was their names.

It was most intense in the countryside, where political alliances
were strongest, there was little or no government to be seen, and
people knew one another; instead of humanizing the conflict,
being neighbors just meant that no one could stay out of trouble
by hiding his political views. In the cities the police and courts
were able to maintain some semblance of order. Urban Colombia
saw little disruption; indeed, business boomed during *La Violencia*, with the economy growing 6.2 percent. In the countryside
the Liberals formed guerrilla armies to defend themselves against
the Conservatives, the governing party. The police ceased to be
crime fighters and instead spent their time killing Liberals. There
was no neutral ground. After the presidential elections of 1949,
which the Liberal party boycotted, the Conservative government
required Colombians to carry identity cards stating that they had
voted in the elections. Being caught with the card was a death
sentence in some places; failing to produce it was a death sentence
in others.

In 1953 the military took over the government and put a stop
to most of the violence. Four years later civilian government
returned when the Conservative and Liberal parties signed a pact

called the National Front, in which the parties alternated in government for twelve years. The pact was later extended until 1974.

The two political parties are no longer at war. But Colombia's many different contemporary *violencias* have their roots in those years. The relationship is most direct in the case of the guerrillas: many of their armies were formed during the political unrest. Medellín's random urban violence, on the other hand, is the result in part of the loss of community caused by the migrations prompted by *La Violencia*. According to Santiago Peláez, the violentologist, three million people fled to the cities to escape the violence in the countryside. "In rural areas everyone knows his role," he said. "In the city all of a sudden you have to compete with everyone else. The traditional sanctions have evaporated. In the country boys are raised with responsibilities. In the city they get no chores. The parish life of the church is lost. The sense of community is lost."

Paradoxically the National Front, the pact that ended *La Violencia*, helped create Colombia's contemporary violence. While placating both parties through the guarantee of alternation in power, it effectively shut the rest of the country out of the government. The oligarchy's traditional domination was now codified in law.

Viewed from the outside Colombia today seems like a true democracy: no military coups since 1953; two parties competing for the presidency; peaceful transitions between parties. But the political system looks different from within. Alfonso López Michelsen, the first president to be elected after the expiration of the National Front, once said elections in Warsaw Pact countries were horse races with only one horse. Colombian elections, he added, were horse races with two horses, but both had the same owner.

The Liberals and Conservatives monopolize Colombia's politics. But the left dominates the country's social organizations. The majority of the unions and organizations of teachers, campesinos, and indigenous groups are affiliated with the left. But this extensive social force is effectively closed out of the political system. The left-wing political parties might have been an option had death squads not ravaged their ranks. "If the rich hadn't been so bullheaded," said Julio Santana, the spokesman for one, Unión

Patriótica, "if they had created a real democracy, if people had room to participate in politics, people wouldn't be killing each other today."

Perhaps the most important way that La Violencia laid the foundation for future violence was by eroding the legitimacy of the Colombian state. The average Colombian was never clear about just what it was the state did for him, but after watching the state not only fail to protect him from La Violencia but actively participate in the killings, his identification with his government—and its laws—could only weaken further. Unable to perceive the benefits of citizenship, Colombians had no reason to accept their society's rules. It wasn't just a matter of perception. The judicial system and the police, two of the most important institutions in making a government work, broke down completely during La Violencia. Crime went unpunished, reinforcing the country's indifference to the law that twenty years later allowed the rise of the drug traffickers.

A state of siege established in 1949 to try to control La Violencia decreed that crimes against the "public order" would be treated not as simple crimes but as political crimes—Class A crimes—and judged in military courts. These public order crimes included practically all offenses against the means of production and the governing class, such crimes as robbing a bank, kidnapping a coffee producer, or stealing cattle. All other crimes were Class B crimes. In effect, this established a military court for crimes against the rich and a civilian court for crimes against the poor.

The government promptly lost interest in the civilian courts. The Supreme Court ruled the dual court system unconstitutional in 1987, on the ground that military courts should not be judging civilians. But by then the civilian courts had suffered decades of neglect. In 1987 the government allotted just 2 percent of the federal administration budget to run the justice system; the legislative and executive branches got 27 percent. Judges receive four hundred thousand new cases each year and are able to process only seventy thousand of them. Three quarters of the men in Medellín's jails have not yet been tried; those who are finally acquitted will have already spent years in jail. No laboratories exist to examine evidence, and no one possesses the training to use them in any event.

The result is impunity. A National Police study calculated that

1 in every 10 crimes is reported to the authorities, and of those crimes, 1 in 100 results in a sentence, meaning that 999 of 1,000 crimes go unpunished. "We've reached the point where anyone who is judged for a crime feels he's getting arbitrary treatment," said Fernando Navas Talero, assistant attorney general for human rights.

Justice has been privatized. The recognizable elements of justice—arrests, trials, plea bargaining, sentencing—do not exist within the state in Colombia, but in a perverse way they exist privately. Colombia does not extradite criminals, but death threats force the extradition of judges and witnesses. Criminals are punished not by the state but by such groups as Death to Car Thieves. Debts are squared not in bankruptcy court but by *sicarios*. As with the breakdown of the state in general, it is a vicious circle. The more people take revenge into their own hands, the more crimes are committed, the more the climate of impunity flourishes, and the greater the strain on the system of justice.

In March 1988 two massacres took place on the Honduras and La Negra farms in Urabá, a zone of northern Antioquia. The massacres came to public attention not because they were unusual in themselves but because they had been investigated, an extremely unusual occurrence. The investigation was one of justice's few accomplishments in 1988, but its findings exposed just how grim and disheartening is the task facing the justice system as it fights Colombia's violence. It brought to light the links between the traffickers and the military, and between drug violence and political violence, shadowy forces underlying much of Colombia's ferocity. All the different pieces of Colombia's violence—the drugs, the history of political brutality, and the impotence of the justice system—converged in the story of the two massacres. Here was Colombia's violence distilled and crystallized.

I needed to strip away Medellín's veil of progress and civilization to see violence at its purest. I took a small plane from Medellín to Urabá. Men shooed the chickens off the runway as we approached and landed. Stepping down from the plane felt like descending into a hot bath. I climbed into the back of a truck to get into the nearest town.

The lush spread of cattle ranches and banana plantations that unfolded as we drove had been carved out of the jungle just thirty years before. But in those years Urabá acquired the savagery that had taken four hundred years to develop in the rest of the Colombia. Today Urabá is the most violent place in the country. When people in Urabá need to escape, they go to Medellín for a little peace and quiet.

Settlers began to move here during *La Violencia* to grow bananas and escape the carnage in "civilized" Colombia. In 1959 the United Fruit Company, under the name Frutera de Sevilla, came in and bought the colonizers' land. People who wouldn't sell were forced out or killed. United Fruit recruited unskilled, illiterate local fishermen or itinerants to pick bananas. The workers, who knew little of laws or labor codes, accepted starvation wages; at times they were paid in scrip to be redeemed at inflated prices at the company store. The banana growers paid no taxes. The workers' houses had thatched palm roofs and no floors. There were no roads, schools, health clinics, or clean water.

In 1964 and 1966 workers formed the first banana pickers' unions. Their leaders were killed; new ones stepped into their places. Soon the unions had allies: left-wing guerrilla groups. The Colombian Revolutionary Armed Forces (FARC) and the People's Liberation Army (EPL), spotting rich soil in which to sow their message of revolution, came to Urabá, feeding off the anger of the banana workers and the small farmers forced off their land by the landowners. The guerrillas paid the landowners back in their own coin. An official of Augura, the association of private banana growers, said that guerrillas had killed 60 farm managers and 160 crew leaders; 80 percent of the landowners now lived in Medellín and traveled to Urabá only undercover. By 1988 guerrillas were extorting protection fees as high as three thousand dollars a month. Some landowners had been kidnapped by the FARC and returned after paying ransom, only to be kidnapped again by the EPL.

The traffickers have, at various times, formed alliances with the guerrillas. Certain fronts of the FARC and National Liberation Army (ELN) guard jungle labs for money. But the narco-guerrilla connection is tiny compared to the narco-right. The traffickers became rich and began to buy Colombia's farms and ranches. As landowners they sought protection from troublemaking peasant organizers and guerrillas who kidnapped their family members. Their alliance shifted from the guerrillas to the military, which shared their political views. Death squads were formed, organized by the landowners, staffed by soldiers, and now financed on an unprecedented scale by traffickers.

The addition of traffickers to Colombia's political violence was like pouring oil on fire. From 1986 to 1990 right-wing death squads or bands of *sicarios* claimed more than eight thousand civilian victims. Most of these were peasant union members and organizers. (The figure does not include guerrillas killed in armed combat.) The monthly report of the Bogotá Permanent Human Rights Commission is simply a phone book-size compilation of the nation's murders and massacres. Eighty-two massacres took place in the first half of 1988 in Colombia; the Honduras and La Negra massacres were merely two of the weekly massacres in Urabá.

I made my way to the Honduras farm, which lies a half hour's drive from Apartadó, Urabá's capital. The dirt road cuts through miles and miles of banana trees, their fruit encased in blue plastic bags to keep insects away. According to the investigation report I had read, in late February 1988 men wearing the uniforms of the Voltígeros Battalion, Urabá's local army unit, pulled up at a Honduras farm soccer game, shouted antiguerrilla slogans, and roughed up the workers on the field. Later Voltígeros officials drove through the steaming clearing where the workers lived. They were accompanied by former guerrillas who pointed out workers they claimed had guerrilla sympathies.

At twelve-thirty on the morning of March 4, 1988, fifteen men parked on the dirt road, walked into the clearing, rapped on the doors of the workers' white cement houses, and yelled, "You're all guerrilla sons of bitches." The visitors read a list of men's names. Seventeen of the men came out of their houses. The visitors forced them to the ground and shot them. Then the killers went to the La Negra farm, a few hundred yards away. As they pounded on the doors, they shouted that residents were hiding arms inside. They hauled three men outside and killed them.

The few families who were home at Honduras when I visited were newly arrived; everyone who had been there at the time of the massacre had moved away, said a man repairing a motorcycle. The tiny cement houses where the single men had roomed were nearly empty. In one there was a pair of purple slippers; in another a small suitcase lay open. At La Negra a banana worker lounging in a pair of jogging shorts told me that the three men killed were union leaders. I asked about their politics. He shrugged. If they had been guerrilla sympathizers, he wasn't about to tell me. A large pig followed me back to the car.

A few days after the massacre, the DAS, or investigations police, began to look into the killings, interviewing fifty people who had witnessed various parts of the crime. Forty-five days after the massacres, the DAS had assembled a sordid tale with a cast of army officials, right-wing politicians, wealthy landowners and drug barons.

The investigation report traced the Honduras and La Negra massacres to the nearby rural zone of Córdoba and a wealthy rancher and cocaine trafficker named Fidel Castaño, who calls himself Rambo. His story reads like a movie script. He founded his death squads after guerrillas had kidnapped and killed his father in the early 1980s. The DAS concluded that Rambo employed two thousand men in his army and enjoyed the support of twenty thousand more in the region. Investigators found dozens of bodies, bearing signs of torture, in mass graves on his property. They also found that police in one town had a special radio frequency set aside to communicate with him.

Rambo ran a school for *sicarios* with more than a thousand graduates. Among the instructors were Israelis, Germans, and North Americans. The school was financed by the Mafia and run by right-wing police and army officers and the mayor of the town of Puerto Boyacá, who was widely thought to be the head of the region's paramilitary death squads. (At the entrance to Puerto Boyacá a billboard proclaims the city the "antisubversive capital of Colombia.") Once in Urabá, Voltígeros soldiers showed the *sicarios* whom to kill.

On the basis of the DAS investigation, a judge in Bogotá indicted Pablo Escobar and Gonzalo Rodríguez Gacha, who was widely known as the traffickers' military chief. She also indicted the mayor of Puerto Boyacá, a police captain, and several officers of the Voltígeros Battalion.

And that's as far as she got. When she tried to fly to the site of the *sicarios'* school, her plane was hijacked to a remote runway, where police held her all day, then returned her to Bogotá. She told a reporter that when she went to request the military's co-operation from Defense Minister Rafael Samudio, he responded that she was a leftist trying to discredit the military. "And if you don't have a leftist past, we'll find one," he added ominously. She left the country. Her father, a prominent Liberal governor, was killed. The second judge on the case was killed.

When Rodríguez Gacha, the country's second most wanted drug trafficker after Escobar, was killed by police in late 1989 after the crackdown following Galán's death, Rambo and his paramilitary groups continued their alliance with others of the Medellín traffickers.

Outside Urabá the marriage of drug violence and politics is a less visible but much more serious threat to the future of the state. The traffickers have taken the lead in a campaign of death against the entire political left, now killing their ideological adversaries as well as their business opponents. Rambo is widely suspected of ordering the killings of two leftist presidential candidates in 1990. Both opposed extradition, but both were leaders of small left-wing parties created by former guerrillas. Bernardo Jaramillo, shot to death in Bogotá's airport, was the candidate of Unión Patriótica (UP), a legal party formed by former FARC guerrillas in 1985. Carlos Pizarro, the dashing son of a Colombian admiral, was the candidate of the M-19, whose guerrillas signed a peace treaty with the government in 1990, piled their guns in a heap under a Colombian flag, and registered as a political party. As a reward for renouncing violence and accepting democratic rules, Pizarro was shot to death on a commercial airliner seven weeks later. Despite his legendary audacity, he had been shot only once before in his twenty years as a guerrilla; it was also while he wore a suit, during official peace talks with the Colombian government. In truth, it was much safer to be a guerrilla than to be a leftist politician. More than a thousand of Unión Patriótica's members were killed in the party's first five years.

Yet there were always more members, more candidates. One of Unión Patriótica's officials was the mayor of Apartadó, surely one of the country's riskier jobs. I gave his secretary my name and stood and waited with dozens of other people in the white adobe room. After half an hour an uncombed man in a red T-shirt who seemed to be in his early twenties approached me. "You're waiting to see me?" he said.

"I'm waiting to see the mayor," I replied.

He laughed. "I'm the mayor." He put on a bulletproof vest. "I have to go see a new medical post," he said, "but I'll be back in half an hour."

When he came back, he took off his vest and shoes and sat down. His name was Ramón Castillo, and he was really thirty-five and a lawyer. He had become mayor six weeks before my visit, he told me, but six weeks were a long time in Apartadó. One man who had been mayor the year before had resigned early in disgust, saying, "Four months are like four centuries here." The next mayor had to leave; she got too many death threats. Castillo showed me his latest death threat, a letter addressed to him and four other UP mayors, signed by a group called Death to Northeastern Revolutionaries.

He put on his shoes and his bulletproof vest and shoved his .38 into his briefcase. "I had to get permission from the army to carry this," he said, not commenting on the irony of a democratically elected mayor's asking the army for permission to protect himself from death squads that likely were staffed by its own soldiers. A year later Castillo left the country. His successor, Diana Cardona, also from the UP, was killed in early 1990.

UP members patiently tried to explain to me that the left-wing parties offered the only way to work for peaceful change; their stubborn assumption that this was possible to do left me more mystified than ever. "You can recruit guerrillas on every street corner," Julio Santana, the UP's spokesman, told me when I went to see him in Bogotá, to try to fathom the mysteries of his party. "Political leaders are harder to find." And getting harder to find each day; seventy-three more UP members were killed in less than two months in early 1990. Santana showed me a twenty-six-page computer printout of UP's dead. "We accept the law," Santana said. "We are a legally recognized, peaceful political organization. If we do endorse the guerrillas, the government has every right to jail us. I wish they would jail us. It would be better than what is happening to us now."

* * *

"MANY PEOPLE THINK THE UNIÓN PATRIÓTICA PEOPLE ARE THE 'good Communists,' " said Colonel Eduardo Arévalo, the press spokesman for the armed forces at the Defense Ministry, his feet up on his desk. "It's a lie. They go back and forth between the UP and the guerrillas. Hell, they're really guerrillas."

Arévalo is a friendly, lively, informal man. He has another important quality, from a journalist's point of view: He is completely blind to the implications of his argument. Anyone who doubts that the military is killing the left merely has to listen to Arévalo deny it. I asked about the indictment of the Voltígeros officers for the Urabá massacres. "That judge is on the extreme left," he said with a wave of his hand. "What you've heard is just propaganda. Besides, a civilian judge can't investigate an officer. She should pass the case over to the army.

"These so-called paramilitary groups are not the army," he continued. "It's just a convenient word the left uses to blame us. What really happens is that people see a Unión Patriótica man in a suit and tie in the Senate, and even though he's wearing a tie and he's a senator, people recognize him as a guerrilla, so they contract a *sicario* to kill him. We can't have him just arrested; the judges will let him go. You don't understand what we're up against. The judges here either are threatened by the subversives or are leftists themselves. Many of the people in the law here have links with the extreme left. Most of the law professors in the National University are extremely left-wing. Amnesty International is manipulated by the Communist party. That's well known." A better spokesman could have figured out how to negate military involvement in the death squads without instantly confirming it. But military officers never seem to learn. When an attorney general accused 59 soldiers of participating in the death squad Death to Kidnappers in 1986, the military high command accused him of instigating a war against the military. The attorney general's name then appeared at the top of a list of thirty-two people targeted for death for crimes against "our military institutions." We have nothing to do with the death squads, the military was saying. And if you say we do, we'll have you killed.

"You can't compare left-wing and right-wing violence," Arévalo said as we walked out the door. "When your body is infected, you need to create antibodies. Sometimes the antibodies have bad side effects, but it's not the same kind of thing as the infection itself. Colombia is infected."

I asked how the infection should be fought. He thought for a while. "Sometimes you have to cut off a finger to save the patient," he said. "Argentina is a good example." The Argentine generals in the late 1970s had killed or disappeared more than nine thousand people. "The surgeon had to take drastic action. But it came out fine. The patient survived."

Urabá had acquired a new chief surgeon before my visit: Voltígeros commander General Jesús Armando Arias. I asked him why in a zone where there were three soldiers for every two banana workers, in a zone where I had been stopped and asked for my papers twice in a half hour car trip, the army had never arrested or fought a member of a death squad. "In spite of the presence of so many troops, there are still guerrillas here," he said. "That doesn't mean we help or tolerate them. We just can't find them. The same is true with the death squads." The first indictment had been handed down for the Honduras and La Negra massacres, a Voltígeros lieutenant named Pedro Bermúdez. "The indictment was a mistake," Arias said. "Maybe he's from another brigade. He's not one of ours."

While waiting to talk to the general, I had fallen into a conversation with another Voltígeros officer. We were sitting on the grass in lawn chairs, drinking orange soda and watching the recruits play soccer. It was a most entertaining game, mainly because the field was pure mud and the players kept slipping into puddles. The officer—he didn't want me to use his name or rank—offered his analysis of the political situation in Urabá. It wasn't complicated.

"The Unión Patriótica and the unions are guerrillas," he said. "Have you talked to the mayor?" I said I had.

"Well, he's a guerrilla."

I asked him about the case of Lieutenant Bermúdez, who, for all I knew, might have been one of the mud-soaked soccer players. "That judge is civilian and had no jurisdiction to indict him," he said. "First of all, Bermúdez is in intelligence, and his job is to talk to everyone, so that's why he was caught talking to the death squad. Only a military judge can have a soldier arrested for something done in the course of duty. A military judge should investigate to find if there is a reason to detain him, but I don't think he'll find one."

Of this I had no doubt. There were some contradictions between what the general and the officer had said. Bermúdez, who, according to the general, did not exist, was, according to the officer, in the intelligence unit. According to the officer, Bermúdez was conversing in the course of his duty with death squads—death squads that were able to operate freely, according to the general, because they had eluded being spotted by the army. In a very different way from that which the officers had intended, they were getting their message across. They, along with the traffickers and the landowners, are in a war with the left, all the left, and in a war the victims have no rights and killing them is committing no crime. Whenever new evidence comes up linking the military with the death squads, the officers deny it. But the more they deny it, the more they tell the truth.

"I AM OPTIMISTIC," ENRIQUE LOW MURTRA, THE JUSTICE MINISter, told me back in Bogotá. It was his last day in office. Low Murtra, I thought, would have the wisdom of his ten months on the job and the frankness that usually accompanies imminent departure—not to mention the tranquillity that came from his plan to move to Argentina. I hoped to hear justice's real possibilities for bringing law to Colombia. He was bald, with liver spots and a constant tremor; it was hard to believe he was only forty-nine. He had sent his daughter out of the country and could not even go to Sunday mass without his escort: a bulletproof car with another car in front and a motorcycle on each side, and his bodyguard with machine guns—sometimes six men, sometimes twelve or fifteen. (The bodyguards could not protect him forever; on May 1, 1991, Low Murtra was assassinated in Bogotá.)

Finding a justice minister on his last day in office was no great trick; Barco ran through ten of them in his four years as president. Low Murtra, who left because of a political dispute, was the only one to resign of natural causes. The others were sacked because they suddenly started to back away from extradition while it was still government policy, or they resigned after evidence of their corruption had been uncovered or after one too many death threats.

I asked Low Murtra about the dangers to judges, how Colombia could fight crime if fighting crime required justices to commit collective suicide. "Judges are not as strong as they should be and will be," he said. But he added that judges received better protection than before. "We're building bunkers in military barracks to protect them," he said.

Another improvement, Low Murtra said, was that he had won a small increase in the department's budget. He also pointed to reforms in the Judicial Police. I told him that I'd talked to the man in charge, who told me that he was sending judges to investigate rural cases in canoes, alone or with one assistant, usually paying for the trips out of their own pockets. "I feel a little frustrated," Low Murtra said, smiling.

His real reason for optimism, Low Murtra said, was that a Bogotá judge had indicted Rodríguez Gacha for the Honduras and La Negra massacres, and an indictment of Escobar was in the works. "It is a very good sign," he said. "It means we're getting stronger."

Low Murtra was not talking about prison for the traffickers, or trials, or even arrests. It was a simple indictment, and not even the first; Alvaro Medina, among others, had done it. That an indictment was a victory indicated the scarcity of victories in Colombian justice.

FOR A FEW GLORIOUS MONTHS AFTER THE MURDER OF GALÁN IN August 1989, public outrage and President Barco's determination turned the justice system into the muscular and single-minded team of Low Murtra's dreams. Police arrested traffickers, jailers held them, and they stayed put until they were loaded onto planes for their extradition to courts in Tampa or Jacksonville. But the crackdown's very success created a backlash so destructive that Barco had to abandon it. When the traffickers began replying with bombs in schools, shopping centers, and ordinary neighborhoods, Colombians began to rebel. The government was obviously not equipped to wage war on the drug traffickers, many people believed, and since it was not so equipped, it should not have provoked their wrath. Even former aides to Galán were calling for dialogue with the traffickers as the key to stabilizing Colombia.

The backlash had several parts. One was anti-U.S. sentiment. Even before the crackdown I heard people express their anger at the United States for asking Colombia to destroy its own institutions when they didn't see the United States getting tough on money laundering or the sale of guns or chemicals used in processing cocaine. With the crackdown the feeling intensified that Colombia is not corrupting the United States; the United States is corrupting Colombia, and Colombians don't hear any thanks for the tremendous cost of their sacrifices. "Let's not turn Colombia into the Vietnam of the war on drugs" was a standard applause line of presidential candidate Ernesto Samper in the 1990 campaign. The U.S. plan is "educational videos in the United States, bombers for Colombia," he said at a press conference, "persuasive chats in the consumption centers and helicopters for Colombia." The spectacle of Washington Mayor Marion Barry as a political candidate after dozens of witnesses had detailed his use of crack was a source of endless bitter amusement for Colombians.

"The United States' problem with drugs," Medina's widow, Luz Estela, told me, "is not the pain it causes but the dollars that are leaving the country as a result. You don't really care about drug addiction. It's public; it's tolerated; there are even magazines that teach you how to smoke. You just don't want us to get the money." I would guess that the majority of the Colombians I met believed this to be true, and they aren't all anti-gringo leftists: Luz Estela defines herself as a conservative, and she can hardly be considered soft on drugs.

A second phenomenon was a shift in the way Colombians viewed the sins of traffickers. With the crackdown the traffickers' crime became not narcotrafficking but the narcoterrorism destroying the state and threatening ordinary people. Although drug addiction is a terrible problem in Colombia, the country has so many terrible problems that worrying about drug addiction is a luxury Colombians cannot yet afford. If drug addiction worries the gringos, many Colombians think, let the gringos take care of it up there.

It was the widespread view in Colombia that the best way to fight narcoterrorism was to give up the fight against narcotrafficking. If the state had simply allowed the traffickers to go about their business, they would not be killing judges, cops, journalists, and presidential candidates, and bombs would not be blowing up innocent bystanders. Most Colombians I met thought that the way to end the violence was to quasi-legalize cocaine, to treat it as marijuana is treated in the United States.

The government seemed to agree. It began its crackdown only after the traffickers had killed Galán, a prominent member of the political elite. The crackdown was concentrated on Escobar and his noisy, politically opinionated, and violent Medellín traffickers, while leaving alone the rival traffickers from the city of Cali, who are less vocal and simply interested in doing business. And when the traffickers showed that they could raise the stakes indefinitely, the government backed away.

THE CRACKDOWN BROUGHT THE ISSUE OF *PLATA O PLOMO* HOME to every Colombian. Suddenly, even those with no previous contacts with the drug world had to worry, twenty-four hours a day, about the traffickers' bombs. They worried when they sent their children to school, as they shopped, even as they walked on city streets. They soon grew weary of living in terror because of a problem they believed belonged to another country. They responded in the natural way: They wanted to make peace.

But cocaine's hold on Colombia was much more complex and much more sinister. Cocaine had transformed all it touched in Colombia. Just as it made the country's traditional political violence more widespread, random, and pervasive, so it intensified the violence of Colombia's streets. Just as it corrupted the guerrillas and the military, so it corrupted civic life. Colombia is addicted to cocaine. It provides employment—perhaps half a million Colombians worked in cocaine in 1990—and hard currency. It has helped destroy, through *plata o plomo*, the institutions that might otherwise have restrained it.

But as I spent time in Medellín, I began to see a more chilling aspect of the drug's impact. That was its effect on ordinary people, the ease with which Colombians learned to live with cocaine.

In a religious and moralistic country trafficking is now an accepted, even admired, activity for a large number of people. Corruption and violence have become routine, ordinary, for all but a few Colombians.

Medellín is not under siege. Life is not conducted to a constant Muzak of gunfire; people do not have to dodge bullets to cross the street. The city is modern and pretty; life goes on. Residents, therefore, can think of violence as part of everyday life. A middle-class Paisa can live a normal life, if avoiding any type of political or union activity, choosing neighbors and relatives who also avoid any political activity, taking extra care when driving not to scratch a car owned by undesirables, and never leaving the house after dark can be considered a normal life. Their insistence that life in Medellín is perfectly ordinary is symptomatic of how its people have learned to live with violence.

I found myself in a bar one night with an agreeable Medellín couple who own an art gallery. After a few shots of aguardiente liquor, the topic turned from the art scene to how foreign journalists have invented Medellín's violence because it was a good story; "vultures" was the word the woman used.

"I don't know," I said. "There was a man shot right in front of my hotel one evening by two *sicarios*. I've never seen a murder anywhere else I've been."

She leaned forward in her chair. "But that's nothing," she said. "That happens all the time. I've seen that four or five times myself."

Initially such blitheness struck me as the product of either extraordinary courage or mental illness. Later, after talking with dozens of people who were similarly nonchalant about experiences the average person would consider terrifying, I came to see it as a necessary defense mechanism for living in places like Medellín. Maybe that is what courage is. Violence has become "normal" in Medellín because it is not possible to live in a society in which massacres and assassinations occur daily and still retain a capacity for horror and pain. There's just too much of it; one goes numb.

But below the surface something infinitely more disturbing is occurring. The vast majority of the people I met in Medellín have severed the link between the violence and its perpetrators. While they condemn the killings, the notion that someone is responsible for them seems to have disappeared. Medellín's priests, bankers, judges, and politicians speak about the cocaine problem with concern. But they talk about it in a fog of passive voice, as if the problem were as anonymous and unpredictable as a sudden storm, for which no one is responsible and about which nothing can be done. They are free to condemn the violence while paying respect to its perpetrators.

The psychological accommodation necessary to live with Medellín's violence was a mystery to me until I completed the journey myself without even realizing it. My guide was a man named Gitano, a former policeman. A mutual acquaintance had arranged for Gitano to come to my hotel one evening. When he rushed into the hotel lobby, he grabbed me by the hand and pulled me out onto the street, where a man had been shot just as Gitano was arriving. By the time we got there, three minutes later, the body, alive or dead, had been removed, and a crowd of about twenty people was pressed around bloodstains in a doorway. A man opened the door and yelled for the crowd to scatter. "It's over. Now leave, everybody," he said. It was seven-thirty on a Wednesday night, just getting dark, and all the stores were open. Hundreds of people must have seen the hit, but when we started asking, no one had seen it. Finally Gitano spotted two friends who owned a barbershop. They said that two young men on a motorcycle had shot four times at a man walking in the street, who then shot back at them twice. Then the motorcycle sped away.

We went for a walk around downtown Medellín. It was fully dark now. Gitano, which means "gypsy," was twenty-six. Good-looking, he wore his hair in a long ponytail and was dressed in tight tattersall jeans and a red shirt open to the waist. He had left the police force for reasons that were murky and was working as a private security guard. Guayaquíl, the neighborhood we were visiting, was full of storefronts. All we could see when we peered in the doors was the glow of *basuco* cigarettes rising and falling like fireflies. People were sleeping on the sidewalk. On Bolívar Street there were prostitutes, one or two on every corner, in miniskirts, heels, and tight blouses. They were tall for Colombian women, and there was something strange about them. . . . Gitano was laughing. "They're all men," he said.

Gitano seemed to feel at home. I was beginning to get the idea that the line between the cops and the criminals in Medellín was a blurry one. The typical policeman was a slum kid with a third- or fourth-grade education—exactly the profile of a trafficker. "A policeman is a human being who wants to live," Gitano said. "They send you to arrest someone who is certainly very dangerous and certainly not alone." With a sweep of his hand he indicated the *basuco* houses. "How do you arrest someone in there? You can't arrest these people. I would arrest them with lead," he said, pretending to shoot. "You have to be violent. No one should trust the police here."

I asked about corruption. He laughed. "Everyone thought that I joined the force to get rich," he said. "It wasn't true. I was broke the day before payday and the day after." But going a little easy was tempting, he said, both for the cop's safety and for his billfold. "The police are fighting mafiosi who make two or three million pesos a month. A policeman gets fifty thousand a month, and that's only if he's married. What would you do?" *Semana* magazine estimated that 80 percent of Medellín's city police had some business relationship with the traffickers.

"I have to talk to two *sicarios* tomorrow," Gitano said later that night. He said a friend of his was looking for some people to kill his father. "His father is not a good person," he said. "He treats the family badly." He asked me if I wanted to come. I said I didn't want to go to where they worked, but maybe we could meet somewhere else.

Journalist Silvia Duzán conducted a series of interviews with *sicarios* and their families; *Semana* published some of her research. In Medellín's northeastern neighborhoods she saw bands roaming the slums headed by boys as young as twelve. Even if they make some money, they don't move out of their neighborhood; outside they are nothing. Instead, they live with their mothers, whom they tend to idolize and protect, and use their earnings to add another story to the house or buy their mothers appliances. They are deeply religious, praying to the Virgin of Carmen to guide their aim, lighting candles before going out on a job. Javier, a *sicario* of fifteen, told Duzán, "I'll die soon, but they'll remember me for having given my mother a nice refrigerator."

One of Duzán's interviews was with a twenty-year-old named El Angel, head of the vigilante group Self-Defense of the Northeastern Communities of Medellín. El Angel said he had started by killing a rapist. "The next day we just hung back and listened to people talk, and we realized people were pleased with the killing," he said. He and his friends moved on to killing drug addicts and *sicarios*, and by the time of the interview he had killed about three hundred people. "We are just responding to the problems the government doesn't resolve," he said. "Here the police never come, and when they do, they become accomplices of the thieves. The community gives us force and backing." (Silvia Duzán was killed on February 26, 1990, in Magdalena Medio while interviewing three peasant leaders for a story on a town's new peace plan.)

The afternoon after our conversation Gitano came to my hotel with the friend, César, and two *sicarios*, Rodrigo and Gilberto. We went to the restaurant on the roof, with a breathtaking view of the city and the mountains, and ordered coffee. We maintained an uncomfortable silence as the waitress poured the coffee. Finally I said, "What do you do?" It was an awkward scene. I wanted to ask, "So which of you are the *sicarios*?" but it seemed indelicate.

César said he worked as a private security guard. Gilberto and Rodrigo said they do "whatever comes up."

I decided to plunge right in. "That includes killing people for money, right?" I asked.

Gilberto nodded, but it was clear he didn't like the word I had used. *El asunto* ("the business") was the word they used.

The *sicarios* seemed nervous. They said they both were twenty-two. They looked younger, both with acne, Rodrigo dressed in jeans and a T-shirt, Gilberto in a fancy sweat shirt and tan pants, with elaborately styled long hair. Rodrigo was married, he told me.

They said they had first killed people when they were sixteen. Rodrigo had started unintentionally. A friend of his was feuding with another man and asked Rodrigo to shake him up a bit. Rodrigo knifed him, and the man died. "It was an accident," he said. He said he was nervous the first time he did a hit for money. Now experienced in the trade, they use the time-tested method of a motorcycle and a .38 and alternate who does the driving and who does *el asunto*. "We always have to worry that the person is carrying a weapon," said Gilberto, "or that he has a godfather who'll get us back. We don't work in our own barrio or where we're known."

But Rodrigo said they feel in control. "In the moment when you pull the trigger, your heart races and you concentrate very hard. It's like a high."

Their rate schedule was variable. Rodrigo said that he and Gilberto often help out their friends. "We advance them money, or we just work for free," he said. They said they would charge a person they didn't know a million pesos for a hit ($3,300). I suspected they were exaggerating; the *sicario* who had killed UP presidential candidate Bernardo Jaramillo told police he made $750 for his trouble. Most of their hits went more cheaply, they said, and sometimes they took payment in cocaine or jewelry.

When they accepted a client, they would sit down and go over in detail the routine of the object of *el asunto*. Then they would spend two or three days following him. Sometimes they cut in the police if they needed help.

I asked if they had any moral qualms at all. "We don't really think of the person but of their family," said Gilberto. "It's true, the family is going to suffer. But we mostly think about the money we make; it's our work. Besides, in most cases they are bad people. We're doing everyone a favor."

Gilberto had been offered a job as a bodyguard for a small-time trafficker. The money was good, a hundred thousand pesos a month, but he turned it down. "It's too delicate," he said. "The man has too many enemies. If someone was going to kill him, they'd kill his guards as well."

They said they had no interest in becoming drug dealers themselves. "My brother is trying to get me to come work with him," said Rodrigo, "but it's very dangerous to work with drugs. You don't want to be walking around with a quantity on you." Rodrigo mentioned that he worried about word getting back to his family if he became a dealer. He was less concerned about his family's finding out about his current profession. They said that there was a higher possibility of getting arrested, or "falling," in drugs than in their business. Gilberto had "fallen" once, spending eighteen months in jail for theft, and it wasn't a pleasant experience.

"What does your family think you do?" I asked.

"This and that," Rodrigo said.

A woman had told Duzán: "The mothers don't ask when kids come home from school with articles they stole from their class-mates. They end up washing their boys' clothes stained with other people's blood, without saying a word."

I asked them what they wanted for the future, say, five years from now. "Five years from now—I don't think that far ahead," said Gilberto. Even saving money for tomorrow was a problem. "You have no idea if tomorrow you'll be in jail or get hit yourself, so I usually use up all my money in one night." He put a finger to his nose, imitating the use of a local product.

Rodrigo was more of a dreamer. He was hoping to score one huge contract, make a lot of money, and go to Miami. He knew a lot of people who had done it.

"Getting a visa is a problem," said Gilberto. He looked at me.

"What a shame," I said.

They were eager to end the interview and get down to business. I left them talking to César about their deal.

The next day it hit me that I had witnessed a murder being planned and had done nothing about it. A week earlier I would not have thought this possible; now the idea of doing something had not even occurred to me. What could I do? Asking for details had struck me as imprudent, and the police, overwhelmed with murder, would pay little attention to a story about one not yet committed.

But more than that, the sicarios' hit hadn't seemed to me like murder. I had severed the connection between the four men in my hotel rooftop restaurant and the imminent death of César's father. After only a short time in Medellín I was thinking about violence in the passive voice, as something that just happens to people.

IF I COULD SLEEP THROUGH CONSPIRACY TO COMMIT HOMICIDE after ten days in Medellín, it should not have surprised me that people who had lived here all their lives were capable of con-demning the traffickers' corruption of the city's youth in speeches financed by the traffickers' money. It should not have surprised me even when these people wore cassocks. Many priests boast of accepting donations from the traffickers; the Catholic Church in Colombia is a tower of ambiguity where violence is concerned.

Father Elías Lopera Cárdenas is a lawyer and theologian in Medellín's archdiocese, whose offices occupy the third floor of a modern brick shopping mall with an atrium in the center and a Hardee's on the first floor. Speaking a floor above a shop that billed itself as selling "Shoes and Fantasies," Lopera criticized the violence and consumerism of Colombian society. "We live in a very aggressive society," he said. "We've lost respect for life." He spoke forcefully, leaning forward, punching the air with his Coke-bottle glasses. "Young people think happiness is to have money. The sixteen- or seventeen-year-old risks his life to get money for a television. Kids say when they're big they want to be mafiosos. We're learning the laws of the Mafia: Pay me or I kill you."

He said that he had heard the dying confession of a man known to be a *sicario*. The man confessed to Lopera that he had once stolen some money. "Is that all you have to confess to?" Lopera said.

The man nodded.

"Aren't you a hired killer?" Lopera said.

"But that helps people," the dying man replied. "It helps the people I kill because they have a very hard life. It helps the people who hire me, and it helps me because it gives me money to live."

Lopera mused for a while about the fallen morality of the city.

I asked him why the church accepted money from the traffickers. "We don't always know who gives the church money," he said. "If the priest is clear about it, he won't accept it. But a lot of the times when we pass the collection plate, we don't know who puts the coin in."

"We're not talking about coins," I said.

"Money isn't bad or good," he replied. "We need money to create development. We have a demographic explosion here, and we need money to help people. The state sells cigarettes and alcohol, but that doesn't make the state immoral. Most people welcome the money. It helps the economy to accept the money, but you have to do it with reflection. I've thought a lot about this. I have a reputation as a deep thinker here."

Deep thinking had produced some curious conclusions. Lopera had worked in Pablo Escobar's campaign when the drug lord ran and was elected to Colombia's House of Representatives, and in 1983 he had moderated a panel about extradition that Escobar had sponsored and participated in. "I knew him when he was a congressman," Lopera said of Escobar. "He thought about Colombia. He talked about ending poverty. When I knew him, he was a good person and had good ideas. The press talks about atrocities. But if he's bad, the state should prove it. It's not up to me."

Possibly only a lawyer, which Lopera is, and a deep-thinking lawyer at that, could have reached the conclusion that the jury was still out on Pablo Escobar. Escobar has not, of course, been tried. Colombian law presumes innocence until guilt is proved, so Escobar is an innocent man. Lopera's civil libertarianism would have been admirable had he been in a country that had a judicial system capable of finding witnesses willing to testify, a judge willing to preside, police able and willing to make an arrest and obtain evidence, and jailers willing to hold the accused once he had been convicted. But this is not a description of Colombia.

Mario Arango is the dean of Medellín's department of moral ambiguity and one of the city's strangest men. When Arango's first book—*The African-Indigenous Ancestry of Colombian Institutions*—came out in 1971, his mother had sighed and asked, "Mario, my son, why don't you do something that can make you a living?" Arango caught on quickly. When I went to see him, he was one of Jorge Ochoa's lawyers and an adviser to Escobar, and his most recent book on drug trafficking was about to become a best seller. He had also been economics editor of Guillermo Cano's paper *El Espectador*, head of the economics department at the University of Medellín, and president of a local college. He had recently been elected to the Medellín City Council.

He was a little dandy of a man, with a big mustache and a potbelly, dressed in a striped shirt and plaid pants that clashed horribly. We drank coffee in his study, overlooking a garden populated by giant turtles. A portrait of Joseph Stalin hung on one wall. Arango had studied in the Soviet Union. His argument was that drug trafficking should be welcomed because it is good for capitalism.

"The United States should be very thankful for the drug

traffic," he said. "It has brought thousands of people into the consuming society, people with an appreciation for the United States. It has amplified demand for your products and kept the economy from falling into crisis. If not for that, we'd have a whole country of guerrillas. What's better for capitalism? Drug trafficking? Or guerrillas?"

His latest book, *The Impact of Drug Trafficking in Antioquia*, contained a survey of twenty Mafia chieftains' life-styles and opinions, such tidbits as the information that 40 percent consider themselves devout Catholics, 80 percent send their children abroad to be educated, 80 percent believe that drugs are dangerous, 90 percent oppose the sale of *basuco* in Colombia, and 60 percent have at least two girlfriends in addition to their wives.

I asked Arango about Escobar. "A very intelligent man," he said. "Wise, with a clear vision of the political and economic problems of the country and the world and a good sense of social service. He's charismatic. He's very attractive in the way he communicates with people; he makes himself liked."

I sensed that he didn't care for the portrait he was painting of himself. "Just because I'm a lawyer for drug traffickers doesn't mean I support them," he said. "I'm just against extradition." He said the Ochoas paid him very little, but he would not specify how much. It was principle, not money, that had attracted the team of lawyers to work for the Ochoas. "There are four ex-Supreme Court justices," he said, "including two ex-presidents of the Supreme Court. And a former member of the Council of State. People of great moral quality."

Another of Arango's books was called *The Ideology and Thoughts of Rodrigo Lara Bonilla*. He had been a good friend of the justice minister. "He was a real leader—brilliant, intelligent," he said.

I asked him if it made him uncomfortable to be working for the men who had had Lara Bonilla killed.

"Oh, I'm not really their lawyer," he said. "I'm just a student of cocaine trafficking, and they called me up to clarify a few legal concepts. It's one of Colombia's principal problems, and I study the problems of Colombia."

Here was a man who could live with contradiction: He was/was not a Mafia lawyer, he did/did not support the traffickers, he was a supercapitalist who admired Stalin, and he didn't let it bother him when his clients had his friends murdered.

THE TRAFFICKERS DO NOT OWN EVERYONE AND EVERYTHING IN Medellín, but they own what they want to own. They have not bought into the city's factories on any important scale, but this seems to be by their own choice. Running a textile factory isn't very glamorous. It is hard work, offers small rates of return, and, most important, is subject to government controls and strict reporting of financial transactions that make it a poor way to launder dollars. Cocaine money goes instead into farms, luxury goods, and more glamorous, harder-to-monitor businesses that are better at hiding money's origins: contraband cigarettes; hotels; restaurants; discos; horses; fighting bulls. Many of the soccer teams in Colombia are owned by the traffickers. Colombians have invented new words to describe the businesses: That team plays narcofutbol, they say, or we're going to a narcodisco.

The way the traffickers help their business through sharing their wealth is by now famous. In the judicial system, a government lawyer told me, the prosecutors are the least corrupt, but it is a question of logistics, not morals; it is simply easier for the Mafia to win cases by bribing policemen or judges. There are many, many corrupt judges, he said, many corrupt officers in the army, investigations police, customs office, and, above all, the police. Others told me that the only rival to the police in matters of corruption is the Congress. Campaigns are expensive in Colombia, and there are no burdensome government regulations concerning financing. Possibly the only two men in the Colombian Congress who did not take secret donations from traffickers were Luis Carlos Galán—and Pablo Escobar.

Perhaps as important as the outright bribes, the government as a whole accepts a more subtle legal payoff. It seemed to have decided that while cocaine has brought the country so many problems, Colombia might as well enjoy cocaine's benefits. The economy is healthy by Latin American standards, growing steadily at more than 5 percent a year in the late 1980s, and with a yearly inflation rate in 1987 of 22 percent, equivalent to the monthly rate in Peru, Argentina, and Brazil. As during *La Vi-olencia*, business has never been better; amid the violence and chaos of 1989, investment rose 60 percent over the year before. This is in part because of prudence; Colombia borrowed little during the 1970s and is not burdened with a huge debt. But partly it is because of cocaine, which in the late 1980s was bringing at least $1.5 billion a year back into the country—as much as the hard currency earned from the export of Colombia's legal drug, coffee. Cocaine money, spent mainly on luxury goods, does not create as much solid investment in the Colombian economy per dollar as does money from legal exports. But it doesn't hurt, and each president has done what he can to make sure the traffickers bring the money home and change it to pesos through the state rather than privately, thus ensuring that the hard currency sits in a state bank.

The government offers a trafficker with suitcases full of dollars several ways to turn the money into untraceable clean pesos, no questions asked. Starting with López Michelsen in the mid-1970s, each Colombian president has offered a tax amnesty, allowing a citizen to repatriate money held abroad without paying taxes. The Barco administration offered nineteen kinds of amnesties. Not coincidentally, the amnesties also permit the laundering of cocaine dollars.

The most brazen way to launder money is through the Banco de la República's Ventanilla Siniestra ("Left-Handed Window"). The window was created during the government of López Michelsen, when the marijuana boom had just started and millions of illegal dollars were entering the country.

On the day I went to the Left-Handed Window of the Banco de la República in Medellín, four men in their twenties wearing tennis shoes and jeans were removing envelopes stuffed with hundred-dollar bills from their shirts and passing them through the window. No one ran to call the police. The transaction took an hour. Mine was quicker. I walked up to the window and said, "I'd like to change fifty thousand dollars, please."

The woman behind the counter didn't look up. "Name?" she said.

"Mary Tyler Moore," I said. I signed my new name and said, "Better make that fifty dollars." I changed $50 and left. The rate I got in the bank was slightly better than the street black-market rate. In the first three months of 1991, the Left-Handed Windows of the Banco de la República brought the government $300 million in hard currency.

Plata o plomo affects the press as well. Newspapers and television generally cover the Mafia only when publishing the statements of government officials on the subject. If the government were to keep quiet, it would be possible to read the newspapers for years in Medellín without realizing that the city had a problem. "Even if I were suicidal enough to write a story and had good information, the paper wouldn't publish it," said Ricardo Aricapa, who has worked for newspapers, magazines, and television. "On the one side, you have fear. On the other, the shareholders, owners, politicians, and advertisers all are in league. If they did publish any significant information, it would go on the last page under the movie listings."

"Until a year and a half ago here you could write what you wanted," said a friend of mine in 1988 who worked for a newspaper in Medellín, a man I'll call Arturo. "I wrote about corruption in the army, the Mafia." He had been covering one particular crime for a month when he started to receive death threats on the phone. What did you do? I asked. "I stopped writing about it," he said. He looked at the picture of his small daughter on the windowsill above his desk. "I have no desire to leave a widow and an orphan. I have no reason to become a hero."

When he was a student, Arturo had sympathized with the guerrillas. Then he had become disillusioned with the revolution, married, found a good job, and decided the system wasn't so bad after all. Had he lived in the United States, he could have been an Ann Arbor peace marcher turned Chicago corporate lawyer. On the day before I left Medellín, I mentioned to another reporter that I had found some parts of the city easy to understand, that some people lived here just the way they would live in my country, and I cited Arturo as an example. The man told me that the year before—the day after Arturo had written a particularly hard-hitting article on the traffickers—two *sicarios* had come looking for him when he left the paper one night. He escaped by hiding under a car while they shot around it. In all our time together, all our long conversations about people in the city who become heroes, Arturo had never mentioned that to me.

*   *   *

MEDELLÍN'S ATTITUDE TOWARD THE TRAFFICKERS IS DIRECTLY related to social class: The poorer you are, the more of a hero Pablo Escobar seems. Indeed, only when listening to young Sandinistas in Nicaragua talk about Che Guevara or women in Argentina's slums talk about Evita Perón did I hear anything comparable to the adoration expressed by poor people in Medellín for Don Pablo.

In April 1983 the Medellín River flooded, destroying the garbage dumps on its banks and the shacks of several hundred families who made their living picking through the mounds of trash. A week later a stocky man of thirty-four, wearing black pants, a white short-sleeve shirt, and a cheap watch stepped carefully through the garbage to talk to the families that were starting to put their shacks back together. It was Pablo Escobar. He promised the families he would build them new housing. He created a corporation, Medellín Without Slums, and a month later 360 families moved into a new barrio.

The houses in Barrio Pablo Escobar (no one uses its formal name, Barrio Medellín Without Slums) sit on a hill overlooking the city. They are brick, small, and sturdy, with plumbing and electricity and gardens filled with Medellín's famous flowers. The residents pay only for electricity and water. They, of course, cannot say enough good about Don Pablo. "We had never seen a rich man build houses for poor people before," said Juan Francisco Flores, a seventy-year-old man with no upper teeth who gave me a tour of the neighborhood. "We call him the father of the poor."

Everyone had heard rumors about the source of Don Pablo's money, but like Father Lopera, they weren't jumping to conclusions. "I'm not in favor of drugs, mind you," said a man scooping rice into bags in a small store. "They've destroyed many of our young people. But we don't always know how people get rich. All we know is that he brought us here. We can't accuse him of anything."

"We are very poor, and it's a worldwide problem," said Flores. "They ought to do something in the United States."

At the foot of the barrio is a church, a small brick building with a Virgin in the glass window. Escobar's mother put up some of the money to build the church, and the residents held bake sales and bingo games to raise the rest. There is no priest, however; the archdiocese, in a sudden fit of moral rectitude, declined to provide one. "We have to say mass in our houses," said Flores. "It's a clear injustice. Don Pablo is the only man around who has a full heart."

Isaura García, a woman of sixty-seven, with pictures of Christ and Rita Hayworth on her walls, told me that she had a friend who could not support her two children. García suggested that she write a letter to Don Pablo. She did, and Don Pablo gave her a house. "Who else would do that?" she said. I could think of someone else: That's the way Eva Perón worked: social justice as a five-year-old would design it. But it was hard to picture Escobar resolving, like Evita, to answer every single letter or shaking his fist at the heavens in anger that some people had a lot and some had nothing. It is not social justice that motivates Pablo Escobar.

In 1982 Escobar was elected to Congress, running with Jairo Ortega, a congressman who had been dean of the law school at the University of Medellín. Campaign posters described Escobar as "Defender of natural resources with effective programs, outstanding sportsman, sports promoter in various neighborhoods, industrialist, and constructer." The last items were true, in a way, and as for the first one, well, who was going to tell Pablo Escobar that he was not a defender of natural resources? According to Orión Alvarez, who worked for the two congressmen, Escobar was mainly interested in the legal immunity that congressmen enjoy.

But people wanted to believe he was Robin Hood. His investment in houses and soccer fields in poor barrios could not have totaled more than a few million dollars. On such pocket change the richest and most ruthless criminal in the world acquired a reputation approaching popular sainthood. As with Evita, the poor of Colombia feel they can write a letter to Don Pablo and a magical, powerful person will reach down and take care of them, exactly what most poor people want when they pray to their Catholic saints, only the mail works faster. Everyone I talked to in Medellín knew about the houses, about the soccer field lights, and about the traffickers' 1984 offer, rejected by the government, to pay Colombia's foreign debt in return for amnesty. Kids in poor neighborhoods, Gitano had said, play a game. The one who has the best clothes or toys is dubbed Pablo Escobar. "He's built more houses than the government," I heard over and over.

Nowhere are the violence and drug addiction the traffickers have brought to Colombia felt more acutely than in barrios like Santo Domingo, one of the infamous slums of northeastern Medellín at the very top of the hills that stand guard over the city. And nowhere is admiration for the traffickers greater. When I arrived on a Sunday afternoon, there were so many people in the street that I thought some sort of carnival was going on. There was no carnival; this was everyday life. People were sitting on the steps outside small houses built into the sides of hills, radios blared three different songs at once, women laughed and chatted in groups, and men drank beer. In a corner store that sold a few pastries and soft drinks, a group of boys had congregated. They told me that many of their friends had died from smoking *basuco*. Jairo, fourteen, said that his twenty-two-year-old cousin had been shot by *sicarios* in the doorway of his house six weeks before because he couldn't pay for his *basuco*. A boy in a torn gray shirt said that his father had been killed in a knife fight over a drug sale. "My dad sold drugs, too," Jairo said. "But he's still alive."

I asked them what they thought of Escobar. "He's done a lot for the people," said Bairo, a curly-haired boy of twelve wearing a red soccer shirt. The others nodded.

"He's lowered the price of food," one said.

When Escobar inaugurated the lights at the neighborhood soccer field four years before, a gala event with a marching band—Escobar himself played in the first match—Bairo had gone to see him. "He's a very important man," he said. "I'd like to work for him—run a factory maybe." Another boy said he'd like to fly planes for Escobar. Another said he could already drive and could maybe drive a bus. One boy said he'd like to run a factory or a farm; a farm would be better. This was clearly a favorite topic of conversation. Other boys came over. I think they thought I was recruiting.

"I'd buy a big house," said one.

"I'd go to the movies every day," another said.

"You all say that smoking *basuco* is bad," I said. "You all know people who have been killed. Why do you want a job that hurts young people?"

"I'd use my money to help the poor," Bairo said. "Like Pablo."

Escobar's résumé—his beginnings as a robber of gravestones, two short jail terms for car theft and small-time coke trafficking—is one that most Medellín slum boys can identify with. In 1976 Escobar was one of them; ten years later he had become one of the ten richest men in the world and in the process had told the gringos, the government, and privileged Colombia to go to hell. A Mafia career offers poor kids the chance to be feared and respected by their peers, to carry a gun and die in the street, or, if they survive, to possess fabulous wealth. There are few other ways for the poor to get rich in Colombia, which was never a country of great social mobility. But cocaine has created twenty thousand new millionaires in Medellín alone, most of them from origins similar to Bairo's. While the poor revere the traffickers, the traditional bourgeoisie of Medellín has little use for them, or rather for their white shoes, ranchero music, and taste in decorating, which runs to statues of nude women with light bulbs for breasts. In 1990 mafiosis were still barred from membership in the conservative Union Club and Country Club.

But it was only a matter of time; parents worried about their children's social circles. "Your kids say, 'Dad, I'm going to a party at John Doe's house,'" a financier told me. "I tell them to be careful; you know what kind of family that is. But the kids say 'I don't care. It's his father—not him.' They mix with mafiosis in school. The Mafia parents want their children to be socially accepted. They send them to the best schools. In a few more years you'll have a generation of young executives, sons of Mafia families, with nice table manners and degrees from U.S. universities. It's like Joseph Kennedy. He made his money in bootlegging during Prohibition. His son was President of the United States."

The Mafia's unpolished habits are not welcome in polite society, but its money is. El Poblado, the beautiful, wooded neighborhood with stately old trees on Medellín's east side, used to be the home of the city's industrialists and ranchers. Now the traditional rich are returning to the middle-class neighborhood of Los Laureles, and the mafiosi are moving from slum neighborhoods into El Poblado. Although new home construction was dropping in Colombia as a whole, it rose 15 percent in Medellín in 1987, and El Poblado was the reason. The neighborhood is full of new high-rise luxury apartments, and its main street is lined with Mercedes and BMW dealerships and shops offering Persian rugs, saddles, Italian clothing, and paintings, many run by traffickers' girlfriends; a boutique is a popular birthday gift.

I asked my taxi driver about a building I had heard of in which each apartment had a private swimming pool. He shook his head. "They're already all sold," he said.

"I'm just looking," I said.

He took me past two white stone towers under construction, each with twelve apartments, each apartment with a pool hanging like a balcony outside its living room.

One measure of the traffickers' acceptance is that they have become the husbands of choice for Colombia's traditional wives of choice, beauty queens. In Colombia girls of five compete to become queen of their kindergarten class. By the age of sixteen they can be Coffee Queen, Cattle Queen, Corn Festival Queen, Flower Queen, or Miss Antioquia. The newspapers devote endless coverage to the pageants and their contestants. *El Mundo* runs a regular column called "Queens"; when a Miss Antioquia failed to show up for a banquet at a local civic organization, the columnist clucked for weeks about her unreliability and suggested darkly that she should be replaced.

Missing a banquet is occasion for a major scandal; dating a mafioso is normal. The local version of a royal wedding was the 1983 marriage of a former Miss Colombia, María Teresa Gómez Fajardo, and Dayro Chica, a former stableboy for the Ochoas (one of his jobs was to lead the family's small children around on ponies) and waiter in their restaurant. Chica gradually rose through the organization to become a buyer of horses and fighting bulls—and a trafficker in his own right. The wedding was held in the Rodeo Club and cost five million dollars; guests from out of town were given round-trip plane tickets. María Teresa was driven up to the club in her wedding present, a white Mercedes covered with orchids. The Ochoa family gave the couple a chess set with gold pieces. "For the first time, a pawn takes a queen," the card said. *El Mundo* published extensive pictures and interviews from the wedding for three days running without ever mentioning just what it was that the groom did for a living.

"The good families here used to have a priest and a doctor," Luz Estela de Medina said. "Now they also have a mafioso. He's usually the best-loved son because he gives the family so many things. Mama wants to enjoy life; brothers and sisters like riding in a new car. It may seem obvious why someone who just started a new job would have a car, but they don't want to know."

"Before Alvaro was killed," said Clarita, Judge Medina's twenty-three-year-old sister, "I never paid any attention to whether I was mixing with the mafiosi. You're not conscious of it until it hits you." Clarita studied nutritional science at La Salle University, a school for Medellín's children of privilege, not a place the Mafia would be expected to penetrate. But she said she could hardly find friends who didn't mix with the traffickers. "They invite you out, give you presents of clothes and jewelry, take you to the best restaurants. Now I never accept. I won't even set foot in the shopping centers they own." Her former best friend married a trafficker, she said. "She likes to dress well, have different rings for every day. Well, I like it, too, but not that much. I don't see her anymore."

Pablo Escobar's son was a third grader at Colegio San José, a school affiliated with Clarita's college. On the last day of school the year before, the boy's father came to pick him up. Clarita saw Escobar waiting in the car with his bodyguards and went home crying. "I went to the principal and said, 'How can you allow the son of a gangster to go to school here?' He told me, 'Who are you to judge that boy?' "

No such welcome existed for General Miguel Maza. Had Maza been a trafficker, there might not have been a problem. But Maza was, instead, the crusading head of the investigations police. By 1990 various attempts on his life had killed seventy-three bystanders, but no one had yet won the million-dollar price Escobar had put on his head. Maza lived near the Lycée Français, and he was receiving a steady stream of letters from the students' parents, asking him to please move out of the neighborhood.

Clarita's rejection of the traffickers had become a problem. "I see people in white shoes with a lot of gold jewelry, and I react too strongly," she said. She was seeing a psychologist to try to get rid of these abnormal feelings.

*　*　*

I MET ONE MORE OF MEDELLÍN'S MALADJUSTED BEFORE I LEFT
the city. Clemencia Hoyos is a young law professor at the University of Antioquia. With its rolling lawns and old trees, the
campus looks as idyllic as any Ivy League university in late May.
Couples holding hands stroll amid the trees, and students study
on the grass. Posters advertising concerts and political meetings
cover the walls. I walked with Hoyos past a building of classrooms
whose outer wall was a heap of bricks. The day before, she said,
a bomb had exploded there at seven-thirty in the morning. The
shattered wall and the glass that still lay on the sidewalk were the
only visible evidence of the fact that this pastoral university has
become one of the most dangerous places of employment in
Colombia.

Hoyos had been vice-president of the university the year before.
To put the university in perspective, she said, it would help to
see the black appointment book she had kept during that year.
In 1987 the university had stopped making education news and
had begun to appear, with horrifying frequency, on the police
pages. Her book was a year's record of murders. There was something almost every week: "July 17, 1987: found cadaver of vet-
erinary student José Abad Sánchez, tortured, circumstances of
death unknown. August 3: anthropology professor Carlos López
Bedoya assassinated. August 14: Pedro Luis Valencia, professor
of public health, assassinated, shot at 7 A.M. in his house, fifteen
rounds of machine-gun fire in his back." And on and on, sixteen
murders of university students or professors in the last four months
of 1987 alone. Hoyos kept a black dress and shoes in her office;
there was no sense in going home to change every time she had
to go to a funeral.

Most of the murder victims were political or human rights
activists, and many had been killed while attending the funerals
of other professors and students, creating an endless spiral of
violence. On August 21, 1987, two professors of medicine, Le-
onardo Betancur and Héctor Abad Gómez, both Liberal party
members and officials of the Medellín Human Rights Commission, were shot and killed on the street on the way to the funeral
of a union leader.

Hoyos's officemate Luis Fernando Vélez, a law professor, had been one of the few surviving officials of the city's Human Rights Commission. One evening in December 1987 he called Hoyos at home. "They want to name me president of the Human Rights Commission," he said. "Oh, God, what can I do?" He had a wife and four children, he said. But he accepted the job. On December 11 Vélez gave a speech in the university about the obligation to work for human rights and the dimension of the task in Antioquia. A week later he was driving home at ten-thirty at night when his car was stopped and he was shot twice in the head.

Hoyos found out about Vélez's death when she heard it on the radio in her mother's house. She had gone home for a visit because two days earlier her downstairs neighbor, a professor of chemistry at the National University, had been shot to death.

In one year eight of her friends were killed. "They used to call me *la gorda*—the fat girl," she said over lunch one day at the university's cafeteria. I looked at her in her khaki pants and Hawaiian shirt, with her punk haircut. She laughed. "I'm eight kilos skinnier now," she said. "I lost a kilo every time someone was killed." In August someone had broken into her house and rifled through her books and papers. Nothing was taken.

"We have no sense of nation," she said. "The cardinal is fat, and the church is fat. There was a big scandal seven years ago: The church's widows and orphans fund went bankrupt; all the money had been stolen. The guerrillas—ten years ago some people had sympathy for them. Now they're worse than the right. The Mafia has bought everyone. Congressmen do nothing but steal money and go to Europe. Everyone knows the army is killing people. Everyone knows the Supreme Court declared the extradition treaty unconstitutional out of fear. Everyone who gets money leaves.

"I know a pediatrician whose wife—they were separated—contracted a *sicario* for a million pesos to kill him," she said. "The *sicario* arrived and said to the doctor, 'Give me a million and a half pesos and I won't kill you.' What have we come to? You can't even trust your own *sicario*.

"Last year," continued Hoyos, "two lawyers called me who were working for Jorge Ochoa fighting extradition. They offered me money to go to New York and interview a few people. They said I had good credentials, and I would have to do nothing that wasn't completely legal. I said no. I told them that not everyone wants to work for Pablo Escobar."

I asked if she found it difficult to teach law in that environment. "I tell my students that what I teach has nothing to do with reality," she said. "I teach religion—what *should* happen. If I tried to teach the law as it really works, I wouldn't have enough material to start class."

Juanxu, her downstairs neighbor who was killed, had saved all his life to build a farm and leave Medellín. He had just bought the bricks when he was killed. "I spend all my money," Hoyos said. "I'm not going to save one peso." She has begun to dream at night about being shot. "If they want to kill me, it will be easy," she said. "Everyone knows where I live. I have parties and leave the door open." She has stopped reading the paper and listening to the radio. She has stopped going to funerals. "Juanxu isn't missing a thing," she said.

Alvaro Medina was not the only one who would die of Quijote in Medellín. There were a few others. It was possible that I had met all of them—a dozen or so people in a city of 2.2 million, a handful of people who, against all reason, continued to believe in Colombia as a nation. There was no explanation for why Medina indicted Escobar, or why Ramón Castillo ran for mayor in Urabá, or why Enrique Low Murtra decided to become justice minister, or why General Maza still pursued Escobar despite a million-dollar price on his head, or why anyone joined Unión Patriótica, or why Luz Estela, after everything the family had gone through, was considering becoming a judge. "I want to raise my sons not to be such good people," she had told me. Who could argue with that? It was best for the family and best for the boys; it was what any normal, rational person would want. But there was always the hope, however remote, that she would fail.

TWO

THE
GOOD
SAILOR

THIRTEEN YEARS LATER THEY STILL MEET, EVERY THURSDAY at three-thirty in the afternoon, a few hundred people gathering to walk slowly in a circle in the Plaza de Mayo around a statue of Liberty with her shield and spear. They wear white kerchiefs cross-stitched with "Irene Krichmar, Miguel Angel Butrón, Desaparecidos, 18/6/76, Argentina," or "José Valeriano Quiroga, Desaparecido, 28/6/76." Over the years, as they walked, the word "disappeared" metamorphosized into a transitive verb in the global vocabulary, and "to be disappeared" and "to disappear someone" entered the world's consciousness, placed there by their children. Each week they are grayer, fatter, and they walk more slowly, but the Mothers of the Plaza de Mayo are determined to walk in the plaza every Thursday until their children appear once again, which means they will walk forever.

Not all are mothers. Some are grandmothers, husbands, wives of the disappeared, fathers, brothers, relatives of all kinds, and people who come simply to show their support for the Mothers of the Plaza de Mayo. In the first months they all were mothers. Then, in the late spring of 1977, when the military junta was a year and a half old and had disappeared more than sixty-five hundred Argentines in what came to be known as the Dirty War, a young blond man with the face of an angelic five-year-old and a Kennedy smile appeared in the plaza. He explained that his name was Gustavo Niño, that he was twenty-six years old and a student, that he came from Mar del Plata, a six-hour drive from Buenos Aires, and that his brother had been disappeared. For a while then it was sixty women in their forties and fifties and one young man.

Gustavo was obviously from a good family, María del Rosario Caballero, one of the Mothers, told me when I first met her in 1988. But he was far from home, and student life was hard. He wore the same blue pullover sweater almost every day. "He always looked a little scared, and we took care of him. He quickly became the pet of Azucena Villaflor, our founder. New people who joined the group often thought he was her son," said Caballero. The Mothers had chosen to walk in the plaza in front of the presidential palace so the junta members could see them from their offices. It was dangerous, even more dangerous for a young man, especially one as passionate as Gustavo. Gustavo once got into a fistfight with a policeman who tried to break up a demonstration.

Gustavo jumped into the work, always suggesting more meetings, stronger slogans. He went to all the commemorative masses. He became part of another group of people—relatives of the disappeared, friends, even two French nuns—formed to raise money to buy a full-page ad in *La Nación*, Argentina's leading newspaper. The ad—a respectful letter requesting information about the whereabouts of the disappeared—was to run on December 10, 1977, and be headlined WE ONLY ASK THE TRUTH. On December 8 the group met to raise the last few pesos for the ad in the Santa Cruz Church, a brown cement church in a working-class neighborhood. Gustavo came with a blond girl he introduced as his sister. "Gustavito, what are you doing here?" Caballero said. "This church is surrounded by strangers. It's dangerous, you shouldn't be here."

"How could I miss such an important day?" said Gustavo. They passed the collection bag around. Then Gustavo got up and said he was going out to get some fresh air. As he was leaving, he pulled some bills from his pocket and waved them, as if waving at certain members of the group. The strangers who had been hanging around outside ran into the church, weapons drawn.

"Drug arrest!" shouted the men. Five Renaults pulled up. The men shoved seven of the group, one of them a forty-three-year-old French nun, Sister Alice Domon, into the cars, and sped off.

Caballero was screaming. "Shut up, you crazy old lady," one of the men yelled back. "Do you want to come with us?"

"I couldn't see if they had taken Gustavo," Caballero told me.

A few days later Azucena Villaflor and the other French nun, sixty-two-year-old Léonie Duquet, disappeared as well.

Testimony later came from survivors of the Navy Mechanics School or ESMA concentration camp that Villaflor, the nuns, and the rest of the group ended up in the ESMA's torture chambers. While she was being given electric shocks, Sister Alice asked about the fate of the "blond boy."

"We were sure they had taken Gustavo," said Caballero. Then on Thursday, at the usual time in the Plaza de Mayo, the women saw him, standing against a wall, half hidden in the shadows. "We were shocked," she said. "He looked terrible."

"I have to talk to you," Gustavo whispered.

"Are you crazy?" said the Mothers. "Get out of here, run, go, it's too dangerous." And Gustavo left.

It was only later that a member of the group who was exiled in France wrote to say that a blond man with an angelic face, going by the name of Alberto Escudero, had joined an Argentine solidarity organization in Paris. "We think he's really working for the navy," the woman wrote; the navy had a Paris office that infiltrated exile groups. The woman sent along a photo. Alberto Escudero was Gustavo Niño.

Over the next few years Gustavo Niño's face became famous around the world. In 1981 an Australian magazine printed photos of Gustavo, now using his real name, Alfredo Astiz, taken while he was the naval attaché at the Argentine Embassy in Johannesburg, South Africa. Then, in 1982, there appeared a photo of Lieutenant (Junior Grade) Astiz, this time with a beard, signing a document of surrender aboard the British warship *Plymouth* after the war in the Falkland Islands. Another photo: Lieutenant Astiz, still bearded, looking solemn, flying from London to Buenos Aires after his interrogation by the British. Yet another photo: Astiz, now a full lieutenant, in uniform in the backseat of a car in 1985, leaving the Federal Court Building after his indictment for the disappearance of Dagmar Hagelin, an Argentine-Swede whom he had apparently shot in the forehead one morning, put inside the trunk of a car, and taken to a concentration camp. And still another: Astiz in his white navy dress uniform, passing behind Ragnar Hagelin, the father of the Swedish girl, accuser and accused.

But then the photos changed; the smile returned: a very tan

Astiz in a lounge chair at the Yacht Club beach in Mar del Plata, his hair tousled in the wind. Astiz dancing in Le Club disco, shirt sleeves rolled up. Astiz standing on the Yacht Club beach in swimming trunks, chatting with another naval officer who had served with him in the Falklands. Lieutenant Commander Astiz, in pea jacket and white navy hat on Navy Day in May 1988, photographed in Bahia Blanca, where his ship, the destroyer *Hercules*, had anchored, looking like a young Robert Redford, laughing, his teeth on display to the world.

It was this last photo, reprinted in a Chilean newspaper, that arrived one day at my desk in Chile. I looked at it for a long time and that day decided to try to understand the world of Alfredo Astiz: a citizen of the most European and developed country in Latin America; a member of the most civilized and aristocratic of its armed forces; the son of a navy commander father and a blue-blood Dutch mother; a lover of Van Gogh and Calder and classical music; well traveled, well educated, and well read—and an officer of the operations department of Task Force 3.3.2 during the Dirty War, the most notorious group of torturers and murderers of the most notoriously murderous junta in modern Latin American history, and directly and personally responsible for the kidnapping of hundreds of people who suffered unimaginable torture and then vanished forever.

WHILE COLOMBIA'S VIOLENCE HAS ITS ROOTS IN A LACK OF SOCIAL order and the government's inability to place rules on a noisy, chaotic society, in Argentina the junta that came to power in a military coup on March 24, 1976, created exactly the opposite situation. The junta, which called its government the Proceso de Reorganización Nacional, or El Proceso—which is also the title of Kafka's *The Trial* in Spanish—suffocated Argentina with social order. The noisy or chaotic simply evaporated into the air. At root, however, the problem was the same: a disregard for law and politics as a way for countries marked by enormous social contrasts to solve their problems. And the results were the same. The junta billed its violence as a war against the guerrillas, principally the group called the Montoneros, who claimed to espouse the nationalist, populist thought of Juan Perón, the general whose presidency in the 1940s and 1950s shaped modern Argentina. But the Dirty War also wiped out the ranks of such dangerous terrorists as Argentina's journalists, psychiatrists, social workers, and labor leaders.

When it was all over and Raúl Alfonsín, a civilian, was elected president of Argentina in 1983, he named a group of prominent Argentines to form a National Commission on the Disappeared. The commission sent its members all over Argentina and to Spain, Mexico, Venezuela, and other countries to collect testimony, eventually gathering fifty thousand pages. The commission found that the government had produced—or, rather, not produced—more than nine thousand disappearances. A distillation of the testimony was published under the title *Nunca Más* ("Never Again").

Nunca Más is, as the British legal philosopher Ronald Dworkin writes in the Introduction, a report from hell: stories of prisoners whose wounds were infested with maggots; a woman who bit through her own tongue from the pain of electric shocks; anal rape with electrified metal rods. File 2819, the testimony of a man imprisoned in the army's Campo de Mayo, reads:

> *We prisoners were made to sit on the floor with nothing to lean against from the moment we got up at six in the morning until eight in the evening when we went to bed. We spent fourteen hours a day in that position. . . . We couldn't utter a word, or even turn our heads. On one occasion, a companion ceased to be included on the interrogators' list and was forgotten. Six months went by, and they only realized what had happened because one of the guards thought it strange that the prisoner was never wanted for anything and was always in the same condition. . . . The guard told the interrogators, who decided to "transfer" [kill] the prisoner that week, as he was no longer of any interest to them. This man had been sitting there, hooded without speaking or moving, for six months, awaiting death.*

Miriam Lewin was nineteen when she was taken on May 17, 1977. I went to see her twelve years later. She had been one of Astiz's prisoners. She was a student at the University of Buenos

Aires and a member of the Peronist University Youth, an organization created by the Montoneros that did campus political
work. According to other prisoners, Lewin was a low-level Montonera, although she herself denied doing anything more than
political organizing.

In any case, at the time of her capture she was carrying a
cyanide suicide pill, as the Montoneros did, and she stuffed it
in her mouth. The soldiers wrested it out before she could bite
through it. Members of the air force brought her to a secret jail
and tortured her in a room with a swastika on the wall; Lewin
is Jewish. She was told to write a self-criticism, repenting her
past activism. She wrote it, then read it in a wig and glasses before
a TV camera, as her captors directed. For some reason, the air
force then turned her over to the navy. On March 26, 1978, she
was hooded and handcuffed, her feet were chained, and she was
stuffed in the trunk of a car and brought to what she later found
out was the ESMA, the Navy Mechanics School. She remained
there until January 10, 1979, when she was released—in a way:
permitted to go home, carefully watched, required to spend her
days for the next year in forced labor for the navy.

I met her ten years after her release, in her small apartment
in an old building in a working-class neighborhood of Buenos
Aires. I was trying to meet as many former ESMA prisoners as
I could, in hopes of understanding the Dirty War and Astiz. A
small woman with shoulder-length blond hair, Lewin was working in the Buenos Aires office of one of Argentina's provincial
governments and in her free time writing for a left-wing magazine. Her apartment was filled with skateboards, toy soldiers
blocks, and the shouts of her two young sons.

"Astiz took me out to dinner," she said.

I didn't understand. "He did what?"

"He took me out to dinner. It was when I had been released
from the ESMA, but was still being watched. Astiz was being
transferred to the embassy in South Africa, along with Admiral
Chamorro, the head of the ESMA. He came by one day and
took me to dinner and to a bar in Belgrano for coffee.

"He told me that Admiral Chamorro invited him to dinner
with another officer so they could meet Chamorro's daughter and
a friend of hers. Chamorro kept saying, 'You young men have
to think about getting married,' and winking a lot. When they

started to talk about politics, Astiz began praising Fidel Castro and the Montoneros but talking as if he were serious. The daughter and her friend were scandalized. Chamorro at last decided he was joking."

"He took you to dinner to tell you that?"

"He said he wanted to say good-bye. He said he respected me and believed sincerely that I had been rehabilitated. He wrote his addresses in South Africa and his family's address in Mar del Plata on a napkin in green ink. 'In case you need anything,' he said."

I was thinking: He doesn't sound like a monster. Many things Lewin told me about her prison stay surprised me. She had been physically tortured only during her first days in the camps. She had been given work to do, translating articles. She had been allowed to call her family. This was not the Dirty War I had heard about. Before I left Miriam Lewin's apartment I asked her, as I did each time I met a former prisoner, if she could put me in touch with others who had been inside. Like Lewin, the others told me that they had held jobs and that navy officers had taken them out to dinner both while they were in the ESMA and after.

I pondered this for a few days, and then it suddenly hit me that the stories I had collected about the ESMA all had something in common: They came from the survivors. But the purpose of the concentration camp was not to create survivors. It was to assure that very few people survived. Every prisoner who came through the gates of the ESMA was assigned a number. In the ninety-two months of the ESMA's existence the numbers topped five thousand. There were several hundred who survived: tortured and released after a few days. Fewer than a hundred were, like Miriam Lewin, kept for years in a hallucinogenic hell in which the line between prisoners and guards had blurred, never sure whether the officer knocking on the door was taking them to the torture table or out for a steak. For reasons I understood later, these people were mainly Montoneros. The others who passed through the ESMA—between four thousand and forty-five hundred people, the vast majority of whom had never taken up a gun—died in torture or in the weekly "transfers." A prisoner who was "transferred" was given a Pentothal injection to keep him from struggling and to spare the plane crew psychological trauma and was "sent up" on a Wednesday—for some reason always on Wednesday—in a Fokker plane as part of a group of twenty prisoners and dumped into the sea.

"Now you'll ask me, why would we waste an injection on those prisoners? But we did," Admiral Horacio Mayorga later told me. His attempt to convince me that the navy tortured and killed its prisoners in a civilized way is consistent with the myth Argentines have created about themselves: that solely an accident of geography has placed the Argentines—they of Italian, British, and Spanish descent, with their white skin and manicured nails—in Latin America, an island of Old World refinement stranded in a barbaric sea. Their neighbors of Indian heritage and darker-skinned Argentines are derided as *cabecitas negras* ("little black heads"). The military boasts of its European roots and its mission to save Western civilization. The junta of the Dirty War considered itself a junta of gentlemen, the coup "a conscious and responsibly taken action not motivated by an interest in or a desire for power," according to the initial announcement of General Jorge Rafael Videla, the junta's president.

Of all the branches of the armed forces, the navy is the traditional service of the upper class. Just as Argentina looks down on its Indian neighbors, that is how the tall, white, educated men of the navy view the army and the police. They are almost diplomats, the gentlemen of the navy. But by the time it shut its prisons in November 1983, just days before Alfonsín took office, that gentlemen's camp, the ESMA, could claim the distinction of being the largest death camp of the Dirty War.

THE NAVY MECHANICS SCHOOL, ON THE AVENIDA LIBERTADOR in Buenos Aires, is white with a red terra-cotta roof. Pines dot the lawn in front of the portico with four columns and the seal of the Republic of Argentina above. The concentration camp itself was located in the ESMA officers' club, a three-story building with a basement. Prisoners slept on the third floor and in the attic. The basement held an infirmary, a photo lab, and torture chambers. One of the torture rooms was soundproofed and, when not otherwise occupied, served as an audiovisual studio. The officers slept on the first and second floors. On the third floor was the Hold, a giant warehouse where goods stolen from prisoners' homes were kept. At the end of 1977 a set of offices known as the Fish Tank was installed, so named because the offices were separated by transparent acrylic walls. The Fish Tank, monitored by closed-circuit television, was where the prisoners worked.

I talked to various people who had been tortured in the ESMA. One was María Elisa Landín, a schoolteacher who was fifty at the time she was seized. Military officials had broken into her house five times, looking for her son Martín, helping themselves to household goods on each visit. On the sixth visit they took Landín and her husband to the ESMA, where she was tortured with electricity applied to her breasts and vagina and beaten until she passed out. "Here we are the only gods," her torturer said. Later the couple was freed. Shortly afterward their son disappeared.

Landín believed that the motive for her torture was not a search for information—her torturers must have realized that it was unlikely she would know her son's whereabouts—but the desire to punish her, perhaps to reduce her son's interest in politics, perhaps to create a warning to others, or perhaps simply to illustrate just who was the master of her life and death.

In the first years of the Alfonsín administration the Buenos Aires weekly *Semana* printed two long interviews with Raúl Vilariño, who had been a junior official in the operations department of Task Force 3.3.2. Torturing was not his job—that fell to the intelligence people—but he had witnessed torture. Vilariño was a *cabecita negra*, a short, stocky man with dark skin from a poor family. At the close of the Dirty War he left the navy and contracted problems of conscience, which led him to knock on the door of first *Semana* and later the courts.

This is some of what Vilariño said:

> *I was probably responsible for the kidnapping of about 200 people. Let's say that half were guilty. Of the 50 percent who weren't, a quarter had a certain ideology, although just because they have certain ideas doesn't mean they'll do terrible things . . . and the rest, well, how many times do people send you to a place and you have the address written down and you still have to ask if you are at the right place? We couldn't go around asking if guerrillas lived here. We couldn't always act with courtesy, if*

that is the word. I don't deny that we made five hundred thousand mistakes. They were because the facts we had weren't right. Or because scared people put up resistance that was misinterpreted, because we were anticipating seeing 500 armed guerrillas.

Everyone we arrested was always guilty. I thought we must be wrong sometime. But no, everyone had done something. . . . I asked to watch a torture session to see if people really admitted to all those things.

There was a door where someone had written "The Path to Happiness." Behind that door was the torture chamber: electric shock machine, an iron band of a bed connected to a 220-volt machine, a electrode that went from zero to 70 volts, chairs, presses, and all kinds of instruments. You can't imagine it all: cutting instruments, puncturing instruments, bags filled with sand to beat people without leaving marks. Many of the methods were copied from the Federal Police.

Have you ever been shocked by a refrigerator or another electric appliance? Add a hundred and multiply it by a thousand. That is what a person feels when he is tortured, a person who might be guilty or might not. . . . I'll tell you about a case, a seventeen-year-old girl named Graciela Rossi Estrada. She was a sad-looking girl. Because they needed more hands, I was asked to be present. It began with the simple methods of the average villain in a grade B police movie: cigarette butts, poking her, pulling her hair, beatings, pinchings. As they apparently didn't get what they wanted to hear, they started with electricity. After a half hour of receiving blows and electric shocks, the girl fainted. Then they took her very delicately by the hair and legs and heaved her into a cell, into a pool of water so she'd swell up. Four or five hours later she was in terrible shape from swelling, and they brought her back to the torture chamber. Then she'd sign anything—that she killed Kennedy or she fought in the Battle of Waterloo. That's why I saw the facts gotten from torture weren't real most of the time; they were just used to justify arresting the person.

> *Once I asked Father Sosa [a Catholic priest], who worked in the camp, if this all seemed right to him, and he said, "You have to think like a surgeon. If you have to amputate a disease, you can't think about how the patient will look."*
>
> *Some days trucks would come in with firewood. They'd put firewood on the ground, then bodies, then more wood, then they'd set the pile on fire. They'd also burn cars if they didn't want them to be found. Mengele [the nickname given to the camp doctor] commented that the bodies, while they were burning, were curling up. The people were being burned alive. He said next time he'd cut their tendons.*
>
> *One of the lovely systems Mengele invented to torture pregnant women was with a spoon. They put a spoon or a metallic instrument in the vagina until it touched the fetus. Then they give it 220. They shock the fetus.*
>
> *[Question:] What did you do, watching that?*
>
> *I vomited. What else could I have done?*
>
> *Were there people who enjoyed it?*
>
> *Of course.*

Vilariño's experience was in some ways very typical of the ESMA and in some ways not at all typical. It was typical in that other people witnessed or suffered the events he witnessed; the testimony of the prisoners left no doubt that what Vilariño described took place. And there is no doubt that everyone in the ESMA knew that such things were going on. It was not typical in that it came to light. There must have been many officials who did not believe that everyone detained was a terrorist. There must have been others who questioned, as Vilariño did, the whole basis for the ESMA. But they always deferred to the greater wisdom of the navy. It was not a matter for civilians. No one else confessed his crimes in a thirty-page interview in a national magazine.

Task Force 3.3.2 had a few dozen members at any one time, divided into intelligence, operations, and logistics. Its members were volunteers, and joining the task force was considered in the navy something like joining a religious order because of its strictness—they lived in the ESMA and could spend nights with their families only three times a month—and because of the level of commitment required.

The task force was formed in May 1976, two months after the junta took power. The junta saw its principal task as killing those who opposed it, an assignment carried out mainly by the army and Federal Police. The navy's representative on the junta, Admiral Emilio Massera, created the task force to allow the navy to participate in the "antisubversive fight" and thereby increase its power with respect to the other services. Massera himself, code-named Zero, went out into the street to help in the baptismal kidnapping.

The task force's operations department carried out up to six missions a day, kidnapping prisoners on the street or breaking into their houses. Operations would then blindfold and handcuff each prisoner and bring him to intelligence. Intelligence would torture him, usually with an electric shock machine. A member of the operations department would be present to hear what the victim had to say, in case it could generate a new mission. This routine, which went on twenty-four hours a day, greatly enriched the Argentine vocabulary. Among the words it contributed were *chupado*, ("sucked up," meaning kidnapped), *traslado* ("transferred," meaning thrown out of an airplane into the sea), *mandado para arriba*, ("sent up," the same thing), and *da maquina* ("give the machine," meaning to apply electric shocks).

The work was not without its rewards. "The boys should be compensated for the risks they run," Massera liked to say. When a prisoner was sucked up, his goods were sucked up as well, ending up in the Hold, a warehouse for books, television sets, mattresses, washing machines, paintings, furniture, and clothes. One woman who was sent to work in the Fish Tank was greeted by her entire living-room set—wicker chairs and couch and a stereo—which was now in service in the Fish Tank's lounge. As a rule the truckloads of goods that arrived at the ESMA did not stay long before making their way to the homes of various navy officials. Rear Admiral Rubén Chamorro, the ESMA's director, was said to be a collector of tango records.

In late 1976 the task force began an experiment surely unique in the annals of repression. A few prisoners, perhaps a hundred (Miriam Lewin among them), were not killed. They were kept alive for two purposes: to be reinfiltrated into the Montoneros to capture more of their colleagues and to write speeches and produce materials to serve the political objectives of Admiral Massera. It was a plan that matched the audacity of Massera, he of the lush eyebrows, the movie star smile, the ironic wit, who escorted starlets and loved night life, who went sailing one afternoon with his mistress's husband and came back alone.

"I was dancing with Massera at a New Year's Eve party," a woman I met, the daughter of a navy family, told me. "To make light conversation, I asked him if it was true that he was still seeing a certain starlet. He smiled and said, 'My dear, when I finish with a lover, I have her killed.'

"I assumed he was joking," said the woman. "But I wasn't really sure."

Massera felt cramped in the gray bureaucracy of the junta, hidden behind the stiff-collared formality of Jorge Videla, the army general who was the president. When the junta adopted a Thatcherite economic policy comparable to General Pinochet's in neighboring Chile, Massera formed the Social Democracy party (he even tried to get himself recognized as Argentina's official representative to the Socialist International), which emphasized Perón-style populism, and he believed he had the potential to become a caudillo, or strong man, in the manner of Perón.

For help, he turned to the Peronists under his power—the captured Montonero guerrillas and their sympathizers inside the ESMA. They, under threat of death, prepared his press briefings and wrote speeches, articles, and broadcast scripts for use in the media Massera controlled. Massera would use a Montonero prisoner entering the ESMA as a political adviser or have him killed as a dangerous subversive. Or both. In September 1978, when Massera left the junta, his political ambitions intact, he gathered the ESMA's long-term residents in the Dorado room on the ground floor for his farewell. "We've all lived through unpleasantness," Massera, wearing a suit, told his prisoners. "The fact that we are in two different groups is merely circumstantial. I hope someday we will meet again, a cup of coffee on the table between us." Then he shook everyone's hand and walked out the front door, and the members of his Montonero think tank were led back upstairs and locked into their leg irons and hoods.

"It was hard for us to understand," said Miriam Lewin ten years later. "Massera was so incredibly arrogant. He wanted to use our technical skills and intelligence to win popular support. He thought that since the Montoneros and Peronist Youth had been so successful, we were the key to making him the new Perón."

"Why did you go along with it?" I asked.

"We used it to assure that we lived," she said. She was cooking brussels sprouts for her children. "I'll begin at the beginning," she said from the kitchen. "When I got to the ESMA, transferred from the air force prison, I was taken to the Fish Tank and an officer named Scheller spoke to me. He said that they thought I was recoverable and that if I behaved, I would have some contact with my family. I got sent to the basement. I could hear voices of other prisoners who were obviously moving around and saw people washing dishes and working in a photo lab. I didn't understand what was going on."

She found out that there were two kinds of permanent prisoners in the ESMA. The Mini-Staff, a tiny group, was made up of the real collaborators: people who had broken under torture—or, in some cases, even before being tortured—had turned in their compañeros, and had gone out into the street with navy officials to spot people, some becoming more ferocious in their collaboration than the guards. A few prisoners kept working for the navy for years after. Coca Bazán, a hard-line Montonera, eventually married Rear Admiral Chamorro, the equally hard-line head of the ESMA, accompanied him to South Africa, and, after his death, entered an ashram in India. Another, Mercedes Carazzo, who held her silence under torture and for months afterward, finally broke when the task force killed her husband. She then fell in love with his killer, Lieutenant Antonio Pernia, and began working with the navy, traveling with Pernia to the navy's pilot center in Paris, where Astiz had gone. The ex-guerrilla-turned-religious-fanatic then dragged the torturer who had killed her husband on a tour of the cathedrals of Europe.

The others, like Lewin, made up the Staff. These people had not turned in their compañeros or had done so only under torture, against their will. They worked with the navy in the sense of doing translations or writing speeches but never cracked ideologically.

"An officer asked me what I knew how to do, and I said I could translate English and French," Miriam Lewin said. "So they put me to work doing translations and writing material to promote tourism that would later be used by the Foreign Ministry, the Argentine government's shortwave radio station, or Channel thirteen, all of which Massera controlled. Other people worked in the library, did stenography and filing, made audiovisual material, or worked in the photo lab producing documents. One prisoner was told to write a history of Argentine unions to show that they had always been infiltrated by subversives." Others worked for Massera outside the ESMA, administering properties stolen from prisoners.

"You learned to simulate being recovered," said Lewin. "They brought you in for talks, and you repented having used violence, or you said your former Montonero bosses were traitors who went abroad to live and left their troops in Argentina as cannon fodder." The best strategy was not to become too convinced all at once; the navy men were not stupid. Lewin and the other Staff members lied twenty-four hours a day. They lied to their captors and they lied to their fellow prisoners. They could confide in no one; who could tell which prisoners were simulating collaboration and which were the real collaborators? It was true guerrilla theater.

"It was risky," Lewin said. "If they took you out to spot people, they would start by bringing along another prisoner who was a real collaborator. Then what happened if you saw someone you knew? If you didn't point him out, the real collaborator would rat on you."

Her son was refusing to eat the brussels sprouts. "Would you prefer carrots?" Lewin asked. She went into the kitchen to grate carrots. He turned his attention to a large doll in a military uniform. I asked what kind of soldier it was. "A general," he said.

Lewin came back. "We had to be very careful always to seem recovered. If some loco wanted you to fall in love with him, you fell in love with him. It was like giving your wallet to the guy with the gun."

The chief loco was Jorge Acosta, who ran the task force. Known as El Tigre ("the Tiger"), Acosta was clearly a psychopath. One minute he could be kissing a wanted prisoner through the man's hood, overjoyed at seeing him on a torture table of the ESMA, the next minute twisting the dial on the electric shock machine higher and higher, his face contorted with concentration.

Acosta, an insomniac, haunted the ESMA at night, waking up the women at three in the morning to tell them some idea about how to fight the Montoneros, and they listened, nodding at every detail, until he finished. At any hour of the night a prisoner could wake up to feel the breath of an officer hovering over him, peering at him as if he were an insect in a box. On their breaks, instead of going to the officers' mess, the navy officers often went to the Fish Tank to drink coffee and talk to the prisoners. Sometimes the men didn't go home at night, even when they could. This was in part because they were dedicated Montonero hunters but in part because they had never met women like the Montoneras before. One night three officers took seven or eight women prisoners out to dinner. The prisoners always agreed to go, in order to ingratiate themselves, to show how recovered they were. Acosta was almost shouting at them in the restaurant. "You know that our relationships with women since we met you are practically destroyed," he said. He said that they all had married daughters of other navy officers, women who didn't know how to talk. The prisoners, on the other hand, could discuss books, movies, politics.

But the women always said what the navy men wanted to hear. The simulations were convincing to the navy officials because a lot of prisoners really *had* broken. When I talked to the ex-Montoneros, ten years after their imprisonment, they were still horrified that so many people in their ranks—people with years of ideological training and activism—had turned in their superiors, their best activists, even their best friends. "We felt defeated," said Lewin. "In 1974 those who were captured didn't break. We thought we were growing; we thought the people were with us. The situation was different; morale was high. Later we began to feel that each person who fell was just one more of thousands who fell. If your chief fell before you and turned you in, and you've lost thirty-five friends, your husband, and your brother, by the time you fall you already have a sense of death and defeat. After a while you start to think, How is it that my chief collaborated and me, I'm just a poor foot soldier, why shouldn't I save my life?"

But collaboration was no guarantee of survival. Many people

who broke and fingered compañeros were killed. Many who didn't turn in anyone walked out alive. When Massera left the junta in 1978, he had no intention of leaving his think tank to Admiral Armando Lambruschini, his successor. Massera still wanted to be president and still needed the slave labor of his prisoners. So the "recovered" prisoners began to work outside, in institutions Massera controlled. Lewin went to work in a real estate office administering property stolen from other prisoners. Then she went to the press office of the Ministry of Social Welfare, which was under Massera's direction, and spent her time preparing press clippings for Massera to read each day.

As she became more and more "recovered," she was given more freedom. First she was allowed to call her parents once a month, then more frequently. Then she was allowed overnight visits home. I asked her why she didn't just escape on those overnight visits. "I asked myself that at times, too," she said. "The answer is that we had emotional ties to those inside, and we were always told, 'If someone escapes, everyone inside gets sent up.' " Finally, still working for Massera, still watched and visited by ESMA staff, she was allowed to live in an apartment. When she and Carlos García, another prisoner, decided to marry, they had to ask permission of Commander Luis D'Imperio, who had replaced Chamorro as head of the ESMA. In March 1980 the couple asked permission to visit Lewin's aunt in New York. Permission was granted. They returned to Argentina four years later, after the junta fell.

WHEN TASK FORCE 3.3.2 WAS BORN IN MAY 1976, LIEUTEN-ant (jg) Alfredo Ignacio Astiz was twenty-five. A recent graduate of the Naval Academy, he was stationed in Mar del Plata, a resort city and naval base in the province of Buenos Aires. There he received instruction in how to raid buildings, follow suspects, and infiltrate suspicious groups. To Astiz and the other fighters in the antisubversive war, working in the legendary task force was the fulfillment of a dream. Astiz applied for a transfer and in January 1977 came to the ESMA as a member of the operations department.

He was good at his job. There was some risk involved—occasionally he had to kidnap people who were, in fact, armed guerrillas—and Astiz led several operations a day. When he was scheduled for a day off, he would ask if any shifts were left uncovered and if there was one, he volunteered to fill it. He quickly acquired autonomy and influence, leading raids and kidnappings and helping plan new ones. He did not torture—that fell to the men in intelligence—but he frequently watched torture sessions in order to act quickly on new information the sessions might yield. He was physically strong, regularly scoring goals when the task force's soccer team played the prisoners' team, and others thought him brave. When he was sent out to find a subversive, he came back with a subversive. He came back with hundreds of them, all subversives by definition, having been captured by Astiz.

On January 26, 1977, Astiz made a mistake that, along with the infiltration of the Mothers of the Plaza de Mayo, turned him into an international symbol of the Dirty War. It was eight-twenty on a summer morning in El Palomar, outside Buenos Aires. Astiz and seven other heavily armed operations officials had spent the night staking out the house of Norma Susana Burgos, a Montonera leader who had been kidnapped earlier. They wanted Burgos's Montonera colleague María Antonia Berger. A tall, blond, athletic woman fitting Berger's description came walking toward the house. The men approached her, and she began to run. Unaware that she was not Berger but Dagmar Hagelin, a seventeen-year-old Argentine-Swede, Astiz ran after her.

"When Dagmar was more than thirty meters ahead of her followers, Lieutenant Astiz knelt down, took out his regulation pistol, and fired (only one shot) at the teenager, who fell flat on the pavement," witnesses are quoted in *Nunca Más*. "Astiz ran towards the victim and kept his gun pointed at her whilst Corporal Peralta also pointed his gun at a neighbor, Oscar Eles, a taxi driver, and made him get into the taxi. Driving to where Dagmar lay, they put the victim's bleeding body into the trunk."

Several things are unclear about Dagmar Hagelin's story. It is unclear if she was a very low-level Montonera or just a sympathizer; she was living in an apartment that she had rented under a false name with a friend, and she spent her evenings typing pro-Montonero propaganda. It is unclear why witnesses who first identified Astiz as the man who shot her later changed their testimony. And it is unclear what happened to Dagmar. She was spotted by prisoners in the ESMA, in a wheelchair, her head bandaged, unable to talk. Vilariño, in his interview with *Semana* magazine, said he saw her in a navy rehabilitation institute in Mar del Plata. And then she was not seen again.

The Swedish government demanded that Astiz be extradited for trial. Argentina refused. The French government later also requested Astiz's extradition to try him for the kidnapping of the two nuns. Inside the ESMA it was an open secret that Astiz had gotten burned—bad luck to have gotten stuck with Europeans —and the cases were considered too hot to discuss. New prisoners were told in whispers not to talk about the Swedish girl and not to talk about the Flying Nuns, as they came to be known after they had been sent on the weekly Fokker excursion and pushed into the sea.

Astiz felt alive in the ESMA. "He loved to talk," recalled Elisa Tokar, a prisoner whom Astiz had personally captured on a Buenos Aires street. "He was always in the Fish Tank with us when he could have spent his free time in the officers' club. We didn't want him with us. If he was there, we had to pretend to be working." He especially liked to talk to the prisoners who had come from good families and had good educations, people who he thought were his cultural equal. "In Paris I never missed the museums and exhibitions," he told prisoners, going on at some length about the Calder mobiles and his pied-à-terre in the Rue Lecorbe, pronouncing the French as God intended it. He spoke perfect English. An uncle in Holland had introduced him to Van Gogh, whom he loved. He read books. A friend of his told me she found *Nicaragua: Tan Violentamente Dulce* ("So Violently Sweet"), a book about Sandinista Nicaragua by the leftist Argentine writer Julio Cortázar, in Astiz's car. He was spotted coming out of the movie *Rosa Luxemburg*.

"He used to talk to me about music," said Tokar. "I love rock music. He hated rock and loved classical music. We would talk mostly about music, or he would ask me what I thought about some political event. I always tried to say what he wanted to hear. He hated Peronism. He hated any kind of populism."

And he hated Admiral Massera, who had blocked his father's ascent to rear admiral many years before. It was more than a family grudge. He hated Massera's political ambitions, his populism, and his corruption. He hated the way Massera and Chamorro and Acosta stole. Astiz never stole. He thought Massera was betraying the navy. He believed fervently in the navy, in its level of culture, in its old-fashioned code of behavior and adherence to hierarchy and orders. "He was a little señor sailor, an English gentleman," said Tokar. "He was very superior with his subordinates and very respectful of his superiors. And he used *usted* when he talked to the older prisoners."

"We were watching TV one day, and a black doctor from the United States came on," said Miriam Lewin. "I think he was a Cancer Society official. Astiz said scornfully, 'He can't even speak decent English. It's the North American guilt complex that they put blacks in important positions like this guy. But the blacks don't have the brains for it. Look at Africa. The only country in Africa that is developed is South Africa.' He had such contempt for the *cabecitas negras*. He always said they didn't like to work, that they spent everything they earned on liquor. They didn't work, so they couldn't progress."

Astiz dedicated entire days to explaining his social theories to the prisoners, and they spent their time assuring him—with growing resolution—that he was right. He scorned Jimmy Carter, whose experiments with human rights were endangering the capitalist world. Margaret Thatcher was his ideal leader. The telegram of congratulations he sent her on her election victory came back to haunt him when, five years later, he signed an unconditional surrender in the Falkland Islands War aboard one of her ships.

In his book *The Swiss Trail*, Juan Gasparini, a grade-school classmate of Astiz's, recounted his impressions when they met again twenty years later in the ESMA, their wildly diverging paths resulting in a reunion of sorts. One of Astiz's nicknames was El Rubio ("Blondie"). "Why should I lie?" Gasparini wrote. His former schoolmate was a son of a bitch, "but with me, El Rubio was a different man." Astiz arranged phone calls to Gasparini's family and got him released from the camp after twenty months—eleven of them spent in leg irons—in spite of the fact that Acosta had him marked for "transfer."

One Saturday night, when Astiz was the senior official on duty, he came to Gasparini's cell and yelled for a subofficial to remove his leg irons. "I'll take responsibility for him," Astiz said, and he drove Gasparini downtown. Their first stop was a book-store. "Buy what you like," said Astiz. "You'll go crazy in that cell." Astiz paid. Then, at Astiz's urging, they went to La Paz, the signature café of Buenos Aires's leftist counterculture. Astiz drank cognac after cognac, and the two men talked about books, rugby, politics, war. "You don't have to pretend with me," Astiz said. "We have our pants down here. I know you, and you know I won't kick you around. When they brainwash you with that social justice stuff, there's no cure. Or do you think I'm like El Tigre [Acosta], who thinks that by taking you out to dinner and buying you a few trinkets I'm going to change how you think? You're basically the same, although with all that's happened to you and what you've seen, you'll stay out of trouble. You don't have to tell me you've changed. You know I'm not El Tigre. Everyone knows I hate him, and I hate Massera, who ruined my old man's career. El Tigre is sick. But even so, we agree on what has to be done: We have to kill all those who can't be recovered because if two or three stay alive, in a few years the whole dance will start again. You can rest easy. You'll get out. While I'm here, Tigre won't cause you problems. I'll take care of you. You'll see."

"And I saw," Gasparini wrote. "And that's how it was."

When Silvia Labayru, the prisoner who posed as Astiz's sister when he infiltrated the Mothers of the Plaza de Mayo, had a baby, Astiz took her out of prison to register it, presented himself as her husband, forged the man's signature, then gave the baby to its grandmother. He took another prisoner to see her dying father and later escorted her to her father's wake. Years later, when the woman testified against him in the trials during the Alfonsín government, Astiz told friends he felt shocked and be-trayed.

"Unfortunately we needed symbols," said Elisa Tokar. "I'm sorry it was Astiz. I wish it had been Acosta."

"He had a better relationship with those prisoners who didn't break under torture," said Carlos García. "Acosta liked the ones who broke; he liked to see people on their knees. Astiz wasn't like that. He had a bad relationship with the collaborators on the Mini-Staff. I remember once Astiz went out to a meeting that was going to take place with a collaborator who was going to identify people. There was a problem and the meeting ended in a shoot-out. The collaborator later said to Astiz, 'I was so worried, I thought something had happened to you.' Astiz told me about it later. He said, 'Four hours ago this man was a great Montonero soldier. Now he's worried about me and not his compañeros. He makes my skin crawl.' "

"He was a kind of worthy enemy for us," said Lewin. "He wasn't corrupt. He didn't rape. He was fighting subversion and communism, not trying to get rich. His vision of the world was terribly Neanderthal, but he was convinced of what he was doing. He was there to 'save' his country."

"I don't share that 'worthy enemy' idea," said Graciela Daleo, one of the most hardened Montoneras. "A worthy enemy would have fought fairly or would have tried us in the courts. Astiz might not have enjoyed repression, but he was part of a system that kidnapped defenseless people, maintained them in inhuman conditions, and killed them."

AT LEAST ONE OTHER PERSON IN BUENOS AIRES SHARED MY FAScination with Alfredo Astiz. Horacio Méndez Carreras is a lawyer. On December 20, 1983, ten days after Alfonsín was sworn in as president, Méndez Carreras received a call from the French government asking him to build a case against Astiz for the murder of the nuns. The next year he picked up another client, the Swedish government, interested in the Dagmar Hagelin case. He began these cases as Alfonsín brought the junta members to trial, but watched the possibilities for justice grow slimmer as the armed forces did everything within their power to block the trials, obligating Alfonsín in 1986 to pass the Full Stop Law setting an end to the trials and in 1987 to pass the Law of Due Obedience, exonerating lower-ranking officials from trials on the ground that they had been only following orders. With the Due Obedience law, the possibilities disappeared entirely.

"Montgomery had a photograph of Rommel over his desk. I had a photo of Astiz," Méndez Carreras said. The photo, clipped from a magazine, was of Astiz in a red sweater, sitting in a restaurant booth, his head in his hands. On June 5, 1987, the day Due Obedience became law, Méndez Carreras burned the photo.

The first time I saw Méndez Carreras, in August 1988, he was still working on an ESMA-related case. The regional commanders, people who had given orders to ESMA Director Rubén Chamorro, were high-ranking enough to fall outside the jurisdiction of the Due Obedience and Full Stop laws; they could still be tried. By the time I came back a year later, the new president, Carlos Menem, had ended even trials of high-ranking officers; no case was possible against Astiz or the ESMA. The navy promoted Astiz and, protective of the man many considered a symbol of the heroic junior officer (and eager to thumb its nose at Alfonsín), assigned him to greet children on the destroyer *Hercules* on Navy Day. For Méndez Carreras, Alfredo Astiz was now just a hobby.

Méndez Carreras and I spent entire afternoons in the small suite of offices he shares with another lawyer, trading anecdotes, playing "What else do you know?," and looking over transcripts of the trials. "He's terribly concerned about what all this does to his social standing," Méndez Carreras said. "He goes to polo matches. In Bahía Blanca he belongs to the Golf Club, and he's always surrounded by young men who treat him like a hero. He teaches them scuba diving.

"He has an apartment in Buenos Aires," he continued. "He took out a second mortgage on his apartment so his brother-in-law could buy a car. What an altruist!" I couldn't help laughing at the quantity of Astiz trivia Méndez Carreras knew. "Did you know that when he was assistant naval attaché in South Africa, he was decorated twice by the South African government? He loved South Africa and always talked about how much he admired the country. He bought a BMW there."

The last time I saw Méndez Carreras, he mentioned that Astiz was likely to go to a polo match the following weekend to watch the son of a mutual friend play. "I'm going to go," he said. "I'm going to wear a gaucho costume with a big hat, and when I get close to him, I'm going to walk right up and say, 'I just want to know one thing, Alfredo. Where are the nuns? Are they in the sea or buried somewhere? Where are the nuns?' " He didn't get the chance to ask his questions; the match was rained out.

"I dream about him," Méndez Carreras said. "I had a dream where he was on trial, and Dagmar was in a crib next to him. I went to see an analyst about it."

* * *

I TOOK THE TRAIN TO MAR DEL PLATA, WHERE ASTIZ WAS BORN and where his family still lives. In the summer Mar del Plata is a resort, packed with vacationers; but in the winter it is bleak and rainy, and only two surfers and a few dogs were to be seen on the beach. The house where Astiz was born—on November 17, 1950—is a modest two-story dwelling of white stone and brick, with a balustraded balcony.

His family had moved six years before to another part of town, a neighborhood filled with retired navy officers and their families. The family's new house is modern, with a rock garden and a picture window, decorated with Oriental rugs. Alfredo's sister, María Eugenia, a model with long, streaked hair, answered the door and called her father. Alfredo Astiz, Sr., a balding man with shining eyes, wearing an argyle sweater and socks, corduroy pants, and Wallabees, came to the door. I liked him immediately.

"I'm not going to talk about Alfredo," he said. "I'm very sorry. You went to all the trouble to come here. Just for showing up you deserve better." But he invited me in.

We sat on the living-room sofa. "I couldn't tell you much even if I chose to," he said. "I never asked Alfredo Ignacio about what really happened. I decided to let him talk about it when he wanted to."

We began to talk about the trials in general. "I don't think people have the right perspective," he said. "The trials were unacceptable. Pardons would not be acceptable because they imply that something wrong was done. The junta's comandantes were tried for things that were considered to be crimes only after the fact. Justice here is a joke! Look what happened to Alfredo. He was found innocent in a military court. Later he was retried in a civilian court. They knew he was innocent. They were really putting the whole armed forces on trial."

Astiz Senior told me that he had retired from the navy in 1975 as commander of the cruiser *Belgrano*. He had lived for two years in Washington, he said, taking courses at the Inter-American Defense College. "But I never learned English. Alfredo speaks good English because when he was young, we sent him to English classes." Astiz Senior liked the United States but feared that people there did not understand what had happened in Argentina.

Alfonsín, he said, did not deserve the reputation he enjoyed outside Argentina. "He was surrounded by Marxists," he said. "I'm going to give him the benefit of the doubt. I don't know if he was a Marxist himself. But he let himself be used by the left."

We called a taxi. "I've talked more than I should have," he said. "I hope you understand why I don't want to talk about Alfredo. If you come back again under different circumstances, you can stay here with us, and we all can go to the beach."

WHEN ALFREDO ASTIZ, JR., WAS GROWING UP, HIS CLASSMATES called him Brother Sailor because he talked only about the sea. When he went into the navy officers school after high school, it was as if following a predestined course.

"That's how the navy works," said Pilar. Pilar was a childhood friend of Astiz's from Bahía Blanca, the navy city south of Mar del Plata, where the family moved when Astiz was young. "The fathers are naval officers, right-wing, anti-Peronist to death. Their attitude is elitist, class-conscious, anti-Semitic. The sons then go to navy school, where the professors tell them they should be running the country."

Pilar—not her real name—also came from a navy family. She grew up thinking exactly like Astiz until, to the horror of her father, she insisted on going to college, where she discovered that there was more to the world than Bahía Blanca had taught her. "Bahía Blanca is Disney World," said Pilar. In Bahía Blanca children go to navy schools in navy buses, their families attend mass with navy priests in navy churches, they spend their weekends at navy clubs, they get well at navy hospitals or are buried in navy cemeteries. A sailor who says something stupid is derided: "Don't be a civilian." The only opinions heard and read are navy opinions. "The same people own the radio, TV, and newspaper," Pilar said. "When a constitutional government is elected, they go into mourning. When there is a coup, they celebrate.

"A woman who isn't married at twenty-four is a spinster. If she goes out with a lot of boys, she is a whore. The principles are very strict with regard to sex and family. Daughters of navy families marry young officers. I don't know why they all don't turn out blind and retarded. You live for appearances. It's a religion of appearances. The women never study. Your career is your husband, and you are a decorative element. There are a lot of very unhappy people there."

And the boys go into the navy, where, beginning at fifteen, they sniff the heady salt breezes of prestige and majesty: the white uniform; the ship cutting a clean path in the water; the foreign ports. The navy is a science; it has a history. "The army is for brutes," said Pilar. "The navy is like diplomacy."

Mothers loved Astiz, said Pilar. They thought, *What a nice boy, and such a good family.* Politically his family was like the rest. "It would not have occurred to them to object to what Alfredo did. My family, for example, thought he was a hero. We kidded about his reputation; we joked that we wouldn't let him hold the baby because he'd torture it. If he did anything wrong, they deliberately didn't want to know. They weren't indifferent to what he'd done; they supported it. In a way, Astiz represents the young naval officers. If Alfredo falls, they know they'll all be in the same boat. In my house, if people were being arrested, we said, 'It must have been for something.'

"I once asked Alfredo, 'Why was the torture necessary? I understand the kidnappings. But why torture?' He told me you have to get information fast, before other people get away. He's at peace with what he did."

I called Jorge Sgavetti, Astiz's best friend. Sgavetti, a navy man's son, works in an advertising agency. A handsome, forceful man with a mustache, dressed in a camel's hair coat, he came to my hotel for coffee. I told him I wanted to talk to Astiz.

"You're not the first reporter who's tried to see Alfredo," he said. He questioned me for a few hours: Who was I, had I voted for Carter, what did I think of Pinochet, what did I think of the antisubversive fight?

He would say nothing about Astiz but did promise to call him on my behalf. I spent a few days in Bahía Blanca waiting, walking on the windswept pampa. Jorge finally reported that he couldn't get hold of Astiz; he was probably at sea or on vacation.

On the morning of the day I was scheduled to leave Bahía Blanca I hired a taxi to take me to Puerto Belgrano, the navy base a half hour's drive away. The base was lush with grass and trees. I walked through the gates with Marito, my taxi driver. I was interested in how navy officers lived, so we went to visit some houses. We stopped in front of a house where a woman was tending her garden. She said her biggest problem was trying to get along on the salary of her husband, a low-ranking officer who made about $140 a month. But there were benefits, she said: private schools for the kids, a social club with tennis courts and a golf course, and a hospital. She had cancer, she said. She and her husband left the base very seldom.

We went to talk to several more families. I knew that Astiz lived on the first floor of the officers' house. Was he at home? If he was, would I be able to get past the guard? Would he see me? What would happen if his superiors found out a reporter was trying to reach him? I decided it was better to wait for Jorge to arrange something.

As we approached the gate to leave the base, the guard asked us for our passes. "Passes?" I said. No one had stopped us when we entered. The guard called the base police, who took us to the police station. We were interrogated by a very minor official, then by a minor official, then by a less minor official. Finally they separated us, put Marito in a small room, and sent me to the Intelligence office. I was met by Lieutenant Commander Ernesto Alcayaga, the head of Intelligence, a smiling, chubby man. He looked through my passport, taking special note of the assorted Nicaragua stamps. He asked me where I lived. Chile, I said. "With whom we recently almost went to war," he said amiably.

"Whom do you work for?"

"I'm a free-lance," I said.

"You took a taxi to the base? It's expensive to take taxis when you have no employer."

I explained that the bus schedule would not have allowed me to get to the airport in time for the afternoon flight to Buenos Aires. I was very happy that the baggage handlers in Bogotá's airport had recently stolen my camera. I was happy that I had been taking notes in English.

"Why did you come to the base?"

I didn't want to tell him about Astiz. "I'm writing an article about how low military salaries are," I said. I was trying to remember if I had told Marito anything on the ride over. We had talked a lot.

He sighed. "I think you are going to miss your flight," he said.

A man came into the room. He had been questioning Marito. "He has no documents," he said. "He said he left them in the car. Should I go with him to get them?" Alcayaga nodded. The officers called the taxi company and also a rug business the driver ran on the side to verify his identity.

Alcayaga took me outside and we got into an orange Ford Falcon. "Why don't you tell me whom you visited?" he said.

We stopped at the house of the woman with cancer. Her husband was at home. They did not appear overjoyed to be visited by the head of Intelligence. But the woman said I had spent about ten minutes with her and said that yes, we had discussed the hardships of living on a military salary. Alcayaga looked surprised. We drove back to his office.

"You want to know about living on a military salary? Ask me," he said. I got out my notebook and asked him some questions. Finally I said that I had no more questions for him if he didn't have any for me. He said he didn't. "Next time you want to be a tourist on a navy base," he said, "ask permission. There's a flight leaving for Buenos Aires tonight. Why don't you take it?"

They had finished interrogating Marito, and we drove back to Bahía Blanca. He laughed and said that he regarded the whole day as an interesting adventure. I gave him a huge tip. When I arrived at the airport that night, Lieutenant Commander Alcayaga was there, waiting for me. He watched me as I stood in line to get on the plane, a little smile on his face.

ARGENTINA'S FIRST ARMED FORCES WERE RAGGED BANDS OF GAU-chos in the service of local landowners. The first national army was an equally disorganized and ill-equipped group of volunteers who assembled without the Spanish viceroy's blessing to defend Argentina, still a colony, from a British invasion in 1810. With independence in 1816 came the need for a real armed forces. In 1869 the Military Academy was established.

In 1873 Argentina bought its first Krupp cannon, and Germany thereafter became its principal supplier of arms. When Julio Roca, president of Argentina at the turn of the century, decided he wanted a professional military, he turned to the world's most successful army for training, the German Army. In 1900 the Superior War College was created. Four of the ten professors were German. Argentine officers went to Germany to study as well.

"Our rules were almost a direct translation from German," said Colonel Luis Perlinger, who had entered the War College in 1937. When I spoke with him, Perlinger was sixty-seven, retired from the army, and working on a doctorate in political science. He was the son, grandson, and great-grandson of Argentine military officers. "My mother's milk had a military flavor," he said. "The conversation at our table was about lieutenants and colonels. When I was young, I dreamed of a heroic death, a cornet playing, the coffin wrapped in a flag."

We were sitting in Perlinger's study, the walls lined with photos of his military forebears and his diploma from Franco's army in Spain. I asked him about military education. "There was no education," he said. "It was training. Education provides you with concepts of good and bad. Training produces robots. I was trained. In the German Army they gave you a puppy when you came in. Then, after the puppy had grown up with you, they ordered you to kill it. That is training. That is why there were SS officials and why Argentine soldiers just followed orders.

"I never heard an official openly say he was pro-Nazi. But we all were taught to be antidemocratic, antiworker, antipopulist. If people didn't start out right-wing, they got that way very fast."

The professionalization of the Argentine Army also brought politicization. In a country that had a much weaker civilian government than Germany, the military began to believe that civilians existed to serve a military purpose. The armed forces became a strong interest group that pressured the government for more arms, more resources, and military solutions to Argentina's problems. Until the late 1920s the army busied itself with its traditional work, fighting wars to extend or protect Argentine territory. But as the wars died out, the military found itself with nothing to do. The new "professional" Argentine Army—disciplined, European-trained, taught to think of itself as its country's savior—began to question why it should be receiving orders from civilians who were undisciplined, unprofessional, not trained in Europe, and obviously making a mess of Argentina.

The navy was subject to different influences. Its founder, the man who organized Argentine naval forces to fight in the war of independence, was William Brown, an Irishman. The Royal Navy, considered the world's preeminent fleet, became the Argentine model. Argentina bought its ships from the British; rival Brazil was a client of the United States. As World War II approached, Britain, worried about its supplies of grain and meat, created the Argentine Merchant Marine. But Britain did not exercise the same sway over the navy as Germany did over the Argentine Army. Naval officers did not go to Britain to study; Britain did not colonize the Argentine Naval Academy. The navy's conservative political views were largely a result of its social composition. In the navy, filled with members of the Anglophile upper class, men isolated themselves further on bases or ships. Neither on land nor at sea did they mingle with common Argentines.

In 1928 Hipólito Yrigoyen was elected president for the second time. Yrigoyen was the caudillo of the Radical Civic Union party, the party of Argentina's immigrants, named Radical for its advocacy of universal suffrage. Yrigoyen's second presidency marked fourteen years of uninterrupted power for the Radicals, and the oligarchy despaired of regaining control. Then Yrigoyen began to talk about rooting out corruption in the armed forces. It was too much for the already peeved and restless military. In 1930 General José Uriburu, who had been director of the Superior War College, overthrew Yrigoyen and became the first modern military dictator to rule Argentina.

In his message to the Argentine people he justified the coup as "responding to the clamor of the public against inertia, administrative corruption, anarchy in the universities, politicking as the first task of the government, international discredit and always, always, actions that denigrate the armed forces." It was the first of fourteen military coups Argentina was to see over the next sixty years.

During World War II Argentina's economic interests were with the Allies—Argentina sold beef and wheat at exorbitant prices to Britain—but the government's heart lay with the Axis. In addition to the military's ties with Germany, Perón had been military attaché in Italy early in his career and had never concealed his admiration for Benito Mussolini. Not until March 1945 did Argentina declare war on Germany, and then only under pressure from the United States. After the war, with the German Army demolished, the Argentine Army had to look elsewhere for tutelage. That job now fell to the French, who brought to Argentina a new military concept: counterinsurgency.

In 1955 Lieutenant Colonel Carlos Jorge Rosas, then studying in France, returned to Argentina to become the assistant director of the War College. At Rosas's request, France sent him two lieutenant colonels. For the next four years Rosas and the French gave classes in counterinsurgency at the Military Academy, teaching students who twenty years later formed the juntas of El Proceso.

The failure of France's counterinsurgency forces to contain revolutions in the former colonies of Algeria and Indochina had not dimmed French enthusiasm for the strategy. It seemed logical. Since the new nuclear equilibrium made conventional war improbable, the new style of war was the subversive revolution. Thus the task of both sides was not the defeat of an enemy army but the physical and moral conquest of a people. The military had to fight not an external power but an internal subversive threat, the spearhead of the universal advance of international communism. It was a rather mystical doctrine with the aura of a medieval crusade. "We must emphasize that the character of this conflict corresponds to the religious wars of the past: ideological," Rosas lectured in 1957. "Its probable consequences: the survival or disappearance of Western civilization." With the stakes so high, anything less than total war was not just a mistake; it was a sin. The enemy received no quarter. The conventional laws of war did not apply.

The leaders of the Argentine military loved counterinsurgency. First, it gave them something to do. In his 1964 book *The Crisis of the Army*, Argentine Colonel Mario Horacio Orsolini wrote that the French theories "filled the void produced by the almost complete disappearance of the possibility of war between our country and its neighbors." And communism was a much more dramatic enemy than Paraguay or Bolivia, an all-powerful force of darkness slowly engulfing humanity. The army's 1966 training manual—required reading for every soldier—set out this vision of the world:

> Communism wants to destroy the human being, family, fatherland, property, the state and God. . . . Nothing exists in Communism to link women with home and family because, proclaiming her emancipation, Communism separates her from domestic life and child raising to throw her into public life and collective production, just like men. . . . [T]he father is the natural head of the family. The mother finds herself an associate of this authority. . . . According to the will of God, the rich should use their excess to alleviate misery. The poor should know that poverty does not dishonor, nor making a living with work, as the example of the son of God proved. The poor are more loved by God.

The French doctrines also gave the military a reason to deepen its involvement in politics. There were no battlefields; this was total war. A war against an internal enemy meant using propaganda, psychological operations, and infiltration of political groups. Politicians, always considered inept and ineffective, were now thought of as the enemy or the dupes of the enemy. The civilians were always talking about north-south issues, when the military saw the real threat as coming from the east; the politicians' ineptitude was allowing subversion to penetrate Argentina.

Captain José Luis D'Andrea Mohr, now retired, entered the War College in 1956, the same year as Rosas. "We never studied Marxism in depth," he said. "We studied it just enough to declare war on it. We began to get instruction in how to fight revolutionary guerrillas—of which there were none in Argentina. We were taught we had to be on guard, that the enemy was everywhere: orthodox Peronism, combative labor unions. We were trained to be ready to take possession of gas plants or city halls when the revolution broke out. We did exercises, running up to a radio station to take it—without informing the people inside, of course. We had lists of names of people such as radio station directors or city government officials who were our objective."

On New Year's Eve 1959 a young Cuban lawyer with three thousand guerrillas overthrew the U.S.-backed dictator Fulgencio Batista, establishing what quickly became a Communist state and confirming everything the Argentine military had suspected about the need to be ever-vigilant. Fidel Castro's victory was also seen as alarming by another power that had previously taken little interest in Latin militaries: the United States.

The United States had established the Inter-American Defense Board and training schools both in the Canal Zone and on the U.S. mainland after World War II, but the schools had never received much attention from the Pentagon. Jarred by Cuba, however, in 1962 the United States adopted counterinsurgency strategy. Like its French counterpart, U.S. counterinsurgency doctrine had one overriding goal: to defeat communism. International communism was seen as a disease that could afflict any third world nation. "The outstanding lesson of the Indochina conflict," said General Maxwell Taylor, chairman of the U.S. Joint Chiefs of Staff, in a speech in 1965, "is that we should never let a Vietnam-type situation arise again. We were too late in recognizing the extent of the subversive threat. We appreciate now that every young emerging country must be constantly on the alert, watching for those symptoms which, if allowed to grow unrestrained, may eventually grow into a disastrous situation such as that in South Vietnam."

The U.S. version of counterinsurgency differed from the French in that it accompanied its military actions against guerrillas with halfhearted attempts to provide an alternative to revolution—halfhearted because the important measures, such as taming brutal militaries, were forbidden because they could interfere with the antiguerrilla fight. In the jargon these programs were known as nation building. Former Assistant Secretary of State for Inter-American Affairs Nelson Rockefeller wrote after a fact-finding mission for President Nixon in 1969 that the military was "the essential force for constructive social change . . . the question is less one of democracy or lack of it than it is simply of orderly ways of getting along." Civilian governments were messy and noisy. They had no chain of command. It was easier to modernize the military, so the United States worked on that, believing that a modern military would pull the rest of society along. With President John F. Kennedy's Alliance for Progress, local armies became even more active modernizers, constructing bridges and digging roads, building their nations.

Counterinsurgency doctrine has enjoyed success twice in history. Britain employed it to smother a left-wing insurrection in Malaya, and the Philippines, directed by U.S. counterinsurgency guru Edward Lansdale, used it against the Huk rebellion. Since then it has failed everyone and everywhere: the French in Indochina and Algeria, the United States in Vietnam and El Salvador, and U.S.-backed troops in countless other nations. At times it not only failed but also spawned more of the brutality, state terror, and corruption that feed guerrilla movements.

The paradox of U.S. counterinsurgency is that within the United States the military behaves in an exemplary manner. The armed forces are completely under civilian control. Generals play little role in formulating policy. No one argues that cuts in the defense budget or the election of a liberal Democratic president could provoke a military coup.

Yet when the United States trains militaries abroad, the civil-military relationship that emerges is quite a different one. The difference occurs in part because in the business of containing communism, the U.S. military's job takes place outside its borders, the United States having no real guerrilla movements to contend with at home. But militaries in U.S. client countries are taught to contain left-wing insurgencies within their own populations. And most are armies with long histories of exaggerated power. The money and time poured into modernizing a military such as Argentina's reinforce the soldier's idea that he can do a better job of running his country than any civilian and that his ties with the United States are better than a civilian's. When hospitals are constructed and roads dug by the army instead of the Ministry of Public Works, the message to soldiers is clear: While civilians dither, the military builds.

Counterinsurgency doctrine fuels the armed forces' suspicions not only of their government but also of their people. Asked in 1977 about a woman who was in a wheelchair when she was captured by the military, General Videla replied, "One becomes a terrorist not only by killing with a weapon or setting a bomb but also by encouraging others through ideas that go against our Western and Christian civilization." Videla's remark is not a large leap from General Taylor's warning that subversion must be discovered and obliterated before it happens; the early symptoms of subversion are also known as politics.

"I went into the navy because I wanted to defend Argentina," former officer Julio César Urién told me. "I was idealistic. But the job they had waiting for me was not what I expected. In 1970, instead of training us to defend the frontiers, we were trained to be an army of occupation. School was a constant drumbeat of the evils of Marxism. If you wanted to reach a high rank, you'd better have the right ideology. The enemy was Peronism; the United States could do no wrong. The arms, the manuals were all from the United States. The uniforms had 'USA' on the pocket."

How much of the Dirty War was "Made in the USA"? Formally, very little. In 1977, over the objections of former Secretary of State Henry Kissinger, the U.S. Congress cut off all aid to the Argentine military because of the junta's human rights violations. Historically Argentina has been the Latin American country most independent of the United States, receiving (for its size) the least amount of military aid and sending the fewest officers to U.S. training schools. But this was a relative independence, for between 1950 and 1978 the United States gave the Argentine military $250 million and invited 4,017 Argentine soldiers for training in the United States or the Canal Zone. Among them were General Videla, who attended the School for the Americas in 1964, and Admiral Massera, a graduate of the Inter-American Defense College in Washington in 1963.

What they learned is a subject of endless mythologizing among the Latin left. María del Rosario Caballero of the Mothers of the Plaza de Mayo told me flatly that the Argentines went to U.S. training schools to learn how to torture. I never personally found any evidence of this, although U.S. instruction in torture and the presence of U.S. personnel during torture sessions in Brazil and Uruguay are chillingly documented in former *New York Times* reporter A. G. Langguth's book *Hidden Terrors*. The Argentines seemed capable of devising tortures on their own; the electric shock machine is a descendant of the indigenous electric cattle prod used on the great Argentine ranches.

The School for the Americas' role was more subtle. Its purpose, and that of other training programs, is to teach foreign soldiers to use the tools the United States gives them. These tools include more than tanks and machine guns; the most popular courses center on another weapon of war, counterinsurgency strategy. Between 1970 and 1975 more soldiers took "Urban Counterinsurgency" and "Military Intelligence Officer" than any other courses. Other popular classes were "Riot Control," "Psychological Warfare," "Counterguerrilla," and "Public Information." Even seemingly technical courses contain heavy doses of counterinsurgency; the syllabus for "Automotive Maintenance Officer" in 1969 listed talks on "fallacies of communist theory, communist front organizations in Latin America and communism vs. democracy."

Torture was not on the syllabus at the School for the Americas. But neither, according to soldiers who studied there, was it explicitly condemned. "Our instructors were people who served in Vietnam," said Ernesto Urién, Julio César's brother, who studied at the School for the Americas while an Argentine Army officer in the 1970s. "In informal talks the theme of torture would come up, and they'd say, 'Do what you must to get what you need. The tools you choose, legal or illegal, are up to you.' "

The Pentagon managers of the International Military Education and Training Program, the supervisors of the training schools, bristle at the charge that the program is insensitive to human rights. Spiro Manolas, a big, patient man who runs IMET, smiled wearily when I brought up the subject. "Our goals are first, to create rapport with the United States," he said, "second, to ensure the operability of equipment they get from us, third, human rights awareness."

I asked how this message was taught. Manolas showed me an IMET document listing student field trips to businesses, banks, newspapers, and agricultural experiment stations. "They see the progress made here by women and minorities," he said. "I've had people say to me, 'I didn't think the U.S. was a law-abiding society, and here I see people stop at traffic lights.' They come into the Pentagon and see black soldiers at the door. They see a department store with stuff on open shelves and no one stealing it. You don't need a course on that. They would rebel if we gave them Civics 101. People say, 'I've seen that democracy can work.' You don't say, 'Now you Colombians, don't cut people's heads off.' You'd lose them."

"It would be embarrassing," said Ralph Novak, the Latin

America specialist who sat in on the interview. "We can't force it down their throats. We can just show how we behave."

We talked for a while about whether IMET risks strengthening militaries at the expense of civilian governments; there is, after all, no civilian equivalent to IMET. "There's no time to train civilians," Manolas said. "I agree that it isn't the role of the military to build the institutions of society. Hopefully, in time civilians will do it. In the meantime, there is an immediate problem to be addressed."

"I use the analogy of calling the fireman or the interior decorator when your house is on fire," Novak said.

What bothered him was that the United States broke relations with Latin American firemen precisely when the blaze was hottest. "Carter's attitude was cut them off—Salvador, Chile, Argentina, Somoza," Novak said. "You're a human rights violator, okay. We won't work with you; we won't try to change you. These countries say to us, 'Look, you do business with the Soviet Union, China. We're your friends, and because we have an internal problem in which we might have been too harsh, you cut us off.' If we had kept working with Chile and Argentina, we could have kept contacts with certain officers, nibbled around the edges, making people aware of how things work in the United States."

This idea of friendship kept popping up. IMET could not have stressed human rights because that would have conflicted with the United States' first priority: to "create rapport" with Latin militaries, as Manolas put it. Secretary of Defense Robert McNamara testified before Congress in 1962: "I need not dwell upon the value of having in positions of leadership men who have first-hand knowledge of how Americans do things and how they think. It is beyond price to us to make friends of such men."

I asked Manolas how IMET evaluates its success. He showed me a booklet called *U.S. Training of Foreign Military Personnel*. Table 1 is headed "IMET Trainees Achieving Positions of Importance." The explanation at the bottom said the chart includes "General or Flag Rank officers who have achieved prominent positions (e.g. President or Chief of State, Minister of Government Departments, Member of Parliament . . .)." In the eleven countries in the inter-American region, 223 officers had achieved membership in this group, people like Anastasio Somoza, Manuel Antonio Noriega, and Emilio Massera.

But Manolas and Novak seemed to think that these men would discard their lifelong cultural beliefs after a visit to the Macon, Georgia, *Telegraph and News*, as if *I Dream of Jeannie* and *The Cosby Show* weren't already broadcast into almost every Latin American living room, as if Latinos didn't already know by heart those gringo idiosyncrasies like the due process of law, which the United States could indulge in only because it didn't have to fight the Communist threat. And with a few key phrases—yes, yes, I see now how democracy can work—the Latinos had the Americans hoodwinked.

The United States let itself be hooked. The Latinos would not, as Manolas said, put up with lectures about human rights. But there are more subtle ways to send a message about respect for civilians, and instead, the United States seems to communicate the opposite: It's a tough world out there. A man's got to do what a man's got to do.

"The U.S. military men made it clear to the Argentines that human rights was a policy they had to sell during work hours. But over cocktails, they confided, 'Between you and me, you're all right,' " said Horacio Mayorga, a retired Argentine admiral, recalling the days of the junta. "They said, 'You kill all the guerrillas you can, but do it so you don't make a public scandal.' That was the promise the first junta had. In public, of course, they say just the opposite."

U.S. General Gordon Sumner, the head of the Inter-American Defense Board, gave a speech to the U.S.-Argentine Chamber of Commerce in October 1977, calling for an end to U.S. sanctions on Argentina. In private he went further. "The message that Sumner was passing along was that Carter was a crazy liberal Democrat, an aberration to be tolerated that would soon pass," said Jack Child, an Army lieutenant colonel who acted as Sumner's translator. "He believed that by sanctioning Argentina for human rights violations, we were helping our enemies. After Reagan was elected, he said, 'Now things will get back to normal.' "

Julio César Urién could see the practical translation of such policies in his navy classroom in 1971 every day. "In September 1971 I was sent to the ESMA in Buenos Aires," he said. "We were two hundred people divided into groups of eight, and we each spent two months with a different official. It was what later became operations and intelligence at the ESMA. I think the idea was to compromise everyone. We acted like paramilitaries, learning how to follow people, kidnap people, and afterward how to break them."

How to break them?

"Torture," he said. "I took a course in antisubversive maneuvers in Tierra del Fuego. I was assigned to be the chief Communist. We did exercises where they actually tortured me with electric shocks, hanging me from a bar and with the 'submarine'—forcing my head underwater. Then they studied my reactions. They taught us that torture is a moral way to fight the enemy. They isolate you from society. They bring priests in to say, 'Yes, that's all right.' Your weekends are restricted. If you had a university degree, you were contaminated; the long-haired students were the enemy.

"Some soldiers did have a problem with learning to torture. But the conditioning was that if you don't torture, you're weak."

When I met Urién, he was no longer in the navy. He had been one of those soldiers who had a problem with learning to torture. Urién's father had been a friend of Perón's, and he was reared in a Peronist household. Perhaps because of that or because he was not from a military family, Urién broke away, far away, from the teaching he received in the navy. More and more disillusioned with military school, in the early 1970s he secretly joined the Montoneros. When Perón returned to Argentina from his exile in Spain, Ensign Julio César Urién led an aborted pro-Perón uprising among fifteen young navy officials. He spent the next eight and a half years in jail and was freed when Alfonsín became president.

Urién became a prisoner; his classmates, the jailers. Among his classmates was Alfredo Astiz. "Astiz was a good person," said Urién. "He was a good rugby player and always got good grades. He had a tremendous amount of admiration for the United States. He always went above and beyond the call of duty. If I had stayed in, I might have ended up like him. He's a product of the policy, a faithful keeper of orders. He's not on the margin of the navy. He *is* the navy."

* * *

IF THE MILITARY'S BRUTALITY WAS THE PRODUCT OF YEARS OF methodical indoctrination, the viciousness of the Montoneros, its principal target, seemed more the spontaneous expression of a wild, formless anger. Argentines claim that it is virtually impossible for a non-Argentine to understand the Montoneros and almost as difficult for many Argentines to do so. Even some of the Montoneros themselves, looking back, marvel at the movement's rage, or *bronca*, as Argentines call it, and vengefulness. But the Montoneros' irrationality was the entirely rational outgrowth of years of *bronca* in Argentine politics, a grand tradition of intolerance, vindictiveness, and resentment.

The Montoneros' patron saints set the tone. General Juan Perón had been a military attaché in the Argentine Embassy in Rome in the early 1940s. When he returned to Argentina, he joined the plotters of a 1943 military coup and became labor minister. He then hijacked the booming union movement, building it from above along Fascist lines, turning it into his personal power base. After Perón was elected president in 1946, he built a corporate state with labor as its base, creating new unions and expanding state ministries and businesses with the funds that Argentina had stockpiled during World War II. Argentina under Perón became a hothouse, its huge manufacturing sector isolated by one of the highest levels of protection in the world. The ranchers who had run Argentina watched in horror as Perón shut them out but opened his doors to immigrant workers.

Perón's wife, Evita, was the illegitimate child of a poor family in the pampas who dyed her hair blond and became a radio actress in Buenos Aires. As first lady, she gave speeches threatening to burn down Buenos Aires's wealthy Barrio Norte. She set up her own foundation, where she sat at a desk for sometimes twenty hours a day, giving out sewing machines, bicycles, toys, or cash to grateful, weeping petitioners.

Together the Peróns presided over the last of Argentina's good years. In the 1930s Argentina was the fifth-richest country in the world, with a per capita income in 1937 equal to that of France, and more autos per capita than Britain. Of all the Europeans, only the Swiss and Hungarians had more doctors per person than the Argentines. Evita Perón, on her triumphant postwar tour of Europe, signed agreements to donate food aid to postwar Italy and Spain. In 1949 the Eva Perón Foundation gave money to the poor of Washington, D.C. After Perón, Argentina became part of the third world, its industry protected into stagnation, its society polarized, its decline nurtured by the inefficiency, corruption, and demagoguery that Perón was largely responsible for institutionalizing. Perón was successful only in imitating fascism's censorship and intolerance. The discipline and efficiency escaped him; he was a Mussolini who could not make the trains run on time. But Argentines still live off the heady memory of Perón's days.

Perón was forced from power by a coup in 1955, and Peronism was outlawed; but the people did not forget them. In 1973 Perón returned from exile in Madrid to be elected president; by then he was a senile, conservative man who headed a faltering administration, and he died after less than a year in office. He left the country in the hands of his vice-president, the woman he had married after Evita's death, María Estela (Isabel) Martínez de Perón, a dancer thirty-five years his junior whom he met in the Happy Land Bar in Panama City. The power in her administration was held by a Rasputin, her private secretary and personal warlock José López Rega. The government was quickly consumed by chaos, corruption, and 700 percent a year inflation. But Peronism failed, and still the people did not forget Perón.

Evita had died of cancer at the age of thirty-three, the same age as Jesus, a woman reminded me at one of the yearly masses commemorating her death. Upon Evita's death the food workers' union sent a telegram to Pope Pius requesting her canonization. The idea went nowhere with the pope but took hold in Argentina; in the late 1980s Argentines still hung garish painted photographs of the Peróns on their walls, pinned medals of Evita to their sweaters, and commemorated the very second of her passage into immortality. Schoolbooks pictured her with a halo, and a second-grade text offered the following prayer: "Our little mother, who art in heaven . . . Good Fairy who laughs amongst the angels . . . Evita, I promise you that I will be good."

The Argentine obsession with the Peróns borders on the necrophilic. General Pedro Eugenio Aramburu, who helped overthrow Perón, stole Evita's body and shipped it out of Argentina.

The Montoneros' first spectacular crime was Aramburu's execution, in part as revenge for his kidnapping of Evita's corpse. In June 1987 someone broke the outside locks on the mausoleum housing Juan Perón's remains in the Chacarita Cemetery, lowered himself to the second level, bypassed the security glass, cut a hole in the side of the coffin, and sawed off Perón's hands. A letter sent to Peronist leaders demanded eight million dollars in ransom, and a letter from Isabel that had been buried with Perón was enclosed in the ransom letter. The Peronists called for a day of mourning. There was a four-hour national strike and a transit stoppage. Three months after Perón's hands disappeared, they turned up in a flask of formaldehyde about forty kilometers from Buenos Aires.

The Montoneros' idols were not the flesh-and-blood Perón and Evita but the Peróns of myth. The real Peróns were anything but revolutionary. Evita's strategy for social change was to give alms to those who came begging. In Perón's second term of office he was a doddering right-winger who would not even receive the leaders of the Peronist Youth. But during that time the Montoneros closed their eyes to repeated snubs from Perón and his tolerance for López Rega's right-wing death squads. They continued to call themselves the soldiers of the true Perón.

The Montoneros took their name from the bands of irregular fighters in Argentina's war of independence from Spain. The organization's leaders, notably Mario Firmenich, came from right-wing Catholic student groups. Its ideology was muddier than Perón's. The Montoneros formed in 1968 with an announcement by a group formed largely of students that they followed a doctrine of "Justicialist [the formal name for Peronism], Christian, and nationalist origin." What they seemed to want was vague: to "liberate" Argentina from imperialism and the oligarchy, although they were not Marxists as such and had no ties with organizations or countries outside Argentina. In 1970, when the party had probably only about twenty members, it burst onto the national scene with its kidnapping and murder of General Aramburu.

Aided by the publicity from Aramburu's death, the Montoneros' political wing organized or took over such front groups as the Peronist Workers Youth, the Union of High School Students, and the Peronist University Youth, which received 44 percent of the vote in student elections at the University of Buenos Aires in 1973. By then the Montoneros could draw hundreds of thousands of young people to political rallies.

The Montoneros also created a "People's Army," a spookily accurate mirror of the army it opposed. Within its ranks, organized into platoons, columns, and companies, dissent or weakness was considered betrayal. If a member talked under even the most brutal torture, he or she could be condemned to death by the Montonero war council. They were messianic zealots; the Young Peronist slogan was "For the enemy, not even justice."

In 1968 Argentina suffered 84 acts of armed political violence; by 1972 the number had risen to 745. By the end of Isabel Perón's government in 1976 bombs were exploding every three hours.

At first the actions of the Montoneros and their allies the Trotskyist People's Revolutionary Army were generally directed at property. They blew up banks and other symbols of bourgeois society. The few people they killed were soldiers or police linked with the right-wing death squads. In September 1974 they pulled off the kidnapping of Jorge Born, the director of the Argentine grain multinational Bunge & Born, and his brother Juan, the chief officer, killing two bystanders in the process. The kidnapping was the most profitable in world history: The Montoneros walked away with more than sixty million dollars, plus trucks of food and clothing for slum dwellers and new contracts for Bunge & Born workers. But with each year the Montoneros' violence grew more indiscriminate.

It was not the Montoneros, however, who were responsible for the bulk of the violence in Argentina. By 1974 right-wing death squads, some backed by Isabel Perón's secretary, López Rega, were killing more people than were the leftist guerrillas. The next year the army wiped out the People's Revolutionary Army, which never had more than five or six hundred guerrillas.

The Montoneros were stronger, with at most five thousand troops (the Permanent Assembly for Human Rights uses the figure of fifteen hundred), but they held no territory and toward the end of Isabel Perón's government were losing political support.

More important, there is considerable evidence that Mario Firmenich, the Montonero leader, was serving two masters, the other being the Argentine Army.

Martin Edwin Andersen, a reporter who lived in Argentina for five years, builds the following case for Firmenich's double life. First, the Montoneros took public credit for two very unpopular assassinations—in fact, committed by López Rega's right-wing death squads—that cost them public support. Second, the press conference Firmenich held when the kidnapped Jorge Born was released took place in a clandestine safe house that really belonged to the state's intelligence service. Third, Firmenich was the only Montonero leader to survive the destruction of three different groups of Montonero leaders in the seventies. Fourth, the army captured Firmenich's pregnant wife on the street in July 1976 and, in a complete reversal of its normal policy, placed her in a regular jail, released her son when he was born, and kept her capture a secret for five years. Fifth, the only Montonero chiefs killed were from the Marxist wing of the party, not Firmenich's Catholic wing. Sixth, the military operations Firmenich ordered in the later years were suicide missions for the young cadres that carried them out. (One example: Firmenich had a public press conference in 1979 to honor Montonero militants, who appeared before the cameras in uniform. A month later he sent them "clandestinely" into Argentina, where, of course, they were immediately caught and killed.) Finally, Andersen says he talked to a U.S. intelligence official who had frequent contact with Firmenich's handler in the Argentine military.

The Dirty War was over even before it started. When the junta took power, the People's Revolutionary Army had been wiped out, and the Montoneros cowed, broken, and probably infiltrated at the highest level. The junta's war was not a war; it was pure and simple repression. From 1969 to 1979, according to *La Nación*, a right-wing Buenos Aires newspaper, leftist terrorists killed 790 people. From 1971 to 1979 government forces or paramilitary death squads killed or disappeared at least 10,483, the sum of the cases reported in *Nunca Más* and deaths in supposed battles reported in newspapers. In the single month of November 1976 fewer than 20 people were killed by the left while 600 were killed or disappeared by the right. In the entire period of the Dirty War the navy lost 11 men: 6 officers and 5 enlisted men. In the ESMA, where about 4,500 prisoners died, Task Force 3.3.2 lost 1 sailor.

The fact was that the left had never been a serious threat, and the military knew it. A directive written by Videla six months before the coup estimated the ranks of the People's Revolutionary Army at between 430 and 600. In April 1977 the junta estimated the Montoneros' strength at 2,843 to 2,883 people. A year later an internal junta memo referred to the "virtual annihilation of the subversive organizations with the loss of approximately 90 percent of cadre." Yet the repression continued. The junta exaggerated the Montonero threat to have an excuse to wipe out Argentina's nonviolent left.

DESPITE THE FACT THAT ARGENTINA'S CHAOS IN THE MONTHS before the coup was largely right-wing chaos, the military once again heard the call to step in. The junta's rule began with the customary announcement that had been dusted off and put back on the radio with each military coup since 1930. General Videla said on March 25, 1976, one day after the coup:

> The armed forces have assumed the direction of the state in fulfillment of an obligation from which they cannot back away. They do so only after calm meditation about the irreparable consequences to the destiny of the nation that would be caused by the adoption of a different stance. This decision is aimed at ending misrule, corruption, and the scourge of subversion.
>
> During the period which begins today, the armed forces will develop a program governed by clearly-defined standards, by internal order and hard work, by the total observance of ethical and moral principles, by justice, and by the integral organization of Man and by the respect of his rights and dignity . . . and the task of eradicating, once and for all, the vices which afflict the nation.

The rationale was the same, but this coup was different. Previous coups had been the work of charismatic caudillos who filled their Cabinets with civilians. This coup was carried out by a group of colorless men—Massera was the exception—who brought the armed forces as a whole into power. What was also new was their ferocity, unmatched in South America in the century. "First we must kill all the subversives," said General Ibérico Saint Jean, who became governor of the province of Buenos Aires, "then their sympathizers; then those who are indifferent; and finally, we must kill all those who are timid."

As the real subversives were by and large dead by the time of the coup, the military turned its hand to labor leaders, intellectuals, student leaders, and the few progressive priests and nuns. They killed schoolchildren who, as Montonero sympathizers, picketed for lower bus fares. They imprisoned Adolfo Pérez Esquivel while he was a nominee for the Nobel Peace Prize he received in 1980. A left-wing priest, Orlando Yorio, was told inside the ESMA, "You aren't a guerrilla, you're not involved in violence, but you don't realize that when you go to live in a slum, you are bringing people together, you are uniting the poor, and uniting the poor is subversion."

Father Yorio was not the only priest in the ESMA, but he was one of the few who were not on the staff. "When we had doubts, we went to our spiritual advisers, who could only be members of the vicariate, and they put our minds at ease," Admiral Horacio Zaratiegui told a magazine. Indeed, the Argentine Catholic Church did endorse the military's conviction that fighting leftists was the Lord's work. This was perhaps not surprising in a country whose government still approved the appointments of new bishops and paid them a salary equivalent to 80 percent of that of a federal judge, a country in which the papal nuncio quoted St. Thomas to bless army troops.

Priests observed torture sessions and helped in disappearances. Of Argentina's more than eighty bishops, only four spoke out against the repression, and one of them, Enrique Angelelli, was murdered in what was proved to be a staged car accident. The thoughts of most of the bishops could easily be confused for the wisdom of the junta. "Disappeared?" said Juan Carlos Cardinal Aramburu in 1982. "Things should not be mixed up. Do you know that there are some 'disappeared' persons who today are living quite contentedly in Europe?" Or this from Bishop Carlos Mariano Pérez of Salta: "The Mothers of the Plaza de Mayo must be eliminated." Or this from Archbishop Antonio Plaza of La

Plata in 1985: The trials of the junta members are "revenge by subversive forces and garbage. . . . [T]hey are a Nuremberg in reverse, in which the criminals are judging those who defeated terrorism."

IT IS PERHAPS A TENET OF HUMAN NATURE THAT THE PEOPLE raising questions about a war are seldom those who won it. Certainly the navy officials I met seemed unvanquished, at least publicly, by doubts. "I'm very glad you called," Admiral Mayorga said on the phone. "In the United States and Europe there is a lot of misunderstanding about the antisubversive war. I feel the only people who understand it are the people who lived it, the Argentines." He invited me to visit him at his home so he could explain the war to me.

Mayorga retired from the navy in 1973 and now spends his time raising bees. His house is filled with ornate furniture and Oriental rugs, but the entry hall is blocked by three picnic tables covered with bright plastic; the kindergarten next door uses his house for a lunchroom every day. He himself, he said, had been president of the PTA in his children's school.

"This is not a banana republic," he said as we settled down in his living room with cups of strong coffee. "People talk about us as if we were savages, Africans. They talk as if we were not people."

"Why was it necessary to torture?" I asked.

"We had to fight like they fight!" he said. The Americans did it in Vietnam, he said; the French, in Algeria. The war against subversion could not be won without torture. "When the plane with the Uruguayan soccer team went down in the Andes, people had to eat the dead," he said. "They were not cannibals. But they ate to live. We, too, ate to live.

"I've vomited more than once after seeing horrible things. We are condemnable. We've killed people without trials that we knew were guerrillas. But we knew the judges would free them. We couldn't ask judges for permission to raid a guerrilla stronghold. It was terrible to be torturing human beings. But we did it so others didn't suffer more. As a good Christian I have problems of conscience. A French general said that if you want to combat subversion, you get down in the mud and get dirty; if not, give up right away. We must condemn the torture. The day we stop condemning torture—although we tortured—the day we become insensitive to mothers who lose their guerrilla sons—although they are guerrillas—is the day we stop being human beings."

What was important, said Mayorga, is that the navy fought like gentlemen. "The image is of women being raped, boys who robbed, indescribable torture. But those were lies. Why would the soldiers have raped? The women were dirty; they went for a long time without bathing. The men had no need to rape. They were fighting right here in Buenos Aires, with lots of women around. There was no robbery. If a group of men took a suitcase and it was found to contain half a million dollars, it would be returned down to the last dollar. The suitcase would go in one place, the keys in another. We are navy officials! We are not going to soil ourselves for a gold watch."

I changed the subject, to Astiz. A military man who is tried in a military court is required to have, in addition to his lawyer, a defender who is usually a respected senior official. For his trial, Astiz had chosen Mayorga, who accepted with enthusiasm and offered his living room as headquarters for the preparation of Astiz's defense.

Mayorga spoke of Astiz as he would of a son. "Women are crazy about Alfredo because he's handsome and appealing. But he broke up with his girlfriend when all this started, telling her, 'You don't want to marry me. They're going to shoot me.' He's been here many times at my house and always said he wasn't going to live more than a few more years."

When Astiz and his military lawyers met at Mayorga's house, the most junior officer ran errands. That was Astiz. One day, as he returned from the grocery with two bottles of Coca-Cola, one of the men looked up and remarked, "Here he is, the angel of death." The men looked at the baby-faced soldier carrying the Coke bottles and cracked up.

"That same day, as he was leaving," Mayorga said, "Astiz took me aside and said, 'I want to thank you so much for inviting me here. You came out of your comfortable retirement to defend me. Not everyone would do it.' I said to him, 'Nonsense, you were in the streets risking your life so that people would not kill me.'

"You know," Mayorga said, "I have friends who are leftists. I enjoy talking with them. I have nothing against leftists who fight with ideas." There seemed to be no one, however, who fell into this category. The Mothers of the Plaza de Mayo, he said, were running arms. The nuns were terrorists—"not leftists but terrorists. Why were they taken and not others who worked there?" The Center for Legal and Social Studies, highly respected for its human rights work, was, he said, "the legal front of the revolutionary left." Even gray and sober President Alfonsín was suspect. "Some say he is a Marxist. I think he is naive. He has a lot of Montoneros among his advisers. His policy is to sow hate, saying that we're all killers."

The press? "Don't get me started," Mayorga said. The Europeans were the worst, but the North Americans were almost as bad. "Journalists only interview the Mothers of the Plaza de Mayo," he said. "They never try to understand what really happened."

"I want to understand what happened," I said. I told him that I wanted to talk to military officials, especially in the navy, especially in the ESMA, about which I had heard many stories whose veracity was hard to determine. Mayorga thought for a while. "I can introduce you to someone who worked in the ESMA," he said. "Call me next week."

When I called him, he invited me to return to his house the following Tuesday at five in the afternoon. Someone would be waiting, he said.

HE ASKED ME TO CALL HIM ONLY JORGE. HE WAS A LIEUTENANT commander on active duty and had not asked permission of his superior to see me. He was of medium height, balding slightly, with heavy jowls and large ears, in his early forties, wearing a blue suit and red tie. At first Jorge seemed nervous. He had miscalculated the driving time and had arrived a few minutes early, so he had been walking around the neighborhood—there was a light drizzle—until the hour of the interview. But as he started to talk, his nervousness disappeared. He said he would answer every question I asked honestly, and if he could not answer, he would respond with "no comment." He smoked throughout the conversation, which lasted three hours. He was articulate and obviously intelligent; his manner was pleasant and engaging.

Jorge said that he had served in the ESMA from 1977 to 1979, coming into Task Group 3.3.2 as a lieutenant, and that at various times he had worked in all three branches: operations, intelligence, and logistics. He had been Alfredo Astiz's immediate superior.

"The propaganda," he said, "is that this was a military government that repressed its political opponents. That is false. It was a war against an armed guerrilla organization, the most powerful terrorist organization in the world, that had fifteen thousand militants and another thirty thousand sympathizers in the universities. This is very important. If you don't look at it as a war, it makes no sense. We had to fight in the enemy's camp. If the enemy was in the street in civilian clothes, that was where we had to go."

I asked him about the work of the ESMA. "We got plenty of offers from people volunteering to participate—even retired officers," he said. "We all lived there, twenty-four hours a day. It was like going to sea for four months. The guerrillas were fanatics. They lived for the war. We had to do the same."

"I'd like to hear about torture inside the ESMA," I said.

Jorge looked at me. He was silent. Then Admiral Mayorga interrupted. "I told Miss Rosenberg last week exactly why we were forced to use torture to get information rapidly," he said. Jorge looked at Mayorga.

He took a deep breath. "To understand why we needed to use torture, you have to understand how the enemy worked," he began. He then went into a long discourse on the cell structure of the Montoneros, emphasizing their discipline. "If by nine-thirty at night one of the Montoneros did not arrive at his house, his partner would take the arms, documents, and money and leave and burn what she could not carry. We'd get there the next day and there'd be nothing left. If a Montonero didn't call a predetermined contact two days running, the organization would give him up for dead. We could have captured a guerrilla and not touched him, trusting that the light would dawn on him in a week or so and he'd tell us everything. But he'd just look at his watch, smile, and say, 'What time is it?' A few hours and we would have lost. His compañera would have left and his organization been dissolved. Try combating that with the Geneva Convention. You read them their Miranda rights and they would have died laughing.

"That we raped, that we burned people with cigarettes—that's all lies. What we did was use electric shocks, applied to their legs with high voltage. People can't stand it, and it does no permanent damage. A lot of people decided to collaborate even without torture once they saw how we acted, how we treated them: that we were naval officers, not savages, that military men are not evil with Nazi faces. I still have personal friends among the ex-prisoners. I'm the godfather of a prisoner's child."

"You yourself tortured?" I said.

He nodded. "It was horrible," he said. "The prisoner would be tied down, and I'd have to interrogate him. I felt destroyed. When you think about the 'enemy,' it's depersonalized. But it's not that way. . . . You have to get used to it.

"At first, I'll be honest, it was hard to accustom ourselves to put up with torture. We're like everyone else. The person who likes war is crazy. We all would have preferred to fight in uniform, a gentlemen's fight where you all go out to have dinner afterward. The last thing we wanted to do was interrogate.

"With the other branches of the service it was different. The police did their interrogations with an unhealthy rage. But they have a lower intellectual and human level."

"Did the United States teach you how to torture at the School for the Americas?" I asked.

Jorge laughed. "The School for the Americas was useless," he said. "We had to learn how as we went along. I read a lot about the French methods in Algeria. That helped a little."

He was proud of what they had invented and told the story as if recounting a thriller. "When I caught someone, I didn't ask him, 'Are you a guerrilla?' I would say to him, 'You are a guerrilla. Your chief is this guy. You live at this address. Now tell me about Mary and Joe.' He, of course, says nothing. But five minutes later we produce Mary and Joe, who are alive and working with us. It destroys him psychologically to realize that his collaboration is inevitable."

"But surely you occasionally made a mistake," I said. "A lot of innocent people died."

"In the first phase of the war everyone who was captured was executed," he said, lighting another cigarette. "We knew if we put them into the courts, they would ask for all the guarantees of the system they were attacking. They'd have been freed." He thought for a while. "Let's say that ten thousand guerrillas disappeared. If we hadn't done it, how many more people would have died at the hands of the guerrillas? How many more young people would have joined them? It's a barbarity, but that's what war is. In World War II fifty million died, twenty-five million of them civilians. And that was a clean war. A clean war.

"We had the backing of the church," he continued. "Not that priests said, 'Go ahead and torture,' but that the church said there were two groups here and we were the ones who were right. In January 1977 the military vicar said we had to rid the country of the guerrillas. I really feel that any armed forces with a decent level of culture and human feeling would do the same as we did."

I said I wanted to know about Astiz.

"Astiz was directly under my orders," Jorge said. "Everything he did was something I ordered him to do. He was one of the youngest, a junior-grade lieutenant. Now the press has made him into a combination of James Bond and Josef Mengele. But everything he did was following an order."

What about the nuns? I said. Were they terrorists? He smiled and put out his cigarette. "No comment," he said.

"Where are they now? Are they buried somewhere?" I asked, hoping to obtain an answer to the question that was plaguing Horacio Méndez Carreras, their lawyer.

"No comment," he said again. "But I will say that the Mothers, when they first began, had associations with terrorist groups."

"And Dagmar Hagelin?"

"Dagmar was a guerrilla," he said. "And she was not Swedish. Her grandfather was Swedish. She was Argentine. And she was never in the ESMA. It was another working group that took her. Astiz had nothing to do with it.

"I ask you, if we were such savage murderers, how is it that the armed forces kept the people who served in the ESMA in service and even promoted them? How is it that we voluntarily went to the trials and some of us are in jail? I ask you, if Astiz had been such a savage assassin, would the whole navy have defended him? That would make everyone an assassin like him."

THE JUNTA EVENTUALLY FELL. BUT IT WAS NOT BECAUSE OF PUBLIC outrage against the repression, nor did the junta collapse under the weight of its corruption or because of the economic havoc it wreaked on Argentina. It collapsed because it lost a war. Trying to divert attention from a disintegrating economy, the junta invaded the Falklands and Georgias, groups of islands 350 and 1,000 miles southeast of Argentina that had been ruled by the British since 1833. Even though the Argentines enjoyed the advantages of surprise and proximity, the invasion failed. Nearly 1,000 people died, 712 of them Argentine.

The attack suffered from the typical myopia of dictatorship. The president of the junta, General Leopoldo Galtieri, believed that Britain, a democracy, lacked the resolve to win or even fight the war. The invasion was carried out in early April, a moment chosen for its political, not military, value; it was 5 degrees below zero Fahrenheit in the Falklands. Galtieri never expected that the United States, dependent on the Argentines to train the contras fighting Nicaragua's government, would back Britain. And blind to Argentina's international pariah status on account of its human rights violations, Galtieri was convinced that his Latin American neighbors would rally to his cause. He never prepared for a real war.

The Argentine armed forces commission that investigated the Falklands disaster, the Rattenbach Commission, later wrote, "Soldiers had one month of instruction. Great Britain enjoyed air superiority and total sea domination. The attack was made when the Argentine Intelligence chief was visiting the United States. The decisions made favored the enemy." The men had so little food that some had to steal to eat. Some had never fired a rifle before. Recruits from the tropical north were sent to the islands in light jackets. Argentina, afraid the British would sink its aircraft carrier, the *Twenty-fifth of May,* kept it anchored in port.

To take the Georgias Islands, about seven hundred miles east of the Falklands, the navy sent just fourteen men, dressed in light clothing, armed with automatic rifles, explosives, and one machine gun, commanded by a lieutenant who had just returned from a diplomatic tour in South Africa. The lieutenant was Alfredo Astiz.

Astiz's invasion of Puerto Leith, a boarded-up whaling village on the Georgias, was the continuation of a military career based on victory over the defenseless. But when the British arrived a week and a half later, with HMS *Endurance,* HMS *Plymouth,* a destroyer, and six helicopters, Astiz surrendered without firing a shot, violating the Military Code's Article 751: "A soldier will be condemned to prison for three to five years if, in combat with a foreign enemy, he surrenders without having exhausted his supply of ammunition or without having lost two thirds of the men under his command." British airplanes flying over the Falklands spilled out pamphlets for Argentine troops reading, "Do what Captain Astiz did. Conscious of the superiority of British forces, he surrendered with all ceremony." A photo of Astiz signing the surrender document on HMS *Plymouth* was sent around the world. When the French and Swedish governments realized just whom the British had captured, they asked for custody of Astiz, and the British navy took him back to England, prisoner of war of the prime minister he so admired. The Geneva Convention, a document that the British, at least, took seriously, mandated his return to Argentina a few days later.

Galtieri resigned in disgrace, and his successor, General Reynaldo Bignone, called elections. The Peronist candidate lost to Raúl Alfonsín, a decent and unassuming small-town lawyer of the Radical party, who emphasized human rights in his campaign. Days after his victory Alfonsín appointed the commission that was to investigate the violations and eventually write *Nunca Más.* He ordered the Armed Forces Supreme Council to try the nine leaders of the first three juntas for murder, torture, robbery, illegal arrest, and additional crimes. The trials were later extended to cover other military officers. Alfonsin retired more than fifty generals. He cut Argentina's defense budget by almost 50 percent.

The trials were unique in world history. They were not Nuremberg-style prosecutions in which the conquerers drew up new rules by which to judge the conquered. Rather, the courts were those of an elected government putting members of a previous regime on trial solely for acts that were crimes at the time of their commission, with full respect for the due process of law.

The decision to begin the trials in military courts was an attempt to allow the military to clean its own house. The trials were subject to review by a civilian court, the Federal Appeals Tribunal, which could also call new witnesses. If after six months the Armed Forces Supreme Council had not completed its hearing, the case would move to the civilian courts.

The military showed no interest in cleaning its own house. The Armed Forces Supreme Council would not try the junta members, and the case moved to the majestic Buenos Aires Federal Appeals Tribunal on April 22, 1985, and lasted for six months, heard by judges appointed under the military government. The tribunal's galleries were always packed, television cameras captured the proceedings, and a record of the trial was published weekly.

The junta members declined to cooperate, attending their trials only when required. For the first time in their careers they and their attorneys showed meticulous concern for due process. Admiral Massera's seventeen-minute speech in his own defense, written and delivered with his usual eloquence and bravado, summed up the junta's attitude. "I have not come here to defend myself," he began. "No one needs to defend himself for having won a just war." Massera said that if the war had been lost, "none of us would be here," because judicial institutions would have been replaced by people's tribunals. The generals had "won the war of arms but lost the psychological war," he said. Those who had lost the war were now accusing the winners and wished to apply "human rights" only to terrorists.

On December 9, 1985, the court handed down its opinion. Hundreds of pages long, the opinion acquitted four of the defendants and convicted five, sentencing Videla and Massera, who had commanded the army and navy during the worst years of the repression, to life in prison. Videla was convicted of 16 counts of homicide aggravated by the defenseless state of victim, 50 counts of homicide aggravated by commission by a group of three or more, 306 counts of aggravated false arrest, 93 of torture, 4 of torture followed by death, and 26 counts of robbery. Massera's list of crimes was similar.

At the same time the courts opened the possibility of private suits against military officers. One of the first was the suit against Astiz brought by Ragnar Hagelin, Dagmar's father. The Armed Forces Supreme Council won the right to try the case. "I did not participate in the arrest of any woman on a public street," Astiz testified. He said he learned of Dagmar's case "through the newspapers." He had never heard of the prisoners the prosecutor named, and he didn't know what the "Fish Tank" in the ESMA was.

"Are you affected by the journalistic campaign against you?" asked the prosecutor, ever probing.

"Profoundly," Astiz replied. "Socially, I have been repudiated in various circles. I couldn't even visit my parents in Mar del Plata."

The Armed Forces Supreme Council then declared Astiz innocent on the ground of double jeopardy, announcing, to Hagelin's surprise, that Astiz had already been tried—in secret military courts in 1981—and been declared innocent for lack of evidence.

Astiz's trial then moved to the Federal Appeals Tribunal. Astiz attempted to create a mistrial by appearing at the identification lineup in his military uniform. But the trial proceeded. The court found him responsible for Dagmar Hagelin's illegal arrest (it refused to presume her death and so did not try him for murder) but ruled that the statute of limitations had run out on the case.

Meanwhile, Astiz was also being tried as part of the general prosecutions for his participation in the ESMA's crimes. The ESMA officials agreed to testify at the trials, but their collective memory was poor. El Tigre testified about the ESMA: "There were no detentions as such. It was like someone goes to a police commission and they're asked, 'Is this what you did?' If he said he did nothing . . . he could leave."

Still, the military trials contained some inspiring moments. One was this bit of testimony: "A soldier always follows orders; but an official is a gentleman as well as a soldier, and if he always takes refuge in due obedience, he would be betraying the confidence the nation places in him when it entrusts him with its most precious things: the care of its land and traditions and the blood of its children." These words—from Astiz's military trial on April 21, 1986—were spoken not by the prosecutor but by Astiz himself. But ever the good naval officer, he went on to say, "I feel free in my professional conscience, given that my superiors, who make up the institution, never sanctioned me for the things that are questioned today."

The military court dropped the ESMA cases, among others, in December 1986, and the cases moved to civilian courts. El Tigre Acosta again began his testimony by saying, "I have no knowledge that there were prisoners in the Mechanics School."

Meanwhile, rumblings that eventually put an end to the trial were taking place within the armed forces. During Astiz's trial for Dagmar Hagelin's detention, the navy high command warned Alfonsín that officers were threatening to revolt if Astiz was convicted. Many officers saw Astiz as the symbol of the young naval officer. He had fought bravely in the ESMA, and as for his surrender in the South Georgias, well, Astiz had simply gotten screwed. Fourteen men to hold an entire island? The military was facing the prospect of years of public trials blackening its name and honor. The pressure grew on Alfonsín, who was well aware of his country's history of coups. In December 1986 he proposed the Full Stop Law, which stipulated that all cases needed criminal complaints filed and attempts to hear the defendants made before February 22, 1987, sixty days later. Any case not filed by that date would not proceed.

The Full Stop Law outraged the left but did little to assuage the military. By the end of the sixty days more than three hundred cases were still legally in process. When one major, Ernesto Barreiro, refused to be judged in a civilian court, nearly four hundred of his supporters in the military rebelled during Easter Week of 1987. Soldiers took over three bases in nine days in Córdoba, suburban Buenos Aires, and Salta.

Argentina reacted with vehemence. Nearly half a million people massed in the Plaza de Mayo to support Alfonsín, and fifty thousand civilians surrounded the rebels' military compound. They surrendered. But the military had apparently made its point. Three days later the Federal Supreme Court suspended the trial

of seventeen officers of the ESMA. A month after the Easter
Week uprisings, on May 13, 1987, Alfonsín asked Congress to
adopt the Due Obedience Law, ending the prosecutions of officers
of lieutenant colonel or lesser rank, who, he said, had been only
following orders. In effect, the law granted amnesty to almost all
active-duty officers. A still-broader version of the law was enacted
on June 5. Trials could proceed afterward for about eighty retired
and two active-duty officers. And Horacio Méndez Carreras
burned his pictures of Astiz. Astiz, acquitted in secret military
courts of Dagmar Hagelin's kidnapping in 1981, became the only
officer below the rank of general to be found innocent in the
Dirty War.

Juan Gauna, Alfonsín's defense secretary—one step below the
defense minister—is a man with a mournful face and permanent
bags under his eyes. When I interviewed him in 1988 in his
office, dominated by a large cross, he had dealt with two military
rebellions—a third was coming—and the two laws marking Alfonsín's retreat on the question of trials. "The danger of a classic
coup did not exist," he said. "The system had a lot of latent
problems that can grow into a complete break, a battle between
the civilians and the military. Then you have general disobedi-
ence and a government without the power to put it in back in
the box. That is anarchy.

"The military feels punished," he said. "They are permanently
on the defensive. There is no sense in having the whole thing
fall apart. We have to preserve the institutions of the country."

Gauna believed that the Due Obedience Law had solved the
problem. "Before this government this ministry was a puppet of
the armed forces. Now that's reversed; we give the orders." He
smiled weakly. He did not look like a man who gave orders.

The military problem had not been solved. Alfonsín, who was,
after all, technically the commander in chief of the armed forces,
refused to approve Astiz's promotion to lieutenant commander.
The navy threatened a revolt if Astiz was not promoted. A deal
was reached: Alfonsín agreed to promote him and then retire him
from service. On December 23, 1987, Astiz became a lieutenant
commander. But the navy did not retire him.

In January 1988 there was another uprising. It was defeated.
Eleven months later there was another one. The rebels surrendered the next day to troops loyal to Alfonsín.

The rebellions slowed as the military found less and less to rebel against. The junta comandantes were still in jail—if four-bedroom luxury cottages with gardeners, cooks, valets, phones, and visitor privileges could be thought of as jail. Their freedom of motion was nominally restricted, but whenever Massera or Videla got the urge to step out, he merely had to request medical treatment at a Buenos Aires hospital. Newspapers in 1989 ran photos of Massera walking unescorted on Buenos Aires streets.

Little by little, even that pathetic remnant of the triumph of law was unraveling. In October 1989 Alfonsín's successor, Carlos Menem, who had himself spent nearly five years in the junta's jails, pardoned 39 military officers convicted of human rights violations, 174 military officers involved in the uprisings, a few who had been convicted of botching the Falklands War, and 64 Montoneros. Only 6 military men—including Massera and Videla—and Firmenich were still in jail, and Menem pardoned them on December 29, 1990. Videla said upon his release that his only crime was to "defend the nation against subversive aggression and prevent the establishment of a totalitarian regime." Not even the pardon was the "full vindication" he felt was called for. In December 1990, one day before George Bush arrived in Argentina during a South American tour, with Menem promising that a pardon was imminent, there was another rebellion.

The postjunta Argentine military is run by the men who had been the junior officers in the Dirty War and the Falklands. Many of them retain the ideology of the Dirty War but now feel even more isolated from their countrymen, who seem ungrateful for the military's sacrifices. The concept of military honor— "Honor is the richest treasure a soldier can possess: to maintain it without stains and marks is the most sacred duty of all the members of the armed forces," General Bignone declared in 1983—has become an idea floating in space, disassociated from correct behavior or victory on the battlefield. It is an end in itself. A military that brought Argentina world censure for its brutality, its economic bungling, and its decision to start a ridiculous war that it waged with grotesque incompetence, demands to be honored, simply for existing.

* * *

THIRTEEN YEARS AFTER THE START OF THE DIRTY WAR, THE NAVY Mechanics School continues to shadow the lives of the men and women who inhabited it. The conversations of former prisoners were tinged with guilt, not necessarily for having talked under torture but simply for having survived. "I didn't turn in anyone," Graciela Daleo, the toughest Montonera, said to me three times in our first interview.

"I was only able to free myself from the ESMA a year ago," said Elisa Tokar, who had physically left the ESMA eleven years before. "I felt still kidnapped. I felt as guilty as the kidnappers because I had lived. I felt there must have been a reason. I didn't turn in anyone. But even typing was betrayal. I could have said, 'I won't type for you.' I can't judge anyone. I used to feel very harshly toward people who collaborated. I know one man who turned in four people without ever being tortured. I can't judge him now. I don't know what his situation was. Maybe I'd do the same."

Late one night I went to a Buenos Aires coffee shop to meet another ex-prisoner, a woman who had felt too weak to testify in the trials. "I talked under torture," she said. She was twisting her napkin. "I have never spoken about this before. They tortured me, and I gave them the names of another family. They told me they were going to visit the family, just to talk. Then they came back. My torturer came back, and I asked him what happened. He looked at me and said, 'The man is dead. He took his cyanide pill and died.'

"I started to cry. He was crying, too, the two of us, alone, crying. He said, 'Look, this isn't your fault. It's all my fault. I got the information from you by torturing you, and we planned it wrong. This is my fault.' Then he took me to a bar, and we both got drunk."

And what about the ESMA's other survivors? Many of the men in the armed forces had not wanted to torture. They did so because they risked their careers, at times their lives, if they refused. But to torture is not the same as to push a button in a missile silo. A torturer must look his victim in the eye and hear him scream. He must make him scream. The victim of torture would not be the only one with scars.

"I once saw Scheller getting psyched up to torture," said a

former prisoner, Nilda Actis, speaking of her torturer. "He was as if possessed by the moon. He was walking down the hall screaming, kicking doors, yelling at us." But this raging animal had another side. "About a month after I was captured we were talking," Actis said. "He had asked me about my life, and I was telling him. He interrupted me and said, 'Someday I'm going to ask your pardon for what I did to you.' I said that I would never pardon him and that he would never ask to be pardoned because he was convinced that what he was doing was right and he'd keep on doing it."

The French torturers in Algeria were the men who later staged acts of terrorism and tried to assassinate Charles de Gaulle and overthrow his government. Raúl Vilariño, the corporal who repented in the pages of *Semana* magazine, told his interviewer, "I saw how people lost their sensitivity. They were so involved in the routine that it seemed normal. The victims were pieces of meat. In torturing, they didn't care about the screams. They lost their table manners. If you don't let an animal see hot blood, he's a tame animal. But what happens to a person, to people who are used to seeing blood? What do they work in now? Selling real estate?"

I tried to track down Vilariño. The last man who interviewed him said he had been in and out of jail for credit card fraud and failure to pay his bills. I called his family in Coronel Suárez, a village in the pampas. It had been years, they said, since they'd heard from him.

Jorge Acosta, El Tigre, had been dishonorably discharged from the navy. Having lost the focus for his energies the task force provided, he had become wild and experienced discipline problems. The denouement came when he posed for a magazine photo in his navy uniform, passing his cap to a woman in an indecorous manner. He was also indicted for bank fraud.

These men destroyed themselves. It was Vilariño's destiny because he had judged himself and found himself guilty. It was the destiny of Acosta, a psychopath, because he could not judge himself at all. The men who could create another ESMA were not these men, but those who had reached a different verdict: the "worthy enemies," the men who had not raped, stolen, and tortured but had simply fought for their beliefs.

"I feel free in my professional conscience," Astiz had said at his trial. Was it true? This man, who had haunted his victims in the streets of Buenos Aires and still haunted them in their dreams, was he haunted himself? This man, who had brought hundreds to the torture table, was he tortured himself?

Astiz had gone to visit Dagmar Hagelin after he shot her. I was told this by former prisoners who had witnessed the meeting and by Pilar, his boyhood friend, who had heard it from him. Hagelin was in a wheelchair, her head bandaged. "I'm the one that shot you," he told her. Trying to make conversation, he noted that they had Nordic features in common. He had confused her with someone else, he said. He asked her forgiveness. Whether she understood what he was saying was unclear.

While still using the name Gustavo Niño, he had gone back to the Mothers in the Plaza de Mayo the week after he had participated in their kidnapping. "I have to talk to you," he had whispered, urgently, from the shadows. What was he going to tell them?

Astiz had said through his friend Jorge Sgavetti that he would not talk with me. I knew he had never talked to reporters. But I wanted at least to see him, hoping to get some insights, even from a glimpse of him or from a brief encounter, of who he was.

Sgavetti told me that Astiz came to Buenos Aires on weekends to see his girlfriend. I went to Ezeiza Airport one cold August day to meet the navy flights that came from Puerto Belgrano. Five minutes after I sat down in the airport lounge, a navy plane landed, and Astiz got off and walked through the gate. He was shorter than I expected, and his hair was sandy blond. He wore a gray tweed coat and a blue striped shirt and blue tie. I recognized him immediately. I walked up to him and said "Señor Capitán," and he stopped. After I explained why I wanted to speak to him, he said that he could not talk to me, that he was a military officer on active duty, and that he was not allowed to speak without permission, permission we both knew would not be given.

He was charming, very courteous, and his smile was dazzling. His face, even at the age of thirty-nine, was that of an angelic child. "I wish you luck, señorita, but those are the rules of the game," he said, and Alfredo Astiz had always followed the rules. His private nightmares would remain closed to me.

But it didn't matter; the little I could see was enough. When our conversation ended, Astiz turned to another officer. The two men started talking, and Astiz laughed, with his head tilted back and his teeth flashing as he strode away, just as in the newspaper photos. His laugh was mocking, victorious, the laughter of a man who knew he would walk in liberty for the rest of his days.

THREE

DIALECTIC

B Y THE AGE OF TWENTY-ONE JAVIER HAD ALREADY BEEN A
Shining Path guerrilla for eight years, four of them spent
in various prisons for various "revolutionary actions." When I
met him in a small prison in Peru's south in 1988, he was in
the last week of his most recent sentence, this time for blowing
up some banks. Upon his release the Peruvian magazine *Caretas*
published an article that Javier later showed me proudly, asking
why such a dangerous terrorist was roaming around free. He had
given me his address and told me to look him up when I was in
Lima. Two years later I did. He was surely back in the mountains
or dead, I thought. But I went to the address he had given me
and found that Javier, the guerrilla, was living with his mother.

The family—Javier, his mother, various brothers, Javier's
niece—lives in a working-class Lima neighborhood in a house
the men built themselves. Twenty-six years later, it still lacked
parts of the roof, doors, and plumbing. The walls are hung with
crucifixes and pictures of Christ. His mother, Blanca, was in her
late fifties, a widow who had worked hard all her life in the postal
service. "If you only knew how much trouble he gives me, señorita," she said in her soft voice. "That boy, he lives only for
politics. Why don't you take him to the United States? Find him
a job?"

"I *am* working, Ma," Javier said. Upon his release from prison
he had gone back to the mountains, but he had gotten sick and
returned to Lima. Now he was twenty-three, working in a stock-
broker's office during the day—a situation in which he saw no

irony at all—studying law at night, and dedicating his free time to the People's War.

It was going well. The People's War marked its tenth birthday in May 1990. The Shining Path, or Sendero Luminoso, is a Maoist movement that seeks to wipe out the old order and impose a "People's Republic of the New Democracy," a society modeled after Mao's Cultural Revolution. Sendero's Mao is Abimael Guzmán, a shy, paunchy philosophy professor—bachelor's thesis: "On the Kantian Theory of Space"—who taught at the University of San Cristóbal de Huamanga in Ayacucho, one of Peru's poorest and most backward states. He founded Sendero with a strike over the issue of tuition in 1969 and, using teachers and students to spread his gospel, began to build the movement. In 1976 he resigned from the university, and two years later Sendero vanished underground. Guzmán began to call himself Presidente Gonzalo; his followers proclaimed him the fourth sword of world revolution: Marx; Lenin; Mao; Presidente Gonzalo. The people's revolution began in earnest in May 1980, when Sendero arrived in the highland village of Chuschi on the night before Peru's first elections after twelve years of military rule. The guerrillas burned the ballot boxes. Shortly after, Lima awoke to the sight of dead dogs hanging from lampposts in cloth slings marked "Teng Siao Ping son of a bitch." The few Peruvians who noticed the exotic and enigmatic Sendero could not take it seriously.

Ten years later Peruvians were taking Sendero Luminoso very seriously indeed. Among contemporary guerrilla movements, only Pol Pot's Khmer Rouge is comparable in brutality. Sendero women flirt with police; when the officer lets down his guard, they slit his throat and take his weapon. A Sendero chief and her fighters stop a truckload of local government officials; after killing them, the Senderistas cut out their eyes and tongues. A ten-year-old boy carrying lit dynamite walks to the door of a Lima bank and explodes.

In the name of erasing the old order, a company of Senderistas entering a highland village will kill anyone associated with that order: the local mayor; the health post's nurse; the peasant organizer managing farm cooperatives; the bank security guard; the European agronomist combating sheep fever; the peasant who owns too large a plot of potatoes; the student who goes to the airport to pick up a political candidate arriving from Lima. In

April 1990 guerrillas entered two Andean villages and killed seventy-four peasants, many of them old people and children.

Customarily the Peruvian Army moves into a village a few days after Sendero leaves. The army's treatment of villagers is almost indistinguishable from that of the guerrillas. It rounds up all those it suspects of sympathizing with Sendero: the housewife who cooked a meal out of fear for her life; the local government officials whom Sendero suspiciously allowed to live; leftist peasant organizers; neighborhood leaders; sometimes a town's entire population of young men. They are taken to the army base and usually not seen again.

By the war's tenth anniversary the guerrillas and the government had killed a total of twenty thousand Peruvians. Despite the government's repression—or, more likely, because of it— Sendero is growing. In 1990 Senderologists in Peru estimated that the group had between five thousand and seven thousand guerrillas, and many more civilians sympathized or lent political support of various kinds. Sendero controlled a small liberated terrority in Peru's jungle. In most of the country's mountainous highlands, or altiplano, Sendero was strong enough to have paralyzed all government activity. And its guerrillas could carry out sabotage and assassinations in every region of Peru.

I first met Javier in Pocollay Prison, off a dirt road six kilometers from Tacna, a town on Peru's southern border, in March 1988. A Jesuit priest I knew had told me that there was a Senderista in Pocollay. I arrived on a day for women's visits and told the guard I was Javier's friend. I was searched and sent to a central courtyard. The guard brought Javier out a minute later. He was a skinny kid missing a front tooth. We first went into the warden's office to talk, but the warden was sitting at his desk, shuffling papers. "I'm supposed to receive visitors in privacy," Javier said.

"Go wherever you like," said the warden.

We went to Javier's cellblock and bought two bottles of Kolin Kola cherry soda for a nickel apiece and sat on the cement steps in the sunny courtyard to drink the soda and talk about the People's War.

Javier first said politely that he was not interested in speaking to anyone from the United States. I said that people in the United States would be interested in hearing what Sendero had to say. He hesitated for a moment, then said that there were a lot of misconceptions about Sendero and that it might be good to talk for a while. He also seemed glad for the company. He explained Sendero's mission to me, what the People's War was about and why it was destined to be victorious in Peru. He went to his cell and brought me some copies of Sendero's newspaper, *El Diario*, and some early tracts of Presidente Gonzalo. I read them and came back the next day, duly enlightened, and we talked more. He told me he was due to get out of prison in a week or two. Before I left, he gave me his mother's address in Lima and invited me to look him up.

Two years later he greeted me like an old friend. He was fatter than he had been in prison—"concentration camp food will kill anyone," he said, laughing—and had new glasses and a new front tooth. He was wore black jeans and a yellow checked shirt and carried a notebook with Donna Summer's picture on the cover. He said he was in college to make his mother happy; he had spent many years causing her grief, and it weighed on him. The official story was that he had retired from Sendero, but Blanca seemed to suspect the truth. "My eldest son never gave me any problems," she told me. He was a neurosurgeon. "But this one . . ." She swept her arm in the direction of Javier, who was sitting at the table.

Javier's sister was a Senderista as well, Blanca said, fighting somewhere in the mountains. Blanca was taking care of the girl's seven-year-old daughter and had started formal adoption proceedings. As she described her two wayward children, she got angrier and angrier. "What kind of kid goes around killing people?" she said, standing and waving her arms. "Down with the terrorists! Death to the terrorists!" Javier had heard this before. He sat calmly eating grapes, spitting out the seeds.

"The system kills people with hunger," he said. "Sixty thousand children die before their first birthday each year in Peru. What's going to help them?"

"I pray," said his mother. "I say prayers for them."

"That's great, Mom," he said. "You just keep on praying."

After a few more minutes of this Javier said we had to be going. I was relieved; I had never interviewed a guerrilla in front of his mother before, and I was not comfortable with all the ground rules.

"I don't know what more I could do to please her." He sighed as we walked out of the house. "You think this is easy? Everyone weakens. I'm sentimental about my mother. I hate knowing I cause her pain. She wants the best for her children. But she's ignorant. She suffers and blames it on 'Senderista killers.' But I'm firm. Men can be wrong, but the party is never wrong. As long as we have the party, we'll triumph. We are condemned to victory."

I told Javier that I was writing a book. I didn't agree with his views, I said, but I wanted to understand Sendero. He agreed to help. He did not ask permission from his superiors to talk to me—he certainly would not have received it—and I, in turn, agreed to change his name and those of his family members in the book.

I saw him every night for a week and met most of his family. Some of them knew about his activities; some did not. He told only one set of cousins, clearly sympathetic to Sendero, that I was a reporter. His aunt served us coffee and crackers—possibly all the food the family had—as his cousins gathered in their tiny, shabby living room to listen to Javier talk. To the rest of his family, and to classmates and fellow Senderistas, Javier introduced me as a primary school teacher from the States who lived in Chile, a tourist in Peru. One night we dropped in on another family of cousins who lived behind the Congress Building in central Lima. Three teenage girls were watching a Venezuelan soap opera on TV and painting one another's nails. Javier headed straight for the kitchen and left me to the girls' affectionate torture of endless questions about TV programs and fashions in the States. "You haven't had any trouble in Peru, have you?" one said. "You haven't run across any terrorists?"

Terrorists? Aside from the one raiding your refrigerator? "Oh, no," I said.

About half the time I liked Javier. He was funny, smart, and sarcastic. He agonized over his mother, spun intricate plots to win back his ex-girlfriend, requested new tennis shoes from Chile—preferably Reeboks—and nagged me to take care of my head cold and get some sleep. But at times a switch would flip in his head, and a tape of *Pensamiento Gonzalo*, the thoughts of Presidente Gonzalo, would begin to play.

"Presidente Mao [Sendero's term for Mao Zedong]," Javier would say, "said it's not enough to say it once, you have to say it many times, and I'm not tired of saying it to you: We are developing a growing and victorious people's war." He never seemed to tire of saying it to me. "We fight only to give power to the people," he said. We spoke just as the Sandinistas were preparing to leave office in Nicaragua. "Look at Nicaragua—so many deaths in that war, and for what? To turn power back to the bourgeois? That is an inconclusive revolution. They don't understand that the purpose of fighting is to turn power over to the lower classes. A Nicaragua will not happen in Peru. Presidente Gonzalo won't permit it."

I had to learn his code. The "Fascist genocidal government" meant the government of Peru's president, Alan García. The political right was the "reaction"; the traditional left, as Mao put it, the "revisionism." The "correct way" or the "way of the people" meant violence. "The bourgeoisie will let the revisionists have their congressional seats. But they'll never give up power except through violence," Javier said.

The society he wanted was China under Mao or, at second best, Russia under Stalin, but even Stalin had gone soft. "Gorbachev betrays the people's interests," he said. "True revolutionaries are still fighting."

What do you think of what happened in Tiananmen Square? I asked. We were walking through the menacing, dimly lit streets of Lima's Pueblo Libre neighborhood, near his university. "A very hopeful and uplifting event," he said. The massacre? I said, incredulous. He waved me away. "You're focusing on the wrong thing. The reactionary propagandists talk about that. But that was just counterrevolutionaries killing counterrevolutionaries. The important thing is that there were students in the square with Mao banners, people who still believed in the violent way. The people were present.

"To ensure that new generations don't weaken, we must have a cultural revolution," he continued. But Mao's had not gone far enough. "When Deng Xiaoping began to exhibit counterrevolutionary tendencies, he was sent to care for pigs to proletarize him. And look what happened. If he had been liquidated, he wouldn't have caused all these problems. Mao was only the head of the party, while others headed the state and the military. We've learned from that. The party has to control everything. Absolutely everything."

"Do you want a Maoist revolution all over the world?" I asked. "In Scandinavia?"

"Yes," he said. He got dreamy-eyed. "I often imagine a swarm of peasants taking the city, just like in the Long March. It's utopian, I know. Can you imagine it here in Peru?" I shook my head. "You're such a pessimist," he said.

"And don't you think you're a fanatic?" I said.

"Presidente Gonzalo has never told us that we are fanatics," he said.

SENDERO BREAKS MOST OF THE RULES OF GUERRILLA WARFARE. Latin America possesses a rich tradition of guerrilla activity, and Peru has a group that follows that tradition. It is not Sendero but the Tupac Amaru Revolutionary Movement (MRTA), which began armed action in 1984, a much smaller group than Sendero. The MRTA reveres Che Guevara. It publishes intellectual tracts, seeks to form alliances with left-wing groups, sends its troops out to do the necessary political drudgery of organizing, and tries to ingratiate itself with the poor sectors of Peru.

To Sendero, the MRTA is just one more brand of bourgeois revisionism; Che Guevara, wrote Presidente Gonzalo, was a "chorus girl." Senderista columns have ambushed the MRTA's guerrillas.

Sendero models its revolution after Mao's, but China, along with Cuba and the Soviet Union, repudiates Sendero for its viciousness. Sendero receives aid from no one; its fighters make their weapons or steal them by killing police or soldiers. In the spirit of fair play, Sendero has bombed the Soviet and Chinese embassies in Lima as well as the U.S. Embassy. It does not try to explain its actions, and leaders seldom give interviews, even to El Diario, the group's newspaper. It directs its principal brutality not against rightists—who "sharpen the contradictions," thus serving the revolution—but against campesino organizers and labor leaders of the left, who "divert the campesinos' attention from the central task, which is the People's War."

Although Sendero claims to represent the Indians, who make up 60 percent of Peru's population, a group that suffers from racial discrimination tantamount to apartheid, there is very little that is native about Sendero. The names scrawled on the walls of Ayacucho are not those of Peruvians but Jiang Quing and Lin Biao, and Sendero's literature treats Peru as if it were as homogeneous as Denmark. It is class, not ethnicity, that matters to Sendero. And it terrorizes the very people it seeks to win over.

"The party decides everything," Javier said. Instead of trying to organize the masses, a traditional task for guerrillas, Sendero simply tells the masses what to do. "People don't want words; they want deeds," Javier said. "You talk to the masses in simple language, and the simplest and clearest is with bullets and dynamite." The guerrillas repudiate the strikes called by Peru's unions. A Sendero strike is an "armed strike," supported not out of solidarity but out of fear, as businesses that open their doors are bombed and workers who venture out on the street are shot.

Yet Sendero grows. In the late 1980s Sendero prompted the government to place more than half of Peru under a state of emergency, with basic constitutional rights suspended. Sendero runs clandestine people's committees that administer schools and rudimentary health clinics in large sections of rural Peru. Since 1986 the movement has developed a base in Lima, especially in the city's free universities; Sendero won the student elections in Javier's university, San Marcos, in 1988.

Sendero's stronghold is the five states that make up the mountainous spine of Peru, particularly its birthplace, Ayacucho—Quechua for "corner of the dead." At the funeral of guerrilla Edith Lagos in 1982, a crowd equivalent to half the population of the capital city of Ayacucho followed her casket to the cemetery, singing Sendero hymns. When the group calls an armed strike in Ayacucho, every house is shuttered and locked. After Sendero boycotted the municipal elections of 1989, Ayacucho's results had to be annulled when three quarters of the ballots came in blank or spoiled.

Sendero does not control the altiplano, but it is strong enough to ensure that the government doesn't either. There are no development workers and only a handful of government officials, the rest having been killed or driven out by Sendero. Sendero had killed at least ten mayors of Ayacucho before the annulment of the municipal elections ensured there would be no more candidates. Only teachers remain, and then on the condition that they teach Presidente Gonzalo's version of history. In some states the only remaining representatives of the Peruvian state are soldiers—tense, skittish, guns always drawn, often too terrified to venture out of their garrisons after nightfall.

In the late 1980s Sendero consolidated its rule over the coca-growing Upper Huallaga Valley, wresting control from Colombian traffickers who had turned the valley into a Peruvian Wild West. Sendero came in, organized the coca growers, and put an end to the chaos of the Colombians. Now the Upper Huallaga is where the People's Republic of the New Democracy comes to life.

Sendero quickly imposed a puritanical morality. Adulterers, alcoholics, coke addicts (aside from those who practice the indigenous custom of chewing coca leaves), and homosexuals receive preliminary warnings and, if they persist, are then shot. Landowners who mistreat their workers or businessmen who charge usurious interest are executed after perfunctory people's trials. As unattractive as it is, many Upper Huallaga residents welcomed Sendero's regime. When the Peruvian government attempted to eradicate the coca fields, Sendero killed the eradication workers and quickly stopped the program. The peasants hate eradication, which not only wipes out their livelihood but also leaves them in the very uncomfortable position of owing the Colombians coca leaf they no longer possess. Sendero also forces the Colombians to pay the Peruvian campesinos better prices. For its part, Sendero exacts from the Colombians a 5 to 15 percent "tax" on leaves sold and also charges them to use local airstrips. Senderologists estimate that Sendero makes from twenty to thirty million dollars a year in the Upper Huallaga Valley.

I asked Javier how Sendero reconciled its strict morality with protection of the coca farmers. "Peru's campesinos have always lived off coca leaves," he said. "Coca has an exalted place in Peru's history and religion. The drug traffickers come in and exploit the situation. We just want to impose conditions that don't take advantage of the campesinos."

"But at least in my country, the people most hurt by cocaine addiction are the poor and oppressed," I said.

"What do we care about the poor of the United States?" he said. "When did the United States ever care about the poor of Peru?"

A new recruit, said Javier, takes part in discussion and study

groups in which Peru's problems and Presidente Gonzalo's solutions are analyzed. Then a compañero might become a courier
or carry out other tasks in the network of civilian supporters.
When he is ready to take up arms, he sometimes gets them by
killing a policeman. The act of violence binds him to Sendero
and makes it hard to retreat later to "legal" Peru.

Javier would not say if he himself had killed anyone, and he
would tell me little about his early experiences. At thirteen or
fourteen he was recruited in junior high school, when the People's War was in its infancy. His mother and brothers said he
had always been a sentimental child, greatly affected by Peru's
poverty. He had, it seemed, always joined organizations: He was
once a Boy Scout and a devout Catholic. "But I realized that
you can't change things by yourself," Javier said. "It has to be
collective action. It was hard for me to stop believing in God. It
still is. But this is the way."

Javier's father had been a policeman. He died in a car accident
when Javier was young. But Javier was sure he would understand.
"To be honest, at first I had a lot of trouble with the idea of
killing police," he had told me in jail in 1988. "But now I have
been educated, and I understand why it is necessary. They educated me well. I think if my father were alive, he'd approve."

THE WALL THAT SPLITS WHAT USED TO BE GLADYS MENESES'S
property in two is a solid, thick wall, eight feet high and made
of concrete. It runs from the front of her yard to the back. It is
the only part of her property that is well constructed; the wall
around her yard is only four feet tall in parts and made of piled-
up stones. I could have knocked it over with my fingers.

The wall was two weeks old when I met Gladys for the first
time in 1988. Gladys had never heard of Sendero Luminoso.
She had not even heard of Peru's president, Alan García. Gladys
was twenty-three and lived in Tacna, seven kilometers from the
Pocollay Prison, where I had met Javier. That was all she and
Javier had in common. Her life was the absolute antithesis of
his. He was in college; she had left school at eleven. He was a
fighter; she, a victim. He talked a lot; she spoke very little. But
it was Gladys who helped me understand the paradoxes of Javier.

I began to understand how Sendero, with its worship of violence and its fanaticism, could be gaining support in Peru when I helped Gladys Meneses try to tear down the wall.

I was in a health post in Natividad, a poor neighborhood of Tacna, asking some questions about tuberculosis when Zenobia, a nurse, introduced me to Gladys, a short, dark, waif-thin woman with delicate features and black, wavy hair. "You want to hear a story?" Zenobia asked. "Why don't you talk to her?" Gladys was sitting on a wooden school chair, grimacing from the pain of a tuberculosis shot in her left hip. Ten minutes later, when the pain had subsided, we went into the next room. Her son Marco, who seemed to be three or four but I later found out was six, climbed up and down a dentist's chair while we talked.

It was the third time in two years she had started tuberculosis treatments, Gladys said. The first time the health post ran out of free medicine. The second time the whole city, including the tuberculosis ward at the hospital, ran out of medicine. In December 1986, when the health post ran out, she decided to sell part of her small piece of land to be able to pay for medicine. She sold half her lot to a man I'll call Jorge López, who owned a chain of bars. The price was twelve thousand intis, then about six hundred dollars; at the time of my visit it was worth a hundred dollars. He had paid her in dribs and drabs, with no interest or adjustment for Peru's tremendous inflation. He still owed her two thousand intis. At the time of the purchase that was a hundred dollars; but when I met her, two years later, it was only twelve dollars, and inflation was rising so fast that in another month it would be six dollars. Now López had told her he was waiting for a brother-in-law to pay him some money he owed before he could pay Gladys. But the brother-in-law, it seemed, was in no hurry.

López had warned Gladys that if she told anyone about his delay in paying, he would make sure she lost the rest of the house as well. To show her he meant business, he had beaten up one of her brothers. But she had told Zenobia about it, and at Zenobia's urging now she told me, cautioning me not to talk about it with anyone. Two weeks ago he had built the concrete wall down the middle of the yard and told her that his brother intended to move in on the other side.

I asked Gladys if she had family. "My husband abandoned

me," she said. She had her two boys, Marco, six, and Mario, two, and two older brothers—both mentally unstable alcoholics—whom she housed and cared for. Her last job had been as a dishwasher in a restaurant, earning twenty or thirty cents a day—well below the minimum wage—and lunch for herself and the children. She was so hoarse she could hardly talk; the tuberculosis had gone to her throat.

I explained that I was a reporter and asked if I could speak with her again. She told me to come to her house the next morning. After Gladys left, Zenobia came in with a tray of medicine. She said she had gotten Gladys some clothes for the boys from the Mormon church she attended. "You know, I'm used to hearing stories like this from the immigrant women who came here from the highlands," she said. "But Gladys can read. The husband who abandoned her is a science teacher. Maybe you can help her."

The next morning I went to Gladys's house, three blocks from the health post, on the one paved road in the Natividad neighborhood. The door to her yard was made of a sheet of blue tin attached to a piece of thick cardboard by nails driven through Coke bottle caps. A plank propped against the door served as a lock. Her house consisted of one small dark room. In it were two small beds, a table with some pots on it, a heap of old clothes, an old tricycle that was still too big for Marco, and a wooden school chair. On the wall was a colorful poster featuring the products of Bayer herbicides, some small pictures of saints, a poster of a chubby blond girl praying—"I pray for Mommy and Daddy," said the text—and a large picture of a blue-eyed Jesus.

The dirt yard contained a water pump and a fire pit for cooking and was strung with wash. Dog excrement was everywhere. At the back of the yard was a small cubicle of woven straw. One of her brothers slept there, Gladys said, and one slept out in the yard. Parts of the wall around the yard had fallen in; at some points you could step over it easily. I never saw a toilet, and I never asked.

My visit was full of the little rituals of class. To her I was *misti*, a Quechua word for the highest, the finest, the patron. The gulf between us was unbreachable. Gladys had only one chair, and on my first visits, before we got used to sitting in her house, Marco—always wearing the same sweater that hung to his knees—would push the chair out into the narrow passageway between the house and the new concrete wall. I would not sit down—she was sick, not I—and I motioned to Gladys to sit. She would not sit. So we both stood, and Mario played with the legs of the chair. I asked her repeatedly to call me Tina, not señorita. She nodded—the *misti*, of course, is always right—but always called me señorita. I toyed with the idea of asking her to use the informal *tu* instead of *usted* for "you" but decided that this was carrying cultural imperialism too far. So I did the next best thing. I called her *usted* and Señora Gladys. She must have thought I was crazy.

Gladys's story was not the saddest I had heard in Latin America. I had met hundreds of people in worse circumstances: street beggars; people who had no roof at all; children starving to death. At first I was tremendously affected by seeing such poverty. Then after a while I started getting numb; giving away a coin or two when people asked and not thinking about it anymore. So much poverty was overwhelming. It blocked me from focusing on the person and made me focus on the poverty, on the metaphysics of why there was so much poverty, and once my mind had made a tour of the realities of life in the third world, it seemed my hundred pesos would provide little relief. What could my hundred pesos do? It only meant that the same beggar would ask me again the next day.

But Gladys's wall was different. It shifted the picture away from the wide angle and made me focus on a detail and a person. Here was an injustice that could be rectified.

I told her that I had been thinking maybe I could help with the problem of the wall. I could find a lawyer to take the case, I said. I asked her some questions. No, she didn't have a lawyer, but López did. She said she had signed a lot of papers; but his lawyer had them all, and she had no copies. She was afraid of López; she didn't want to live in the street. But yes, if I helped, she would sue him.

I was thrilled. Gladys wanted to fight the system. Here was proof; given a little support and encouragement, she would stand up for her rights. I was sure that with a good lawyer we could win this case. "You know he has no legal grounds for kicking you out of your house," I said. She just looked at me. I gave her a bag of oatmeal I had bought for about ten cents in the market. Her face lit up, the first emotion she had shown since we met.

Tacna, where Gladys lives, is a dusty town of 170,000 on the Chilean border, the relatively prosperous capital of the wealthiest state in Peru. Tacna sits in the middle of the driest desert in the world. The houses are built of concrete or white adobe brick and blend in with the surrounding sand. The trees in the center of the main avenue, the Avenida Bolognesi, are the only touch of green.

Central Tacna is small, but in the surrounding mountains new immigrants settle into *pueblos jóvenes* ("young towns"). The newest *pueblos jóvenes* are checkerboards of straw sheds in the sand, little more than tents, with no water or electricity. (The *pueblo joven* in which Gladys lives, Natividad, is one of the most established and one of the few that feature such amenities.) Seventy percent of the people in Tacna, and practically all the people who live in the *pueblos jóvenes*, are immigrants from the Peruvian highlands, the Quechua- and Aymará-speaking Indian sierra where Sendero got its start. Tacna's immigrants are mainly Aymará Indians from the nearby state of Puno, a bleak, harsh highland governed by droughts and floods. Some of the men speak Spanish, but practically none of the women do. They come to try to work in Tacna's thriving contraband market, selling goods smuggled over the border from Chile. A man usually travels down from the highlands in the back of a truck and stays with cousins while he looks for work in construction or in the contraband market. When he finds it, he goes back to Puno to bring his wife and children.

Accustomed to a rural life of caring for sheep and growing potatoes, the immigrants build their small shacks of woven straw, weighting the roofs with stones to keep the wind from blowing them off. Although they now live in a hot, dry, crowded city instead of in a cold, sparsely populated highland, they live essentially as they did in Puno, the only way they know, speaking Aymará, dressing the way they always dressed, the women in four layers of skirts, sweaters, and bowler hats even in 85-degree afternoons. The women sell food on the street; the boys shine shoes or wash cars for a few pennies a day. Because of its large immigration—Tacna has quadrupled in size since 1950—the town is short of basics; there is enough water, for example, to supply just over half the population. It is a hard life, but if people wait long enough, there is the promise of electricity, water, and a job in the contraband market. As far as I could tell, no one ever goes back to Puno to live.

Gladys's social mobility ran in the other direction. A few years before, she was healthy, with a husband and a job. When I met her, she was sick, unemployed, and responsible for four dependents. After we had been working on the lawsuit for a week and she seemed more comfortable with me, I asked her if she would be willing to tell me about her life. I told her it would help people understand how poor people lived. If she didn't want to answer a question, I said, she didn't need to. I had worried that she might feel obligated to talk to me, but she was immediately enthusiastic. For the first time she invited me into the house, and we sat on the beds. Mario sat in the school chair and listened.

She was one of the few Tacnanians born in the city. Her father, a carpenter, came here from Puno twenty-five years ago, her mother from Tarata, a quiet village in the mountains. Her parents separated soon after Gladys, the youngest of four children, was born, and her mother, Benita, moved to the house where Gladys lives—now part of one of the city's most established *pueblos jóvenes* but then considered to be somewhat out in the country. Benita made a living taking in washing.

Gladys left school when she was eleven to work for a middle-class family. She lived in their house, cooking and taking care of their babies, going home to see her own family on Sundays. When she was fourteen, her mother sent her to work just across the border in Arica, Chile. Her salary was much higher than it had been in Peru, and she could earn even more for her family in contraband, bringing shirts across the border to sell in Tacna. But soon her mother took sick—menopause, Gladys said. Gladys came home from Arica to run the shirt business and to feed, bathe, and attend to her mother and take care of her two mentally unbalanced older brothers. Her older sister was already married and had her own family to look after. When Gladys was sixteen, her mother died.

"One day I ran into a school friend on the street," Gladys said. "She invited me to the movies." Gladys had never been to the movies; she had never gone out at all. Her friend's boyfriend brought along a friend of his, a man named Marco. After spending the evening talking to Gladys, Marco took her back to an empty room at a friend's house. She never saw him again. She stopped "getting sick" every month after that, she said. But she didn't understand why.

She had gotten a job in a small restaurant. One day her sister came to visit, and Gladys complained to her that she had gotten fat. Her sister took a good look. "You're pregnant," she said. She explained how it worked. Gladys told her friend to find Marco and tell him that she was pregnant. He sent back word that he was not interested in seeing her. She went into the hospital and had a caesarean section.

When she came out of the hospital, she and little Marco went to live with an uncle and aunt. Then one of her brothers got sicker, and Gladys moved back home to take care of him. For a while he was in a mental hospital. Gladys had to provide a mattress for him, and she gave him hers, sleeping at a neighbor's because she had no bed.

She went back to work in the restaurant, taking Marco to work with her each day, putting him in a box while she washed dishes and waited on customers. She earned the equivalent of about twenty dollars a month in salary and tips, she said. In addition, she and Marco ate for free and ate well, meat or chicken most days. Marco learned to walk in the restaurant. She worked from seven in the morning till nine at night, came home, washed diapers, and fell into bed.

After two years of this life a man named Mario came into the restaurant to eat. He started coming in more and more frequently to see Gladys. He told her he wanted to marry her. He didn't mind that she had a baby. For the next three years Mario, a taxi driver who lived with his younger sister and brother and was putting them through school, came to see Gladys every day. Although Mario's family didn't like her and kept telling him to look for a more educated woman, Gladys was thrilled. He was tall and handsome, she said, and educated; when his brother and sister finished school, he went to school himself and became a high school science teacher. What's more, he treated her well. He gave her money, and he even built a door for her house, a solid wooden door, not like the cardboard, tin, and Coke bottle cap door to her yard. Then Gladys became pregnant again. Fine, said Mario, let's get married and have a baby. But then he went on a weeklong trip to the mountains to visit relatives, and when he came back, he had changed his mind.

"How do I know it's mine?" he said. "You work in a restaurant and meet a lot of men." When she was seven months pregnant, he stopped coming to visit. She was devastated. She had considered herself married to Mario. "I will never get married again," she said. "I've been tricked twice. They're all like that."

A month later she went to the police and asked for help. She had no money to support another child. The police were kind to her and arranged a court date. Mario came with a lawyer, and the judge said that he could not hear the case unless Gladys had a lawyer of her own. Gladys heard that the local bar association provided lawyers—usually law students—free of charge. The woman she talked to at the bar association told her to come back after the baby was born, that she'd have a better case then, but Gladys never went back.

After Mario was born, Gladys was fired. The owners of the restaurant had tolerated one baby; they would not tolerate two. From time to time an uncle gave her money for food, but it wasn't much. "I wasn't eating," she said. "I worried all the time." She could not find a job that would allow her to bring her sons to work.

One day, as she was leaving the house, she felt sharp chest pains and began to cough up blood. She went to the hospital. Her tuberculosis test was positive. She weighed less than eighty pounds. The doctor wanted to keep her in the hospital, but she had no place for the boys and insisted on going home. She went to the health post three blocks from her house for shots every morning. But after two months the post ran out of free medicine.

It was then that she decided to sell half her property. Her uncle Carlos had been working as a driver, administrator, and caretaker for Jorge López, a man from Cuzco, who owned some bars. Carlos was far from satisfied with López—he owed Carlos for months of back pay—but Gladys was desperate. By the time she got the first payment weeks had gone by since she had stopped getting her tuberculosis shots. She would have to start the treatment all over. She felt better and decided to wait.

López hired Gladys to work for him at La Pirámide, a bar he owned across the street from the Mercado Bolognesi, Tacna's largest contraband market. Gladys worked from eight at night till eight in the morning in the bar, leaving Marco and Mario sleeping in the house alone. She kept the cash register and helped tend bar, occasionally managing the place by herself. She came home in the morning, cooked breakfast for the children, and fell asleep. In the afternoons she cleaned, took in some washing, and played with the boys.

By this time Marco was already a little man, she said. He was only five, but he sometimes had tea ready when she came home in the morning. She did not have enough money to buy the uniform he needed to go to school, so she taught him in the house. She had taught him to read some letters of the alphabet. Carlos bought him a notebook and some pencils, and she proudly showed me how Marco had copied letters. "He knows songs, he knows how to pray, and he can make paper airplanes," she said.

López paid her wages of six hundred intis a month, which at the end of her tenure amounted to under ten dollars a month, one quarter of the legal minimum wage—one sixth of the minimum that Gladys, a woman working a twelve-hour shift at night, was legally entitled to. At times, Gladys said, López was months late in paying her.

At Christmas 1987 Gladys decided she wanted to take two days off to be with her family. She had a good holiday, taking Marco and Mario to a Christmas fair. When she came back to work, López told her she was fired. She had gotten sick again, she was visibly ill, and he didn't want tubercular barmaids. She started the treatment again and again had to stop; this time the entire city ran out of medicine. López also owed her a month's salary. In February 1988 he put up the wall dividing the lot.

When I met her two weeks later she had just stopped working in another restaurant because she was too weak. She bought food with the money her uncle gave her and the sums López paid her for the lot. She was getting the shots again; this time the tuberculosis had spread to her throat.

Gladys said she did not feel alone. Her uncle Carlos, she said, gave her some money for food, bought things for the boys, and took care of her when she was sick. She had a neighbor who was kind to her, a woman who sold contraband fruit in the market and occasionally brought Gladys her leftovers at night. "She's like my mother," Gladys said. A drunk sometimes came around to bother her, Gladys said, and her neighbor always ran over to chase the man away.

I asked her why she thought she had such a hard life. "At times I've sinned," she said. "I ask God for pardon." She said she prayed a lot, pointing to the pictures of Christ on her wall. When she was really sick, she said, she had conversations with her mother at night. "She answers me in my dreams," she said. "I dream that she's here in the house, cooking for me, and when I come home from work, she had food ready. 'Come into the house,' she says in my dream. 'Come in and eat.'"

Gladys's story was almost too unrelievedly grim to be true—a tale by Dickens—yet I believed her. Her doctors, her former employers, and people who knew the Lópezes or knew Mario all confirmed what Gladys told me. In the end I believed Gladys because she could have invented the story only if she had realized that it would shock or move me. But she didn't tell it that way. It wasn't pathetic or dramatic; it was just her life, and she had no expectation that it could have been any different. She had seldom had a relationship with anyone or any institution outside her immediate family in which she was not victimized. She had probably never met anyone before who was surprised by this.

"Did you know there's a legal minimum wage?" I asked.

She had heard the term but didn't think it applied to her. "I thought that's how they pay," she said. She was right, of course; that was how they pay. But she wouldn't have complained in any case. "I didn't want to lose the work," she said.

Gladys's concept of law was hazy at best. When I asked her if she had asked López to add interest when he stretched out the payments on the property, she just stared at me. She had no birth certificate for herself or her children, no title for her house. She had never gotten any help from the government. The few times she had tried—to get Mario to pay child support or to cure her tuberculosis—she had been disappointed. She had never voted, she said. For a while, she said, she liked this government because prices weren't going up. But now they were rising again.

J‌USTICE IN T‌ACNA RESIDES IN A BLOCK-SQUARE BUILDING ENCLOS-ing an interior courtyard, just off the central plaza next to the cathedral. I went there the day after my first visit with Gladys. A friend had suggested that I go see a judge he knew, a man who might be able to tell me what to expect and what Gladys needed to do. By seven-thirty in the morning the courthouse was already filled with people engaged in the national pastime of waiting in long lines to talk to bored-looking men sitting behind manual typewriters.

I waited in a line outside the office of the lowest court, and when my turn finally came, I told the man behind the typewriter that I wanted to see the judge. "He's busy," the man said. The judge's door was open. I stuck my head in and waved. He was a young man, sitting at his desk in a suit and tie in a bare room, working on some papers. I had never seen anyone in a suit and tie in Tacna before—not even the mayor. I mentioned my friend's name. The judge told me to come in and sit down.

We talked for a while about the Peruvian legal system. The constitution of 1979, he said, was a document to be proud of. Poor people could be assured that their rights were protected. Everyone accused of a crime, for example, was entitled to a lawyer.

"Of course, this doesn't function in practice," he said. "We aren't really very organized or disciplined. No one wants to take the case of an indigent. Theoretically you have access to a lawyer if you're accused of a crime, but what happens? The court pulls in a lawyer, and he accompanies you. But he doesn't fight on your behalf."

I told him about Gladys's case. "It pains me to hear of it," he said. "We almost never get such cases. Poor people don't initiate lawsuits. Maybe if we went into the *pueblos jóvenes* to talk to people, we might be able to learn about cases like hers. Then we'd really be a Justice Ministry. But we don't really do that type of thing. We think only of our own pay. Being a lawyer is very lucrative. It's not a service profession; it's commerce. Many judges are also corrupt. It's good business."

"Who's the buyer?" he asked. When I mentioned López, he leaned back and smiled. "I know that man," he said. "If that's the man who bought the lot, you don't have to tell me anything else for me to know that something unjust has gone on. He's a delinquent. He runs a chain of bars; some are really whorehouses.

I closed one of them, and he's making a lot of trouble. He's got a group of lawyers, and he delays and delays and delays."

He told me that Gladys needed to have the title to her property and a copy of a document stating her own evaluation of its worth. She needed a copy of the sale document sealed by a notary. If she had written López letters asking him to pay her the money he owed, those would be useful, too.

Gladys had none of those things, she told me a few days later. She had written no letters; she had no papers from the sale. Everything she had signed was in the possession of López's lawyer, and to ask for a copy was to alert him that she was contemplating legal action. Because the transaction had not been notarized, López could easily have altered the document. She had never declared the value of her property, which was still in her mother's name. She did not even have the title. All she had were some light and water bills. She gave me a few. The light bill was marked "Order to cancel service." She answered my questions listlessly. She seemed to have lost her enthusiasm.

I was losing mine as well. Without any of the documents she needed, I couldn't see how she could win. I went to her house the next morning to tell her I thought we should forget about it. She wasn't at home, but through the crack in the door I could see Marco, in the same too-long sweater and blue pants as always, sweeping the floor, valiantly struggling with a broom twice his height. I watched him for a while. Then I called Patricia Fuentes, a lawyer a friend had recommended, and asked her to take the case.

Fuentes is a large, smiling woman, the daughter of one of Tacna's most prominent lawyers. We sipped lemonade in her living room while I told her about Gladys. She seemed almost optimistic. It was too bad that Gladys didn't have any papers, but she could get them, Fuentes said. It might take some time, but it was probably a good thing to do even if she didn't want to sue anyone. The best argument Gladys had, she said, was that López had bought the property in bad faith, deliberately paying less than two thirds of the legal value. "That's illegal under Peruvian law," she said. "I think she can get her property back. I think she can win."

The next day I went to see Gladys again. She hadn't been at

home the day before because it was her twenty-fourth birthday, she said. She had gone to talk with López about the money. "He bought me two beers for my birthday, and he deducted the price of four beers from the account of what he owed me," she said. She said she saw him write it down but thought it was better to say nothing. He was about to pay her, she said. He had just closed a business and would give her money when he got the license to open a new one.

I explained to her what Patricia Fuentes had said. She was silent. "He's beaten up my brothers," Gladys said. "I don't want him to throw me out of my house."

"He can't throw you out of your house," I said. "You don't owe him anything. There's absolutely no way he can do it." She looked at me. She didn't believe what I was saying. I wasn't sure I did either.

The next time I went to Gladys's house I brought Patricia Fuentes with me. Gladys's uncle Carlos was there. Carlos, who clearly had the legal mind in the family, wanted to sue López because he himself had worked for him for eighteen months, managing his bars and doing general errands, and had never been paid. López had kept saying that he would pay everything he owed him next month; but the months came and went, and he never did.

"What do you mean he didn't pay you?" said Fuentes. "How could you keep working for him without getting a salary?" He shrugged. "How is any judge going to believe this?" asked Fuentes.

She asked Gladys who López's lawyer was. His name was Wilbur Valdivia, Gladys said. "That can't be right," said Fuentes. "I know Wilbur. He's a clerk for a judge. He can't do that and be a lawyer at the same time."

"That's right, he works for a judge," Gladys said. She said that they had always done their business in a judge's office.

"That didn't seem odd to you?" Fuentes said.

Gladys said nothing.

Gladys talked to Fuentes about how they could try to get the sale documents without tipping off López. "Why don't we say that we need all your papers because your tuberculosis has worsened and your family wants to be prepared?" Fuentes suggested.

Gladys thought that was a good idea. We agreed to meet in Fuentes's office in a few days.

When we arrived for the appointment, Gladys was silent and petulant. Fuentes told Gladys and Carlos that she had been to see López's lawyer, who was still working for the judge. He remembered Gladys and said he would turn over her papers on Monday. Gladys said nothing the whole time. She seemed to have lost interest in the lawsuit. I was about to leave Tacna and would come back in two or three months. We decided that Fuentes would get Gladys's documents in order and, when everything was assembled, would proceed with the suit.

Gladys's suit, it was becoming apparent, did not represent her abandonment of passivity. It was the essence of passivity. Whenever we talked about what she needed to do—rather, whenever I talked to her about what she needed to do—she was silent. She had simply found a powerful, white, rich person who she thought was on her side. If I could handle the suit for her, she probably thought, I could win, because a gringa rated higher on the scale of influence and power than even López. Or maybe she thought that I was nuts and that the best thing to do was to humor me. She had no confidence in her power to direct her destiny but had boundless confidence in my power to do so. I was more *misti* than ever.

And I was beginning to believe that Gladys was right. I had stopped wondering why Carlos would work for a year and a half for López without receiving his pay, why Gladys put up with wages that would not supply her family even with potatoes, why people lived twelve to a room with no water or electricity, why the poor whimpered and accepted the countless other small blows of daily life. They had no other choice.

There are people in Tacna who don't know their own names. Fuentes told me that she sometimes visited a mothers' center in a *pueblo joven* where her husband worked as a doctor to help the patients with some simple legal work. The most basic task was getting people legally registered, with names and birth dates. The problem was that few of the women knew these facts about themselves. Their employers chose names for them when they came to Tacna from Puno. "Well," Fuentes would say, "what would you like to be called? What would you like for your birth date?"

Most of the women who didn't know their names chose to be called María. For a birth date they chose December 8, the day of Purísima celebrating the Virgin Mary. Fuentes ended up with a clinic full of Marías born on December 8.

The word "rights" is a popular word in Peru. President Alan García talked about rights all the time. In 1979 a new constitution had been written. A document that is now published in every phone directory in the country, it provides for freedom of speech and assembly, decent wages, access to justice, and guarantees of good working conditions and equality for women, children, and Indians. It is an excellent constitution and at times bears some resemblance to reality. Progressive, educated people like Fuentes and the judge I spoke with are very proud of it. They talk a lot about the rights of the poor in Peru.

But the poor in Peru don't talk about rights. They recognize the constitution for the bit of poetry it is. If they have heard the word, they think, as Gladys thought about the minimum wage, that it doesn't apply to them. Rights exist only for the powerful, meaning, of course, that they do not exist at all.

In late April 1988, two months after we first met in the health clinic, Gladys's throat closed up, and she had to fight for breath. Her weight dropped to ninety-two pounds. On April 22 Zenobia, the nurse from the health post, took her to the hospital. The doctor warned her that if she didn't stay in the hospital, complete her course of treatment, and rest, she would be dead in three months. Zenobia suggested that she put Mario and Marco into the local children's home.

Gladys stayed in the hospital for thirty-eight days. She had just gotten out when I returned to Tacna. The transformation was astonishing. For most people, going to the hospital is a hazardous adventure. Patients have to bring their own sutures, sheets, and bandages. The strong infections circulating often ensure that a mother who brings in a sick child will never see that child again. But for Gladys the stay in the hospital had been wonderful, almost like a vacation. She had gained thirty pounds, mainly because her uncle Carlos brought her food every day—chicken, beans, noodles, hearty things—to supplement the hospital meals. She made a few friends among the nurses. She had met a twenty-eight-year-old orderly who worked there. He brought her gifts—magazines and tapes to listen to. She told him she had two children, and he said he would keep seeing her anyway. But she didn't trust him, she said.

The children, who had visited her in the hospital every Sunday, loved living in the children's home. They finally had other kids to play with. Mario, who had been extremely thin, was now chubby. Marco, too, had gained weight. He was noticeably more outgoing, not the grave little elf I had known. At the age of seven he was going to school for the first time.

But Gladys missed her children and her house. Carlos told her that strange men had been coming around. This worried her; she had been robbed the year before. Someone had broken in, not very difficult to do, and taken her iron, radio, and television set. The loss of the iron was particularly serious; she had been taking in washing to make money.

She went back to her house; the kids moved back, too, although Marco continued to go to school at the children's home. She went to the hospital most days to see her new boyfriend. She especially liked to visit in the evening, when the night nurse gave her food. It was like going to a restaurant, she said. This provoked screaming matches with her uncle Carlos, who called her a whore. "Stay home and rest and take care of your boys," Carlos said. Carlos and Gladys were barely speaking.

When the health post in Natividad, Gladys's *pueblo joven*, opened in 1968, the staff treated 3 cases a year of tuberculosis. In 1987 the post treated 70 cases. In the first week of June 1988 alone it treated 17 new cases of tuberculosis, all in children. Tacna's incidence of tuberculosis, 143 cases per 100,000 people, was the third highest of the twenty-five states in Peru. Immigrants from the highlands, where it was too cold for the tuberculosis bacteria, come with no natural defenses to a hot climate, where the bacteria thrive. They eat poorly and often have other infections that weaken their defenses. They live in tiny rooms crowded with relatives and sometimes animals, facilitating the disease's spread.

Abigail Martínez, a social worker at the health post, said that 41 percent of tuberculosis patients abandoned their treatment programs before they were cured. Some quit for easily explainable reasons. Gladys, for example, had quit twice because there was no free medicine. But even when there was medicine, almost half the patients stopped their treatments.

Martínez was taking a survey of why people quit. I looked at a few sheets on her desk. One man responded that he had stopped his treatment because he was working in the contraband market; his very long day did not allow time to come in to the health post for his shots. Other people answered that they were afraid of injections, that the pills had bad side effects, or that going to the health center took too long. A common response was "I felt better, so I stopped the treatment." Martínez said that most immigrants did not understand why they had to keep taking pills even after they felt better. One man wrote in "alcoholism." A few people said they preferred the services of *curanderos*, practitioners of traditional medicine, some of whom make diagnoses by passing a chicken or a guinea pig over the patient's body, then killing the animal to read the disease. "One man said that the pills don't do him any good but that the *curandero* cured him with a dead cat," Martínez said.

"Some things a *curandero* can take care of perfectly well," said Dr. Fulgencio Llasaca, the doctor at the health post. With his mustache and long sideburns he looked like a Miami used-car dealer. Before working in Natividad, he worked in Locumba, a small town a two-hour drive north of Tacna, where patients preferred to take their problems to the two *curanderos*. "A skin inflammation, for example, responds well to herbs," he said. "And some things, like headaches, respond if a *curandero* tells a patient to cut out salt or get more rest. But a kidney infection . . ." He said he had made friends with Locumba's *curanderos*. When he saw a seriously ill patient who preferred the advice of the *curandero*, Llasaca took the *curandero* aside and explained the necessary treatment, the *curandero* prescribed it, and everyone was happy.

The best *curandero* in town, patients at the health post said, was Patricio Torres, who lived a half block away. I thought a visit might show me something about how Peru's Indians saw the world. Besides, my back hurt. I turned the corner and asked three teenagers playing soccer in the street for Don Patricio's house. "Which Don Patricio?" they said.

"The doctor," I said, ever respectful of native customs.

One boy laughed. "This is it," he said. "But he's not a doctor. He's a warlock."

An old woman answered the door, and I stepped into blackness. When my eyes became accustomed to the single thin line of light that escaped the curtain, illuminating swirls of dust and cobwebs, I could see dark blue walls and a concrete floor. Two chairs covered with ancient upholstery occupied one end of the room. The old woman sat on a wooden bench at the other end next to an old man. She had only two teeth. "Are you ill?" she said.

"I came to ask the maestro some questions," I said. "My sister suffers from headaches."

She clasped her hands over her belly and stretched out her legs. "He's the best," she said. "There are three *curanderos* in Tacna, but none as good as Don Patricio." She told me why they had come. The couple's granddaughter had been scared by an animal on the beach a year and a half ago, and since then the girl cried all night. "During the day she's fine," she said. "But at night she doesn't stop crying. We've been to a doctor, but it didn't help. We thought since she cries at night, there might be some forces involved." I nodded.

"Did you bring an article of clothing?" she asked. She unrolled a baby's shirt from a newspaper. "He'll look at this and might be able to tell what's wrong with her. You should have brought an article of your sister's clothing. Or hair, if she suffers from head-aches. Hair would be good."

The *curandero* opened the door to show out his patient, and the old couple went in, leaving me alone. A few minutes later they came out. "He says to bring the baby tomorrow," the woman said. I was ushered into his office. It was a small room with a white table covered with a blue-flowered Japanese cloth. Two bottles of baby powder sat on the table. The walls were hung with family photos and a picture of Jesus on the cross.

Patricio Torres said he was seventy-eight years old. With his full head of curly black hair and his athletic build, he looked fifty. He wore a white undershirt and an enormous silver chain hung with keys. I asked about the old couple's grandchild. "My impression is that the baby was scared by a spirit, which has taken her over," he said. "Tomorrow I will see the child, and we'll call the spirit." He said he was born in Sama, an hour's drive from

Tacna, and had become a *curandero* after getting out of the army in 1935. He worked a lot with herbs and jungle plants, sometimes finding prescriptions in a book on herbal medicine on his desk and wisdom from his uncle, who was also a *curandero*. He was born with the gift, he said. "I'm teaching myself telepathy now. I find I have a facility for it. Everyone is born with some talents." He said he had nothing against doctors; he occasionally visited a doctor himself. "But the doctor can't find everything," he said. Sometimes, he said, he cured people with cards, the forty-card Spanish deck, and sometimes with animals. "If you have something evil in your house, for example, I'll come with a guinea pig. We'll let the animal go, and it will go right to where the problem is."

I asked about passing animals over the patient's body. "I do that," he said. "A chicken usually works. You can pass a chicken over the patient and then kill it and open it up. The sickness will show up as a red stain. If there is no stain, then the patient is well. It works just like the X ray a doctor takes."

He leaned over the desk. "Do you know what it means," he whispered, "if the animal dies while you are passing it over the patient?"

"Bad news?" I said. He nodded. "It must be hard to tell the patient," I said.

"You can't tell the patient," he said. "He'll die sooner. You tell a family member to make the patient comfortable. But you have to be careful." He showed me back into the dark waiting room.

To Tacna's poor, especially the immigrants from Puno, the *curandero*'s chicken is the familiar medicine they have used all their lives. What seems like black magic is the health post's fabulous tales of invisible bugs and magic needles to ward off disease and the goings-on inside the fortress of a hospital where people go in but never come out. The science of the rich is the magic of the poor, and vice versa. The formal institutions of society, easily understood by middle- and upper-class Peruvians, are unfathomable to the poor, who correctly do not view such institutions as courts or hospitals as useful for solving their problems. And the methods chosen by the poor are incomprehensible to wealthier Peru.

It was in Ite that Jeff Thielman, a North American volunteer in Peru, began to understand the tragic height of the wall separating the two worlds. Ite is a desert oasis of six hundred people, with no electricity and one hand-crank telephone, a two-hour drive from Tacna. Jeff was working at Cristo Rey, a Jesuit school in Tacna, and had gone to Ite to supervise Cristo Rey's students in their annual construction project, this year a kindergarten. It was Sunday afternoon, and Jeff had taken the day off and gone swimming with a priest and two nurses working in Ite. That was when Sebastián Anquise's baby died.

At four in the afternoon they got back to find Sebastián, a skinny, cross-eyed twenty-one-year-old, was waiting for them at the health post. He had been waiting for four hours, and he looked devastated. Sebastián's wife had given birth that morning, he told the group. He had delivered the child and cut the umbilical cord with a razor blade. The baby was sick. "Why didn't you call someone when she went into labor?" the nurse asked. Sebastián kept his head bowed.

The group went down the hill to Sebastián's house, a one-room concrete box with two tiny windows and holes in the roof. There was one single bed for Sebastián, his nineteen-year-old wife, Herenia Molloni, and their older baby. Next to it lay some pots crusted with food and a few pieces of clothing. Flies were everywhere. It was the worst poverty that Jeff, who had just arrived in Peru, had ever seen. The newborn baby was lying at the foot of the bed, wrapped in a filthy piece of cloth, dead. It had lived just eight hours. There were so many flies on the baby's face, Jeff wrote in his diary, that it looked as though its eyes were open.

Jeff, the nurse, and the priest put the baby in a box and buried it the next day under a metal cross and a flower in Ite's tiny hillside cemetery. At the funeral Sebastián passed around a bottle of Coke and a single glass.

The baby had been born six weeks premature, the nurse told Jeff the next day. Herenia had been hitting herself in the womb in hopes of aborting the child. The nurse had suggested to Herenia that she have this child, then begin to use some sort of birth control, but Herenia didn't want to. She told the nurse that on Sebastián's wages, they could not support the child they already had, let alone a second one.

A week later Jeff went back to Sebastián's house. Sebastián was earning fourteen intis a day—then worth eighty-four cents—in his job as a farm worker for a local patrón. The minimum wage was twenty-three intis. Where he had come from, in rural Puno, he had been earning only ten intis. He told Jeff his life was much better here in Ite, that the climate was not as harsh and the pay was better.

Jeff started to ask other people about salaries. Rosa, the nurse, said that most workers were paid only fifteen intis a day, and women got only ten. Jeff met a woman who lived in a metal toolshed in the back of a patron's house. She told him she made five intis a day. It was the same story all over. Sebastián knew he wasn't being paid the minimum wage, which was twenty-three intis, he told Jeff, but there was nothing he could do.

Jeff thought there was something he could do. It was summer, and he would not have to start teaching at Cristo Rey until the school year started. He had been looking for a way to spend the intervening two months. He found it in Sebastián's house.

"I made the decision that day that I was going to shake the town up," he said. He would spend the next two months, or whatever it took, trying to get Ite's landowners to comply with the law and pay their workers the minimum wage.

He took his project to Fred Green, a World War II marine pilot turned Jesuit priest who ran Cristo Rey. Green, who has lived in Peru since 1959, told Jeff not to waste his time. But after thinking it over, he told Jeff to try it. "You might learn something," Green said.

Jeff started the project when he got back to Tacna. On Friday he rode his bike downtown to see Oscar Galdos, the head of employment and social security in the Labor Ministry. Jeff explained what he had found in Ite, which fell under Tacna's jurisdiction. Galdos told him this was a problem all over Peru, adding that he thought that they could do something about it but that transportation to Ite was difficult.

The next Tuesday Jeff went back to Galdos and volunteered to pay for gas for the trip. Galdos directed Jeff to another official, who wasn't around. Jeff went to talk to a third official. She listened to his story and said she would call him the next day. She didn't call. Jeff went to her office a few days later. She was talking to another woman while her officemate read the paper. She said she was working on the transportation problem. For the next six weeks, until school began at Cristo Rey, Jeff spent every day with a government official. They all wanted to go to Ite, they told him. But there was a meeting that day, or it was someone's birthday, or no car was available. "What a fool I am," Jeff wrote in his diary.

The school year began, and for two weeks Jeff did not make his daily pilgrimage to the government offices. When he went back on May 13, there was a new man in charge. "He really wants to help me," Jeff wrote in his diary. "I talked to him and he said he'd talk to the mayor of Ite." But a month later nothing had happened. In desperation, Jeff made a hundred copies of the minimum wage law. Ite's mayor had a house in Tacna. Jeff gave him the copies. He promised he would distribute them but assured Jeff that all the farmers were paying minimum wage.

After twenty-eight years in Peru, Father Green had developed divine patience in the face of the absurd. Every year, he said, Cristo Rey asked the Peruvian government for construction materials for its project. "It's a lot of work to get local food and housing for thirty boys," Green said, "but our biggest problem is getting the government to provide us with a few bags of cement and some steel rods. There is no shortage of cement, but it takes months of visiting offices again and again to get it. It's the same rigmarole every time, for the most part dealing with the same people."

A year after the death of Sebastián's baby I went to Ite with Jeff. Sebastián was still not being paid the minimum wage. He and Herenia were now living in a straw shed next to a sheep corral. There was one small bed. On the bed were two children. The new baby, a boy, was born just ten months and seventeen days after Herenia had given birth to the baby Jeff had helped bury. He was born on Christmas Day, and the couple had named him Jesús.

OSCAR GALDOS, THE SOCIAL SECURITY AND EMPLOYMENT CHIEF whom Jeff had pestered, was reading the paper when I entered his office and asked to speak to him. We talked for the next two hours. On the wall behind him was a poster from the National Debureaucratization Program. "Debureaucratization is the responsibility of every Peruvian," it said.

I asked him if it was true that some employers did not pay the minimum wage. "The great majority of employers," he corrected me. "It is a disgrace, but the supply and demand for work allow this to happen."

There were many reasons the government did not carry out inspections, Galdos said. His office would not initiate an investigation without a complaint from a worker. I tried to picture Sebastián finding a way to make the two-hour trip to Tacna to denounce his employer. Then, said Galdos, there is the transportation problem. "We don't do many rural inspections because we have no cars," he said.

"When was the last time you did one?" I asked.

"Well, we've really never done one," he said. When the government inspects the Southern Peruvian Copper Company's mines in the area, instructors travel in Southern's cars, accompanied by Southern officials.

Galdos, like Jeff, viewed himself as a fighter blocked by the system. "This is the history of Peru," he said. "It is the legacy of hundreds of years of colonial rule. The worker is always exploited. He doesn't know the laws and usually can't read and write. There are hundreds of terrible cases in the country, thousands. What we need is a huge campaign on the part of the government to improve education and health." Without these sweeping reforms, he said, there was no point in trying.

He chuckled when I asked him about the impatient gringo who had dogged him the year before. "Jeff came in and began banging on my desk, saying, 'I want these guys to pay minimum wage.'

"I said, 'Fine, I want it, too.' I told him, 'You want to make a revolution?' I said I was a revolutionary, too.

"I wanted to help him. I tried to get transportation. But the problem is, if we arrive to investigate and the patrón thinks his workers have denounced him, he will fire them. We have experience with this. We've gone into restaurants and questioned the owners about what they pay their kids, and the next day the boys lose their jobs and are out in the street.

"There was a man in my office this morning. He was fired from his job because he has tuberculosis. Because of an error his doctor made in the dates of his treatment, social security is not going to cover his illness. What can I do? I could be his lawyer, but there are hundreds of cases like that. We need to solve not just one case but all of them. I'm like a doctor who sees so many deaths that one more doesn't mean anything."

Galdos was part of a species of government official that seemed indigenous to Peru. Everywhere else I had been, including Washington—especially Washington—government officials avoided reporters. If I did manage to land an interview with an official, he spent the interview either denying that the problem in question existed or redefining it with an avalanche of jargon and statistics. If he were really good at his job, I left his office shaking my head, unable to remember just what it was I had come to ask him about. He knew, and he knew that I knew that he knew, that his vision had nothing to do with reality, but the rules prohibited him from admitting it.

Not in Peru. Bureaucrats in Peru seem eager to talk, and they paint their work in the worst possible light. Instead of denying that problems exist, they usually maintain that things are even worse than I had thought. They may or may not be less useful and efficient than their counterparts in other countries, but they are the only ones who spend hours analyzing their own uselessness and inefficiency. Every statement about their office, the government, or the country seems to begin with the words "lamentably," "unfortunately," or "disgracefully." At first I thought this was a healthy trait—finally, a place capable of self-criticism.

But it isn't a sign of health. The words absolve people like Galdos of the necessity to try to change the system. Bureaucrats are not defensive only because they are completely disengaged. That's the way it is, and that's the way it always will be, the theory goes. Peru will not change until a man on a white horse sweeps the old order aside. Nothing works, so people come to believe that nothing *can* work. Few people try to make things work, so nothing works.

In Peru the future is a gift of the past, and it is the rare man who can alter his destiny. The self-made man, object of such fervent worship in the United States, does not exist in most of Latin America, least of all in Peru. Here the rich make their money the old-fashioned way; they inherit it. Even the laziest, stupidest rich man dies rich. The cleverest, hardest-working poor man will always be poor. Success is the product of contacts and social station, not of talent or industry.

As a result, there is not much point to hard work, but it is extremely useful to cultivate friendships with as many important people as possible. For people with friends in high places, government is very efficient indeed. The people with the power to bring about changes in Peru—those with money and influence —are, of course, the very people who see no reason to change anything. Corruption and inefficiency are mutually reinforcing. "I see very little change since 1959," said Father Green, who has watched dozens of efficiency campaigns come and go. "If anything, there's more inefficiency all the time. The state bureaucracy grows, and there are more hands each paper has to pass through, and more stealing." In many government offices in Peru the only indications of García's efficiency campaign were signs announcing ALL TRANSACTIONS ARE FREE. LET'S NOT FOMENT IMMORALITY. The signs, of course, meant exactly the opposite— a clear signal that in this office, money talks.

Most people in Peru were clear about the need to avoid the government entirely if they wished to get something done. Hernando de Soto, the founder of a Lima think tank, the Foundation for Liberty and Democracy, invented a fake clothing factory and undertook the necessary legal transactions to establish a formal business. De Soto's researchers were told to pay only the bribes that were absolutely necessary. The operation took 289 days and cost $1,231 in bribes. A computer printout of the necessary legal steps ran more than a hundred feet long. Legalizing a fictitious store in which to sell the fictitious clothes took 43 days and cost $590. Getting a license to build a house took 6 years and cost $2,156 in bribes. Just getting the land required 207 different administrative steps in 48 different government offices. Setting up a large covered market—the kind found all over Peru—would have taken 17 years if anyone had ever tried to do it legally, but no one ever had. No wonder, De Soto wrote in a controversial book, El Otro Sendero ("The Other Path"), that 48 percent of the working population in Peru shunned the bureacracy, building its houses and setting up businesses entirely in the "informal" sector and, of course, paying no taxes.

Gladys Meneses might not have recognized it, but she was a shining example of informal Peru. She took no interest in the state, and it, in turn, took no interest in her. She had never legally married, had never gotten a title to her property, never paid taxes, never gotten birth certificates for her children. Her only connection to the government was in the form of electricity and water bills.

That Gladys had the opportunity to pay electricity and water bills made her part of a privileged minority in Tacna. The majority of the *pueblos jóvenes* enjoyed neither electricity nor running water. Natividad, the *pueblo joven* of about ten thousand residents where Gladys lived, was one of the most established *pueblos jóvenes* in Tacna, with a relatively good health clinic, three primary schools and a secondary school, several markets, and a neighborhood center with basketball and soccer courts that were filled and noisy all day.

The neighborhood had been founded in the time-honored way, in a middle-of-the-night land invasion. One of the original settlers, Ruperto Luque Huanca, was now a justice of the peace, whose office, a cubicle containing a desk with a typewriter and three school chairs, was next to the basketball court in the neighborhood center. Over the noise of a twilight basketball game he described the original land invasion of sixty families on September 8, 1960. It was just a sandy plain, he said, but you had to start somewhere.

"We had been living in straw huts, and the government promised us houses, but nothing happened," he said. "Instead of waiting for the bureaucracy, we just went at night and put up tents, using wooden sticks and sheets of woven straw." The landowners woke the next morning to the sight of sixty tiny huts and the smell of coffee bubbling over outdoor fires. The police never came to evict them, Luque said. This was part of the strategy of a land invasion; once it was done, it was hard to throw out the settlers without a battle. "The government had been saying all along it would give us land," Luque said. "Maybe they were relieved when we just did it ourselves."

This was a pretty good statement of government policy in general. Natividad, like most places in Tacna, improved only when residents did things themselves. After waiting four years for the government to build a school, in 1964 residents built it themselves. The government dawdled fourteen years before installing water pipes. Three years later Natividad's neighborhood organization decided it didn't want to wait another fourteen years for electricity, and the board took out a bank loan to put in an electrical system. The government then managed to do its part: connect Natividad to the rest of the city and flip the switch. In a fit of civic responsibility in 1979 the city government put sewers in Natividad.

The people in the *pueblos jóvenes* build their own houses. A family usually begins by making a cube of woven straw. Then it acquires bricks of adobe or concrete, piling them in a corner until there are enough for the beginnings of a wall. People live for years in houses with no walls. A ceiling means you have arrived; some houses in Natividad even have two stories and are the envy of the block.

The majority of Tacna's workers create their own jobs; 60 or 70 percent of the city's workers sell contraband goods in one of the four huge markets or on the street. This is a relatively new profession. In the mid-fifties and sixties a few women had earned their living smuggling Chilean fruit, powdered milk, and Nescafé across the border. The volume rose in 1970 with the ascent of Salvador Allende's government in Chile, whose socialist policies subsidized basic goods; Peruvians bought cheap products in Chile and smuggled them into Tacna. But contraband grew to mammoth proportions shortly after General Pinochet's overthrow of the Allende government in 1973, when he opened a duty-free zone in Iquique in Chile's north, a hundred miles south of Tacna. Traffic in fruit and coffee became traffic in televisions, personal stereos, and French perfume. "When Iquique first opened, about three hundred people were trafficking," a local businessman said. "The authorities let it go, thinking it was a tiny problem."

Today more than a hundred thousand people in Tacna make their living from contraband. The smugglers hike through the desert, which still bears mines installed during a recent Chilean-Peruvian dispute (one smuggler had his legs blown off). Or they bring goods over from Chile by rowboat and bury them on the beach for Peruvian contacts to dig up later. The easiest smuggling route is directly through customs officials, who are not shy about demanding bribes.

Any product a normal human being would think of owning may be bought in the Mercado Bolognesi, the oldest of Tacna's four contraband markets, organized just after Iquique opened. The market is a huge building covered with a roof of cement, cartons, straw, laminated steel, planks, and blankets, a perfect reflection of the chaos inside. Some of the vendors display their merchandise in beautiful glass booths; others use only planks covered with cartons. There are hundreds of different products: shoes here; clothes and handbags in the next row; electronic keyboards; dishes; perfume; phones in the shape of Coke bottles; toys; auto parts; and Chilean fruit, powdered milk, and Nescafé. Prices for electronic goods are competitive with the cut-rate New York stores. I saw watches for thirty-one hundred intis—thirty dollars—Sony radios and tape decks for sixty-eight dollars, television sets for seventy-five dollars. Chilean wine was selling for less than it sold for in Chile. I bought an army knife for three dollars. When I tried to use the corkscrew to open a bottle of contraband Chilean wine the next day, the knife broke in two.

To an emigrant in Puno, a journey to Tacna must seem as overwhelming as a trip to the moon. The poor start their own small businesses, build their own houses and schools, and form their own neighborhoods. The aggressiveness, risk, sweat, and initiative this life demands are the local equivalent of running a Wall Street hostile take-over. What I had confused for people's passivity was a simple distinction between actions that could improve their lives—move away, get into business, build a school —and ones that are a waste of time. It took nineteen years of determined work for Natividad residents to make their neighborhood a decent place to live. If they had waited for the government, it might have taken centuries. They built the contraband markets that provide employment for most of the city without any help from the government. They trust the kind of medicine they can understand. They depend on their families and few others. They know just enough about the legal system to be certain that it will never do a thing for them. They know whom and what they can trust and whom and what they cannot. Heading the latter list is anything to do with the government or with *misti*.

MARCO MENESES WAS FINALLY GOING TO SCHOOL. IN OTHER countries, going to school would have enabled him to improve his lot and might have trained him to raise questions and make changes that could benefit society as a whole. But there was little chance that education would do this for Marco Meneses in Peru. He was at the children's home school at seven-thirty every morning, in time for breakfast, in the uniform of gray slacks and sweater the school gave him, and he went home to Gladys after dinner at five. When I stuck my head in the window of his classroom on my tour of the school, he was sitting at his desk, clutching his notebooks and beaming. Later I saw him playing on the grass outside, whirling his arms over his head like a helicopter, running in a circle with the other students, flushed and smiling.

Brother José Lobatón, the school's director, had studied philosophy in Lima. "But they don't teach us to think, to question, in the philosophy courses," he said. "It's just copying what the author of the particular book thinks. There's no discussion. Here we stop kids in class when they say what they think. It's terrible. Education here is a ritual. It's like going to mass. History, for example, is raising the Peruvian flag and praising our heroism. It's good that we respect our traditions, our folklore, but it's very superficial."

Part of the problem, he said, was that good people did not want to be teachers. At the school in the children's home the new teachers made seven thousand intis a month, then just about forty dollars. You could survive on that if you were a single man or woman living with your parents, as many teachers were. Teachers who were sent to rural areas, however, had to pay their transportation, food, and housing from that meager salary, and many teachers solved the problem by simply not showing up. It was common for rural schools to have teachers only a few days a month. "Why would anyone want to be a teacher when he could be out selling contraband?" he said.

The school's first-grade class was held in what was euphemistically called the library, although the shelves were bare. The second-grade classroom was a tiny locker room. Fifteen students, their seats jammed together, were copying phrases from the blackboard. Many of the students, said Ruperto Espinoza, the head teacher at the school, couldn't really read or write but had become expert at copying what he wrote into their notebooks. "I dictate, and they write," he said. "When I teach history, I explain the history of their country, and they write it down." Espinoza, who was teaching the second graders, called two of his students to the front of the room. "Write, 'The flag is red,' " he said. Neither could. "You see, they can't write," he said. "Only about half these people should be in second grade. The rest really should be repeating first grade." He didn't bother to lower his voice, nor did he show the students how to write the sentence. I asked about discussion and group participation. "We don't do that," he said.

I went to a class that combined the third and fourth grades. There were twenty-eight students, ranging in age from eight to sixteen. They were reviewing their notebooks, preparing for a science test. The teacher, María Elena Pérez, said they would be asked, among other things, to label the hands of a watch and to name the instrument used to measure temperature.

She said that the students who lived at the home generally did better academically than those who, like Marco, returned to their own homes every night. "Here we make them study," she said. "At home the mother will get up early and go to work and doesn't really know if the children do their homework." But there were difficulties with studying in the children's home, she said. "Our library isn't very complete," she said.

"There's not a single book in it," I said.

"That's what I mean. It's not very complete," she said.

According to the census of 1961, 43 percent of Peruvians over the age of four had completed a year of school. Attendance has improved greatly since; in 1987 the average adult Peruvian had completed almost the fifth grade. In Tacna the average was higher: almost seventh grade. But going to school is not very different from *not* going to school. The vast majority of schools have no books or materials. "The majority of kids in high school have never read a book," said Father Green. Learning history means memorizing dates and places; learning science means identifying a thermometer, not understanding how it works. Learning to write means copying hieroglyphics without, perhaps, ever learning to read. Education, one of society's few ways of correcting its own mistakes, is a word without meaning in most of Peru, one that many students will never learn how to spell.

WHILE THE CHILDREN OF PERU'S ELITES ATTEND THE UNIversity of Lima or the Catholic University or study abroad, those who come from working-class families are likely to go to Peru's largest university, the National Major University of San Marcos, the oldest university in the Americas, a free school in a poor barrio of Lima. Javier took me to a law school class. To get to San Marcos, we had to take two buses from his house, ending up an hour away in the neighborhood of Pueblo Libre that enveloped the walled University City. Lima's electricity shortage along with a lack of money for maintenance combined to make San Marcos resemble the site of a bomber attack, the whole place littered with debris, covered with sand, and scattered with a few scrawny trees. At night the only artificial light comes from a bonfire of burning garbage.

In the classroom Javier's law professor stood under red block letters written on the wall reading "Long live Presidente Gonzalo, chief of the party and the revolution!" and "Long live Marxism-Leninism-Maoism, Gonzalo thought!" Two posters showed a young Mao with the slogan "Workers of the world, unite!" Outside in the hallway I waited under a "Death to *yanquis*!" slogan while Javier talked to a friend.

Sendero graffiti covers almost every inch of wall. As I walked by the arts building, a rare stretch of clean wall above the third-floor windows caught my eye. "Thanks for pointing it out to me," Javier said, laughing. "I'll have the compañeros take care of it tonight." Sendero murals decorate the staircase landings and building lobbies: paintings of Presidente Gonzalo, in an open-jacketed suit, with glasses and a paunch, holding a sword or a red hammer and sickle flag. Under the murals were long tracts, fifteen or so paragraphs, written in longhand in red marker on computer paper. Javier read them to me in hushed tones. "Crush the New Counterrevolutionary Revisionist Movement: Gorbachev Betraying the People's Revolution," was the title of one. There was a speech by Mao written in smaller letters. "Read it to me," Javier said. He needed new glasses.

"A revolution is not a dinner party," I read, "or writing an essay or painting a picture or doing embroidery; it cannot be so refined, so leisurely and gentle, so temperate, kind, courteous, restrained, and magnanimous. A revolution is an insurrection, an act of violence by which one class overthrows another."

He nodded, savoring each word. As we walked away, he quoted

more Mao: "Nothing is impossible for him who dares to scale the heights."

We went into the university's snack bar and ordered coffee, which was served in huge mugs, and sausage sandwiches. "I'm paying," Javier said.

"What a macho you are," I said, and he laughed and put his money away.

After dinner we went upstairs to a classroom whose walls were covered with murals of Marx and Lenin. A group of nine children, some of whom looked to be around seven, wearing Andean wool caps with earflaps and extremely serious expressions, played flutes and drums. After each song they chanted, "Viva Presidente Gonzalo! Viva the People's War!" The students got up from their chairs and followed the musicians, young pied pipers, into the hallway to dance. "The People's Revolution is a party," Javier murmured.

Sendero had been burrowing in at San Marcos since the late 1970s but first appeared publicly in June 1987, when the red flag with a hammer and sickle was raised during a student demonstration. The next year Sendero's slate of candidates won the student elections. But the movement has lost support since; its strong-arm tactics—hanging dead dogs on campus to intimidate informers, for example—alienated some students.

But San Marcos is still fertile recruiting ground for a movement that was born at another free university, the University of San Cristóbal de Huamanga, in Ayacucho. Shortly after San Cristóbal de Huamanga reopened in 1959 after sixty-five years of dormancy, it received an infusion of funds from European governments and the U.S. Alliance for Progress. The university's attractive salaries lured some of Peru's leading scholars from other provinces. Among those academics was Abimael Guzmán, who had been a brilliant philosophy student in the aristocratic city of Arequipa. Ayacucho's university quickly became the most modern outside Lima. At the same time a left-wing military coup by a populist general, Juan Velasco Alvarado, raised expectations, especially among the young, that great changes were coming. When those expectations were not met, the university—with Guzmán's help—became a crucible for revolution.

Guzmán became the university's personnel director and,

through that position, controlled the curriculum. His teachers replaced "Introduction to Social Science" with "Historic Materialism," "Biological Science" with "Dialectic of Nature." He used teachers as Mao used peasants and Lenin workers, and his disciples went to teach in high schools and colleges around Peru. Velasco unwittingly helped spread Sendero's message by promoting the free universities: In 1960 Peru ranked fourteenth in Latin America in school attendance; by 1980, thanks largely to Velasco, it ranked fourth. Access to education produces social mobility. But it also produces guerrillas. Though Peruvian education does not teach young people to question, it cannot keep them from questioning naturally, and Peruvian society offers few answers. "The poor man who doesn't know he is poor will be poor forever. The poor man who is conscious of his position is a potential revolutionary," Guzmán liked to say.

Alarmed by Sendero's rapid spread, Peru's security forces raided San Marcos four times in the late 1980s. On February 13, 1987, four thousand policemen raided three Lima universities, killing a student and arresting more than five hundred in San Marcos, breaking doors, smashing a statue of Che Guevara, "confiscating"—i.e., stealing—computers and equipment and burning books, with special emphasis on any book bound in red, even burning a copy of Peru's constitution. The university, which already resembled a war zone, was reduced to rubble.

One night Javier took me to a San Marcos square dance. The hall was freshly painted white, decorated with balloons filled with confetti and colored-paper snowflakes. As Javier and I paid admission, smiling young people were eating plates of chicken and rice or square dancing in Andean folk style as men in ponchos played guitars and flutes. We had picked our way through the debris in the unlit streets outside; few places are as menacing as a Lima barrio at night. But inside was all light and laughter, good, clean fun, except that the band's lyrics were a hymn to the People's War, and some of these happy dancers attached bombs to dogs and slit policemen's throats.

"Are they all from the Shining Path?" I asked Javier, somewhat alarmed; there were two hundred people here.

"I can't answer that," he said. "But they all have the desire to serve the people."

We broke into the line to dance to a song that began "Warrior with a Red heart, nothing can stop him." The music was a melancholy wail, like Jewish klezmer music, and as the line dance picked up, I began to feel at home; we were doing the hora. The line snaked in and out, weaving back through itself, faster and faster, and blinded by the confetti and ribbons dripping from my hair, I closed my eyes and let Javier pull me along.

When I asked most Peruvians about how things were in their country, the answer was usually the same: "Terrible—a million percent inflation, garbage piling up, no jobs, no water, no electricity." At the square dance Javier introduced me to one of the compañeros, an engineering student. How are things? I said. "Great," he replied with enthusiasm. "A million percent inflation, garbage piling up, no jobs, no water, no electricity. The forces of history are really on our side."

THE FORCES OF HISTORY, IN TRUTH, HAVE NEVER BEEN WITH PERU. Or with the rest of Latin America. Considering the way the continent was conquered and colonized, it is miraculous that violence is not more pervasive and that Latin American societies function at all. There were no democratic currents blowing in Spain at the time Columbus set sail for what turned out to be the New World. In late-fifteenth-century Spain, the monarchy held absolute power. King Ferdinand and Queen Isabel consulted advisory councils, but no institutions existed to challenge the crown.

For the three centuries spanning Spain's conquest and colonization of America, the single dominant fact of Spanish life was the Inquisition. The Inquisition, which began in Rome in the thirteenth century, was not, of course, limited to Spain. But it was in Spain that the Inquisition reached its greatest intensity.

Much in the Spanish Inquisition later found its echo in modern Latin American antisubversive campaigns. Spain never participated in the Crusades, preferring to reserve its fervor for the Muslims, Jews, Lutherans, and other heretics within its own borders. The church fought the internal enemy with techniques of infiltration and psychological operations that previewed today's counterinsurgency techniques. A secret police of souls with a vast network of spies arose. Devout Catholics had to report anyone who doubted or sinned. Many people reported business rivals or family enemies. Others, through torture or religious pressure, were persuaded to turn in their children, brothers, or parents. Priests tortured small children to reveal their parents' religious beliefs. The supposed heretics were then tortured, and thousands were burned at the stake in autos-da-fé. A heretic's family suffered his shame for generations; his children were barred from holding positions of public trust, and their goods confiscated.

Even the Inquisition's language reverberates in Latin America hundreds of years later: The enemy was "soulless," his motivation part of a "worldwide godless conspiracy of evil"; his tactics "poison the minds of young children, who can only be saved in purifying flame." In 1599 Juan Mariani, an adviser to King Philip III, wrote of the Protestants, "It is a glorious thing to eliminate this pestilent and pernicious race from the face of the earth. When a limb is rotten, it is cut off so it does not infect the rest of the body. In the same way, we must use the sword to separate the state from this bestial cruelty in human form."

The death and emigration caused by the Inquisition and Spain's political decline in Europe led Spain to look elsewhere for wealth and influence. This was the setting in which an Italian sailor named Christopher Columbus arrived at the throne of Ferdinand and Isabel with his proposition to find a direct sea route to the spice lands of Asia by sailing west. The monarchs had rejected Columbus's proposal before. But now, with their coffers dangerously empty, they agreed to gamble. They procured financing from local bankers and gave Columbus diplomatic credentials to use in China and Japan.

That Columbus had happened upon America became clear only years later; he died without realizing he had landed on an autonomous continent. Instead of the great cities and spice plantations of Asia, Columbus discovered a desolate island (in what is now the Bahamas) populated by "savages." From the point of view of profit—the only point of view considered at the time—the trip was a failure.

On his second trip, the next year, he fared no better; he landed with seventeen boats and twelve hundred men in what is now the Antilles, where he found little to have made the journey worthwhile. On his third voyage, however, he reached the coast of what is now Venezuela (he thought it was Japan) and found traces of gold and pearls. This time, when he returned to Spain, Spain took notice, and the conquest began in earnest. Explorer after explorer set forth to follow Columbus's route, hoping to find even more riches.

Those who did not find minerals turned to plantation agriculture, introducing such New World crops as the potato, corn, tomato, tobacco, cocoa, coca, and quinine to Spain. To grow the crops, the Spanish enslaved Indians on plantations called *encomiendas*. In 1501 a royal decree gave colonizers the right to levy a tribute tax on the Indians, with a small part going to the crown and the rest to the *encomendero*. The Indians paid the tax through forced labor, and in return the *encomendero* taught them Catholicism. The forced labor lasted three lifetimes; after a father, son, and grandson had worked for the patron, the family was free. The Spanish imported dogs to hunt down escaped Indians; some Spanish adventurers made their living capturing entire Indian villages and selling the residents to the *encomenderos*.

The system troubled many in Spain, including a handful of radical priests and Queen Isabel, who wrote a petition requesting that the *encomienda*, which she considered slavery, be abolished. The Spanish rulers wrote laws obligating more humane treatment of Indians. But the economic realities were overpowering: Without slave labor, the Spanish colonies were worthless. The laws were simply ignored in America, giving rise to one of the basic operating principles of modern Latin America: *Obedezco pero no cumplo* ("I obey, but I do not comply"). Law had nothing to do with reality.

In 1565 the crown established the post of corregidor, to collect taxes, to help the *encomenderos*, and—ostensibly—to protect the native population. The officials were paid poorly and, after the sixteenth century, had to pay for the position themselves. They recouped their losses through corruption. If government officials were not already their provinces' wealthiest men when appointed to their jobs, they lost little time in becoming so.

The violence and corruption of the conquest reached their height in the two regions where the prize was greatest: Mexico and Peru. The Aztecs and the Incas were the richest and most developed of Latin America's Indians. They had the bad fortune to offer the Spanish gold, highly sophisticated agriculture, and millions of Indians who could be enslaved on the *encomiendas*.

Machu Picchu, the greatest archaeological wonder of South America, was a shrine to the technological command of Peru's Incas: terraced agriculture; hydraulic systems; earthquake-proof buildings that have proved to be more solid than many structures using today's construction techniques. But although the Incas were breathtaking engineers, their society was not, as the Latin American left likes to claim, a model of equality and democracy. A small elite controlled all the land; peasants were forced to labor for the landowners. No Incan was permitted to look his emperor in the eye. The Incas were also imperialists, who, having conquered their neighbors, proceeded to other lands. At the time of the arrival of the Spanish, Atahualpa, the Inca emperor, was ruling from Quito, in what is now Ecuador.

Francisco Pizarro, an illiterate pig farmer who was the illegitimate son of a Spanish nobleman, landed on the Peruvian coast in 1532 and proceeded inward, following the smell of gold. Pizarro requested a meeting with Atahualpa. At the summit Pizarro presented Atahualpa with a Bible and asked him to accept Catholicism and declare himself "servant of the pope and vassal of the king of Spain." Atahualpa, not understanding the concept of a book (the Incas had not discovered the written word), let the Bible fall to the ground. Pizarro's forces then attacked the Incas and took Atahualpa prisoner.

The Inca tried to buy his release, promising two rooms filled with gold and silver. Pizarro accepted; Atahualpa complied. Then Pizarro hanged him. His death established the level of trust between white and Indian that persists to this day.

In the forty years following his arrival, Pizarro proceeded to conquer the whole of Peru. He could do this with fewer than a hundred men for several reasons. First, the Incas were divided, with Atahualpa's enemies initially supporting the Spanish. Second, the Incas initially trusted Pizarro, believing that he and his men were gods. The Incas were also betrayed by their own authoritarianism; after their leaders were killed, the commoners tended to follow whoever replaced them. By 1572 the last ruling Inca, Tupac Amaru, had been killed, and the country fell firmly under Spanish domination. When the Spanish arrived, the Indian population numbered more than 2.5 million; a century later only 600,000 remained, the rest felled by the Spanish and their diseases, principally measles. Pizarro founded Lima in 1535, and it quickly became the most important city in South America, the major port for trade with Spain, and the capital of the viceroyalty of Peru, which ruled Colombia, Ecuador, Bolivia, Chile, and Argentina.

The feudalism of the Spanish crown remained until Peru's fight for independence, which began in 1821. Peru was freed from Spain mainly by Argentine and Colombian fighters; Peru's own elites, fat with the corruption Lima offered as the gateway to Spain, had no interest in giving up their colonial status. After independence, royal feudalism simply gave way to local feudalism. Government was a chaotic series of caudillos and military coups; between 1826 and 1845 Peru had more than thirty chief executives.

MODERN PERU IS THE LEGACY OF THIS HISTORY. PERU'S LEADERS have not been measurably better or worse than those of other Latin American countries. Good men have become president in Peru, but they have found themselves prisoners of the class differences, corruption, poverty, and lethargy of their society. Since the 1960s Peru has been dominated by three very different types of leader: Fernando Belaúnde, who governed in the 1960s as a populist and again in the 1980s as a conservative; General Juan Alvarado Velasco, who led a left-wing military coup in 1968; and the social democrat Alan García, who came to office in 1985. All three tried to better the lives of the poor; each went about it in a radically different way. All three failed, and each failure further shut out the poor from the political institutions of Peru.

García's collapse was the latest entry in the country's catalog of reasons for cynicism about politics. Never in Peru's history had a president taken office with expectations as high as in 1985. García was the first president elected from the APRA party, the American Popular Revolutionary Alliance. APRA had long been the most important electoral force in Peru, but the military had blocked its previous presidential candidates from taking office. García was thirty-five, a beefy six feet four, a man who had financed his studies at the Sorbonne by singing in Paris cafés. He was a spellbinding orator. His confidence in himself and his ability to change Peru seemed limitless. He was not a Marxist, offering the hope that he could convince the wealthy to cooperate in real change as a way of combating Marxism in the long term.

García took office announcing that he would pay the International Monetary Fund (IMF) no more than 10 percent of Peru's export earnings on the country's $13.7 billion debt. This was, in truth, pure talk. That first year García paid 30 percent; his predecessor, the conservative Belaúnde, had stopped paying altogether. But García's public defiance of the IMF rallied Peru behind him.

In his first few months García enjoyed a 97 percent approval rating. The APRA slogan sprouted on walls all over the country: "Only God can save your soul. Only APRA can save Peru." For two years it seemed true. García's unorthodox policy of stimulating the economy by redistributing income to the poor produced growth rates of 8.5 percent and 7 percent, the highest in Latin America. Everyone I talked to in Peru in March 1987 was still enchanted with Alan, as the Peruvians called him. What will happen, I asked a local schoolteacher on a train near Cuzco, when Peru has to start living without imported goods? "It's about time we learned how," he said.

Peruvians got their opportunity only a few months later. The economic boom continued as long as factories could simply put their idle machines to work. But Peru needed new investment, and this did not come. García met with twelve leading businessmen, called the Apostles, who signed letters of intent to invest but then did not invest. The IMF placed Peru on its blacklist, ineligible for new loans, the only Latin American country so distinguished. At the end of 1986 the government was losing hard currency at the rate of a hundred million dollars a month.

As production started to fall behind the new purchasing power, inflation started to climb; it was to total more than 2 million percent for García's five years in office, setting a world's record for sustained hyperinflation. In January 1989 rumors circulated that the military had planned a coup and then called it off, supposedly because the generals decided they could not win a battle with the Peruvian economy. Only the illegal export of coca paste, which by 1989 was bringing in more than a billion dollars a year, kept the country afloat. The minimum wage fell behind inflation; the poor were poorer with each passing day, their buying power lower than at any time in the previous twenty-five years.

Peruvians' disillusion with García translated into disillusion with politics in general. Previous experience seemed to become a disqualification for election. In November 1989 Ricardo Belmont, a radio and television personality with no political record, was elected major of Lima. That year it appeared that Mario Vargas Llosa, a novelist and political outsider, would be elected president. His appeal seemed to be that he was wealthy, white, and European and that he had wealthy, white, European friends. "If Vargas Llosa wins, won't people invest in Peru?" Javier's mother asked me. Connections, as any reader of a Vargas Llosa novel knows, are how things work in Peru.

But Vargas Llosa started forming alliances with Peru's traditional right-wing politicians. He began proposing economic reforms that scared Peruvians: firing state workers; removing subsidies. As Vargas Llosa began to be seen as a political insider, the role of outsider fell to Alberto Fujimori, the Peruvian-born son of Japanese immigrants. The people I spoke with three weeks before the presidential election in 1990 knew nothing about him except that he was Japanese. But that was enough. Rumors circulated that Japan would pay off Peru's foreign debt. Fujimori was a samurai in shining armor; his connections were even better than Vargas Llosa's.

Vargas Llosa and Fujimori, however, were not the only beneficiaries of Peru's antipolitical mood. As government channels became less accessible to the people, Peruvians gradually turned to other, more radical, agendas.

JAVIER WOULD NOT TELL ME MUCH ABOUT HIS OWN HISTORY WITH Sendero. I wanted to know how he had been recruited, what it was like in the early years, what his first tasks had been, where he had fought. "We don't want to personalize the revolution," he replied. I sensed that he also found it painful. His girlfriend in the movement had died. "I only regret that we didn't have a baby, like she wanted," was all he would say about her. And he had been one of a few dozen survivors of the single most brutal event in the ten years of Sendero's war: the massacres in Lima's prisons.

On June 18, 1986, Senderistas in three prisons in Lima—

Lurigancho, El Frontón, and the women's prison, Santa Bár-bara—staged an uprising. They took seven police and guards hostage and presented a list of demands, such as garbage collection and one common prison for all the Senderista inmates. Instead of negotiating, President García called in the military, which assaulted the prisons with bazookas, cannons, and machine guns. When the smoke cleared, 244 prisoners were dead. No one survived in Lurigancho. Javier, who had been sent to El Frontón after his arrest in Puno for blowing up some banks, was one of a few dozen to survive there. He lost practically everyone he knew and afterward was sent to a naval base, where he was tortured, then shipped off to Tacna, where I met him. The day is commemorated ungrammatically in Sendero thought as the "Day of Heroicism."

Finally one night Javier started to talk. It was midnight, and we were sitting in a grubby roast chicken restaurant in Lima's center. Javier was celebrating a perfect score on a property law exam. He had finished his dinner and was now eating mine. "We took the hostages at six in the morning," he said. "And we waited for the attack to begin. At five forty-five that afternoon helicopters began to fly over the prison. Then the attack began, grenades and mortars. We resisted for more than twenty-four hours. I would hear an explosion and look over at where a compañero was and I'd see only dust. I never thought I would survive. I was terrified. Fear is natural; one merely has to transform it into courage. I lost all notion of time." He interrupted himself. "Who came out ahead in that?" he asked me.

"In the short term or long term?" I said. "You lost two hundred fifty of your best militants."

Wrong answer. He frowned and gave me the right one: The genocide unmasked the Fascist dictatorship and showed the world the "heroicism" of the compañeros.

"Because the military shot the prisoners after they surrendered?" I said.

"There was no surrender," Javier said, furious. "There were only wounded compañeros. The compañeros still live and fight in us; they are present at every moment; they showed us how to give our lives yesterday, today and tomorrow for the revolution."

But later he said quietly, "Sometimes I wake up in the middle of the night like I'm still living it."

* * *

THE SENDERISTAS STILL IN PRISON ARE NOW HELD IN CANTO Grande, a sand-colored adobe fortress on the edge of a slum in Lima's foothills. I went early one Saturday, visiting day for women. Reporters are forbidden; I had the name of a Senderista prisoner, and I told the guards I was her friend. I passed through seven different checkpoints; various guards stamped my arm and searched me and the cigarettes, oranges, and newspapers I carried. The open-air center courtyard is the hub of a wheel of various halls, each wedge-shaped with a large, walled patio along its outer rim. The halls, or pavilions, as they are known in prison, separate women from men and political from common criminals. A guard opened the steel gate to Pavilion 1A, the Senderista women's pavilion, which swung shut behind me. The government does not enter here; the guards are afraid, and it is easier to let the prisoners run their own pavilions. This Shining Trench of Combat, as the Senderistas call it, is a model for life after the victory of the People's War, a tiny liberated zone inside Peru's maximum security prison.

Canto Grande provides immates with almost nothing: a few pieces of bread a day, if the guards don't steal it; water, when there is water—about once a week—and cement beds. If inmates want to eat, sleep on a mattress, wear clothes, ease their days by smoking cocaine paste cigarettes (almost all the common prisoners do), or bribe guards to get out of solitary confinement, the goods or money must come from relatives or from such creative capitalism as selling cocaine paste, prostitution, or stealing from weaker prisoners. The cells of the common prisoners are thick with slime, garbage, and rats.

But in Pavilion 1A you could eat off the floor. The main room was hung with red ribbons and metallic streamers, like Christmas tree ornaments, that said RPND. "People's Republic of the New Democracy," explained my hostess, who wore a salmon-colored dress, pink shoes, and purple eye shadow. We sat down on a cement bench at a long cement table covered with cloth. As I talked to Nuria (I have changed her name), each woman who walked by smiled and shook my hand heartily. The women were not Indians; they were whites or lower-middle-class mestizas, of mixed blood. They all were young, from eighteen (those under eighteen go to a juvenile prison) to about thirty-five. I was brought a delicious breakfast of fried plantains, onions, and coffee. At the other end of the table women in visiting-day dresses and high heels grated carrots.

Outside on the open-air patio, posters of Mao and Presidente Gonzalo murals covered the high walls. A banner on one wall proclaimed, "Nothing is impossible for him who dares to scale the heights," the same thought Javier had recited to me on my tour of San Marcos. The women had gathered in a circle to greet guests with a song, accompanied by drums and guitar: "Workers and peasants, together with all our people, directed by Gonzalo, we will construct our state. Let's go, Peruvian people, let's go to war, with dynamite and lead we will topple the old state. I want to be outside in the burning fields, tears, sweat and blood. That's how we sing; that's how we dance."

"That's the romantic part to melt hearts," whispered Nuria.

Today was a special day: One of the prisoners was to be released. Her family had come with her small daughter to pick her up, and as the women danced in a circle and drums played, she cried and hugged the women one by one. Then everyone accompanied her to the door, shouting "Viva" to Presidente Gonzalo and singing the "Internationale," which Sendero has adopted as its anthem.

Nuria said that each morning the eighty-two women in the pavilion get up at six-thirty, bathe with water they collect in bottles when there is water, do group exercises, sing Sendero songs, listen to a compendium of the radio news, and set about assigned collective tasks of cooking, cleaning, making handicrafts to sell, or preparing theatrical programs for visiting days. "In contrast with the rest of the prison, we have no drugs here, no alcohol, no lesbianism. We are living the new society."

Nuria was a twenty-six-year-old journalist awaiting trial as an apologist for Sendero, an activity declared illegal in 1988 in a package of antiterrorism laws. I asked why Sendero was so violent. "Peaceful change doesn't work," she said. "The bourgeoisie will never give up power, so anything they do without being forced to is not really giving up power. It's just a concession to keep power. The revisionists of the left merely serve the old order. Only violence can make them give up power."

She, like Javier, employed the phrases "use violence" and "be on the side of the people" interchangeably. I asked her about Tiananmen Square. She said exactly what Javier had said. "It showed there are still people who want to use the violent way," she said. "Still a small group, but a very hopeful sign."

What about when Sendero kills innocent bystanders? I asked. Or ordinary campesinos whose only crime is owning a bicycle? "Those are just stories told by the reactionary media," she said. But then she contradicted herself. "To set up the new order, we have to erase the old. Every war has a cost." She shrugged. "Are sixty thousand children dying of hunger each year not a cost?"

"I don't know that I could use violence on another person, no matter how worthy the cause," I said. I had read that most of Sendero's military chiefs were women, that the three Senderistas in Lima's Political-Military Bureau in the mid-1980s were women, that some of Europe's most distinguished terrorists were women. But I had a hard time picturing myself slitting a policeman's throat. "How do you learn to do it?"

"It's a process of gradual advances," she said. "You come in unable to do things, but through education you learn to do things you couldn't do before." She interrupted herself. "I've done all the talking. Tell me something about yourself."

I started to tell her where I was living and what I was writing. After a few seconds she broke in. "What do *you* think of the People's War?" she said.

I said that I thought that some great changes were necessary in Peru but that violence was not the way. "You sound almost like a pacifist," she said, horrified.

The cassette playing in Nuria's head was the same as Javier's and the same I was to hear, almost word for word, from the other women in the jail. After talking to Nuria, I asked to see the woman whose name I had been given and whom I was officially visiting, Giselle I will call her, a European who had come to Peru in 1978 and joined Sendero. "It was the right thing to do," Giselle said simply. She said that Cuba had not yet had a revolution; the country was still in the hands of the bourgeoisie and large landowners. Pol Pot had the right idea but lacked the guidance of a Communist party. Albania was ruled by bourgeois revisionists. The Baader-Meinhof Gang "is wrong; they have no ideology, but they are brave enough to take up arms, so deserve credit."

The women had finished cooking lunch. We had soup with pieces of beef and corn and a radish and tomato salad; a carrot cake was baking for afternoon teatime. The show was ready to start. I went out to the patio and sat down with the other visitors. There was a drumroll. The Sendero women marched out solemnly, in perfect formation, carrying red flags or carved wood mock machine guns, all wearing black high heels, black skirts, red blouses, and Mao caps—flight attendants of the revolution. For the next three hours we watched a Sendero ceremony celebrating International Women's Day, with speeches saluting Rosa Luxemburg and Jiang Quing Mao, among others. A woman read quotes from Mao about the difference between feminine liberation and the true emancipation of women that was possible only with the fall of capitalism. They sang tuneless Sendero songs and shouted slogans: "Long live the just, glorious, and correct Peruvian Communist party! Long live the new offensive against the counterrevolutionary revisionists headed principally by Gorbachev and Deng!"

A little boy, the son of a prisoner, read a poem called "Woman, Mother, Guerrilla." "Listen to the shouts of our people," he read while the families watched, smiling. "Today, while you suffer exploitation, lift your head, break your chains of repression! The people's war advances!"

A long play followed, about workers who score a victory over their capitalist exploiters through the guidance of the heroic compañeros of Sendero. The women played multiple roles, donning suits and mustaches for their roles as men.

"It's a monastery," Father Hubert Lanssiers had told me. He had been the Senderistas' chaplain in prison, a challenging occupation, especially for a Belgian priest who was an honorary member of the French Foreign Legion and had been confessor to the Diems. "They are nuns; their life is work and prayer. But at the same time they can be charming and flirtatious. They ask you to bring them hair dye, but they can stick a knife into you and twist it."

I left Canto Grande as mystified about the Senderista mind as when I came in. The slight insight into Sendero's growth that I gained came not from the Senderistas but from the prison itself.

As I walked out of the peace and order inside the walls of the Sendero pavilion into the prison courtyard, I could imagine a sign on the pavilion door: ABANDON HOPE, ALL YE WHO EXIT HERE. The Sendero men were singing in their pavilion, but in the other pavilions the common prisoners were thrusting their arms and in some cases their heads through the bars, begging for money or food and cursing ungenerous visitors. Bowls lowered on strings from the third floor hit my head, accompanied by a rain of spittle. The courtyard stank of garbage, urine, and the sweet stench of cocaine cigarettes. It was bedlam, but it was only a slightly caricatured version of much of the rest of Peru. And if I were forced to decide between serving out my time in the medieval hell of the common prisoners or in the spooky monastery of Pavilion 1A, I knew which I would choose.

MOST OF PERU'S HIGHLANDS IS SENDERO COUNTRY. IN THE NEIGH-boring states of Ayacucho, Apurímac, Huancavelica, Junín, and Cerro de Pasco, Sendero has killed or driven out most government representatives or placed them under virtual house arrest. When Sendero takes a village, it first blows up the municipal buildings and, if there are any, a couple of banks. Next, it holds instant "people's trials" and executes members of the local power structure, with special viciousness for those who belong to the Communist party or other parties of the legal left. Sendero reserves its most intense hatred not for Peru's right but for the campesino organizers and labor leaders of the left. Sendero doesn't want people to make the peasants' life better, but to make it worse, to the point of being intolerable. After the executions Sendero finds the civil registry and lines up everyone in town. The troops tell villagers they are now members of Sendero. They form people's committees and designate a youth chief, a food chief, a health chief. The prudent campesino will cooperate. He will bring food to the troops. He will perform a "revolutionary action," such as robbing a large landowner's sheep, if forced to. And he will keep silent if the Senderistas take his twelve-year-old son with them when they leave.

But no guerrilla movement can survive on fear alone. Many peasants with the opportunity to inform the police about Sendero's whereabouts without endangering themselves choose to keep silent.

The reason for their silence is twofold. On one side, Sendero's moralistic totalitarianism appeals to many. It keeps the men home with their families at night. It offers a crude system of justice to which the peasant can appeal, punishing those who pay the campesino too little or take his land.

That is more than the government ever does. The second reason a campesino might support Sendero is that to him the idea of tearing down the Peruvian state is eminently reasonable. What has the government ever brought but promises and trouble?

The Ayacucho countryside is 165 miles from Lima's upper-class neighborhood of Miraflores, where residents live in high-rise apartment towers and enjoy such luxuries as banking machines and Nautilus health clubs. But the difference between the highlands and Lima cannot be measured in miles, only in centuries. Most of the campesinos in Ayacucho live the way their families did four hundred years ago, and the government has done little to improve their lot. Only one in a hundred campesino families in Ayacucho has electricity and running water. For light and heat, they burn kerosene, when they can buy it, in condensed milk cans. Nearly half of Ayacucho's adults are illiterate. Per capita income is less than a third of Peru's meager average. The average life expectancy is fifty-one years; in Lima it is seventy. Every government, García's being no exception, takes office promising to bring development to the sierra. No one ever does.

Four hundred fifty years after Pizarro's landing, Lima is still the viceroyalty that controls Peru. In the late 1980s Lima gobbled 98 percent of all new investment in Peru. In the sierra, even without Sendero's influence, government exists only in theory.

What the government does provide in abundance is repression. The military's indiscriminate cruelty in fighting Sendero has turned it into the guerrillas' most important ally. Indeed, part of Sendero's strategy seems to be to provoke military brutality, and the security forces seem only too glad to cooperate. The human rights policy of García's predecessor, Belaúnde, was summed up by the statement of his war minister, General Luis Cisneros Vizquerra: To be successful, the government had to kill sixty people, maybe three of whom would turn out to be Senderistas.

García came to office promising something different. "It is not necessary to resort to barbarism to fight barbarism," he said in his inaugural address. But beginning in 1987, García's security forces began to lead the world in disappearances, according to a United Nations report. The government disappeared or killed 6,000 people in Ayacucho from 1982 to 1988 alone, more than twice the number General Pinochet killed or disappeared in seventeen years of military rule in neighboring Chile. A new death squad, the Rodrigo Franco Command, whose links with his APRA party were "undeniable," according to García, killed 150 people in 1989. Violence was coming from so many sides that when the offices of the Red Cross, Amnesty International, and the Andean Jurists Commission were bombed within a few weeks of one another in early 1990, staff members had no idea whether Sendero, the military, or the Rodrigo Franco death squads were responsible.

In the Ayacucho village of Accomarca in August 1985 the army rounded up sixty-nine people, including women, old men, and twenty-one children under five years of age. Soldiers raped the women, forced the captives into three houses, machine-gunned the houses, set them on fire, and then lobbed in hand grenades for good measure. A group of campesinos arrived in Lima to denounce the massacre, and human rights groups flew out to Accomarca in helicopters to investigate. Second Lieutenant Telmo Hurtado, who led the attack, told investigators that the children were dangerous because "the guerrillas begin to indoctrinate children from two, three, four years old." He was later promoted to lieutenant and sent to work at the Peruvian Embassy in Washington.

When police or soldiers are tried for killing a campesino, the trials almost always take place in military courts, where neither murder nor torture is considered a crime. Instead, the accused is tried for "negligence" or "insubordination," charges that at worst result in a three-day prison term. Police have been convicted of human rights abuses in exactly one case, in which a lieutenant and ten of his troops machine-gunned a wedding party and then set the thirty-four victims on fire with hand grenades. By 1990 there had not yet been a conviction of a soldier. The prosecutor's office that had vigorously investigated the killings in Ayacucho, Sendero's birthplace, was closed in 1988 "as an economizing measure."

If the Accomarca massacre had occurred in neighboring Chile, it would have made headlines all over the world; the United Nations would have sent an investigating commission, and Sting would have given a concert to benefit the widows and orphans. But the massacres take place in Peru and so pass unnoticed. This is, in part, because the victims are less visible. They are not white, articulate, middle-class, Spanish-speaking political activists who live in major cities, but poor, brown, illiterate Quechua- or Aymará-speaking campesinos in remote villages where few journalists go. Their widows do not issue press releases or march in white head scarves in front of the presidential palace. They are usually too terrified even to give their accounts to a local investigator in the unlikely event there is one. If they do try to protest, their echo does not travel far; the wall between Peru's Indians and the typical newspaper reader is insurmountable.

The cases also receive scant attention because the victims have the good fortune to be living in a democracy. General Pinochet was a right-wing military dictator; Alan García was a democratically elected reformer committed to social justice. But according to human rights groups' statistics, of the two, it was García's security forces that were more brutal, and Pinochet's that were more likely to be tried for their crimes.

BEFORE MARIO VARGAS LLOSA RAN FOR PRESIDENT, BEGAN TO talk in a candidate's simplified homilies, and forgot what he once knew of Peru, he called his country "an incurable disease." Peru's pathology is capable of producing such opposing mutations as the violent, fanatical Javier and the passive, alienated Gladys. But Peru is also capable of healthier responses. Sendero had for years been trying to gain a foothold in Puno, a highland state whose poverty, underdevelopment, and similarity to Ayacucho should have made it natural Sendero territory. Puno also offers a border with Bolivia, a real strategic asset. But Sendero, after controlling parts of Puno, was having no success establishing a base; the campesinos simply kept telling the police what Sendero was up to, and all of Sendero's terror and persuasion could not convince them to keep quiet. Javier, who was captured in Puno, was one of the guerrillas who failed there. In the fight against

Sendero, Puno was one of the few reasons for optimism in Peru, optimism being a rare enough commodity to merit a closer look.

I sat on my duffel bag in a cloud of sand and squinted into the noon sun. The bag and the blanket and parka a friend had lent me were already covered with a thick coat of dust, and I had not yet left Tacna. The Arocutipas were late. Nelson Arocutipa, an eleven-year-old shoeshine boy I met at a center for working children Jeff Thielman had founded, was going to Puno for vacation. The Arocutipas were from Puno, as were Gladys's father and most of the other new immigrants to Tacna. Nelson lived in Ciudad Nueva in Tacna with his parents, six brothers and sisters, and a huge white turkey. Their house was the usual open-air affair lacking electricity, with a honeycomb of rooms strung with wash. Nelson's father had moved to Tacna seven years before. Nelson, then only four, came with his mother two years later. Today, for the first time, he was going back to Puno to visit. He was going with his sister Sonia, seventeen; Sonia's husband, Raúl Chedda Condori, who was twenty-one and had a job as a cook and barman in a restaurant; and Raúl's fourteen-year-old brother, Dino.

Nelson was happy to have me along, but Sonia, who didn't know me, was less pleased. My motives must have been highly suspect; most people who could afford a bus ticket or even a plane flight did not choose to go to Puno in the back of a truck. A seat on the AeroPeru flight was just under $9. A bus ticket cost about $4 for the thirteen-hour trip. But the Arocutipas would save $1.50 apiece by riding in the back of a truck.

The trucks left each day from Ciudad Nueva's informal marketplace, where four trucks were parked on a stretch of sand. Indian women in blankets and hats sold apples, bananas, bread, and bottles of Coke and Inca Kola, the sticky yellow Mountain Dew-like soda that Peruvians consider their national beverage. At about one the Arocutipas arrived. We chose a truck and put the heavier bags on the roof. I followed them into the back of the truck, and we arranged ourselves on top of the softer bags. The owner's wife, an Aymará Indian in traditional dress like that of her passengers, pushed us into the truck, against the wall nearest the cab. It was steaming hot. Every few minutes the door would open, and the owner's wife would push in a few more people. The truck seemed full when there were twenty people.

After three hours of waiting, the natives, including me, were growing restless. We shouted for the driver to get moving or at least to open the door so that we could relieve ourselves, but the woman only opened the door to scream at us and push more people in. At five we pulled out of the marketplace with thirty-one people in the truck. The owner and his wife had obviously learned how to treat their passengers from watching their white bosses. I felt like a cow. I had very suddenly ceased to be *misti*.

I was jammed into a corner along the wall next to the cab. A man next to me was carrying a cat in a small cloth bag, feeding it bread whenever it started to yowl. A woman in Indian dress, traveling with her ten-year-old son, had a chicken in a bag. The man with the cat was urinating on the floor. I was almost completely covered by the woman to my left, a hugely fat Indian with a white straw sombrero that kept falling in my face. The truck smelled cloyingly sweet, the stench of urine mingling with the smell of coca leaves, which many people were chewing.

The truck bounced along for ten minutes, then pulled into a gas station, where it sat for thirty minutes. The next stop seemed to be the owner's house; it was hard to tell, because our only "window" was an opening where one of the topmost boards forming the side had been removed; it was hard to see out. Finally, at about six we began to climb into the mountains.

What little scenery I could see was as bleak as the moon: long stretches of sand dunes that resembled ocean waves, nothing growing except here and there patches of tumbleweed. Night fell. Some people slept; others talked softly in Spanish or, more often, in Aymará. People ate from bags of bread or bananas they had bought in the marketplace. Nelson Arocutipa threw up.

At the first checkpoint—one of many instituted in Peru's futile effort to keep us from transporting contraband to the rest of the country—I was sick and fainted. The owners took me into the cab of the truck with them. The woman held a two-week-old baby, her fifth, she said. The truck stopped at Tarata, the town in which Gladys's mother had been born. It was nine-thirty. There was no electricity that night. The town, sand-colored adobe and cement, was lit by candles and the stars. People lined the streets, selling skewers of meat and fruit to the passengers on the buses and trucks that came through. I bought a skewer of three thin pieces of beef heart and a potato for fifteen cents.

I returned to the back of the truck, opening the door into bedlam. There was not an inch of floor space, and I stepped on people's legs as I made my way to the front wall, finally jamming back in under the fat woman who kept losing her hat. The girl next to me was vomiting. I slept fitfully, nodding off and waking up as my head rolled to the side. The next time I woke it was 2:00 A.M. The truck had stopped. The driver was apparently taking a nap. A few people yelled to get moving, but it did no good. An hour went by, then another. Finally we moved out again.

By 5:30 A.M. it was light, and we were in the highlands. At Maso Cruz we sat at a checkpoint for forty-five minutes while police searched our belongings for contraband. A few passengers left. Outside, sheepherders in wool ponchos and dashing felt hats and women in layers of skirts and long braids drank coffee at stands along the road. Some of the women were barefooted. More passengers, most of them sheepherders, got into the truck, and it rumbled to life once more. The cat in the bag was apparently sick as well, yowling louder than seemed possible. A thick layer of dust covered us all. Outside, I could see a few stone huts and fields of bunchy, tall grass. Indian women drove herds of llamas.

Six hours later the truck came to the end of the line in the town of Ilave. I could barely walk; the altitude, cold, lack of sleep, and distinctive aromas of the trip had left me utterly exhausted. I said good-bye to the Arocutipas, who were going to Nelson's aunt's house in a small village nearby, and limped up to the central plaza to catch a bus for the city of Puno, the capital of the state that bore the same name. I bought a warm Coke and got in line. On the bus the Indian woman next to me was asking people to hide the tapes and clothing she had smuggled from Chile. She handed out shirts, pants, socks, and cassette tapes to her fellow passengers. I put some men's socks in my duffel bag, but the police who came on didn't open it. We arrived in Puno about one-thirty, twenty-five hours after I had come to the truck stop in Tacna.

The next day I began to talk to people about why Sendero had not been successful in the Puno countryside. At first it seemed inexplicable. The stories I heard from the bureaucrats were the same tales of inefficiency and sloth that I had heard in the rest of Peru. There was, the bureaucrats agreed, no Peruvian government in rural Puno. The poverty statistics were similar to

Ayacucho's. The difference began to be clear when I went to visit the human rights office of the Puno Catholic Church.

Father Luis Zambrano showed me some church publications about human rights in Puno. They were comic books, written to be understandable to local campesinos. One described how policemen had robbed a truck, killed a woman in the ensuing shoot-out, and then blamed her death on a Sendero ambush. The other told the story of a campesino shot by police during a land take-over. Zambrano also told me that the church's radio station had been bombed and that soldiers had threatened local priests and peasant organizers. The organizers had been threatened by rural landowners, as well, and in one case the family of a federation leader had been killed.

What caught my attention about this list was what it left out. There were no stories of mass murders, no wedding parties machine-gunned or entire villages burned. The police and security forces were only moderately vicious and brutal and killed only a moderate number of people. The people of Puno, as a result, were more willing to think of Sendero, which was more vicious than the army, as the enemy.

There was a second reason, just as important, that Puno rejected Sendero. Twenty-four years before, the Catholic Church had founded the Institute for Rural Education, a network of campesino federations that provides training and credit to the peasants and organizes rural unions. When I visited, the IRE was organizing groups of peasants to take over and begin to farm plots of fallow land. In short, the IRE helped peasants get what they needed through community organizing and political action.

This, Bishop Jesús Calderón told me as we drank tea in his office, which was as warm and light as a greenhouse and full of plants and birds, was why Puno was different. Not all of Peru's poor, he said, were Sendero's natural constituency. Sendero took root among those who had no hope of improving their lives in legal Peru. I thought of Gladys and Sebastián. As long as Peru produces people like Gladys, it will go on creating people like Javier.

Like the early settlers of Gladys's neighborhood, the members of Puno's peasant federations band together to get what they needed despite the bureaucracy. The Peruvian government does not provide solutions to people's problems, but in Puno, at least, the government grudgingly allows people the freedom to try to solve their problems themselves.

When I visited, the situation was fragile. Some local land-owners, furious at the land take-overs, had begun to threaten the peasant organizers, calling them closet Senderistas. A few had been killed. But others in the local elite recognized that the organizers were keeping people away from Sendero. Strategically, Sendero was correct to aim at the left. Sendero's most important enemies in Puno were not the soldiers but the campesino organizers—people like Ricardo Vega.

Ricardo Vega dreamed at night of the woman who was trying to kill him. In his dream he tried to picture her face, which he had never seen. What he knew about her was this: She was called La Gringa, a term Latin Americans used for anyone who is tall, white, and thin. She was possibly not a Peruvian. "People who have seen her say she is very young, with a sweet face," he said. "I know she can't live all year round underground. There are times when she must come to a city and walk in the streets and buy bread and sit in a café like anyone else." The fact that Vega did not know La Gringa's face, but that she knew his, made her almost a sexual obsession. Every new woman in the street was La Gringa. "I wonder if I've met her," he said. "I know we'll meet someday."

He hoped when they met, it would not be alone. Vega, thirty-six when I met him, is a sociologist from Lima who first came to Puno while a student at San Marcos, to write his thesis on the campesino federations. He fell in love with the countryside and the people, and in 1979 he moved to Ayaviri, the second largest city in the state of Puno. La Gringa, age unknown, origin unknown, was the head of the local company of Sendero Luminoso. On April 8, 1987, she killed one of Vega's best friends, Zenobio Huarsaya, a former Senderista who had broken with the movement and, against Sendero's wishes, been elected mayor of his village, San Juan de Salinas. La Gringa and two other Senderistas arrived in San Juan's central plaza on a Wednesday morning, captured Huarsaya, and summoned villagers to witness a "people's trial." La Gringa made him kneel on the ground. The villagers threw rocks at the Senderistas and shouted at them not to kill Huarsaya. The Senderistas hesitated. "Kill him," ordered La Gringa. With his wife and children crying and the villagers shouting, "Murderers," the Senderistas shot him through the head. The year before, La Gringa had led the platoon of Senderistas that had ambushed a caravan of local APRA officials. The Senderistas killed seven people. La Gringa cut out their eyes and tongues.

She had told many people in the region that she wanted to kill Vega. The year before I met him, Vega, who was the head of the church's IRE, had organized a march of peasants to take over unoccupied lands to raise their potatoes, sheep, and alpacas. He was supposed to arrive at a local political leader's house at 7:00 A.M.; but his truck had a flat tire, and he was two hours late. When he arrived, the family told him that La Gringa had come in with a machine gun, looking for him. She held the family at gunpoint, then tired of waiting and left.

After the death of Mayor Huarsaya, local campesinos told the police of a Sendero safe house. The police raided the house and killed seven people—several after they had surrendered—cutting off the testicles of one man while he was still alive. Sendero had to leave Puno. Vega heard nothing from La Gringa for a year, but she visited him regularly in his dreams.

I took the bus from the city of Puno and arrived in Ayaviri, population fifteen thousand, at ten on a Friday night. It was March, early fall. The town was cold, gaunt, and deserted. The only people in the streets were two women loading unsold skewers of sheep hearts and potatoes into their carts in front of the church in the central plaza. I found a bed for a dollar in a small hotel. The next morning I got up at five, a little late for Ayaviri, and went to find Vega. Everyone knew where he lived.

A pleasant-looking man with thinning hair, wearing a blue sweat suit, he answered the door. I introduced myself and said I wanted to talk to him, see some of the farms and how the people in the area lived. He shook his head. "I'll be happy to talk here," he said, "but I don't know how you can get out to the countryside. No one's going out today that I know of." I agreed to come back at nine o'clock.

But at seven-thirty Vega came up to me in the street in the central plaza. This time he was dressed in new jeans, a black sweater over a bulletproof vest, and a red scarf. "I lied to you," he said. He was going to the countryside. He had to go to two campesino communities where marches were being planned. The problem was that after having withdrawn from the area for a year following Mayor Huarsaya's death, Sendero had just moved back in. On Wednesday, two nights before I arrived, Senderistas had killed a policeman. The night I arrived they killed a private security guard and fled into exactly the mountains where Vega now had to go. "We had agreed to travel only in caravans," he said. "But I have to go to this meeting, and there are no other cars that can go. We'll be alone. It's up to you."

At nine we left Ayaviri in Vega's truck. In the front with us was an old man in a black suit who had buried his wife that morning. The other seven members of the funeral party rode in the open back of the truck. We would give them a ride as far as the last town before the mountains. In return, their presence would give us protection.

I lit cigarette after cigarette for Vega as he drove. "You gave me a start at the door this morning," he said. "I thought maybe La Gringa had arrived." He said his wife was getting nervous. She thought Ayaviri was getting too dangerous and was talking about taking the two children and moving back home for some peace. She was from Medellín, Colombia.

There were few other cars on the road, a lucky thing, he said, because there was practically no one we could run into who would have been good news. Sendero hated him. The managers of the big farms hated him because the campesinos were taking over their land. The police were in with the big farms. The army, the antiterrorist police, and the paramilitary squads of the government considered him a Senderista. Two years before, after Sendero had attacked a local village, the army came in with a list of "Sendero leaders." The list, curiously enough, contained the names of all the leaders of the campesino movement. The soldiers forced Vega to kneel in the plaza with his hands behind his head. They arrested him and then let him go a few hours later. "It's all part of the salsa," Vega said—part of the mix. It was an expression he used a lot.

Vega had a phone—his phone number was two digits—but it rarely worked. His major link to the latter half of the twentieth century was a stereo, a good one, and although he spoke no English, he had memorized Bob Dylan's repertoire, and we sang several songs together. Vega had written to Dylan, asking him to write a song about the campesino movement. Dylan never wrote back.

Occasionally we passed people driving herds of sheep, men in sweaters and wool knitted caps with earflaps and women, their black hair in long braids, wearing bowler hats, sweaters, and layers of skirts. Vega knew everyone. We stopped every few kilometers to ask about the situation ahead. A man told us that strangers had just moved into Alto Collana, the second community we had to visit. "Sixteen young people. Six with machine guns. One has a red cap," he said.

"Any women?" asked Vega.

The man didn't know. "Be careful with the uncles," he said, using the local code for Sendero. We left the funeral party in town and drove out into the mountains.

Vega wanted to stop and see a friend, the president of the local campesino federation. It would be a condolence call. The antiterrorist police had come through looking for Sendero the Friday before, and in the process they had gone from store to store, robbing people. The next morning the man woke up to find his sons dead—poisoned.

There was no one at the man's house. We stopped at the house of another friend. "Going to see your girlfriend?" the friend said, laughing. He was talking about La Gringa. He said Sendero was in the mountains, but we would probably be safe as far as Bajo Collana, the first place we needed to go. We drove a few more miles. Then we heard a sharp sound. Vega smiled. This was not where we wanted to get a flat. He got out and looked around; we had run over a stone, that was all. He opened the glove compartment, found a bottle of scotch, and took a long swig. As we drove into the next valley, far off on a hill we saw a man sitting cross-legged on the ground, watching.

After another hour or so we reached Bajo Collana. I had been expecting a village, but Bajo Collana seemed to consist of one house. Sixty men and women sat on the ground outside the house, the women in Indian dress, many nursing babies, the men in jeans, old sweaters, and baseball caps, wearing sandals made of tire rubber.

The house was large and had a chapel; Vega told me that its owner, a farmer named Cayetano, was one of the wealthier campesinos. It had no electricity, no water, no toilet, no roof, and a dirt floor. Looking around, I saw benches covered with sheepskin, bags of fertilizer, a heap of potatoes and some bottles of Coke, sweaters, a child's bicycle, and a pretty sheep with long eyelashes and a pink bow tied around its head. That was all. Vega said that Cayetano, his wife, and five children led a simple life: up at five; have a bowl of potato soup, maybe with a bone in it; go to the fields, taking some potatoes for lunch; come home at five; have some more soup; sleep.

Vega introduced me as his cousin. We went with five men, the local leaders of the movement, into the only room with a roof to plot strategy. This group of families was a real success story. In 1986 the men had marched onto plots of fallow land and begun farming, forcing the government to stop talking about land reform and do something, just as the settlers of Natividad had done. The government had given some of the families legal titles to their new plots, but the campesinos today were planning a march in hope of getting title to all the land. We went outside, and Vega talked with the whole group, about how well the movement was doing, how great it was to have their own land, and how they were inspiring other campesinos in the area to do the same.

After the meeting Cayetano gave Vega and me each a bottle of Coke. A man from Alto Collana, our next scheduled stop, told Vega that more than a dozen Senderistas had just arrived in town. Vega thought for a moment, then asked him to bring messages to the group along with his apologies. We drove back to Ayaviri.

A year later, in May 1989, twenty-four Senderistas walked into the Institute for Rural Education headquarters just outside Ayaviri and forced the three guards to destroy the building. The next month Vega heeded his friends' pleas that he and his family move out of Ayaviri into the city of Puno. In January residents told police about the Sendero column's safe house, and the Senderistas were killed—a repeat of what had happened after Mayor Huarsaya's killing in 1987. In March 1990 I saw Vega in Lima. He seemed tired. He said that La Gringa was trying to bring another column into the zone. He had been offered a job running a new Puno-wide Institute for Rural Education, to be funded by the European Economic Community. He was thinking about it.

＊　＊　＊

La Gringa's nom de guerre was Basti Javier told me. Yes, she was Peruvian. And she was a very good company leader. That was all he would say. He had been one of her troops. He said his work in Puno was organizational, going from village to village, talking to campesinos. He knew a few words of Aymará. He could say, "How are you?," "I am fine," and "Hurry up." At night, he said, the Senderistas spent their time talking about what Peru would be like after the revolution.

I asked why La Gringa was out to kill Vega. "The people are seething with revolutionary energy," Javier said. "People like Vega divert that energy and legitimize Fascists."

And Mayor Huarsaya? "He had infiltrated us," he said. "He betrayed us. In accordance of the rules of war, we were correct in killing him."

"You might have been following the rules of war," I said, "but you lost a lot of support because of it."

"We have principles," he said, "but we cannot escape excesses. You can't control the masses. Sometimes we recognize people as torturers, and then we don't spare their lives."

I mentioned that I had met some campesinos in the area who didn't feel as though Sendero really had their interests at heart. He said this was a question that Presidente Gonzalo had thought about and dealt with. "First of all, not all the campesinos are campesinos," he said. "There are rich and poor, and some lend themselves to the repressive forces. Many times the campesino wants only a piece of land and he's happy. But whether he's happy or not doesn't matter. It's whether he has political power. We tell him he has to want more than having a cow. We tell him he'll have to kill his cow when the climate gets bad. You have to educate people. They know whose side we're on when we kill police, judges, and functionaries.

"It's a long process, educating people. You have to explain the class struggle, explain how they have been betrayed by people who claim to represent them. Then you have to talk about their misery, make them understand that we represent them. Sometimes people don't understand."

*   *   *

I SAID GOOD-BYE TO JAVIER IN THE STREET OF LA VICTORIA, A poor Lima neighborhood where we had gone to visit yet another group of cousins. I had kept reminding him that I disagreed with his views, but he had convinced himself that over the course of the week he had made me see things his way, the Sendero way. He began to think of possible titles for the book. "How about *The Revolution Burns in the Andes?*" Javier mused. He walked me out to the street. "Remember to bring me tennis shoes," he said.

He had flagged down a cab. Javier opened the door for me and gave the driver the address. "And drive carefully," he told the cabby. "I'm writing down your license number, just in case.

"I'll see you in the United States," he said. I laughed. "Seriously," he said. "I'd love to visit. Isn't there an American people crying out for revolution?"

"I don't think you'll get a visa," I said.

"Nothing is impossible for him who dares to scale the heights," yelled Javier as the cab pulled away.

GLADYS'S HEALTH WAS IMPROVING THE LAST TIME I SAW HER. SHE was not skinny anymore, she had almost completed her tuberculosis treatment, and the hospital had promised to supply her with enough pills to cure herself for good. She had heard that before, she said, but this time she knew the doctors better and thought they were serious. She proudly showed me her new possession, a pair of bedroom slippers. There was a huge mound of garbage in the yard, but she said that when she was stronger, she would move it out to the street. On one table she had arranged framed photos of Mario with Mickey Mouse, taken at a Natividad birthday party, and the photos of her, Marco, and Mario that I had taken on my last visit. Marco was still going to school and was still thrilled about it.

Gladys said that her legal transactions were still going on. Patricia Fuentes had shown up one day with the new title to her property and was about to get birth certificates for the children.

But the basic troubles remained: She was as poor as ever, she had no job at all, and the wall and her problems with the Lópezes remained. While she was in the hospital, Germán López, Jorge's younger brother, had moved into the lot on the other side of the new wall: Gladys's former property. He had cut the lights to her house and taken the line for himself. Uncle Carlos had called the police, and Germán told them that he had been paying all along, which wasn't true. Carlos showed me a copy of the complaint. Gladys had won that one; a friendly policeman had gone to talk to López, and Gladys kept her electricity.

I wanted to meet the Lópezes, but I had promised Gladys I wouldn't bring up her suit or even mention her name. So I went to La Pirámide, where she had worked, one evening at about five, just to see what it was like. The bar had recently reopened after being closed for a few months. It was striped with different shades of blue outside and pink inside. Plastic mermaids hung on the walls. Five Indian women were drinking from a huge bottle of Inca Kola at one table, relaxing after a day in the market. I walked outside and stood next to Germán López, whom I had seen going into his house a few times as I walked up the street to visit Gladys. I said I was waiting for a friend. We started to talk. He said he was from Cuzco but liked living in Tacna. He was thirty-two, I knew from the legal complaint, but he looked younger. He had a very sweet face. My imaginary friend never showed up, and I left after a few minutes.

Germán López, I suddenly realized, probably didn't own more than two pairs of pants. It had never occurred to me before, but if he was living next door to Gladys, his economic situation could not have been very different from hers. I had grown accustomed to thinking of the family as direct descendants of Pizarro, part of the exploitative rich who were sucking Gladys's blood. But Germán López lived in a house that was the mirror image of Gladys's. His bar was a dump. His brother Jorge's life was a series of scams and shady businesses that probably kept him scrambling one step ahead of his own creditors. They were rich and powerful only in the eyes of Gladys Meneses.

But to Gladys, the Lópezes' rung on the social ladder was irrelevant; what mattered was that it was higher than hers. She had decided, she said, that she would not sue Jorge López. Nor would she ask him again to pay her what he owed, neither her back wages nor the money for the lot. It was too dangerous for her now, with Germán and his family living on the other side of the wall. Jorge López's threats continued. "I'm afraid he'll throw me out of the house," she said.

But she got along well with Germán's wife, Gladys said. The woman occasionally gave her food, sometimes a cup of tea. When Gladys got well, she said, she would need work. She wanted to get into the contraband market, selling apples and grapes. She would need money to start out, about thirty dollars to set up a stand and buy merchandise, she said. She would ask the Lópezes for a loan.

FOUR

THE LABORATORY

A T THOSE PARTIES IN EL SALVADOR YOUR GLASS IS ALWAYS
full. There is always a woman with dark skin and a white
apron by your side when the need for shrimp arises. I came to
the Qaddafi Gang's party expecting the best, and I was not disappointed.

The Qaddafi Gang consists of eight women in their thirties—
all divorced, blond, tall, and rich—and their male friends. The
women's last names—Wright, Guirola, Magaña, Prietes—are
the names of the wealthy in El Salvador, the oligarchs. The
Prietes family lives in the San Francisco neighborhood of San
Salvador in a two-story mansion of white stone with a columned
portico. Blanca's brother, Francisco, turning twenty-three today,
led me through the house, past pre-Columbian and conquest-
era bronzes and statues, past paintings from India and Japan, to
the backyard. About a hundred of Francisco's friends were standing around or sitting on tapestry couches on the patio. The men
all looked like him: tall, slim-hipped, with dazzling teeth. The
women, equally attractive, were wearing typical Latin American
dress: high heels, tight jeans, and dark hair styled like Farrah
Fawcett's.

A maid brought over a plate of small turkey sandwiches and
cheese puffs. I sat down on the couch with the older crowd of
the Qaddafi Gang, next to a woman wearing a blue silk taffeta
dress with a black fur bolero jacket and black high heels, diamond
rings, and gold bracelets and earrings. Her hair was done in a
perfect Miss America 1964 flip. Her name was María Elena.

That was also the name of her fifteen-year-old daughter, who sat near us and was a copy of her mother, except that she had braces. They had been talking about *quinceaños* parties, the Sweet Fifteen. Times were changing, said María Elena. "Nowadays kids don't want such big parties. They'd rather spend the money on a trip to Hawaii." Her daughter, she added, went to the American School, where her studies were in English.

She asked me when I had arrived. Only a few weeks before, I said. "It's a beautiful country," she said. "The perfect climate, nice people, lots of maids to take care of us."

I had met the women of the Qaddafi Gang earlier in the day at a political rally, where they had told me about this party. But María Elena said people didn't talk much about politics. "We sometimes have a rule at parties: You can't talk about politics, sports, or problems with your servants," she said. I asked her if she worked. She said she had inherited a hacienda in Sonsonate, in the west. She had a hundred head of cattle and grew yuca for flour. The hacienda hadn't been doing well lately, she said; the price she got for milk was low, and imports were expensive. She also changed dollars on the black market. "Now that's a way to make money," she said with enthusiasm.

The rest of the Qaddafi Gang had arrived, and we walked around the swimming pool to a gazebo. There was a bar in the gazebo. It was there I met Roger Beltrán (I've changed his name).

"She'll have a vodka" was the first thing he said.

"I'm drinking soda," I said.

He mixed a screwdriver for himself and another one for me. "Have a vodka," he said. "The Qaddafi Gang treats you like a queen." The name, he said, comes from the first two words of *Cada fin de semana nos emborrachamos* ("Every weekend we get drunk").

He looked tired. He said the workers had taken over the plastics factory he ran after he fired six of them for trying to organize a union. "Tonight is the first time I've left the factory in a week," he said, rubbing his beard. "I've slept there every night. I haven't had a chance to shave. But I was going crazy, so I snuck out the back to come here."

I asked him what his workers wanted. "They want transportation to work, uniforms, better treatment," he said. "They want collective bargaining."

That didn't sound so outrageous, I said.

"We've been losing more and more money," Roger said. "If the union demands more, we'll go bankrupt. The union says they don't care if we shut down. Well, I care. I told them we'll occupy the factory for as long as we need to. My people have arms. Not to kill them but to take care of the business. I have the right to be armed. It's my factory.

"They say they're badly treated," he said. "They say that we run the factory under the influence of drugs and liquor. I race cars, and my brother and I each have a Porsche. They say for every gallon of gas I take bread from the mouths of their children."

Roger was thirty-seven. His grandfather had come to El Salvador from Lebanon. "My father was so poor he left his house when he was sixteen because his parents couldn't feed him," he said. "He worked as a bartender and a waiter, and then he started the factory. We're the people who are building this country. It's the unions who want to destroy it. You journalists never write about how the private sector is being destroyed in this country. You print only the unions' side. You never write the truth.

"Listen, my dear," Roger said. "I'll tell you how journalism works. The journalists are all leftists or paid by the left. I could slip a few bills to a reporter and get a story in *The New York Times*."

"Really?" I said. By this time a number of the others had gathered to listen, and they were nodding. There seemed to be universal agreement on this subject. It was the first lively conversation I had found that evening. After a tortuous twenty-minute conversation about the best skiing spots in South America, I decided it was time to go. It was 1:00 A.M. As I walked out the front, musicians in a seven-piece marimba band were carrying their instruments into the servants' entrance. The party was just beginning.

Among the many foreigners engaged in experimenting on El Salvador since the early 1980s—the U.S. military advisers, Spanish priests, German agronomists—the most annoying to the country's wealthy, it seems, are the journalists, especially the U.S. journalists. There must have been more journalists per square foot in El Salvador than in any other country in the world, all of us prodding and poking as if at a giant guinea pig, measuring the country's reflexes at all hours, examining its sores—and all of us, according to most of the Salvadorans able to read our work in English, misreading the data completely.

Our articles deal principally with war, death squads, and poverty. Such articles do not appear in the Salvadoran newspapers. Complete freedom of the press exists in El Salvador, but the last two left-wing newspapers, *La Crónica* and *El Independiente*, closed in 1981, when their offices were blown up and two of their editors hacked to pieces with machetes. The local papers now cover Chamber of Commerce meetings and publish army high command communiqués. Whenever the poor appear in their pages, it is in photos of gray, pop-eyed, unshaved teenage boys, captioned "Dead subversive."

The vast majority of El Salvador's upper class ignores our queries, throws an occasional rock our way at rallies, spits in our faces, and growls, "Tell the truth." The wealthy are angry because they rarely read their point of view in North American or European papers. They think our reports are distorted, taken out of context, that we do not understand El Salvador.

Over the years I came to believe that in a way the wealthy Salvadorans are right. El Salvador is a cliché of war and poverty. It was easy to write about a civil war that had killed seventy thousand people in ten years in a country of only five million, a place where women with no shoes walk miles over unpaved roads, carrying water that is unsafe to drink back to their houses with no walls. It was easy to write about illiterate sixteen-year-olds, carrying weapons they do not know how to use, killed in battles they do not understand by an enemy who is maybe a cousin; it was easy to write about the vultures circling broken bodies dumped on the black volcanic rocks of El Playón, about the people overcome by sudden urges to leap off cliffs or into Cherokee Chiefs with tinted windows, to reappear much later and very dead, missing tongues or toenails or testicles.

But after a while the names began to sound the same and the teary widows with children clinging to their skirts and the endless funerals blurred together. The stories, including the ones I wrote, were factually true. They described the violence. But they did not help me understand it. They did not give me the truth about El Salvador.

I began to understand El Salvador's violence only after listening to repeated admonishments from the wealthy to tell the truth. They meant not the truth as I saw it but the Truth as they saw it, the basis of which is the belief that the members of the private sector, the productive people who create wealth for El Salvador, are under attack from the twin evils of terrorism and socialist policies. This is the central Truth. There are other, more ambiguous subtruths: that the death squads of which we kept writing do not, in fact, exist—the left invented them to discredit the oligarchy—or that the death squads exist but are simply a necessary response to communism. Sometimes one can hear both these versions from the same person on the same day.

But the details of the Truth do not matter. What matters is that the oligarchy believes in it passionately. Finding the Truth is a question not of metaphysics but of real estate. It was born behind the concrete walls, barbed wire, and bulletproof glass that delineate the world of the upper class like the lines in a coloring book. The Truth is a version of reality distilled and sharpened each day as the rich talk only to one another, as government ministers whisper the names of the rich softly and lovingly, as the army acts as their personal guards and the newspapers as their personal press agents.

One can find advocates for a similar Truth among the wealthy of Colombia and Argentina and Peru. But El Salvador's elite represents an extreme. In a country practically without a middle class, the rich have built their fortress higher than have the rich anywhere else, with thicker walls. In Latin America only Guatemala has an oligarchy more stubborn. Popular myth counts El Salvador's ruling class at fourteen families, an exaggeration, but not by much. The oligarchy is made up of about five thousand people, or 0.1 percent of the population. Its privileges are as unquestionable as religion, and the oligarchy defends them with the fanaticism of crusaders, unwilling to compromise, to acknowledge that it shares its country with others. Those in the oligarchy live inside a bubble, but it is, in a way, their very isolation from the clichéd squalor of El Salvador that links them intimately to their country's misery. Their fanaticism gives rise to guerrillas, who kidnap them and bomb their homes and businesses, forcing them to withdraw further into the depths of their fortified palaces, where they respond with more death squads.

THE QADDAFI GANG WAS CELEBRATING MORE THAN FRANCISCO Prietes's birthday. It was a week before the presidential elections of March 1989, and Alfredo Cristiani, a businessman and the candidate of the ARENA party, was leading in the polls. After centuries of controlling the government, the oligarchy had watched, furious, as a succession of what it considered hostile presidents rose to power, beginning in 1979. Cristiani's election would mark the return of Truth in government to Salvador.

The oligarchy's problems began with the Sandinista Revolution in neighboring Nicaragua. The Sandinista march into Managua on July 19, 1979, set off three principal reactions in El Salvador. Leftists, who for forty years had tried to organize and run candidates, quit politics to form five different armed groups. The five united in 1980 in an uneasy coalition called the Farabundo Martí National Liberation Front (FMLN).

The second reaction came from the United States. Worried that El Salvador would follow Nicaragua into revolution, the Carter administration placed its weight behind a group of reform-minded military officers. On October 15, 1979, those officers overthrew the oligarchy-sponsored president and installed a junta of soldiers and civilian social reformers. The new leaders promised to guarantee human rights and condemned the "economic, social and political structures that have traditionally prevailed." Just three months later, by which time it was evident that the military controlled the junta and that no substantial reform would take place, the civilian members resigned. But the United States stayed on, embarking on the most ambitious counterinsurgency effort since Vietnam. The project included a large military push and a modest program of social reforms designed to placate the poor, thus diminishing the guerrillas' support. In 1980 the oligarchy saw its farms expropriated, banks confiscated, and a government board step in to control the export of its coffee. The wealthy remained fabulously wealthy, their life-style unchanged, but in 1979 for the first time, they were forced to confront a government that listened to other voices. Many fled to Miami.

But others chose a more aggressive response. In 1980 there began to circulate a curious videotape, in which one Major Roberto D'Aubuisson, forced out of the National Guard after the coup, labeled many of the country's labor leaders, university professors, and priests as Communists. The videotape was passed around in the proper circles, and the people D'Aubuisson named, including the archbishop of San Salvador, Oscar Romero, began to die. The next year D'Aubuisson founded a political party, the National Republican Alliance (ARENA).

The United States found D'Aubuisson extremely inconvenient. Not because he was unpopular in El Salvador. On the contrary: D'Aubuisson, a tightly coiled man who always looked ready to explode, with hypnotic eyes and the devil's own laugh, could talk to ordinary Salvadorans. He quickly became the most popular politician in the country and could have easily been elected president. But a President D'Aubuisson would have been a disaster for the United States because the U.S. Congress would not fund the war effort with a man widely believed to be the leader of the death squads in power. When D'Aubuisson's party won the Constituent Assembly elections in 1982, the U.S. Embassy stepped in to prevent the Assembly from naming him president. In presidential elections two years later the United States backed the Christian Democrat José Napoleón Duarte, a onetime social reformer, over D'Aubuisson, with the CIA providing about two million dollars for Duarte's campaign through various channels.

By the next presidential elections, in 1989, ARENA had learned how to deal with the gringos. D'Aubuisson was still the party's soul, but its new face and voice—a white, soft face and a voice that spoke perfect, soothing English—belonged to Cristiani, a Georgetown University-educated coffee grower. When Cristiani defeated the Christian Democrats, the oligarchy in El Salvador would once again be behind the government—and the United States would once again be behind the oligarchy.

The Qaddafi Gang could taste victory. At the ARENA rally where I met them the women were wearing ARENA T-shirts with their gold necklaces and singing ARENA songs. Later that night, in Blanca Prietes's backyard, they talked enthusiastically about getting up early the next day to accompany Cristiani on a campaign swing in the east.

Roger Beltrán was as excited as any of them. After hearing him argue at the Qaddafi Gang's party that journalists print only the left's version of events, I told Roger I wanted to see his El Salvador. He agreed to let me tag along with him in the days before and after the election. "I'll tell you how it is," he said. "But you'd better write the truth."

One morning a few days before the election he took me out for a drive in his black Porsche. We drove to Santa Tecla, thirty kilometers outside San Salvador—a gallon of gas the way most people drive a Porsche, maybe two gallons for Roger. How much of his workers' bread that worked out to I didn't know. He smoked Marlboros and sipped a Pilsener beer in an NFL plastic drink holder. It was obviously not his first of the day. Next to him on the gearbox lay an Yves Saint Laurent wallet and a .45.

The highway between San Salvador and Santa Tecla was lined with billboards bearing photos of the various presidential candidates. Each one we passed had been defaced with a splotch of paint or ink. Roger hooted at the billboards of the Christian Democrats. "During the mayoral elections a friend of mine and I filled dozens of plastic bags from my factory with ink," he said, laughing. "Then we went out and got very drunk and threw them at the posters."

El Salvador would be a different place after ARENA won, he said. "ARENA isn't going to rob so much. They already have money, and the Christian Democrats have robbed everything already. And ARENA's people are capable. The Christian Democrats put people in power who never ran a business. We're going to put an end to this communitarianism." I asked him what communitarianism was. "It's the ideology of taking from the rich and giving to the poor," he said.

"What's wrong with that?"

"You wouldn't say that if you owned a bank," he said. He said that in 1980 his family had five million colones in the bank and in shares of a small savings and loan institution, equal to about two million dollars. "They nationalized the bank and paid us in bonds. You can't even use the bonds for toilet paper."

On the side of the road a woman wearing rubber thongs and

a ragged, dirty green dress carried a plastic jug of water on her head. I asked Roger what he thought about when he saw her.

"That these people need work," he said. "This government has done nothing to help private enterprise. They have no financing for factories. And when the electricity fails, I have to pay my costs, but I'm not producing anything."

I asked if he had thought about leaving. "My father bought a town house in Miami," he said. "We have businesses there. But there I'd just be one more immigrant. Here I'm someone. I walk into a bank and say, 'I am Don Roger Beltrán,' and I get a loan."

He told me that I thought like a gringa. "I know the United States," he said. He had not actually studied there, as most upper-class men had. He had taken an engineering course in Madrid and had lived in London for six months. He often visited Miami, San Francisco, New Orleans, and Washington but had forgotten almost all his English. "People from the States come with democratic ideals that don't function here. You don't have the slightest idea what goes on here. We need to help the private sector. We don't want your leftist ideas." We had returned to San Salvador and were driving through the Escalón neighborhood, one of Salvador's ritziest. He sped through the winding streets, tires squealing. He pointed out a small church. "That's where I go to mass every Sunday," he said.

"You can't win a war with 'democracy' and 'negotiations,' " he said, pronouncing the words with a gringo accent. "How can you negotiate with people who put mines in the road and burn buses? You win wars with bullets. Soldiers come to a hill, prepare to take the hill, and then someone comes running up and says, 'Stop! You can't kill these guerrillas. You have to protect their human rights.' " He pronounced "human rights" with a gringo accent and a fey flip of the wrist.

We drove by the president's mansion. Roger rolled down his window and shouted, "Viva ARENA." He laughed. A minute later we passed the house of Gloria Elena Wright, a member of the Qaddafi Gang. The house and grounds took up a whole very long block. A wall and dense trees made the house invisible from the street. "She has a lot of money, that girl," he said. "A lot of money. Her father had the biggest hacienda in the country, La Carrera. It was so beautiful. You could ride miles and miles on horseback. When they took the hacienda, they paid her father with worthless bonds.

"I'll show you my house," he said. He was just renting it; the house he owned was a few blocks away. It was white, two stories, large but not as huge as Gloria Elena's. Above the door was a sticker with a fat girl with a line through her, like the Ghostbusters logo. He left his cigarettes and the .45 in the car and told the maid to get us beer. She was a slight young woman in a T-shirt and skirt, from the guerrilla-controlled area of Chalatenango. "Cora, are you a guerrilla?" Roger said, laughing. He turned to me. "She better not be."

The house was formally furnished in Japanese style. Bookcases of blond wood were filled not with books but with racing trophies. In the living room was a picture of Roger's nine-year-old son, a student at the British School. "He wants to be a test pilot," Roger said. "He knows all about planes. And he tells me not to worry about the factory. He says, 'Dad, I don't have camouflage pants, but I can fire a machine gun and help you out.' " Roger had bought the boy a .22.

We went up to the second floor and stood on the balcony, overlooking his car. He put his foot on the railing and threw his cigarette butt onto the lawn. "I'm going to get a security guard," he said. He said he slept with his .45 on one side of his bed and his shotgun on the other. We finished the beers. He had to go back to his factory, he said, by now obviously drunk. I said I'd find my own way home.

The next time I saw Roger was the day after election day. I was walking up the Paseo Escalón, the main street in his neighborhood, when he pulled up beside me in a black VW. It was noon, and he had just gotten up. ARENA had done even better than people had expected: Cristiani had gotten 52 percent of the vote, enough to win without a runoff. Last night, Roger said, the Qaddafi Gang had celebrated at Gloria Elena Wright's house, drinking champagne and eating pupusas, Salvadoran cheese and bacon pancakes. Roger had been an ARENA poll watcher.

We went to the Zona Rosa, a five-block stretch of discos and restaurants, and sat down at an outdoor café. "I talked to D'Aubuisson this morning," he said, digging into his fried fish. I wasn't hungry. "He says the final count will show ARENA with sixty percent of the vote." D'Aubuisson's first wife was a friend of

Roger's family, and one of D'Aubuisson's sons had worked at Roger's factory.

"So what's D'Aubuisson going to do now?" I asked.

"He already has his job," Roger said. "He's been appointed to a special post: chief of anticommunism." He winked. "Now we can win this war. You need total extermination or they'll all come back again." He smiled.

I saw Roger again a week later. He had invited me to spend the day at a friend's beach house. He picked me up at nine o'clock. He was driving the Porsche again and was in good spirits. We sped through San Salvador's back roads to the highway.

He told me to get two beers out of the cooler in the backseat. Roger was wearing shorts. One of his legs was scarred all the way up, with a piece of flesh missing below the knee. He had skidded on a motorcycle and wound up being hit by a bus. "That was in my wild days," he said. He had been taking a lot of cocaine. He had gone to a drug treatment center in Pensacola, Florida, to dry out.

Like almost every upper-class Salvadoran I met, he was divorced. "My ex-wife is very beautiful," he said. "But all she was interested in was doing her hair and buying new clothes. I gave her all that. But she had no time for me." He spent a lot of time with Gloria Elena Wright, but he said she was not his girlfriend. "She has three children," he said. "I couldn't marry a woman who has three children."

We arrived at Samuel Aguilar's house in Amantal, on the Pacific beach, two hours later. It was a white stucco house, with a terra-cotta roof, elegantly simple. "It cost half a million colones," Roger said, a hundred thousand dollars. Inside, the house was furnished in spare Mexican style, with white walls and light wood. I changed into my bathing suit and lay down on an inflatable raft in the pool. Samuel's wife and her sister were floating on other rafts. The sister was listening to her Walkman. Roger and I had agreed that he would introduce me as his cousin from the States on his mother's side. If anyone asked what I did for a living, I would tell them, but no one would ask that question of a woman.

Around noon the other guests began to arrive, ten adults in all. Maids took the younger children into the house and went into the kitchen to fry chicken for the kids and prepare seafood for the adults. The older children settled in front of the TV to play video games. The parents changed into bathing suits and came into the pool. The women were attractive and younger than the men. The men were mostly fat and wore a lot of gold jewelry. One man had a new lapis lazuli ring he showed the others. Most of the guests wore ARENA sun visors or T-shirts.

Later, as we sat on the pool's shallow steps under an umbrella, the maids brought out platter after platter of mussels and oysters on the half shell, shrimp salad, huge cooked shelled shrimp with French dressing dip, crabs in the shells, and crabmeat with lemon-butter sauce. When our hands got sticky, we just dipped them in the pool. Two feet away from the pool was a bar with vodka and coconut water, beer, and mixers. "Samuel," Roger was saying, "you treat your friends like kings."

Aguilar's sister-in-law decided she wanted to go beach riding. The Aguilars had two all-terrain vehicles and a motorcycle. We opened the gates to the beach, and Roger started one of the ATVs, but he was so drunk that I didn't trust him even on sand. I climbed onto the motorcycle behind Mario Villacorte, the owner of Mario's disco in the Zona Rosa. "Single passenger only," said a sticker on the side, and I quickly found out why: There was no place to put my feet. On one side there was a plate I thought was a footrest. It turned out to be the bottom of the gearbox, and I burned my ankle on the chain. I ended up putting my feet around Mario. He was slightly more sober than Roger, and I was slightly more sober than Mario. The first time he tried to turn around we flipped over, and the bike fell on top of us. A few minutes later we tried to cross an inlet, and the bike tipped again and was soaked. Now it wouldn't start. We sat in the sand and waited for the others to tow us back to the house.

Aguilar's wife gave me some lotion to put on my legs. When I went back out to the pool, some of the guests were sitting on lounge chairs in the shade. "You're a reporter," said one, Alvaro, a balding man of about thirty-five. Roger, angry at me for not riding with him, had told them. I nodded. He said he worked in advertising and had gone to the University of Texas. "I know the image of Salvador in the United States," he said. "Nobody prints the truth. I recently went back to a college reunion with my two housemates and their wives. They couldn't believe I was supporting ARENA. They had the typical idea: party of death squads, et cetera. They said to me, 'Alvaro, you're not like that.' I said, 'Well, maybe the party's not like that.' "

About three feet away from Alvaro, in the shallow end of the pool, wearing an ARENA baseball cap and a gold chain around his neck, sat Ricardo Sol Meza. Sol Meza was a famous man. He and his brother-in-law Hans Christ were the owners of the Sheraton Hotel in San Salvador. On January 3, 1981, two North American advisers to the land reform program, Michael Hammer and Mark Pearlman, walked into the Sheraton coffee shop to eat a late supper with José Rodolfo Viera, the Salvadoran director of the land reform agency. At another table in the coffee shop sat Sol Meza and Christ with Major Mario Denis Morán, the head of the intelligence section of the National Guard; Lieutenant Rodolfo López Sibrián, his second-in-command; and Captain Eduardo Avila Avila, who worked for D'Aubuisson. According to eyewitnesses, Christ saw the three land reform officials come in, and half an hour later Avila and López Sibrián walked to the front of the hotel. Two National Guard corporals testified that they waited outside the hotel for Avila and López Sibrián, who gave them Ingram .45 submachine guns. Covering the weapons with their windbreakers, the guardsmen walked past the hotel's roller disco into the coffee shop. Christ pointed out the correct table. The national guardsmen pumped forty rounds into Hammer, Pearlman, and Viera, then walked out.

Three months later the Salvadoran government, under tremendous pressure from the U.S. Embassy, arrested Sol Meza and requested the extradition of Christ, who had gone to Miami. Sol Meza was released in August 1981, for lack of evidence. Only the triggermen were convicted; all other charges in the case were eventually dropped.

Roger had been drinking steadily all day and was in no condition to drive home from Aguilar's. I got a ride with Mario and his maid, who held his baby son in the backseat. Mario had just staged a commando raid to steal his son back from his ex-wife. He talked for a while about being a single parent. I asked him if he or anyone else objected to the presence of a man associated with the death squads like Sol Meza. "He's a business partner of mine," said Mario, surprised at the question. "We owned the roller disco in the hotel together. And he was jailed unjustly. I was with him when the shots went off."

We drove by Roger's factory. A sign outside said, BELTRÁN, THE EXPLOITER OF HIS WORKERS. Mario shook his head. He gestured toward an Indian woman walking in the road. "Do you think her vote should count the same as yours?" he said suddenly, in English.

"You don't think people are ready for democracy here?" I said.

"The question isn't whether people are ready for it. It's whether democracy is a good thing. Democracy is a bowl of shit."

IF DEMOCRACY HAS YET TO WIN OVER THE WEALTHY OF EL SALvador, one reason is that they are treated as aristocracy from birth. The boys are brought up to manage the family's wealth; the girls, to spend it. "Here the future leaders do not hold down jobs in a grocery store," said Larry Smith, the director of the American School. "They are used to giving maids and nannies orders to do things for them. They don't take care of things themselves.

"There's a big problem with cheating," Smith continued. "You know there's not even a word for cheating in Spanish? They call it group effort. The parents might tell the kids not to do it, but the message doesn't get through when dad brings junior to school in the morning and runs every red light."

The children of the wealthy do not serve in the army. "They can't," Roger had told me. "Their origin is bourgeois, and the army is proletariat." The draft in Salvador consisted of sending press gangs to poor neighborhoods and rounding up the young men by force; once the army even borrowed a bus from the city bus company, picked up passengers at a bus stop, and drafted all the young men aboard. Duarte made one attempt to draft the rich boys, rounding up kids in the Zona Rosa's discos one night. After a week of pressure from their parents all the boys were sent home.

I arrived in El Salvador in August 1986 and on my first night began my encounter with the Truth. I went for a walk alone and stopped at a gas station to ask directions to the Zona Rosa. Three young men were standing around a truck in the gas station. "Come with us," Roy Beers said, in perfect English. It was Friday night, but Roy was just a little too drunk to go to the Zona Rosa. He had spent the day in the Club Deportivo, the sports club, but evidently the sport he had chosen that day involved vodka and tonic. Now it was nine o'clock, and Roy and his friends Manuel and Mauricio were stuck in a gas station. Roy was leaning against the door of his truck under a No Smoking sign, smoking a cigarette and laughing. The truck wouldn't start. Roy had banged up the door earlier that day, but that didn't seem to be the problem. In Roy's condition, making an accurate diagnosis of why the truck wouldn't start seemed to be the problem.

"You're out of gas," said Manuel.

Roy took out his wallet. There was nothing in it. Manuel handed the gas station attendant a few colones, and soon they were on their way, Manuel and Mauricio to the Zona Rosa, Roy home to sober up. Manuel and Mauricio gave me a ride, and we followed Roy in Mauricio's Audi, to make sure he got home safely. Roy said he'd try to join them later, but it was doubtful. His parents didn't like to let him drive at night because he had already crashed two of the family's cars.

Roy and Manuel were twenty; Mauricio was twenty-three. Mauricio was a cargo pilot, flying the kind of cargo that enabled him to drive an Audi, and he spoke no English. Roy and Manuel affectionately called him *negro*. Roy and Manuel were not *negro*. They were white, they spoke English with the accent and arrogance of California mall rats, and they were rich, the *niños buenos* ("good kids"). Manuel, like the truly wealthy of El Salvador, now made his home in the United States. His family had moved to northern California in 1982 to escape the kidnappings. He attended junior college and planned to become an orthodonist. He came back to El Salvador every summer for vacation and for a ritual August trip to the beach during the celebration of the Feast of San Salvador with Roy, his friend since kindergarten at the American School. "I like it here," Manuel said. "Life is much more relaxed than in the States." I asked if he'd noticed a change in four years. "People have no respect for traffic laws," he said. "Every time I come back it's worse."

I had made plans to spend the weekend at the Tesoro Beach Hotel with some friends. It was near Roy's beach house, where they were driving the next day, and as we left the Zona Rosa late that night, they offered me a ride. "But we want to get an early start," Manuel said.

I waited most of the day for Mauricio, who picked me up at

four in the afternoon. Since they would have to cook for themselves in the beach house, they had some shopping to do. We pulled up at the Americana supermarket on San Salvador's central avenue, the Alameda Franklin Delano Roosevelt. A six-piece mariachi band was playing in front of the frozen foods section. Three of the musicians were blind. "I don't know how to buy food," Roy yelled over the music. "I've never been in a supermarket before." The maid did the shopping in Roy's house. The three finally settled on two cartons of Marlboros, six bottles of vodka, four liters of Sprite, a box of Kellogg's Choco Flakes, cans of tuna fish and refried beans, sandwich bread, milk, and huge packages of potato chips, banana chips, and Cheez Doodles. When they reached the check-out counter, Roy dug out his wallet, then stopped and laughed. Manuel paid. Manuel always paid, he said. Roy never carried any money.

It was dark by the time we got on the road, and the storms that came every evening during the rainy season had started. On the hourlong drive to the beach, the air was cool and patches of sky flashed with lightning.

"Hey," Roy said suddenly, "there's nobody else on this road but us." He said that the night before another friend of theirs had been driving a truck on a lonely street when the guerrillas stopped him, took the truck, and locked him in a house for the night. In the morning the guerrillas came to get him, gave him back the truck, and let him go. Roy began to tell stories. A few years ago, when the violence had been worse, a friend of Roy and Manuel's at the American School was driving in the Zona Rosa when someone—still unknown—shot him in the head and killed him. A few months before, the police had arrested a ring of right-wing army officers that had been kidnapping wealthy Salvadorans for money while pretending to be guerrillas.

"You don't often think about being kidnapped," Roy said, "just when you're driving on a country road alone. When I was at camp in Maryland for three summers, people were shocked that I lived in El Salvador. They asked me if we had cars, if we had TVs. They didn't think you could leave your house."

"You just live your life," said Manuel. "I mean, yeah, there's a war, but people still go have fun."

"I had a teacher in the British School," said Roy. "He was here for two months, and then he left. He said he didn't want to get like us. He said that we didn't even think about the deaths anymore." He was quiet for a minute. "It's true. He was right," he said. "Every day there are more deaths in the paper, and you start to ignore them unless it's someone you know. It doesn't hit you even though you might be next."

There was no electricity along the road, possibly because of the storm, possibly because the guerrillas had blown up a power station. In front of the tattered shacks of cardboard and wood, people sat around fires holding their children and swatting mosquitoes. Occasional flashes of lightning filled in their silhouettes against the fires.

Ahead on the road we saw lights; the Tesoro Beach Hotel had its own generators. The lobby was cool and spacious, with expensive beach clothes hanging in the window of the gift shop. The boys paused. "What the hell," said Manuel. "We'll start on the beans and potato chips tomorrow." We sat down in the restaurant and ordered hamburgers. Downstairs in the disco the Mr. Tesoro Beach pageant had begun.

THE RICH STUDY IN THE UNITED STATES, THEY SPEAK ENGLISH like gringos, they vacation in New York or San Francisco, and they have made their portion of San Salvador into a model-railroad Miami. But this superficial affinity with the United States only highlights the difficulties of spreading the American civic gospel. Probably nowhere in the world is there a group of foreigners as "American" as Salvador's oligarchy, yet since 1979 it has felt misunderstood, even betrayed by the United States, whose material culture it embraces wholeheartedly but whose political system it does not even pretend to endorse.

I pondered this dichotomy during leg lifts at Fitness World. Fitness World of San Salvador has all the equipment of a middle-size studio in the States—wood floor, mirrored walls, workout machines, mats, sauna—and none of the crowds. There are Garfield posters on the wall and fitness and nutrition charts, all in English, as are the magazines in the waiting room. Classes are two dollars each. Twenty dollars buys a month's membership, including weights and sauna. There are low-impact and jazz dance workouts, classes for beginners, pregnant women, women trying to get back in shape after pregnancy, even classes for children. There is rarely electricity, of course; but Fitness World has a battery-operated boom box, and at dusk we did our sit-ups as a secretary held a flashlight.

I had not been to an aerobics class since leaving the United States in 1985; I was less interested in fitness than in meeting rich women to interview. There were seven women in my class, all blond and slim. They wore designer leotards and shiny tights and eye shadow. A man of about twenty-five, wearing bicycle shorts, took the class as well.

Our instructor was named Suzanne. She was a North American married to a Salvadoran who had been living in San Salvador for ten years. She led us through Michael Jackson's "Bad" and some disco hits, counting the movements in English. We stopped to take our pulses and we all chatted in English. It was the birthday of one of the regulars, and we sang "Happy Birthday"—in English.

Fitness World is the inspiration of Gina Guirola, age thirty-two, a tall, friendly blonde who is the daughter of a Salvadoran father and a Long Island mother. Gina went to the American School and to college at Tufts and holds a master's in education from Harvard and a doctorate from Boston University. She was writing her dissertation on motivation in exercise. When her marriage broke up, she brought her baby home to El Salvador and built an aerobics studio in her mother's ample basement.

The name Guirola figured on every list of El Salvador's most important families. I spent an evening learning about the Guirolas from an elderly lady in a Chanel suit and pearls who cared deeply about the subject in part because she herself had Guirola cousins. Gina, the lady said, was the great-granddaughter of Angel Guirola, who came to El Salvador from Spain in the 1850s and made his fortune in indigo. He met Mauricio Duke, one of the New York Lexington Avenue Dukes, who had come looking for gold. Duke took Guirola back to New York to meet his five sisters, and Guirola married Cordelia Duke. The couple had seven children. The boys went to Europe or the United States for their education, marrying into some of the best families in Paris, London, New York, and San Francisco, including the San Francisco Folgers. They were known for extravagant trips and pranks: Eduardo, the second oldest, attended a fancy-dress ball in 1870 in Santa Tecla in drag, causing a scandal when he used the ladies' room.

By 1980 the Guirola family was the second largest coffee producer in El Salvador, after the Alvarez family; fifth in cotton, and among the top ten in sugar. It was second in landownership. The family owned the Banco Salvadoreño, one of the country's largest. In 1980 the state-run Salvadoran Coffee Company reported that the Guirolas netted four million dollars from growing coffee. The men who harvested the coffee made twenty-one cents an hour; the women, eighteen cents.

María Elena Guirola, a Qaddafi Gang member, is a cousin of Gina. Mauricio Guirola was president of El Salvador's Diners Club. Jorge Guirola was the treasurer of the Chamber of Commerce and Industry. Mimi Guirola, a widow, lives in a huge, decrepit Miss Havisham-style mansion in Santa Tecla. Another prominent family member is Francisco Guirola, who had raised funds for D'Aubuisson. On February 8, 1985, he was arrested flying into a Texas airstrip with $5.8 million in cash. He pleaded nolo contendere to violating U.S. currency laws. Another cousin, Antonio Guirola Méndez, was jailed in Guatemala in the early 1980s for trafficking in weapons.

I learned more about the family from Gina's mother, Elena. She sat on a couch in the corner of the aerobics studio—it was between classes—and told me about her life, while her grandson tottered around us. She had been a fashion model with the Powers agency when she met Ricardo Guirola in New York in 1939. She was still beautiful, with short auburn hair. She had grown up on Long Island and before meeting Guirola had thought El Salvador was somewhere off the coast of Italy.

She and Ricardo drove to El Salvador and set up housekeeping at the Guirolas' coffee farm outside Santa Tecla. After a few years they moved to San Salvador, where her husband took over the family bank, and went to the farm on weekends. Then the world fell apart in the space of seconds when, on a trip to the farm, the family's chauffeur, driving the couple's three children, ran into some electrical wires, killing everyone in the car. Shortly afterward, when she was pregnant with Gina, Ricardo died. Then, with the land reform of 1979, she said, she lost the farm.

"A little piece of paper doesn't make up for thirty years of your life," she said. She seemed very bitter.

In the last few years she had begun to work for the first time, buying real estate and renovating houses. "The women of my generation don't have careers here," she said. "It was a sin for a married woman to work. Now it's more open. We're in coffee country. I could have a business making coffee ice cream or coffee candy." She had Salvadoran citizenship. "But even here, among friends, everyone speaks English."

I asked her about El Salvador's problems. Carter and his human rights policy were the problem, she said. "He set us back twenty years," she said. "There was nothing wrong with the military here. Everything was going smoothly. In the United States the military makes mistakes, too. The people Carter put in power were poor, and now they're multimillionaires. The U.S. wanted us to fall into the hands of people like Daniel Ortega."

Wasn't Carter trying to stop the human rights violations? I asked.

"There's no such thing as human rights violations," she said.

While almost every wealthy Salvadoran seems to get through school in the United States without acquiring any beliefs that contradict those of his parents, there is the occasional renegade. "You think we're all monsters," Joy Mejía told me. She is a large, extroverted woman, half Canadian, educated at Wellesley and raised in Paris, who runs a gift shop in the San Benito section of San Salvador. Her son, Pancho, who lives in the States, had come to El Salvador to film a documentary about human rights. I noted some disagreement in the family on that subject. He walked in as I was talking to his mother. "The American press does not understand us at all," she was saying. In the next sentence she started to give me an example of other misunderstood Latins, the Argentine generals. "I don't know why they're persecuted so," she said. "They had to get rid of the Communists for Alfonsín to become president."

"Mom," said Pancho, "you guys aren't misunderstood at all. They've got you exactly right."

The Panchos of this oligarchal society are contaminants in an otherwise hermetically sealed world. The newspapers the wealthy read, *El Diario de Hoy* and *La Prensa Gráfica*, are not newspapers in the familiar sense. A typical headline in *La Prensa Gráfica* was SOCIAL DEMOCRACY AND COMMUNISM SHARE SAME GOALS. A few days before the election of 1989 the army made a historic announcement that soldiers would be tried for the murder of ten villagers in San Sebastián. The case was later trampled to death by the military, but at the time it was the first of its kind. *El Diario de Hoy* could not be bothered to cover it. Its entire front page was taken up with the headline and story ANEP (a business-men's group) CALLS ON PEOPLE TO VOTE.

The recurring subtext of the newspapers is self-pity. *El Mundo*, a smaller and slightly less reactionary newspaper, devoted its whole front page one day before the election to the coffee pro-cessors' prediction that coffee would disappear by the year 2000. But the news pages' constant lament of the impoverishment of the private sector is contradicted by the social section, with its endless photos of overdressed women at their afternoon teas in fancy sweet shops and hotels. *El Diario de Hoy* published half a page on "HELP YOUR DOG AVOID STRESS."

Every day, when I left my Fitness World class, I walked up the hill to the Zona Rosa, with its Pizza Hut, Paradise Steak and Lobster House, and discos such as Mario's, which my acquaintance owned. At the Zona Rosa's traffic circle a man always stood selling rare animals. One day he had a small white-faced monkey on a chain. The monkey was sleeping, curled up in the fetal position with his hands under his head like a pillow. There were two toucans perched on a broom suspended from a tree. One had nestled its bill into the other's neck, and they were sleeping in the heat despite the noise of the traffic. A small dirty beige owl perched on top of a cage. It was not on a leash. "It doesn't need to be," the seller said proudly. It was so well trained, he said, that it would never fly away. Another day he was holding a three-month-old spotted fawn in his arms. The fawn sucked on a cloth moistened with water and salt. At ten dollars the fawns were big sellers, he told me. "But what usually happens is that the children get tired of them, and no one really knows how to take care of them. Then they take them to a farm and let them go. But by that time the fawn is too tame to run from its enemies, and it dies soon after."

*   *   *

THE STORY OF THE OLIGARCHY'S ABSOLUTE RULE OF MODERN EL Salvador begins with the conquest and control of its land, the country's only natural resource. In the 1500s Spanish explorers subjugated the Pipil Indians, who had farmed communal plots for thousands of years, and took their land. At first the Spanish planted indigo for dye. The indigo farms were assigned the best fields, and the Indians were given small plots in the hills to grow their beans and corn. In 1879 chemical dyes were developed in Europe; indigo was suddenly useless. The oligarchy decided to plant coffee, which had been a small crop, responsible in 1859 for 5 percent of exports. It was a fateful decision that further concentrated El Salvador's already concentrated wealth. To grow coffee, a planter must be able to wait five years for the trees to bear fruit. He must be able to hire hundreds of workers at harvesttime, and he must have enough land to benefit from economy of scale. But coffee would not grow on the indigo land the oligarchy already possessed. Coffee required the cooler hills that at that point formed the Indians' communal land.

The government gave the oligarchy whatever it needed. Between 1846 and 1856 El Salvador had twelve presidents, representing various factions of the wealthy but always representing the wealthy. In 1881 the government instituted a land reform in reverse, taking the Indians' communal lands for growing coffee and refusing to provide even subsistence plots in return, in one stroke winning both the land and the cheap labor of a suddenly landless people who had no other livelihood.

By 1928 coffee made up 92 percent of El Salvador's exports. Coffee and El Salvador were perfect for each other. Through its concentration of wealth, energetic people (Salvadorans are famed for working hard), pro-business governments, and good land, El Salvador, the smallest country in the Americas, became the third-largest coffee producer in the world. Coffee controlled the economy; the price of coffee alone determined El Salvador's fortunes each year. As the coffee plantations spread, there was less and less land to grow food, and Salvadorans began to migrate to Honduras to find work and food. Like indigo, coffee was a crop that did not depend on an internal market. Growers had no incentive to pay workers good wages; Salvadoran workers, after all, would never earn enough to buy coffee. It was a business that required little adjustment to the modern world; the government had no incentive to develop schools. In the early 1990s only a few dozen students finished high school each year. One half of 1 percent of the people held 90 percent of the wealth. Coffee ossified a perfectly closed feudal society that seemed as if it would go on forever—until 1932.

On January 22, 1932, a group of peasants armed mainly with machetes seized several small towns in the western province of Sonsonate, where the coffee growers' takeover of the peasants' land had been particularly rapacious. The revolt, brought on by hunger, was organized by a young Communist from San Salvador named Augustín Farabundo Martí. The peasants killed about a hundred people. General Maximiliano Hernández Martínez sent in the army to put down the rebellion, killing thirty thousand people over the next few days, wiping out El Salvador's left. The oligarchy applauded the *matanza*—Spanish for "massacre"—and it became the accepted model for dealing with leftist rebellion. Fifty years later El Salvador's guerrilla army called itself the Farabundo Martí Liberation Front, and a right-wing death squad proudly took General Hernández Martínez's name.

After World War II newly invented insecticides brought the tropical diseases of the coast under control, permitting the planting of cotton in El Salvador. The country was still dominated by coffee, but now cotton on the coast and sugar in the lowlands ate up even more of what had been subsistence plots.

In 1948 the oligarchy found itself challenged for the first time as President Oscar Osorio introduced modest reforms. Although the constitution Osorio drew up in 1950 contained such items as the prohibition of rural unions, it did recognize the right to a minimum wage. For the first time El Salvador had labor legislation, social security, and collective contracts. Osorio's government also instituted an income tax.

The oligarchy was furious. Archconservatives, such as Orlando de Sola, who told me he thought D'Aubuisson too left-wing, are still furious. "The constitution was a socialist constitution that did not recognize the right to life and property before the law," de Sola said. Most simply ignored the new laws. In 1961 only eight thousand people paid taxes.

The reforms did little to curb the voracity of the rich. But that year the Central American Common Market began, spurring the development of light industry. In El Salvador these industries were, of course, owned by and large by the same families that owned everything else. The families' control blocked the rise of a new industrial upper class, but they at least did see the need to join the modern world: educate themselves and listen to foreign ideas. New foreign trade also created a small middle class of technicians and managers. In the 1960s college enrollment increased tenfold.

But the oligarchy saw little reason to loosen its grip on El Salvador's wealth. Its members thought of themselves as nation builders, the people who cleared the jungle, built railroads, created jobs. "My family was convinced we were special; we were saving the country," one member of the class told me. He was the son of a coffee-growing family from a small town. We sat on the patio of his opulent house in San Salvador, drinking coffee and looking at his garden filled with orchids. He had gone into politics and had advocated reform, warning the oligarchy that social peace required compromise. He spoke of the oligarchy as "they," not "we." Most of them considered him a traitor to his class. He had agreed to speak to me on the condition of anonymity.

"We brought lights to our town, water; all the progress was the result of our efforts," he said. "I was raised to be a landowner. On the farms the peasants ask permission of the patrón to get married. It's a feudal society. If an upper-class boy starts shooting his gun in the street in a small town, there is no law to tell him it's wrong.

"The rich didn't go into politics. Other people did it for them. I was the director of a newspaper in college, and my grandmother said, 'Why are you interested in politics? Don't forget you are born rich and you'll die rich. You don't need to be in politics.' She had a tutor to teach her English. She spoke English with an Oxford accent, and she had never left town."

Nominal control of government bounced back and forth between civilians and the army, but the oligarchy never lost power, successfully blocking all serious reform. In 1976 a new land reform agency announced a plan to take land from 250 large haciendas and distribute it to 12,000 peasant families. Business groups accused the government of "trying to destroy the national fabric of society." They recruited the military to block the measure, drove down the value of the currency through capital flight, and beat up and threatened the land reform workers. The government quickly forgot about land reform.

The landless, 12 percent of the population in 1960, rose to 40 percent in 1975. From 1972 to 1981 farm workers' salaries dropped between 20 and 70 percent, depending on the crop and the area. In 1981 El Salvador boasted the most unequal distribution of land and wealth in Latin America. In the countryside 90 percent of the people were illiterate. There was one doctor for every thirty-five hundred Salvadorans, the lowest ratio in Central America. Life expectancy in rural El Salvador was thirty-five years. In 1981 only a third of all Salvadorans had safe water; 39 percent had electricity; 41 percent earned less than $10 a month. In 1978, according to a Planning Ministry study, the basic market basket cost 5,373 colones a year—$2,150. Not even the highest-paid farm worker could make enough to buy half the basic basket goods, and women and children working in farm labor earned just 17 percent of the total cost. Salaries did not even meet Salvador's own extremely mimimum wage requirements; the Planning Ministry found that coffee workers received only 62 percent of the salary they were due. The figure was lower in cotton and sugar.

For forty years, since the 1932 uprising and massacre, the left had tried to redress these inequities through political organizing. But in the 1970s the politicians and their followers tired of waiting and started to form guerrilla armies. Throughout the decade the guerrillas took over embassies and killed policemen, military and political officials, and businessmen. They bombed stores and factories, usually at night, when no one would be killed. They kidnapped dozens of foreign businessmen and diplomats and Salvadoran oligarchs, starting in earnest with the 1972 kidnapping of Ernesto Regalado Dueñas, possessor of the two most important last names in El Salvador. A million dollars' ransom was demanded; it was never paid because Regalado Dueñas was killed first. The Sol Meza family—Ricardo Sol Meza was the Sheraton owner I encountered in Samuel Aguilar's swimming pool—paid a reported four million dollars for the release of one relative. Over the next nine years the oligarchy spent at least thirty million dollars on ransoms, possibly double that. The guerrillas used the money for weapons, food, salaries, supplies, and operations, including more kidnappings.

The guerrillas were no Shining Path. They were, to begin with, not an ideologically coherent group. They had differing ideas about how to run a revolution. Some groups advocated forming alliances with non-Marxist organizations; others disagreed. They disagreed about using strikes and about the balance between urban and rural action. They argued about how fast to push; after Ronald Reagan's election some wanted to try to overthrow the government before Reagan took office, while others thought the time was not yet right. In 1980, at the urging of Fidel Castro, the groups united to form the FMLN.

The same year a group of Marxists, Christian Democrats, non-Marxist leftists, and representatives of workers and trade groups formed the Democratic Revolutionary Front (FDR), a political group that complemented the guerrillas' military actions. The FDR favored using the guerrillas to force a negotiated settlement and endorsed the guerrillas' goals of a planned economy, abolition of the security forces, and a huge increase in social spending. By 1981 FDR-affiliated unions and popular organizations counted on the support of a quarter million people.

That year the guerrillas had roughly twelve thousand troops and were growing in number and power, each soldier highly motivated and abundantly clear about why he was fighting. In addition to what they captured or bought with proceeds from their kidnappings, they received matériel from Cuba via Nicaragua. Popular organizations supporting the guerrillas staged marches that attracted hundreds of thousands of Salvadorans. The guerrillas controlled two of Salvador's fourteen provinces, Morazán and Chalatenango, and ran a makeshift government with schools and hospitals. The FMLN appeared to be ready to take over El Salvador.

THE CARTER ADMINISTRATION, ALARMED BY THE RISE OF THE guerrillas and the success of the Sandinistas, designed a counterinsurgency plan: Head off revolution through reforms. The new junta readily agreed. With characteristic naiveté, the Carter officials thought that the guerrilla threat would be enough to unite the military and the oligarchy behind their plan. Indeed, some powerful Salvadorans did mouth the phrases and play along. But the vast majority rejected the slightest compromise. Unwilling to give up some of their privileges to buy social peace, they chose war. On March 6, 1980, the traditional alliance of the oligarchy and United States snapped as the junta, using a U.S.-designed plan, decreed a land reform. The next day soldiers drove into haciendas all over the country to evict the wealthy from their land.

"For the first time the oligarchs felt that they were not being listened to," my acquaintance the oligarch told me in his garden. "Imagine you are a large landowner. You have always had the army, the church, and the U.S. Embassy to back you up. Then soldiers drive onto your property. They're led by a lieutenant who looks like he's seventeen years old. You say, 'What do you think you're doing on my farm?' and he says, 'This *was* your farm.' It's too much. The whole system you grew up with is falling apart. Economically it's not so terrible. But all of a sudden you don't have the political power, you don't have the army. You aren't asked what you think. And you are not ready for the changes."

The land reform was part of a larger package. The junta bought 51 percent of the nation's banks in order to make credit more readily available to small borrowers. To clamp down on the capital flight that had taken $1.5 billion out of El Salvador in the previous two years, it set up government boards to buy and export local coffee, cotton, and sugarcane. But the most important and most inflammatory move was the land reform.

The program was heavily influenced by Roy Prosterman, who had designed the U.S. land reform program in Vietnam. It was to have three phases. The first expropriated large properties and formed 317 cooperatives, the members of which were the haciendas' farm workers. The second phase was designed to affect 1,700 medium-size farms. The third phase, called Land to the Tiller, was to allow renters and sharecroppers to claim small plots of the land they worked. On paper the reforms were designed to give land to more than 125,000 families.

The state paid for the land with government bonds valued at whatever the owner had declared his land was worth for tax purposes. The landowners who had been undervaluing their land for years were now caught in their own trap; the greedier a land-owner had been, the more he lost now. Machinery and inventory were paid for in cash or more bonds.

But there usually was no machinery or inventory. I found out why when I visited San Carlos de Guirola, the farm whose loss Elena Guirola had lamented. It was in Comasagua, an hour's dusty drive in the hills from Santa Tecla. It was still called De Guirola even though the family no longer owned it. But it had not been expropriated, as Elena de Guirola had implied. Félix Jaco, the farm administrator, told me that to avoid expropriation, she had sold it right before the land reform to a group of two hundred of her friends. Gina Guirola later confirmed this. The owners were still the rich; the coffee harvesters were still landless. When I arrived, the first people I saw were a family of workers cooking coffee, tortillas, and rice with carrots over an outdoor fire in back of the shed they slept in. They were migrant farm workers and earned 140 colones ($28) for fifteen days' work.

Gina had spoken of the farm with nostalgia; she had loved to ride horses there when she was little. "Now it's a ruin," Elena had said. It *was* a ruin. Two kids were playing on a big slide that emptied into a filthy swimming pool. What had once been the family's mansion, built of red brick with tile floors and a breath-taking view of the valley, had been destroyed in an earthquake. Jaco was sitting in the doorway of his small, run-down house, sewing a pair of pants on an old machine. He said the mansion was now used a few times a year for meetings. The only sounds were the cries of the children in the pool and the bees buzzing.

The Guirolas' maneuver was one of the most common ways the oligarchs fought back. Other landowners heavily mortgaged their land, killed their cattle, and sold off the machinery right before the reform. If it had been completed, the land reform would still have left 1.8 million peasants landless. It would have done nothing for the 65 percent of the population that had no permanent jobs on large estates or sharecrop plots. But the land reform stopped a long way from completion. Nine weeks after it was introduced, expropriations under Phase I came to a halt. It had put just 30,000 families into cooperatives. Phase II, which would have affected twice as many people, was never carried out. When ARENA took control of the legislature in 1982, its first act was to gut land reform, exempting three quarters of the farms targeted for expropriation.

The peasants who did get land in the Phase I cooperatives found themselves stuck with no technical help or capital, large debts, and untrained managements. A U.S. Agency for International Development audit in 1984 reported that 95 percent of the cooperatives could not pay their debts. The Phase III Land to the Tiller program distributed only tiny plots, and in most cases the land was not fertile enough to feed a family.

The land reform resulted in the worst possible combination of events: It did little to alleviate El Salvador's inequities and the misery of its poor, but it did provoke the rage of the wealthy. The oligarchy and its traditional ally the armed forces responded to the land reform and the rise of the guerrillas with an unprecedented expansion of their death squads. Tutela Legal, the human rights office of the Catholic archdiocese, documented more than 9,000 killings by the military or paramilitary death squads in 1980 alone. The following year the death squads killed 13,353 people, proportionally analogous to a half million people in the United States. Anyone with a vague connection to those suspected of wanting change—nuns, labor leaders, students, mothers of students, neighbors of mothers of students, cousins of neighbors of mothers of students—was considered subversive. Bodies piled up on roadsides and in the fields and hills around the city. In 1982, as the Reagan State Department certified that the regime had made a "concerted and significant effort" to respect human rights, 13,794 people were killed in death squad violence. In the same period, according to Tutela Legal, the guerrillas were responsible for the deaths of fewer than 60 civilians.

Priests were a favorite death squad target. The right had always accused the church of preaching socialism. The church had never advocated taking up arms, but priests, especially El Salvador's large delegation of Jesuits from Spain, did play a significant role in the growth of the mass organizations that were associated with the guerrillas. Left-wing priests helped organize peasant strikes and trained lay catechists to spread the progressive gospel of Vatican II, encouraging Catholics to organize and work for their rights. A death squad called the White Warriors Union chose as its slogan "Be patriotic—kill a priest."

The oligarchy was particularly enraged at San Salvador's Archbishop Oscar Romero. "He betrayed us," I heard over and over. When Romero was chosen as archbishop in February 1977, El Salvador's wealthy applauded and put up the money for a luxurious investiture ceremony. Romero had been a timid, conservative bishop who declined to denounce landowners who paid less than the minimum wage and had criticized those priests who spoke out against the repression. But as archbishop he published the names of the disappeared. He defended the mass organizations, maintaining that the right to organize was recognized in Pope John XXIII's *Pacem in Terris*. He made an impassioned plea to the army to stop the murder of civilians. "No soldier is obligated to obey an order to kill if it runs counter to his conscience," he preached on March 23, 1980.

The next day, as Romero said evening mass in a hospital chapel, a man pulled up at the doorway of the chapel and killed the archbishop with one shot. Various investigations, including one carried out by the U.S. Embassy, pinned the murder on D'Aubuisson, and in 1982 Captain Eduardo Avila Avila, one of D'Aubuisson's most trusted aides (also implicated in the Sheraton Hotel murders), confessed that at D'Aubuisson's direction, he had personally planned the Romero killing. The judge who carried out the initial investigation was forced to flee the country after an assassination attempt. The case went nowhere. At Romero's funeral police opened fire on mourners, killing forty people.

The death squads that proved so effective in the 1980s were born in the 1970s, the clandestine children of many fathers. Landowners created local death squads to solve their labor problems. One rural death squad started out as a Boy Scout troop. The top military security agency, ANSESAL, which the CIA had founded and equipped, was probably responsible for pulling most of them together into one organization with financing from wealthy businessmen. Soldiers, either on active duty or retired, carried out the killings of leftists whose names they pulled from ANSESAL's files.

The death squads found a new protective umbrella in 1982, when ARENA won the elections for the Constituent Assembly —later called the National Assembly—and D'Aubuisson, the country's most popular politician, was elected head of the legislature. D'Aubuisson and his security chief, dentist and oligarch

Héctor Antonio Regalado—whom the U.S. Embassy later accused of plotting to kill U.S. Ambassador Thomas Pickering—turned his office into the death squads' central headquarters.

José Hernán Torres, one of D'Aubuisson's bodyguards, told *The Washington Post* that men went out each night to kill, sometimes just to have something to do, kidnapping and murdering even their own allies. About forty men arrived each night to get orders from Regalado, chose a weapon from the stockpile on the Assembly Building's second floor, and went out to roam the streets. Torres said that one night they killed a car thief for target practice. Another time Regalado ordered the killing of an assemblyman for taking away a squad member's weapon. When D'Aubuisson resigned from the Assembly to run for president in 1984, Torres said that the death squads moved to private safe houses.

In the rise and subsequent rule of the death squads, D'Aubuisson's fingerprints were everywhere. In 1980 he publicly threatened U.S. Chargé d'Affaires James Cheek, drawing his finger across his throat and saying that Cheek would get what he deserved for leading El Salvador to communism, a reference to the Carter-backed reforms. When the junta cashiered D'Aubuisson from the National Guard, he took ANSESAL's files with him. In May of that year D'Aubuisson was arrested for plotting a coup against the new junta. When soldiers raided the farm serving as the plotters' headquarters, they found D'Aubuisson and Rodolfo López Sibrián (later implicated in the Sheraton murders) with other officers, along with notes of meetings, a phone directory of right-wing military officers and businessmen, and lists of purchase records for submachine guns, silencers, scopes, and ammunition. The material clearly linked D'Aubuisson to the murder of Archbishop Romero and the leadership of death squads. But the military judge in the case was a member of D'Aubuisson's military school class, and the suspects went free due to lack of evidence.

D'Aubuisson was the most direct connection between two naturally allied groups, the oligarchy and the military. The armed forces had traditionally followed orders from the oligarchy, even though soldiers are mostly poor dark-skinned men. Many join the military to take advantage of income opportunities in extortion and corruption, one of the few routes to wealth and power within their reach. With the *matanza* of 1932 the armed forces became more of an independent power, but with the rise of the guerrillas the army reinforced its links with the oligarchy, bonded by their common enemy. The two groups also shared their anticommunism, which had been reinforced in the military by decades of training and strategic instruction in counterinsurgency theory, taught by their patron and ally the U.S. military.

With the rise of the guerrillas, the United States intensified its efforts to reform and repackage the Salvadoran officers. Winning the war also meant winning the hearts and minds of the Salvadoran people, hence the land reform, bank nationalization, and a new emphasis on human rights. The Carter administration set about the dual mission of teaching the brutal and inept military to fight and care about human rights.

It was an intensification of years of effort to train, reform, and professionalize the Salvadoran security forces—and years of failure. During the 1960s and 1970s the Agency for International Development's police aid program "professionalized" three hundred police and National Guard officials through the Office of Public Safety program, and AID cited the program as a "model" in 1972. Among those professionalized in the late sixties were D'Aubuisson and the founder of the paramilitary group ORDEN, one of the country's most feared and repressive security organizations. D'Aubuisson's immediate superior told a U.S. congressional hearing that D'Aubuisson was also on the payroll of the CIA.

Under the Reagan administration the experiment changed. The Carter administration had been serious about real reforms. To the Reagan people, who wanted a quick battlefield victory, human rights were fine as long as they didn't get in the way of efficient operations. They agreed that soldiers could not fight effectively, as Roger Beltrán so elegantly put it, with "one hand tied around their balls." But the Reagan administration had to convince the U.S. Congress that democracy, human rights, and social reform were coming to El Salvador. So to keep the money for the war flowing, it began to emphasize cosmetic change.

The war was costing a lot of money. From 1946 to 1979 U.S. military aid to El Salvador had totaled only $16.7 million. In 1980 alone—under the Carter administration—it was $6 million. By 1988 the figure had hit $85 million, not including war-related funds folded into the economic aid budget. From 1980 to 1990 the United States gave Salvador $1 billion in military aid and at least an equal amount that indirectly supported the war effort.

Creating democracy—or at least the appearance of democracy —was relatively easy. Amid great fanfare in 1984 José Napoleón Duarte was elected president of El Salvador. This allowed the U.S. government to characterize El Salvador as a "fledgling democracy," "young democracy," "fragile democracy"; the phrases varied but always included "democracy." It was nothing of the kind. El Salvador had seen elections before, some of them cleaner than the 1984 elections. But as in most Latin nations, the ability to vote did not make the country into a democracy. People could go to the polls once every five years. But little else had changed. Salvadorans resolved their everyday problems through channels that were anything but democratic. Justice was for sale, unions were repressed, and bureaucrats slammed doors in the faces of the poor.

Another national euphemism was "moderate," a big word at the U.S. Embassy. Cristiani was not the refined facade of ARENA; he was a moderate struggling against the extremists in his party, who incidentally had made him the candidate and gotten him elected. According to the embassy, soldiers did not kill priests and torture civilians. Instead, "human rights incidents allegedly occurred," and U.S. efforts were preventing further such alleged incidents. Every day in every way the moderate fledgling democracy of increasingly human rights-conscious El Salvador was getting better and better.

In 1983 Vice President Bush went to El Salvador and warned that no more money would be forthcoming until fewer alleged human rights incidents took place. Since previous killings had taken care of most of the opposition—there were few people left to kill—his warning was heard. The volume of killings dropped. In 1983 death squads committed half the number of murders of the year before, an improvement of sorts. "If a man beats his wife morning, noon, and night," said a priest in the archdiocese office, "and then he stops beating her in the morning, do we call that an improvement?"

Salvadoran military officials watched in amused disbelief as the gringos funded them, armed them to the teeth, trained and reorganized them, and tried to transform them into a mobile troop of Eagle Scouts earning merit badges all over El Salvador.

Under the watchful eye of U.S. military advisers, Salvadoran soldiers kissed babies, dug roads, and handed out food to villagers. In the armed forces' press office—where all foreign reporters had to go to pick up government press credentials—hung a life-size black-and-white photo of a soldier gravely shaking hands with a little boy while patting another boy on the head. The armed forces parachuted candy and toys into rural villages at Christmas. From airplanes the military scattered pamphlets printed on what looked like hundred-colon bills that said, "Your life and liberty will be respected. The army will protect you!" A weekly television program touted the army's activities. Most of the soldiers saw these exercises as bizarre. But if that's what the gringos wanted to keep the *yanqui* dollars coming, that's what the gringos would get.

Military officials, the men the embassy was lauding as "moderates," learned a whole new vocabulary from the embassy's counterinsurgency phrasebook. In 1989 Armed Forces Chief of Staff Colonel René Emilio Ponce was saying such things as "It hurts the guerrillas much more if we take away their base of support than if we're killing their combatants." When Ponce arrived in a village, he gave out food, clothing, and medicine. Carlos Eugenio Vides Casanova, the minister of defense, received the U.S. Legion of Merit from the chairman of the U.S. Joint Chiefs of Staff in 1989, the citation praising him for "institutionalizing democracy, apoliticizing the Armed Forces, furthering respect for the rights of all citizens."

But Ponce and Vides Casanova had found democracy late in life, a conversion that coincided with the arrival of a billion dollars in military aid. In the early 1980s the old Ponce had been a high-ranking official in the Treasury Police, the most brutal security force in the country. As recently as 1988 he had refused to investigate when witnesses saw troops under his command force two men suspected of guerrilla sympathies to run through a burning field, then chop off their noses, fingers, and ears and shoot them. The old Vides Casanova had commented after the 1979 coup: "The armed forces are prepared to kill two hundred thousand to three hundred thousand if that's what it takes to stop a Communist take-over." He told the Cabinet that the military would not take orders from civilians. "You owe your positions to us. We have been running this country for fifty years, and we are quite prepared to keep running it." Vides Casanova had been the head of the National Guard when its members tortured and murdered a North American backpacker. The judge the Reagan administration assigned to investigate the 1980 rape and murder of four U.S. churchwomen by national guardsmen concluded that Vides Casanova had possibly participated in the cover-up.

By far the least credible rehabilitation was that of D'Aubuisson. After ARENA's victory the U.S. Embassy began to advertise the shiny new 1989 D'Aubuisson, not the sinister psychopathic killer of before, no, sir, but a man we can work with. Ambassador William Walker—who as political counselor at the embassy in Salvador had been kicked out in 1977 for his aggressive criticism of human rights violations—a few months after the election told a visiting U.S. labor delegation that D'Aubuisson was a "Huey Long-style populist."

To the Salvadoran military the Americans were too good to be true. The Salvadorans quickly figured out that they could do anything, really anything, and the gringos would cover for them. If they raped and murdered U.S. nuns, Secretary of State Alexander Haig would testify that perhaps there had been an "exchange of fire," that maybe the nuns were armed. When six Jesuit priests were killed in 1989 on a university campus surrounded by the army, Ambassador Walker suggested to the press that they had been killed by guerrillas dressed as soldiers.

After each massacre or assassination U.S. officials swore that this time they were serious, the money was going to dry up, that continued funding depended on a full investigation and prosecution for—and here the phrase varied over the years—the killing of Archbishop Romero, the nuns, the Sheraton Hotel murders, the murder of four Dutch TV journalists, the murder of civilians in the village of Las Vueltas, the village of Los Llanitos, the village of Las Hojas, Armenia, Mozote, or San Sebastián, the murder of the Jesuits. In the first months of 1990 death squads and security forces killed or disappeared about two hundred civilians—not the chilling figures of the early 1980s but still double the number of the previous year. (The guerrillas disappeared or executed twenty-three civilians during the same period.) Arrests of union activists were up, and torture was widespread. Fourteen of the military's fifteen top commanders had, during the course of the war, led troops responsible for illegal executions or disappearances. But by 1990 not a single officer had been convicted of a human rights violation, and the money kept coming. The gringos were bluffing. They were always bluffing.

And the amount of money was staggering. By the late 1980s AID's program in El Salvador was the fifth-largest in the world, spending $250 million a year—equivalent to more than a month's average salary for each Salvadoran. For the first time in the history of U.S. foreign aid, the United States was putting more into a foreign government's treasury than the recipient country itself. For a century Salvador was almost solely dependent on coffee. Now with the fall in coffee prices and the rise of AID money, the country is almost solely dependent on the United States.

But although AID officials like to boast that the United States spends three times as much on development as on military aid, in a general sense it is all military aid, part of the counterinsurgency campaign, politics as a continuation of war by other means. A study by the U.S. House Arms Control and Foreign Policy Caucus estimated that 70 percent of U.S. assistance went directly or indirectly to the war, counting such items as economic support funds because they free money for the war effort. The military and economic aid is hopelessly intermingled; the United States finances the country's destruction while subsidizing its rebuilding. With the army now involved in paving roads and distributing food, soldiers are bombing a village one day and nailing its houses back together the next.

AT THE SAME TIME AS IT TRIED TO REFORM THE MILITARY, the United States set about modernizing El Salvador's oligarchs. The principal tool was AID's funds for the private sector, which was more than half AID's total program. The idea was for AID to work with the private sector as the U.S. military worked with the Salvadoran military, in the process trying to create a more enlightened oligarchy. AID's agenda, adopted by Cristiani, was "the most comprehensive reform program in Latin America with the possible exception of Chile," an AID official told me. But "reform" is a relative term. In this case it means reversing the previous administrations' AID policies. Traditionally AID promoted land reform so peasants could raise their own beans and corn. Now it promotes the opposite: large plantations with low-wage labor to grow nontraditional export crops such as broccoli. To increase business investment incentives, AID advocates lower taxes for investors, less government involvement in the economy, and more restrictions on union organizing. It conditions its aid on austerity plans that cut social welfare programs. It teaches businessmen how to lobby for private-sector interests. It works to abolish or reduce government agencies such as Incafe, the coffee marketing board, and "get coffee marketing back into the private sector." The Salvadoran coffee exporters could not have designed a more congenial plan themselves. An AID internal memo said that U.S. aid had been "the crucial factor in maintaining the Salvadoran private sector." AID paid for Salvadoran businessmen to go to Guatemala for seminars on "Understanding Politics," their ability to wangle such projects only proving that the Salvadoran private sector already understood plenty about politics.

"This is not the most socially conscious private sector in the world," an AID official told me. AID's remedy is to strengthen the hand of the businessmen, to work with them to develop city-based industrial entrepreneurs to counter the weight of the rural landowners, and, in the process, endow them with a social conscience. "We want to broaden the base, expand participation in the private sector," said the official.

This private-sector version of counterinsurgency, admirable in theory, does not take into account the likes of Roger Beltrán. Roger fits the demographics of AID's new private entrepreneur. He is of Lebanese descent, the grandson of a penniless immigrant, traditionally shut out of El Salvador's upper class. His father founded two factories; Roger manages one, and his brother the other. He is a city man. But if proof is needed that the new oligarchy can behave as stubbornly as the old oligarchy, Roger Beltrán is it.

Roger invited me to visit his factory. He met me at the small outdoor fast-food restaurant next door that feeds his employees and those of a nearby supermarket. It had been nearly two weeks since the workers had occupied the plant to protest Roger's firing of six union organizers. The strikers and some of Roger's managers and guards were sharing the building uneasily, sleeping inside, all refusing to leave. We walked around to the back of the factory to talk to Alfonso, an employee who had favored the takeover but was now tired of the strike and wanted to quit and go home. "We're sleeping on cardboard cartons, and we don't even have blankets," he said.

I asked Alfonso how the takeover occurred. He said that men in hoods had come into the factory during a shift change, turned out the lights, and blocked the doors. "Don't panic. We're on your side," they told workers. They were organizers for the Christian Democrat union. They talked about the miserable working conditions and what workers could gain by striking: collective bargaining; work uniforms; towels; a party at the end of the year.

Roger interrupted Alfonso's recital. "They want dividends every six months. They want transportation to work. The union's brainwashing everyone."

We walked back to the restaurant and ordered chicken and rice. Roger said nine of his heavily armed managers were inside the factory guarding the equipment. "We are Rocky, Rambo, and Schwarzenegger," he said. In front of the factory some women workers came every day to bring food and lend moral support to the men inside. We took our trays and sat down at a table of darker-skinned middle-aged people. "I want you to meet my workers," Roger said. "They'll tell you I'm very strict with them. I make them obey."

"We just want the strike to be over so we can work," said one woman. "I am trying to support my mother."

Another said that her house would be repossessed if she didn't make her payments. She showed me the cheap watch she wore. "This was a present from the bosses," she said. "They even lent us money for school uniforms for our children."

Another woman said that the factory had lent her husband money to buy a soldering kit. "We even pay their life insurance," said Roger, beaming.

He introduced me to Concepción Marina Rivas. After twenty-one years of working in the factory, she said, she earned twenty colones a day (about four dollars), forty cents a day above the minimum wage of eighteen colones. "I have no problems here," she said. Sometimes management suspended workers for a day without pay if they were late or doing a bad job, she said. But this had never happened to her. She had even been interviewed on the evening TV news about how well she was treated. "In my opinion, a good worker makes a good boss," she told me. "If they give me even a piece of tortilla, I appreciate it."

Roger had barred me from talking to union members at his factory, but a few days later I went to the union headquarters downtown, a ramshackle house with an open inner courtyard strung with wash. The union was the CGT, the General Workers' Confederation, which had been founded by the United States as a moderate counterweight to the National Union of Salvadoran Workers, one of the mass organizations largely sympathetic to the guerrillas. Danilo Umaña, the union's human rights director, showed me newspaper ads the union had published condemning guerrilla violence and Marxism-Leninism.

"We backed the Christian Democrats, thinking that El Salvador would respect workers' rights," Umaña said. "We still have no democracy here. But there's some political space." In his opinion, the prospects for workers under ARENA would be grim. "We now have the right to form a union, to strike, to get social security and a minimum wage. We may lose those. We'll have to pressure businessmen to keep their promises about the right to organize. There's a strike going on right now about that. Have you heard of Roger Beltrán?"

He showed me some photos of union members outside Roger's factory bearing signs reading THE CGT DEMANDS OF BELTRÁN: SOLVE THE PROBLEM! and PEACE, FREEDOM AND BREAD. He described the conflict. I asked him whether the strike was legal. "No," he said. "But what is a legal strike? Justice is at the service of the oligarchy. The judge on the case who declared it illegal told us that in her opinion, it was legal, but she ran the risk of being killed if she said so."

María Elena Meléndez, who had worked in the factory, came in. "The day of the strike Beltrán came out armed, with four vigilantes with machine guns," she said. "He walked up to one of our directors, put his arm on his chest, and said, 'I'm going to shoot your insides out.' Then a man drove up with a military haircut. We were scared. Beltrán beckoned our director over with his finger and said to us, 'This man is going to beat the crap out of you.'

"He's very arbitrary," she said. "He'll suspend you because he's mad at someone else or because he's drunk. It can be six minutes to the end of your shift and he suspends you and you lose the day's pay. He comes up and touches the women. He told some people, 'If ARENA wins, you're going to kiss me down to the soles of my feet.' "

Jorge Ramírez, twenty-four, was the strike director whom Roger had threatened. I met him six months after the strikers had been fired. "Beltrán took the catch off his revolver and hit me in the chest with it," he said. "Then he called a guard over, and the man asked me my name and told me to be careful, that something could happen to me.

"When ARENA won, people weren't sure they wanted to stay on strike," Ramírez said. "They thought, things are only going to get worse, and maybe we should hold on to the jobs we have." He smiled. "Now conditions at the factory are worse. We used to have a half hour coffee break. Now the workers say that's gone. I've applied to every plastics factory in San Salvador. They all tell me, 'Ah, you were a striker when you worked for Beltrán.' There are jobs open, but I'm not getting them."

Roger was gloating. He boasted about firing the striking workers and circulating a list of their names to other businesses. "People should know who the troublemakers are," he said. "After all we did for them—giving them loans to live better and paying them well. That strike cost me half a million colones. I had to hire security guards. We lost clients. We lost production. I had to buy M-16s and grenades." He told me he had paid off the union's lawyer to get more favorable terms for ending the strike.

Roger had not changed. He was drinking a screwdriver as he pulled up to my hotel in a new red Toyota pickup truck. We went to a Mexican restaurant called El Zócalo in the Zona Rosa. He knew everyone. We sat down with two friends of his, Raúl Guirola and Mónica Spader. Guirola said he was one of the founders of ARENA. "Nothing moves without the military," he said. "It's the same in your country. The only President who really got things done was Roosevelt, a military man." I didn't ask which Roosevelt he meant.

IF AID NEEDS A WARNING THAT CREATING A NEW URBAN PRIVATE sector offers no guarantees of bringing social consciousness to the

Salvadoran elite, it does not have to go as far as Roger Beltrán. It can look at its own staff. Even some of the Salvadoran businessmen AID had employed to spread its good news do not seem to have absorbed the message themselves.

Mario Valiente, a small, balding man with a mustache, works for AID's creation FUSADES, a group the agency invented in 1984 to modernize the private sector. Valiente directs Fortas, an arm of FUSADES that seeks to fortify such associations (hence the name) as the National Association of Private Enterprise (ANEP) and the Chamber of Commerce. If ANEP got any stronger, I thought, it could join the United Nations.

"Our market research found that the average Salvadoran has business talent but doesn't think of himself as a businessman," Valiente said. "We want to illustrate what free enterprise is and make potential businessmen feel part of the system." He showed me a course outline Fortas had hired professors to teach in five or six universities, in itself an ingenious form of private-sector initiative. It listed classes such as "Private Property and Society" and "The Subsidiary Role of the State." "We're going to try to get it taught in high schools," he said. "Fifth grade, really, is not too young to start forming businessmen. Until our courses came along, students studied Marxism."

We moved on to more general themes, and Valiente asked his secretary to bring us each a third cup of coffee. "The way we have to fight this war is like a boy wooing his girl in a glass room with her whole family watching," he said. "The Geneva Convention has kept us from winning. I push you; then you accuse me of torture. Soldiers catch a terrorist, and they have to let him go. When you have terrorists that kill and destroy, the country has the right to defend itself. We haven't done that yet.

"All right, so this society is a little feudal in the way a patrón treats his peasants," he said. "They think that that's how it's always been and there's nothing wrong with it. When you talk to people, there's no clear conception that they have to better the lives of workers. But you can't do it by decree. You can't have a law saying: Raise the minimum wage. Where are you going to get the money? You have to augment production first. If I raise a bigger crop, I can pay better salaries."

In that one sentence Valiente summed up AID's efforts in El Salvador. USAID created FUSADES and employed Valiente because it believes that helping the private sector raise bigger crops is the most important way to encourage it to pay better salaries.

But the oligarchy never does pay better salaries, no matter how large or small the crop. It never does pay taxes, no matter how much money it makes. While the Guirola family netted four million dollars in 1980 on coffee, it paid its male harvesters twenty-one cents an hour and the women eighteen cents. How much would it have had to net to have paid the women twenty cents? How many gallons of gas would Roger Beltrán have to buy for his Porsche before he would pay a worker with twenty-one years of service more than four dollars a day?

The wealthy pay workers poorly not because they have to but because they can. They pay few taxes not because they have to but because they can. And as long as the law, or lack of enforcement of the law, allows them to pay poorly, to fire union organizers and let others worry about their country, they will continue to do so.

The only time the oligarchs betray the notion that they are citizens of a nation is when they talk about the war. The war arouses their enthusiasm, at least as long as the poor do the dying and the United States pays the bill. In 1983 the United States introduced the armed forces to the National Plan, modeled after CORDS (Coordinated Rural Development Support), the program that AID had managed in Vietnam. The National Plan had four steps: ground sweeps to kill guerrillas, civilian defense patrols, rebuilding projects, and resettlement villages for refugees. In 1986 the National Plan was replaced by United to Rebuild, ostensibly the armed forces' idea but suspiciously identical to the National Plan.

General Adolfo Blandón, then the armed forces chief of staff, presented United to Rebuild in a speech at the Chamber of Commerce and Industry in August 1986. His purpose was to obtain business support for a program of public works designed to keep key villages out of guerrilla hands by providing medical care, telephone service, electricity, and school lunches and by teaching villagers to read and write.

The auditorium was filled to capacity. "A few years ago we were called insensitive," Blandón said. "People said the armed forces were incompetent, that we worked only from eight to five and were only interested in caring for the Fourteen Families. Now we are taking our place in the hearts and minds of our people." He asked for the Chamber's help.

Francisco García Rossi, a coffee grower, stood up. "I have a question," he said. "This government's policies have every day made private enterprise poorer and weaker. Before we give you our help, it is necessary that you in the armed forces use your influence to reverse the socialist process we've embarked on. Do you have the will to fortify capitalism?"

Blandón, not a man accustomed to being outflanked on the right, paused for a long time. "Interesting question," he said. Instead of answering it, he said slowly, "I have always believed in private enterprise, but there must be progress. This is also a form of fighting Marxism. If you don't treat workers well, they are not going to like you, and in truth, there are people right in this meeting who don't treat their workers very well."

For the next half hour businessmen in the audience echoed the question posed by García Rossi: Why don't you coup? "Well, maybe the government does need to change a few things," Blandón finally said. Although visibly annoyed, he stuck to his basic message. The next day *El Diario de Hoy* carried a banner headline: GOVERNMENT NEEDS TO CHANGE, SAYS BLANDÓN. The story dealt mainly with the complaints of the coffee growers. United to Rebuild was hardly mentioned.

Blandón's tiff with the coffee growers illuminated both the progress that El Salvador had made and the barriers to further progress. Three years before, the oligarchy would not have been able to obstruct United to Rebuild because Blandón would never have presented it. But the program meant nothing. The development projects were admirable but imaginary. "That program was never implemented," an AID official told me three years later. "The commission never met. There was just no one interested in it."

IT WAS EVIDENT THAT EL SALVADOR'S WEALTHY WOULD OPPOSE reforms. What remained a mystery to me was why this seemed to be good strategy for winning votes among the poor. As the 1989 election approached, it became apparent that the advocates of reform—the Democratic Convergence party—were faring badly, while D'Aubuisson's ARENA had widespread support.

The Democratic Convergence party had once been the political arm of the guerrillas. Its leaders, Guillermo Ungo (who died of cancer in 1991) and Rubén Zamora, were not Marxists. They arrived at their alliance with the guerrillas only after spending decades trying to achieve change through politics. Both had suffered beatings, exile, and threats; Zamora's brother, who had been the attorney general of the 1979 reform junta, had been killed by a death squad. They had spent the eighties living abroad and visiting most of Europe and Latin America: moderate, educated traveling salesmen for revolution. But in November 1987 they decided to try something truly revolutionary: risking their lives to return to El Salvador and run for office.

Ungo, the presidential candidate, expected to do well in the election. The guerrillas, after all, still had a lot of support, but people were tired of the war. The competition was the corrupt, incompetent Christian Democrats, who had misgoverned the country since 1982, and ARENA. The Convergence proposed a negotiated political solution to the war, an end to U.S. involvement in El Salvador, "real democracy," and an economy based on "people's necessity."

The Convergence's rally in Santa Tecla's plaza began an hour late with large-screen TVs showing videotapes of soldiers shooting at demonstrators. About two hundred people came over to the stage. When the videotape ended, most drifted back to the market stalls on the sides of the plaza. Ungo's second-in-command (who was killed by a death squad ten months later) gave a speech defending the guerrillas' peace proposal. A few people clapped politely.

Then Ungo came through the audience, fifty-six but looking seventy, stooped and tired, wearing a blue safari suit, walking alone, with no security guards or bulletproof vest. The Convergence workers in the crowd, about twenty people, chanted, "You can feel it, Ungo is here."

Ungo gave a speech about poverty and the war. But his voice was passionless, and at times he was drowned out by feedback from the mike and people talking in the crowd.

A man in a Convergence T-shirt shouted through a megaphone, "Ungo, friend, the people are with you."

"Viva!" shouted three men around him.

By the end of Ungo's speech the crowd had swelled to about a hundred people. Convergence workers passed out balloons to the children. Three minutes later the plaza was deserted. A friend who went to a rally in a small town in the west that weekend told me that he saw Ungo give a speech in a field peopled only with a handful of Convergence workers.

The people were not with Ungo. There were several possible reasons. Some were afraid to show their support. Many had never heard of the Convergence, a new party with little money for advertising. Then, too, the Convergence's principal base of support, the guerrillas, was boycotting the election and had threatened to disrupt the voting by occupying villages and shooting at voters and poll watchers, including those of the Convergence party. Or it could have been that people were skeptical that the Convergence could change things, or they just didn't like what Ungo had to say.

The people were with D'Aubuisson. Two days before the Convergence rally I attended, ARENA staged one in San Salvador, which was where I first met the Qaddafi Gang. It began with four processions through various neighborhoods, each march led by a different ARENA politician. I followed D'Aubuisson through the working-class neighborhood of San Jacinto, down a route I walked again a week later to commemorate the anniversary of the death of Archbishop Romero. Today the march honored not Romero's death but the man who had probably killed him. It was a Saturday afternoon, and the noisy crowd sang the ARENA song over and over while waiting for D'Aubuisson to arrive. There were plenty of upper-class teenagers and women in red, white, and blue ARENA T-shirts and sun visors, but most of the people looked as if they were from the neighborhood. They waved banners and ate snow cones. "I wish he would run instead of Cristiani," a young woman at the rally said to me in English. "He's a stronger person, a firm hand." After a half hour D'Aubuisson pulled up in a truck with his wife and the march began. She had dyed blond hair and wore a white ARENA vest, a white ARENA T-shirt, an ARENA necklace and carried an ARENA purse. D'Aubuisson, short, wiry, and handsome, wore a black vest, black boots, and a pistol. Three blond girls wearing too much perfume called his name. He looked at them, put his hand over his heart, and pretended to throw it to them. They screamed the way girls scream at rock stars.

The march grew as it advanced, and by the time we reached the Plaza Libertad, the crowd stretched over several blocks. The plaza was filling up as the other three processions streamed in. In a few minutes it was packed with around twenty thousand people. The platform was hung with red, white, and blue ARENA banners. Over and over the band played the ARENA song, "Tremble, Tremble, Communists," which was so catchy that even most of the reporters couldn't keep from humming it. When the crowd roared out the lines "El Salvador will be the grave where the Reds meet their end," the dignitaries on the podium made an exaggerated thumbs-down motion.

D'Aubuisson walked up to the microphone to huge applause. He began talking about the gringos. "They talk about human rights, but look how they treated the Indians in their own country, without a word about human rights," he said. He talked in staccato bursts.

"The foreigners are doing experiments on us, like laboratory mice," he said. "They never asked us if we wanted a corrupt, incompetent government. We've put up with it for ten years, experimenting on us as if we were rabbits."

"Write it down," said a woman standing next to me. This was Lina Funes, whom I later got to know as a member of the Qaddafi Gang.

"The reporters write lies," D'Aubuisson said. "They say this is the party of the rich. But look around you. The people have never seen a rally this big before."

Lina was poking me. "Write it down, write the Truth."

"We are never going to negotiate, whether the gringos like it or not," D'Aubuisson was saying. "We are going to maintain a permanent dialogue with the guerrillas to tell them what Salvadorans want." He finished his speech to cries of "*Patria sí, comunismo no!*" ("Fatherland yes, communism no!")

Cristiani, a big, athletically built man with a mustache, put out his cigarette and stepped up to the podium. He wore a black baseball cap with a red ARENA flag. His interests were his coffee business, riding motorcycles, and playing squash. He was not a politician; he had not even been a member of ARENA until he became the party's president in 1987. He looked about as comfortable as a plantation owner addressing his slaves. He promised that he would back the armed forces and never let the guerrillas take power. He talked about eliminating the coffee boards and getting farming and the banks back into private hands. "Enough already of Communists and communitarians," he said. He promised to improve schools and hospitals. After enumerating several of the many major Christian Democratic corruption scandals, he concluded with a swipe at a foe he did not name: "the people with the baby faces and the innocent looks who don't understand the damage they've done"—the gringos.

The crowd clapped politely for Cristiani. But it cheered wildly for D'Aubuisson. ARENA was El Salvador's most popular party, and D'Aubuisson the country's most beloved politician. ARENA had the majority of seats in the legislature and controlled 178 of 262 mayoralties in the country. Part of the reason was that the Christian Democrats had been a disaster and life was far worse than it had been when Duarte took office. But there was more to ARENA's appeal than that.

A week before the election I had driven to San José de Villanueva, a village of eight thousand off a dirt road an hour's drive from San Salvador. The mayor was ARENA; everyone I met was going to vote for ARENA—if people were voting at all. "Problems are not solved by politics," said a man with eight children and no job. "Only by God. God is great, and he will respond."

Next to the village plaza, where girls in school uniforms played baseball, some workmen were building a church. I spoke to José Escalante, the construction supervisor. He was not a fan of democracy. "The only person we ever voted for is Duarte, the man we have now, and look at our situation. Better to have rich people running things. They know how to do it, and they won't steal so much."

Over and over I heard the view that government could not change the condition of El Salvador's poor. The rich could do it—not because they were government but because they were rich—or it could be left to God. In Argentina many had substituted "Evita" for "God" in that sentiment; in Colombia it was "Pablo Escobar." It didn't matter; it was an equally fatalistic, unsophisticated, and self-defeating way for people to structure their lives. But what had ever happened to prove them wrong?

El Salvador's social structure, in which a wealthy patron gives his campesinos food, housing, and permission to marry, carried over into all walks of life. It was the only way of life most poor people knew. Many, perhaps most of El Salvador's poor had no desire to organize themselves and no desire to take power. When ARENA's politicians called themselves the party of people who "know how to work and know how to give work," many believed them. D'Aubuisson was the old-fashioned caudillo: strong, handsome, violent, a man who knew how to talk to common folk. And about all those death squad accusations, well, people believe what they want to believe.

THERE WAS NO ELECTRICITY ELECTION WEEK. THIS WAS NOT unusual; electricity comes and goes without comment in San Salvador. But the guerrillas had decided to celebrate the elections by blowing up more power stations than usual and declaring a transportation strike. Most taxi and bus drivers cooperated—some out of support for the strike, some out of fear that the guerrillas would set fire to their means of livelihood. Since water is pumped with electric pumps, there was also no water. And most people had no telephone service.

For a while I was in an apartment where the phone worked but never rang, and I had taken to picking up the receiver every few minutes when expecting a call. A week before election day I changed apartments. The new apartment was closer to the center of the city and had, wondrously, a working phone—thrilling news until I realized there was no one I could call. Work meant walking for hours each day, with no prospect of a shower. My housemate and I had gotten into the habit of going across the street to the Sheraton every morning and taking sponge baths in the rest rooms before getting coffee. There was always water at the Sheraton, which had its own tank. At least we could leave the house. Some of the wealthy who lived behind electric gates found themselves prisoners on their own property.

On election day I awoke to the sound of mortar fire. It was five o'clock, still dark. I turned the tap; no water for the fourth day in a row. I lit a candle, dressed, and walked outside. Dawn was breaking. Dogs ran in the street. The horizon was a silhouette of palm trees against a red-streaked sky. I could hear roosters and birds and, from the Guazapa volcano a few miles away, the sound of machine-gun fire, mortars, and bombs.

The reporters had agreed to go out in groups. A friend picked me up, and we drove to an apartment to meet some other reporters. A photographer who lived in the building ran down the stairs excitedly, talking into a two-way radio. He said that during the night a Reuters photographer had been killed by government security forces.

We drove out toward the fighting at the base of the Guazapa volcano. On the way we stopped in Soyapango, a half hour's drive from San Salvador. Some of the soldiers in their camouflage uniforms and green face paint had marked blue ash crosses on their foreheads; it was Palm Sunday. A girl walked by in a white communion dress. It was seven-thirty in the morning, and people were standing in lines outside the elementary school that served as a polling place. But voting hadn't begun yet; things were running late. Each party had poll watchers, the ARENA people with fancy vests. There were even some Convergence poll watchers. They looked nervous.

Nothing was happening in Soyapango, and we continued on toward the fighting. In the village of San Ramón, at the foot of the volcano, the fighting had just stopped. Like San Salvador, San Ramón had no water or electricity all week. Villagers did have entertainment, however: They had set out chairs in front of their houses and congregated in the street and in the doorway of the corner store to watch the fighting. They said it had started at five in the morning in the village, then moved up the side of the volcano. We stood in the street watching the choppers circle, bombing the volcano. "Are you going to vote?" I asked people, as much to make conversation as anything else.

It was a ridiculous question. The nearest polling place was a half hour walk away, and the guerrillas, who had threatened to harm voters, had made a rather spectacular announcement of their presence that morning. "We'll wait and see," one woman said. The others nodded.

"Lots of fighting around here?" I asked.

"Around here, no, nothing. It's quiet," said the woman. "The fighting was in the next block." She pointed. One could, it seemed, get used to anything. "But two weeks ago we had a battle here for an hour."

Shots—very close now—rang out above the buzz of cicadas. No one even flinched. Soldiers were scrambling down a dirt path. I climbed up the hill, where I found a dead soldier, covered by a poncho except for his legs and hands. He was wearing camouflage, and a blue ribbon was tied around his left wrist. His pack lay on the ground next to him. Soldiers nearby who also wore blue ribbons identified him as a twenty-three-year-old corporal named Juan Alberto Gálvez and said he had been shot in the chest three hours before. Three guerrillas had been killed in the battle, and about ten wounded, they said, but the guerrillas had managed to remove their casualties. This particular battle had started when a soldier wearing camouflage walked through San Ramón early in the morning. Two other soldiers waved to him, taking him for a colleague, and then he opened fire on them. The guerrillas were sometimes hard to identify, they said. So the government troops wore ribbons, changing the color each day.

There were houses about thirty feet from where Corporal Gálvez had fallen. "The guerrillas shoot into people's houses," said one of the soldiers. "We don't. We have to respect their human rights. If we kill a guerrilla, then we are violating his human rights."

"The Red Cross gives food to the campesinos, and it ends up with the guerrillas," said a sergeant. "But we can't touch the campesinos. Oh, no. There were fewer rules to follow before. Now we're screwed."

When we got back to the city, I asked a friend if I could use the shower in his hotel room. There was no electricity, but the Camino Real Hotel always had water. I had not showered in four days, and I had fallen into a ditch during the morning. I took a shower by candlelight.

When I finished, my friend was listening to the radio with a terrible expression on his face. He said that a Salvadoran TV sound man had been killed the night before and that Cornell Lagroew, a Dutch TV cameraman who was a friend of mine, had been killed in the crossfire of a battle in the province of Usulután. We sat staring at his portable radio. Two other reporters I knew were missing. In 1982 four Dutch television journalists had been killed while on their way to rebel-controlled territory in Chalatenango. "A week ago," my friend said, "Cornell was joking that he wasn't going to be the fifth."

Election day saw the heaviest fighting in years. Cornell, the twenty-fifth journalist to die while covering El Salvador, was one of thirty people killed that day. The guerrillas staged simultaneous attacks on twenty-three towns, and there were battles in twelve of Salvador's fourteen provinces. Voter turnout was light. That night most Salvadorans sat in their waterless homes in the dark, listening to the election results on transistor radios. Roger Beltrán and the Qaddafi Gang ate pupusas and drank champagne at Gloria Elena Wright's house. U.S. Ambassador Walker called the voting a "civic fiesta." At Cristiani's inauguration a State Department spokesman said the transfer of power was "an example of the democratic process spreading through Latin America."

It was as if the election had represented a victory for U.S. policy instead of its failure. Despite the $4.45 billion in U.S. aid over ten years, the Salvadorans are poorer than before. From 1980 to 1988 per capita income fell by a quarter. Ten times as many people were unemployed or underemployed in 1988 as in 1980. Only one family in ten had safe drinking water—down from three in ten in 1984. One fifth of the population had fled the country, and one in ten Salvadorans lived in a refugee camp.

"Three billion dollars in aid could have done a lot had it gone to eradicating poverty," said Ricardo Stein, a development consultant on the board of FUSADES. "Instead, it went toward eradicating the poor."

Despite ten years of arms and training for the military, in 1990 the war looked very much as it had in 1980. The guerrillas had lost their patrons in Nicaragua and the Soviet Union; their arms flow had dwindled, their allies were pressuring them to negotiate, and their civilian supporters had been largely assassinated. Yet they could still shut down San Salvador at will, launch a simultaneous offensive in every province of the country, and shoot down army planes. And after forty thousand civilian deaths in the war, the government security forces still retain a taste for wife beating.

After so many years, so much money, so many lives, Salvadorans had turned over power to the same people who had always held power. And the United States once again supported them.

As long as the United States financed the war, El Salvador would continue to hold elections, the generals would express their profound concern about human rights, and the politicians with their manicured nails and polished English would talk about building hospitals and schools. But when the United States loses interest in El Salvador, the charade will be over.

The billions of dollars in U.S. aid were designed to change El Salvador, but it is the gringos who did the changing. The million dollars a day were a bribe to make democrats of the D'Aubuissons, but it was the D'Aubuissons who blackmailed the gringos to keep the money flowing, knowing the desire to win a war led the United States to overlook what it had to overlook. El Salvador had become, as D'Aubuisson said, a laboratory experiment. But it has not tested, as the United States had sought to do, what stimuli can induce killers to abandon their killer instinct. Instead, it proved how little the killers must alter their behavior to continue to receive rewards from the United States. The mouse, after all, also trains his scientist: When he rings the bell, the good doctor brings him cheese.

FIVE

THE
TRIUMPH

THE PASSAGE OF A DOZEN EVENTFUL YEARS HAS MADE IT easy for people in the United States to forget that Nicaragua's Sandinista Revolution of 1979 was once hailed by most of the world as the way to slice through the Gordian knot of repression and passivity that had tied up Nicaragua for nearly five centuries. Neither the Gladys Meneseses nor the Roger Beltráns would have a place in the new Nicaragua. The revolution would replace the old patterns of serf and patrón, servility and repression, misery and wild excess with new habits of equality, dignity, and independence. In place of the blatantly corrupt Somoza dictatorship, which ignored the needs of the poor, the revolution held out the prospect of a dignified wage for the common man, a roof over his head, shoes on his feet, and beans on his table. In place of a government that attacked demonstrators, jailed and tortured opposition politicians, outlawed labor unions, censored the press, and spied on its own citizens, the revolution would treat its people with respect.

"The country I imagined," said Luis Carrión Cruz, "was a place where everyone had the opportunity to receive an adequate education, where health care was a right and not something granted by exception, where all classes could participate." Carrión was thirty-six when I met him; at the time of the Triumph, as Nicaraguans called the revolution, he was twenty-six. A child of wealthy parents, a graduate of a prestigious prep school in the United States, he had turned his back on his privileged world to organize a Christian community in a poor Managua barrio. His outrage at the inequality and repression of the Somoza dictatorship led him to embrace Marxism and then to take up arms with the Frente Sandinista and assume his position as one of the nine comandantes of the revolution who were to run Sandinista Nicaragua.

I had seen Carrión frequently on the television news when I lived in Managua during 1986 and 1987. He was usually dressed in uniform, delivering a passionate speech. But I did not meet him until March 1989, in his office, and my first impression was: This revolutionary looks like a yuppie accountant. He was wearing brown horn-rimmed glasses and an Yves Saint Laurent striped shirt. He was thin, and his hair was receding. He spoke so softly I could hardly hear him, and he practically never looked up, preferring to focus his gaze on the cigar he fiddled with but never actually lit. The only time his voice lost its evenness and he began to talk from his heart was when he spoke not about the country he lived in but about the country he had imagined.

"A revolution fights to construct, to build new things," he said, leaning back in his chair. "I still dream about it. But now I realize that you can't go so fast, that the road is filled with difficulties. You run up against the harsh reality: that you have to defend yourself, that you have to be able to produce what is necessary. I myself was going to work in education." He waved his cigar at the wall of his office. "This," he said, "all this came later."

The "this" he was speaking of was his job as minister of economy, commerce, and industry. He became minister in 1988, placed there to run an economy each year more like that of Pinochet's Chile, ending up similar to the austerity models the International Monetary Fund (IMF) was trying to impose in various Latin American countries as the price of fresh loans, with the difference that the Nicaraguans were not going to get any loans, and they knew it. To stave off complete economic disintegration in January 1988, the government began to fire workers, consolidate ministries, and remove subsidies on food. But the measures were insufficient; the economy did not improve, and in January 1989 President Daniel Ortega carried the reforms further. Overnight most remaining subsidies and exchange controls were removed, and prices rose to world market levels. But wages did not rise, and in April 1989 a nurse, for example, earned 150,000 cordobas a month, slightly more than $20. This was enough to buy one pair of cheap shoes, or to visit a doctor, or to buy beans and rice for two people for a month, but not enough to do more than one of those things. Government budgets were slashed; the health budget was cut by two thirds. People had to bring their own surgical gloves and syringes when they went to the hospital. Schools had no books and sometimes no chairs, and after the early achievements of the revolution in teaching Nicaraguans to read, now the rural poor were slipping back into illiteracy. Between 1979 and 1989 the buying power of a Nicaraguan worker fell 92 percent; Nicaragua surpassed Haiti as the poorest country in the hemisphere.

Before he became minister of economy, commerce, and industry, Carrión had served as first vice-minister of the interior. The sign outside the Interior Ministry proclaimed it the "Sentinel of the People's Happiness," and it was entrusted with the defense of the revolution. That defense included censoring the press, sending shock troops to beat up opposition politicians, arresting strikers, and rewarding "revolutionary vigilance" performed on one's neighbors. Carrión himself was directly responsible for security, for the networks of informers and infiltrators throughout Nicaragua, and the jails that became notorious for their mistreatment of political prisoners.

How had these phenomena crept into a revolution whose idealism I, along with most of the world, admired? Carrión's activities seemed to reflect the revolution's course. I looked him up and found him to be serious, thoughtful, and intelligent. He does not talk in dogma when the occasion does not require it, and he does not hesitate to point out the ironies of his career: that a man who had become a Marxist because he detested brutality and inequality subsequently found himself in charge of meting out first repression and then draconian capitalism to Nicaragua. As Carrión sees it, Nicaragua's problems were the result of the aggression of the United States, a country that could not tolerate a Latin American revolution. All the unpleasant and unpopular measures he was now compelled to take were a direct result of this hostility. All revolutions, he believes, are therefore condemned to endure what the Nicaraguan revolution suffered. "Every single progressive step that has been tried in this continent has been met with destabilization or open war from the United States," he told me.

The United States' economic embargo of Nicaragua, its blockage of international loans, and its invention, training, funding, and maintenance of the contras certainly made up an overwhelming "harsh reality," as Carrión put it, facing the Sandinistas. But there were other less obvious harsh realities that Carrión seemed unwilling to factor in, perhaps because they were by-products of the glories of revolution. The revolution meant that after lifetimes of exploitation the poor and victimized overthrew a dictatorship that served only the rich, that people forced into silence for centuries were now encouraged to participate and organize, that the government no longer desired to keep the poor as "Oxen" (as Somoza liked to say) but taught them to demand power, that beans and rice were now within the reach of every Nicaraguan, that the poor had access to goods before available only to the rich, and that the oligarchy that had been so powerful and wealthy suddenly was neither, and that the local superpower was no longer assured that its interests would come first. These are the ingredients that have come to characterize third world leftist revolution; a government that does not seriously alter the patterns of power is not worthy of the term "revolutionary" as we understand it today.

But these miraculous events may also be described by their obverse sides: Brought to power by war, the revolution arrived with a siege mentality that confused opposition with betrayal and revenge with justice. The new ideology required that Nicaraguans join the committees, cheer at the rallies, and mouth the phrases even after the constant meetings had become oppressive and the words had turned sour. The Sandinistas' mission to raise the consciousness of the poor decayed into the arrogant notion that they, by definition, spoke for the people. With a policy of cheap food, the state paid farmers less for their beans, so they planted less. The system of rationing goods created corruption and speculation. The wealthy sent their money to safer havens abroad, and many with educations emigrated to countries where their skills would be rewarded. The same conditions that characterize revolution make it nearly impossible for revolution to succeed. All Latin American revolutions will end up like ours, Carrión said, and he may be right, although for a larger reason than he believes.

CARRIÓN'S FATHER OPENED THE FAMILY SCRAPBOOK TO SHOW ME a clipping from a 1980 edition of *Barricada*, the official Sandinista newspaper. Luis Carrión, comandante of the revolution, bearded and uniformed, was announcing a reorganization of local government to the cheers of the crowd. On the facing page was a faded photo from 1963 of Luis Carrión receiving a medal as the best sixth-grade student in Nicaragua. I turned the page. There was Comandante Carrión carrying the coffin of a Sandinista martyr. Facing it was a photo of Carrión at age six on horseback, winning a medal in a jumping contest. Another photo: Carrión as a teenager receiving a gold watch as his high school's best student. It is Anastasio Somoza, president of Nicaragua, who presents him with the watch. "He's not political, is he?" Somoza asks Carrión's father.

Luis Carrión was born in 1952, the first son of Luis Carrión Montoya, one of Nicaragua's richest men. Carrión Montoya was the chief executive officer and principal shareholder of BANIC, the most important financial group in the country, and its largest real estate developer. Among the luxury residential neighborhoods Carrión built was Las Colinas in the hills outside Managua. It was there, in a mansion staffed with servants, that Luis and a younger sister and brother, Gloria and Carlos, grew up. On weekends the children rode horses on the family's four-thousand-acre farm.

Within the context of their society Mrs. Carrión was a bit of a rebel. Despite the presence of three maids, Gloria said, the children had to make their own beds. When Gloria rejected the traditional coming-out party and refused to be named sweetheart of the country club, her mother supported her over her father's furious objections.

Of the three, Luis seemed the most unlikely future renegade. "He was the best student, best behaved in the house, the best at everything," Gloria said. "He was disciplined and a little shy. I didn't like him. He was my mother's pet, and I was jealous. He got to go to the movies in the middle of the week because of his grades; he got to go to the boxing matches. We didn't.

"What my father wanted for me was to learn a few languages and marry well," said Gloria, who became the head of the Frente Sandinista women's organization and, later, a *frente* official. "I went to California to study when I was fourteen. I studied at the Sorbonne. I was in New York, in Paris, at the best hotels and restaurants. It was the fulfillment of every aspiration I was supposed to have. But I saw it all and felt, 'There's nothing here. It must be somewhere else.' " During her summer vacations she returned to Nicaragua and worked as a translator for religious groups on a rural health mission.

Their younger brother, Carlos, recalled that one day when he was being driven to school, he noticed signs hanging outside other high schools announcing that students had gone on strike. The signs demanded liberty for political prisoners jailed by the Somoza dictatorship and the readmission of expelled students. "I started to wonder why my school wasn't striking," he said. "I began to think maybe we should do something." A few days later Carlos organized a strike in his high school. He was to spend the last five months before the revolution in jail, twenty-three of those days under torture.

But Luis was the dutiful son, the one who seemed likely to fulfill his parents' expectations that the boy would become not just a banker, like his father and his mother's brother, but a leader in Nicaraguan society. When he was five, he used to go around saying, "When I'm president . . . ," his mother told me. He attended the Colegio Centroamerica, Nicaragua's most exclusive prep school, in the conservative city of Granada, where he learned from the most traditional priests. Somoza could rest assured; he was not political. "I was very naive," he said. "I knew there was injustice, but I didn't know what to do about it."

He started figuring it out in the United States. For his last year of high school his father sent him to Phillips Exeter Academy in New Hampshire. For the first time he was surrounded by organized rebellion. It was 1969, and his fellow students were consumed by the anti-Vietnam War movement. Carrión started going to demonstrations and marches. He wrote letters to President Nixon condemning the "genocidal imperialist war." After

Exeter—where he made the honor roll every term—he enrolled at Rensselaer Polytechnic Institute, a small engineering college in upstate New York. Politically Carrión was waking up, but his classmates seemed to him to be sleeping, interested only in making money. His fellow Latinos, most of whom came from families like his, were particularly reactionary. He took more and more interest in the copy of *La Prensa*, the anti-Somoza newspaper, which his parents sent him each week.

A conservative economics professor assigned Karl Marx's *Communist Manifesto* to Carrión's class. The professor wanted to pick holes in it; Carrión found that it helped him make sense of many of the things that had been bothering him. He began to wonder what he was doing attending classes in the United States when at home, he read in *La Prensa*, students were protesting against the dictatorship by striking and taking over schools and churches. "I felt useless in the United States," he said. He called his father and said he wanted to come home.

"You'll lose my friendship," warned his father.

"If I have to choose between my ideals and your friendship, I choose my ideals," Luis replied.

Carrión Montoya slammed the phone down so hard he broke it.

A few weeks later, in June 1971, Luis Carrión came home and enrolled in the National University in Managua. "I still didn't know what form my involvement would take," he said, "but it was clear to me that to find out I had to be in Nicaragua and part of the political struggle."

FOR THE FIRST TIME LUIS CARRIÓN OPENED HIS EYES TO THE other Nicaragua. More than half of all Nicaraguans could not read; in some parts of the countryside, illiteracy reached 90 percent. ("I don't want educated people," Somoza liked to say. "I want oxen.") Most children under five were malnourished.

Anastasio Somoza distinguished himself from other banana republic dictators only in his genius for corruption. When an earthquake in 1972 killed thirteen thousand people and destroyed or damaged 80 percent of the buildings in Managua, Somoza and his family stole not only the foreign cash that arrived for reconstruction but also the cement, the tents, the machinery, the shovels, even the beans and rice coming from overseas. He was not the most repressive dictator in the hemisphere, but he held his own; the opposition newspaper, *La Prensa*, the unions, and the political organizations were kept in line through jailings, harassments, beatings, and the occasional well-timed assassination. The only tolerated opposition was the Conservative party (the Somozas were Liberals), which dutifully lost more or less regular presidential elections, at times with its candidate sitting in one of Somoza's jails throughout the campaign.

"I rejected the arbitrariness, the political repression, the running over of people in general," said Carrión. "There were no rights. The majority of people was completely excluded from power. It was not even possible to protest." Few Nicaraguans felt their country was their own. The Somoza family owned 20 percent of the country; many people believed that the United States controlled the rest.

"If you were traveling and you said you were from Nicaragua, people said, 'Ah, Somoza's hacienda,' " recalled Moisés Hassán, one of the Sandinistas on the original five-member junta. "What could you say? You had to swallow it. I resented the humiliating situation of the average Nicaraguan, who practically had no rights. If you were walking in the street and met a member of the National Guard—it didn't matter what rank—and he didn't like your face, he could just hit you. It would do absolutely no good to complain, and everyone knew it. I resented the fact that the U.S. Embassy was the center of power, that Nicaragua was subjugated to North American power. There was such a sense of humiliation, frustration, and inequality."

By the time of the revolution resentment against the United States had been mounting for 129 years. U.S. Marines made their first landing on Nicaraguan soil in 1850. Thereafter the United States intervened in Nicaragua more often than in any other Latin American country. In 1856 the U.S. adventurer William Walker got himself "elected" president of Nicaragua, instituting a form of democracy that the Somozas eventually perfected. U.S. President Franklin Pierce formally recognized Walker's presidency.

In 1909 the United States became displeased with President José Santos Zelaya (who was, in fact, a Nicaraguan). The problem was not Zelaya's corruption or his reluctance to leave office after sixteen years, but that he canceled the concessions of some U.S. businesses. Following the threat of overthrow from the United States, Zelaya chose to resign. For the next twenty-four years the country was under almost continual U.S. Marine occupation. By the 1920s several guerrilla bands had sprung up, dedicated to the overthrow of the U.S.-backed government. One was led by a small man in a large hat named Augusto César Sandino. U.S. President Calvin Coolidge sent Henry Stimson to Nicaragua as a special envoy. Stimson succeeded in persuading most of the guerrilla leaders to give up their struggle if American troops would "guarantee order, liberty, and prosperity." The single exception was Sandino, who did not want to see the United States guarantee anything. To keep the peace, Stimson established the Nicaraguan National Guard, an organization whose good conduct would be assured because it would be trained and supervised by the United States.

In 1927 the Marines began their pursuit of Sandino. When they left, unsuccessful, six years later, they turned the National Guard over to Anastasio Somoza García, who had ingratiated himself with Stimson largely because of his command of English, becoming Stimson's translator. After the Marines pulled out, Nicaragua's president invited Sandino to a marathon negotiation session at the president's house. After this conference members of the Guard took Sandino to the airport, and there they killed him.

Somoza was already more powerful than the president, and in 1936 he staged a military coup, formally taking power. He called an election, won by 107,000 votes to 169, and founded a dynasty that was to last forty-three years. He was shot to death in 1956. Somoza's son Luis, the least despotic of the family, turned over the presidency to a puppet front man in 1963. Three years later, Luis's brother, Anastasio Jr., became president. He was training his own son for the job when Luis Carrión returned to Managua in 1971.

CARRIÓN BEGAN TO STUDY MARXISM IN SECRET WITH A DOZEN National University classmates. They demonstrated for the freedom of political prisoners and marched with the teachers' union, the leaders of the anti-Somoza protests. But Carrión and his friends were restless; they felt as if they were playacting. A real commitment, they decided, meant leaving their comfortable homes and the social world of their parents, who could not understand why their children talked so much about the poor yet would not go to charity balls.

One afternoon in November 1971 Carrión and his fellow students knocked on the door of the parish house of Our Lady of Fatima, in the working-class neighborhood of Riguero. Father Uriel Molina, the parish priest, opened the door to find a dozen young men he had never seen before. They told him that they wanted to form a Christian community in his parish and to live and work with the poor. Molina blinked. "Well, all right," he said. An hour later the students returned with mattresses and blankets.

Carrión and his friends chose Molina, who also taught at the Catholic University of Central America, because he was one of the country's few radical priests. Molina believed in liberation theology. How closely this theology—heavily influenced by Pope John XXIII's Second Vatican Council in 1962 and named and developed by Gustavo Gutiérrez, a Peruvian priest—actually skirts advocating revolution is a matter of dispute, but it certainly caused a revolution within the church. It broke the historical trinity of priest, soldier, and landowner. For the first time members of the church placed themselves against the traditional oligarchy and became agents of change.

This was a dramatic departure for an institution that up to then was one of the most powerful conservative forces on the continent. The Catholic Church's evangelism in Latin America had gone hand in hand with the Spanish Crown's pillage. King Ferdinand and Queen Isabel interpreted the discovery of the New World as God's endorsement of their role as the protectors of Catholicism. Wary that the pope, one of the most powerful political figures in Europe, could exercise an anti-Spanish influence in the New World, the Spanish monarchs blocked all papal communication with the priests in America. Tithes collected in America went not to Rome but to Spain. Priests answered to the Spanish crown; they could not even move a parish without first consulting Spain.

Totally dependent on the Spanish monarchy, the priests became agents of the conquest. Unconcerned about the Indians' bodies, the Spanish were very worried about their souls, and they thought the Indians ungrateful when they did not see the new gospel as adequate compensation for their victimization. The church received large tracts of land to supervise the Indians' conversion. The bishops' power was not simply religious but political, some enjoying powers similar to those of regional governors.

Catholicism helped the Indians accept their fate. It emphasized submission to authority, that poverty and servility in this life— suffering as Christ had suffered—would assure the toiling believer of a place in heaven. Peasant uprisings, said the church hierarchy in the 1800s, were part of the "intrinsic evil" of the campesinos, a "primitive form of rebellion against authority and a violent protest against private property."

The traditional church never advocated education for the masses. Its schools serve the children of the elites; the great Catholic universities of Latin America are almost always the most expensive and exclusive. To the poor, the traditional church offers its saints. The believing poor see their saints as intensely personal protectors. Each person has one correct saint among the hundreds to choose from: a saint to watch over bakers; another for shoeshine boys; another for lottery ticket sellers. The saints bring good fortune and bad, their power robbing the poor of control over their own lives, encouraging passivity and silence.

In Nicaragua the priests encouraged their flocks to accept the Somoza dictatorship and the National Guard as the will of God and to pray for the health of whichever Somoza happened to be in power. While the Marines searched for Sandino, Archbishop José Antonio Lezcano y Ortega met with Marine Lieutenant Colonel Elias Beadle, the Guard chief, who asked for the church's collaboration in this latest "pacification" of Nicaragua. The archbishop wrote a letter to his priests, recommending giving the National Guard "all your moral support. In exchange for this cooperation, Mr. Beadle assures me he will correct the mistakes made by his officials and enlisted men in the National Guard." In a grotesque ceremony in the cathedral in 1942, Archbishop Lezcano y Ortega crowned Somoza's daughter Lilliam "Army Queen." In 1956 a new archbishop granted two hundred days of grace to all Nicaraguans who attended Somoza García's funeral.

The liberation theology that Carrión, his friends, and later much of Sandinista Nicaragua embraced offered an alternative. It was a new reading of the Bible, changing the traditional focus from ministering to the wealthy to serving the poor. Instead of a way to keep the poor in their place, Catholicism would be a way to help them improve their lives, educating them not to accept but to question and organize, to demand their rights and recognize injustice.

It is difficult to imagine anything more controversial. Suddenly, following the Latin American Bishops' Conference in Medellín in 1968, a large minority of the priests of the Catholic Church—Latin America's single most powerful institution, for centuries the defender of society's traditions—began to teach hundreds of millions of the Latin American poor to question and rebel. The political possibilities were staggering.

In Nicaragua liberation theology found an early and passionate advocate in Ernesto Cardenal, a poet and Trappist monk, who set up a Christian community on the desolate archipelago of Solentiname in Lake Nicaragua in 1966. Cardenal, who was to become the Sandinistas' minister of culture, soon declared himself one of a group of seven priests calling themselves Brothers in Marx. In the late 1960s the movement spread, giving rise to strikes in the Catholic high schools and the universities and to Christian base communities—small groups that met to read the Bible and organize to solve local problems, often led by lay preachers instead of priests. After the revolution, even as the Catholic hierarchy continued to reject liberation theology, the Sandinistas and most of the country's priests turned Nicaragua into the Latin American mecca of left-wing Catholicism.

That liberation theology would one day enjoy the government's backing would have seemed unlikely to the students who knocked on Molina's door in 1971; they were still worrying about their parents' backing. Their parents had tolerated it when their sons with brand-new Buicks insisted on taking crowded, noisy, dirty buses to the university. But that they would leave comfortable houses to go camp on the floor in a crowded, noisy, dirty barrio was too much. Communism had gone too far. Carrión Montoya went to the parish. Molina showed him in and offered him a glass of brandy. Carrión Montoya waved it away. "No, Father, let there be no mistake," he said. "You are my class enemy. You are forcing our children to change so that they'll join a community of the poor and leave behind the culture of their own class." It was hard for him to call Molina "Father."

The group called itself the University Community. In the morning the students read the Bible; in the afternoon they tried to organize the barrio so that the neighborhood could set about solving its problems. They tried to talk to residents not only about poor sanitation and high food prices but also about what the group considered those problems' root causes. Carrión's specialty was Marxist speeches to Christian base communities about capitalist exploitation and imperialism. In the evenings the students, their friends, and their girlfriends played guitars around a campfire and argued about poetry and politics. On hot nights everyone tried to squeeze into Molina's small room, the only one with air conditioning.

Their political action went beyond the barrio. To protest milk price hikes, they threw nails on the road outside the milk factories to puncture the trucks' tires, then distributed the milk to the poor. "I saw Luis at a protest once," Carrión Montoya told me. "I shouted to him, 'You know that you're killing your mother, don't you?' " In late December 1972 they occupied the cathedral with other like-minded groups, planning to fast for three days to protest the commercialization of Christmas. The fast ended on its second day as the great earthquake struck Managua.

"Luis was never really a Christian," Father Molina said. "He had a restlessness that led him in a Christian direction. He was the intellectual of the group. He prayed, but he was not a man who expressed himself that way. He was one of the most serious, most honest of the group. He never talked about superficial things."

"I was, at that moment, a convinced Christian," Carrión wrote years later. "Christianity gave me the ideological tools to break with the bourgeois ideology that had been inculcated in me by my family and studies, because when you read the Bible honestly, you see that it's a revolutionary book, 'subversive,' as they came to call it under Somoza."

It was not surprising that Carrión and those like him would turn to Marxism. That the Soviet Union in the early 1970s was going through the worst stagnation of the last few decades mattered little to the students. Just as rebellious teenagers believe they will never fall into the little corruptions and compromises of their parents' lives, most revolutionaries regard their movement as different.

What mattered to Carrión and his classmates, in any case, was not the objective reality of communism but the objective reality of capitalism. They knew that the poor had nothing in Nicaragua and the rich had everything. A system that promised a drastic redistribution of wealth became a natural model.

And to be a revolutionary in Nicaragua meant joining the Frente Sandinista. The *frente* had been founded in 1961 by Carlos Fonseca, Tomás Borge, and Silvio Mayorga. Its guerrillas were few in 1971, but they were supported by hundreds of city collaborators organized into Sandinista cells. Many were non-Marxists simply interested in getting rid of Somoza. While the University Community students were watching the *frente* with interest, the *frente* was also studying them. The University Community was building political organizations in the barrios under the protective umbrella of Christianity. The *frente* could use those organizations for its own ends. Nor did the cars, and the houses and farms of the students' parents, escape the *frente*'s notice.

In October 1972 two *frente* activists, Ricardo Morales Aviles and Bayardo Arce, a *La Prensa* reporter who eventually became a comandante, dropped by the parish to see Carrión. Carrión had been waiting. He told Arce and Aviles he was eager to work with the *frente*. The other students said that they wanted to help as well. Father Molina was in Chile at the time, attending a meeting. When he came back, he found that his Christian community had become a revolutionary cell. Gradually the students, assigned to other tasks, began to leave the parish.

Carrión became a city organizer for the *frente*, preaching Sandinista gospel to groups of young Christians. He grew increasingly estranged from his parents. At one point while they were on safari in Africa, Luis and Carlos turned the house into a Sandinista operations center. The compañeros ate three months' worth of the family's food in two weeks. Carrión neglected to replenish the pantry. When his parents returned and demanded an explanation from one of the maids, she told them that a group of strange young men who went out only at night had been staying at the house. "I understand you want to overthrow everything I stand for," Carrión Montoya roared at his son. "But don't use my house and car to do it. Someday you and I are going to find ourselves in opposing trenches." Luis Carrión stole his father's rifles and left for Costa Rica.

Gloria and Carlos went to visit him. The three had taken separate journeys to the same political destination. Carlos was already a member of the *frente*; Luis would shortly be made Carlos's political chief; Gloria would soon start running a clandestine *frente* publishing house. But it was in Costa Rica that they really sat down and talked about politics for the first time. Carrión seemed different, Gloria said. He had grown a beard and was thinner than before. He had always been closed, enigmatic, self-sufficient. Now she found him more open, more willing to talk.

Inside Nicaragua the movement against Somoza was swelling. In late 1977 the *frente* began to launch major attacks on National Guard troops. On January 10, 1978, Pedro Joaquín Chamorro, the editor of *La Prensa*, was shot to death on a Managua street corner, spurring even non-Sandinistas to action. A group of prominent businessmen, priests, and intellectuals, known as Los Doce ("the twelve"), declared their support for the Sandinista struggle and began to tour the world, asking for help. President Carter's administration, which wanted to see a moderate, pro-business government in power, was maneuvering clumsily to ease Somoza out. Even the Catholic Church had joined the anti-Somoza clamor. On August 3, 1978, the Nicaraguan Conference of Bishops, led by Archbishop Miguel Obando y Bravo, who later became de facto head of the opposition to the Sandinistas, wrote a letter calling for Somoza's resignation.

Carrión came back to Managua and lived underground for a time. Soon the *frente* sent him to a ranch in the north for thirteen days of military training. After his training he received command of a brigade in Chontales, in the center of Nicaragua. When he arrived in Chontales, he found his brigade waiting for him: nine men with two .22 rifles and a revolver. Carrión stared at the arsenal. "What were you thinking?" he asked.

"We were sure that one day we'd have contact with the *frente*," an old man replied.

A few days later two more soldiers arrived. With his eleven men—only two of whom had combat experience—Carrión attacked a base in Rama staffed by eight hundred national guardsmen. The attack failed completely, and one of his men was killed and another wounded. But as the fighting intensified in other areas, his troops grew in number and experience. Most of the Guard in Carrión's zone left for the south, enabling Carrión's men to take the city of Jinotega.

By then Somoza's air force was bombing Nicaragua's cities; fifty thousand people were to be killed over the course of the revolution. But it was too late for Somoza. Most of Nicaragua's youth who were not in the National Guard were fighting with or working for the Frente. In June 1979 the Nicaraguan Bishops' Conference wrote a pastoral letter supporting armed struggle as a legitimate means of defeating the dictatorship. On July 17, 1979, Somoza and his mistress boarded a plane for Florida. National Guard soldiers deserted, returning to their homes or fleeing Nicaragua, and the Guard dissolved. On July 19, Managua fell to the rebels. People lined the streets to cheer and throw flowers as the fighters streamed into Managua from all over the country, on foot, on bicycles, crammed into trucks.

Luis Carrión Cruz had fulfilled his destiny. The son of privilege, graduate of Phillips Exeter Academy, politically awakened by the United States and *La Prensa,* he took his place, at the age of twenty-six, as the youngest of the nine comandantes who formed the Sandinistas' National Directorate, which now ran Nicaragua. He had become, in the furthest possible way from his father's wishes, a leader of his country.

TIME BEGAN THAT DAY. "IT WAS LIKE THE COMING OF CHRIST," a friend who was fourteen at the time recalled. "Nothing was ever going to go wrong again." The country was dazed, euphoric. People wandered the streets singing and hugging total strangers. On the afternoon of July 19, 1979, all Managua packed into the central plaza—now renamed the Plaza de la Revolución—waving red and black Sandinista flags and ignoring the speeches of the new comandantes. At night in the barrios there was the crackle of bonfires, the sound of salsa music and of drunk young guerrillas arguing and firing their rifles, and the cries of mothers as sons who had been in the mountains for years suddenly appeared in their doorways. The day after the Triumph, Carrión and Joaquín Cuadra, a member of the University Community who was to become chief of staff of the armed forces, went to Molina's parish house. "We told you so," they said, embracing Molina.

On July 20 the intoxication wore off and the hangover set in. Nicaragua awoke to realize that the regime had not just fallen, the entire state had dissolved. There were no courts, no congress, no army, no ministries, and no bureaucrats. "The nine of us had never gotten together to talk about how to run a government," said Carrión. "We had the *frente* platform, but it was vague. The confusion was total. The immensity of the task, the total anarchy, suddenly hit us. We had to construct a whole state from scratch." The compañeros knew how to run a revolution: They could design posters, spray-paint walls, hold meetings, and make bombs. They could blow up power lines, but they could not reconnect them. They could make endless speeches. But running a ministry was something else. No one would take orders. Everyone had defended his barrio and killed *guardia*; everyone was a revolutionary hero. Revolutionary heroes did not want to be told to mix cement. A mayor's office could be shut down for days because no one knew where to find typewriter ribbons.

But the chaos didn't seem to matter; this was a party. Nicaragua didn't need mayors' offices. This was the workers' state. "Everyone was his own boss," said Moisés Hassán, who was put in charge of reconstructing the city of Masaya. "We expected that all authority would disappear. We expected that with the end of Somoza's corruption there would be plenty of resources for the people and we would have better lives." For the first years the absurdities of Nicaragua—the telephone company headquarters where the phones didn't work, the buses whose drivers chose any routes they pleased—were the baby missteps of a people improvising a new country, proof that Nicaragua was truly Latin and gloriously free.

Revolutionary spirit—the feeling of romance and self-sacrifice called *mística*—made up for a lot. Volunteers, 18,000 of them, went to the farthest corners of the country to teach 150,000 of Somoza's "oxen" how to read. Another 100,000 formed health brigades or worked several days a week in their own cities giving vaccinations. The health workers eradicated polio and malaria, for a few years anyway. "We felt we could organize anything," Carrión recalled. "It didn't matter that there was no money."

To workers, the day of the Triumph was emancipation day. On many farms they could now knock off at ten in the morning, after four hours on the job. Campesinos had access to easy credit, in cash. Factory workers suddenly demanded reduced hours and better wages and shut down their factories with strikes if their demands were rejected.

But as workers found more and more to enjoy in the fruits of the workers' state, the more alarmed the government became. The Sandinistas had inherited a national treasury with enough hard currency to last for two days. Nicaragua had always suffered from an uneducated work force and lack of roads and infrastructure. Now there were more problems: the destruction brought by the war; leaders short on experience and organization; lack of money for imported goods such as fertilizers.

Nicaragua needed more production, not less. But the campesinos tended to see their new credits as the spoils of the revolution, not as a scarce resource to be guarded and invested. They did what they normally did when they had cash: They got drunk, and if there was money left over, they bought radios. The old system of production had been corrupt and inefficient. But at least it had produced something. What replaced it was general chaos. City dwellers now had cheaper food and a weekly basket of free rice, beans, sugar, cooking oil, and—if there was a young child—milk as well. But the peasants were receiving practically nothing for their crops; it was cheaper for them to buy beans and corn at a government store than to grow those crops themselves. Food production dropped. Strikes crippled the factories. The revolution was in danger of starving itself to death.

At the same time the wealthy were moving their money outside Nicaragua, thus fulfilling the constant Sandinista chant that they were betrayers of their country, Somocistas, sellouts, and tools of *yanqui* imperialism. "You couldn't really have expected the Sandinistas to say, 'You beautiful bourgeoisie, we love you,' after most had supported Somoza in a war that killed fifty thousand people," Carrión Montoya commented. But in fact, despite all the rhetoric about nationalizing businesses and industries, the Sandinistas behaved with restraint. Until 1981 the only property and businesses expropriated were those belonging to the Somozas and their associates. Yet this restraint created the worst possible combination of events: Businessmen were too nervous to invest in new stock or machinery and saw no reason to try to work with a government that insulted them at every opportunity. At the same time they enjoyed the freedom necessary to run their businesses into the ground and take their money to Miami.

Trapped by their own rhetoric, which had raised workers' expectations to unrealistic levels and frightened away capital, the Sandinistas began to use coercion. They began to expropriate more land and more factories, announcing each new expropriation to cheering crowds. They stopped talking about workers' and peasants' needs and began to talk about their obligations; the "workers' state" took on an ironic new meaning.

As guerrillas the Sandinistas had encouraged peasants to take over plots on large plantations; as ministers the Sandinistas now punished such land invasions. Wages dropped, and the government canceled the week of paid vacation that workers traditionally took at Easter. On July 27, 1981, the nine comandantes passed a law forbidding all work stoppages and strikes in order to "combat labor indiscipline and anarchy on the job." Dozens of union leaders were arrested. Union elections were rigged. They had to be; the Sandinista unions, mindful of the need to keep production high, often lost elections to opposition unions that promised workers more. Carlos Carrión told me about a roofing materials shop where the opposition union, the Workers' Front, promised the workers fewer hours for the same pay and a cafeteria with subsidized meals. The Sandinista union told workers they would have to work longer for the same pay to help the business stay afloat.

Luis Carrión, in a 1981 May Day speech to the Sandinista union coordinating committee, said workers who joined the militant opposition unions were "tricked and confused by the reactionary and sellout ideas of the bourgeoisie." In a speech in 1984 he argued that Nicaragua must suspend the right to strike in order to save it. "The right of the working class to strike is unquestionable," he said. "But to talk about it in the abstract is wasting time. The question we must answer is, Whose interests would be served by the instability and loss of production that would result? Would it benefit the working class or the people? Evidently not." Instead, he argued, strikes divert the workers' energy from the crucial task of fighting the imperialist aggressors.

"If they get their way," Carrión warned of the gringos, "they would do away with the gains of the revolution and, principally, the right to organize and strike."

UPON TAKING POWER, THE SANDINISTAS ABOLISHED THE DEATH penalty, ended censorship, and dissolved Somoza's National Security Office and the Military Intelligence Service. But the midnight knock on the door, like Somoza's labor code, crept back into official policy. And just as the Sandinistas believed that their measures against workers were an inevitable consequence of the situation, so their growing use of repression seemed to them a natural outgrowth of those harsh realities of revolution.

Somoza and his National Guard had been brutal to the Sandinistas while in office. Now it was the Sandinistas' turn. They did not torture or shoot the former enemy, the guardsmen, as Somoza might have done to his enemies. Instead, they set up special tribunals, judicial steamrollers that in the first two years after the revolution flattened nearly five thousand people, most of them former guardsmen. A judge could decide a prisoner's guilt on the basis of "personal conviction," the *feeling* that a defendant was guilty, rather than on the basis of evidence. Membership in the Guard or support of Somoza was a crime in itself, even if the accused had never stolen a pencil or picked up a gun. Many prisoners were held incommunicado, were never told the nature of the charges against them, and had no access to lawyers. Many were threatened with death during the investigations. The conviction rate was 78 percent.

This was accepted behavior in a society that had always put vengeance before justice, even more accepted during Nicaragua's passionate honeymoon with the Sandinistas. All Nicaragua was Sandinista. In 1980 Defense Minister Humberto Ortega gave a speech to literacy workers. "Do you agree that the Frente Sandinista with this Directorate should continue conducting the revolutionary power of Sandino's working people?" he asked. The crowd roared its approval. "Then this is a vote, a popular election; this is Sandinista democracy." They would hold elections, said Ortega, "to improve revolutionary power but not to raffle off who has power, because the people have power through their vanguard, the Sandinista National Liberation Front and its National Directorate."

In January 1980 the government closed an extreme left-wing newspaper for "inciting labor unrest." Six months later Alfonso Robelo, a politician who resigned from the ruling junta, was denied permission to hold a political rally. In October *La Prensa* was blocked from printing reports of protests on the Atlantic coast. The newspaper was closed for the first time for forty-eight hours on July 10, 1981. These events took place before President Reagan signed the order to provide covert funding to the contras in November 1981 and well before a CIA operation blew up two bridges near the Honduran border on March 14, 1982, signaling the start of the war.

THE WAR CHANGED EVERYTHING. AT FIRST IT INTENSIFIED THE *mística* and patriotism. Nicaragua was under attack, and the vast majority of its citizens closed ranks around the Sandinistas. But gradually the war began to have the opposite effect, by sharpening the harsh realities that now always defined the edges of Sandinismo. There would be little money for books and vaccinations, for repairing streets and importing tractors. The hospitals treated not children but soldiers, some of whom were children themselves. And if once there had been room in the revolution for at least some opposition and dissent, that, too, vanished.

In the months before the war, Vice-Minister of the Interior Luis Carrión's worries were gloriously mundane: building and training a police force, reorganizing the jails to fight common crime. But he always believed war was inevitable. "We always knew we had to be on guard," he said. "I volunteered to come to the Interior Ministry. I understood that in the first years the situation would be complex and that I could play an important role in defending what we had gained." In May 1980 Giorgino Andrade, a volunteer in the literacy program, was killed by a group of former national guardsmen. "I had always known there would be a counterrevolution," Carrión said. "When Andrade was killed, I felt it with my heart as well as my head. I knew we were going to have a terrible war, and we would have to postpone a lot of things."

Two months later the Republican party platform in the United States demanded the overthrow of the Sandinistas. Ten days before Reagan's inauguration Carrión gave a speech warning Nicaragua that bad times were ahead. "We have to spend more on our defense than Somoza spent," he said, "because Somoza had a very powerful godfather in the north and his back was covered by friendly dictatorships. We have to defend ourselves, with our own hands, nails, and teeth if necessary. We have to produce more and spend less. We want to ask our working class that this Saturday morning, which you have off, be replaced by working next Saturday afternoon." The crowd responded with "National Directorate—give your orders!"

The day after the contras blew up the bridges on March 14, 1982, the Sandinistas instituted a state of emergency, jailing political activists and stepping up censorship of the press. By then the existence of the contras, their CIA funding and training by some of the least savory elements of the Argentine military were widely known. *The New York Times* was quoting high U.S. government officials saying that the United States "would not rule out" direct military action. The Sandinistas began to expand their army.

Luis Carrión took charge of the security of Managua. He set up networks of informers, who infiltrated the contras and spied on the barrios. He helped organize the Sandinista People's Militias, whose sheer numbers helped offset their lack of military training; many were directed by thirteen-year-olds who didn't seem to know how to use their AK-47s but clearly relished having one. He brought in East German and Cuban advisers to teach the police how to interrogate prisoners. "We wanted to stop the sabotage, terrorism, and political assassinations planned for the cities," he said. "We tried to develop the capacity to watch the CIA."

Carrión's work had two goals. One was to keep the contras from building the kind of city organization that had served the Sandinistas so well. He was remarkably successful. Remove the Sandinista infiltrators, the joke went, and you'd have no contras left. The contras never managed to paint slogans on even one wall in Managua. Meanwhile, the contra army was crawling with Sandinistas; even the houseboy of Enrique Bermúdez, the contra military commander, turned out to be a Sandinista spy.

The second goal was to show the United States, particularly after the invasion of Grenada in 1983, that an invasion of Nicaragua would not be completed over a long weekend. The militias were proof that the Sandinistas had enough support to arm their citizens, a policy that in most other Latin American countries would have produced instant insurrection. Every time a militia dug a trench or a company held a training drill, Sandinista TV cameras were there to cover it.

If the Sandinistas had not been able to convince Nicaraguans to embrace a one-party state, Reagan did it for them. There were a few who threw their lot in with the contras and the United States, mostly wealthy businessmen and northern campesinos, but the vast majority of the Nicaraguans I met said that although they had serious complaints about different aspects of the revolution, they felt criticism was unpatriotic while Nicaragua was under siege.

After decades on the hacienda of Somoza, Nicaraguans now relished their worldwide celebrity status as the small country that told the *yanqui* giant to stuff it. The country became one huge billboard. Murals showed heroic workers with rippling muscles, their fists striking eagles marked "CIA." Slogans appeared everywhere: "Here no one gives up," "We don't give up or sell out," or the more picturesque "Let your mother give up." The right of Nicaragua to make its own mistakes was more important to most Nicaraguans than the mistakes themselves. Reagan never managed to unite Democrats and Republicans in the United States behind his Nicaragua policy. He did however, manage to unite Nicaragua.

Reagan's second favor was to give the Sandinistas a war they could blame for the problems the revolution itself had helped to create. But this was of limited use; in the end the excuse paled in comparison with the misery the war genuinely created. Seen from Washington, Reagan compiled a record of almost perfect failure in Nicaragua: The Sandinistas outlasted him; the contras were brutal and comically inept; the United States reinforced its reputation as a bully willing to break international law for its own ends and lost influence in Latin America on more important issues. But seen from Managua, the contra war succeeded brilliantly. It ruined the tottering economy and provoked increased repression. If the United States intended the war as a vaccine against future revolutions in Latin America, it may well have succeeded.

"We had no economic policy during the war," Carrión told me. "It was a political policy. The economic policy was determined by the need to defend the revolution. Resources and products were assigned to protect the lowest sectors, the people who bore the heaviest burden of defense. We made mistakes. But we could not have thought in terms of economic rationality in 1984 or 1986."

In Managua the war's most obvious effect was to prevent the cleanup of the chaos that already ruled. When I first arrived in Nicaragua in 1985, the country was two disasters behind. Managua had collapsed like an accordion in the earthquake of 1972, and Somoza's bombings during the insurrection destroyed much of what remained. In 1985, Managua looked haunted. The shards of stained glass had not yet been swept off the parapet of the cathedral on the central plaza. One of the two crosses on the cathedral towers was broken off. Inside, weeds and small trees grew in the dust. The stone was cracked and gray. The stairways were dark and smelled like public toilets. Garbage was all over; even the altar was littered with toilet paper.

I climbed up to the top parapet and walked around the cathedral. Across the plaza is the eternal flame of Carlos Fonseca, the commander in chief of the revolution. To the north lies Lake Nicaragua, a biologically dead lake, killed by discharges from chemical companies. "Downtown" Managua stretches out to the south. A huge seventeen-story white tower—the Bank of America Building—sticks improbably up over the city. Behind it are the only new buildings, the white and terra-cotta Government House offices, which are surrounded by fields, some with horses grazing, and the skeletons of collapsed buildings, concrete bones with no skin or flesh. People had moved into the rubble and hung hammocks from the protruding beams.

The streets and sidewalks are cratered with potholes deeper than I am tall, and there are few working streetlights; going out for an evening stroll is not for the fainthearted. Only two or three streets in the city have names. Addresses—even for delivering mail—are "two blocks south and half a block toward the lake from where the big tree used to be," referring to where the tree had stood before the earthquake, the implied meaning being "Ask someone."

The war produced less evident but more important chaos: ludicrous economic distortions; filling a gas tank cost less than buying a Coke. Meanwhile, the United States blocked multilateral lending organizations from making loans to Nicaragua and pressured Mexico and Venezuela to cut off Nicaragua's cheap oil. The 1985 U.S. economic embargo did further damage, cutting Nicaragua off from the United States, its largest and closest market and source of imports. And of course, the war altered the government's priorities. While in the revolution's first years social spending accounted for 50 percent of the national budget and defense 20 percent, by 1987 the figures were reversed.

The cruelest price was food shortages. Milk production in 1985 was one fiftieth what it had been before the revolution; only families with infant children could obtain milk. By 1985, too, rice, which made up half the average Nicaraguan's diet, was rationed at a pound a week per person. The combination of bad policies and the cost of the war produced rampant inflation, rising from 40 percent in 1984 to 300 percent in 1985, spiraling up to more than 30,000 percent in 1988. Shortly before the war ended in 1988, government economists calculated that its total cost would come to more than $3.5 billion, twice the country's yearly gross national product.

JOHNNY BRICEÑO HAD BEEN DEEPLY IN LOVE WITH THE REVOLUtion. But over the years the relationship changed. At times he and Sandinismo were barely speaking, and toward the end of the 1980s they settled into a comfortable, if passionless, arrangement. It was common. Most Nicaraguans had learned to live around the revolution, not thinking about it very much. In the beginning they were possessed, seeing themselves and their country through the haze of *mística*. But for all but the fiercest Sandinistas, *mística* at some point ran up against those ubiquitous harsh realities and faded into indifference or cynicism. For some this was a painful realization, but they learned to live with that, too.

I got to the basketball courts behind the Government House

late. Johnny was already there, trying to teach a group of teenaged boys and girls wearing their school skirts, knee socks, and white blouses, not to carry the ball and run at the same time. I was guarding Johnny. He had put on twenty pounds since getting out of the army, but he was still a lot faster than I was.

After two games the girls left, and the boys followed them. Johnny beat me twice at a shooting game, Horse. It was growing dark, and we sat down at an outdoor refreshment stand and ordered Pepsis. He was wearing the T-shirt he always wore to play basketball, painted with "Born to Be Nica"—in English. He had made it himself. The T-shirt was the statement of a man who lived in one world while carrying another world inside him. The two worlds happened to be at war with each other—he had been a soldier for one side—but they were peacefully coexisting inside Johnny.

Johnny—he asked me not to print his real name—was born and raised in the other world, in San Francisco, California, of Nicaraguan parents. Ten years before our basketball game, in March 1979, when he was fourteen, he came to Nicaragua for the first time, to visit family. When he got here, he realized that he had walked into a revolution. He had grown up in a rough part of San Francisco's Mission district. He had a knife tattooed on one arm and "nica" tattooed on the other. He knew how to shoot a .22 and a BB gun. But war was something else again. La Nicarao, where he was staying, was a very combative neighborhood. The local compañeros gave him an M-1 rifle and taught him to use it.

By June 1979 he had almost forgotten that he had ever lived anywhere else. "The revolution," he said, "was one of the most incredible things that happened in a million years. It changed the world. Everything would be fine from here on out."

He decided to stay in Nicaragua. His mother sent him the money to finish high school at the American school. When he was sixteen, he went to work as an international supervisor at the phone company. At eighteen he married a fellow American School student, the daughter of a U.S. relief worker.

There were problems, he recalled, but nobody really paid attention. "The *frente* was everything," he said. "Everyone went to New Song festivals to sing hymns to the revolution. Everyone was in the militias, with their brown and green uniforms. We called them Chocolitas after a chocolate milk that came in a bag.

"There was a tremendous feeling of unity," he said. "There were probably a lot of people taking advantage of the situation, but at the time we all could afford to be naive. There was a lot of mismanagement in high places, especially of the subsidized food, but we were too romantic to care. It was so romantic it was unreal. We thought everyone was in this together. On the news they showed Sergio [Vice President Sergio Ramírez] going to pick coffee. We were all like Che."

In May 1983 Johnny joined a special corps of soldiers to put up the first coast-to-coast phone lines. It was dangerous work; the soldiers erected the telephone poles during the day, and at night the contras blew them up. Finally they got a line through. Interior Minister Tomás Borge called Enrique Schmidt, the phone company director in Puerto Cabezas. "It was a great telephone call," said Johnny. "Everyone celebrated, and Borge said, 'Your children will remember you for this historic project,' that sort of thing. The next day the line was blown up again."

The war had started, he said, "but people were still so happy that we thought, "We'll kick their asses real soon." We thought it would be wrapped up right away." He wanted to give up his U.S. citizenship and join the army. But his wife wanted to move back to the United States and have children, and she didn't want the children to be orphans. The family broke up. She went to live in Washington, D.C.; Johnny joined the Sandinista army.

"I didn't feel any conflict about being from the States," he said. "I didn't grow up in white America; I never felt like an American. And I bought the whole thing here: how the U.S. was the one that supported the devil. I didn't hate the United States. By the time I had to kill people I had learned that the enemy had a face, and the face was the contras. In the bush it never crossed my mind that the United States was part of this. But then you never think of anything in the battlefield."

At first, he said, being in the army was romantic. "I wanted to kill all the motherfuckers, come back, get a Camilo Ortega medal for bravery and a hug, and be a hero." We were on a bus heading toward Johnny's house to watch the sixth game of the Nicaraguan baseball championships on television. The bus was jammed. I was sitting on a soldier's lap, holding on my lap a package of something greasy that belonged to a female soldier who hadn't gotten a seat.

We got off the bus and walked a few blocks through a working-class neighborhood to the small house Johnny shared with his brother. The baseball game was almost over. He went to his closet and took out his Camilo Ortega medal for bravery. He was one of three soldiers in his battalion of six hundred to win one. "You want to buy it?" he said. But he kept it in the pocket of his only suit.

We talked about the war. "We were the good guys. We were going to stand on one side and shoot at bad guys, who held knives between their teeth and kidnapped campesinos. The campesinos would hate them and love us," he said. "Little did I know that they *were* campesinos."

His trainers, mostly Cubans, taught him that if he fought by the book, then he wouldn't get shot. "Combat was abstract," he said. One day he was doing reconnaissance when the company ahead of him ran into three hundred contras. Fifteen Sandinista soldiers were killed. It was Johnny's first sight of newly dead men. "I felt, *Hey, we don't die. We're the good guys.*"

A short time later the contras ambushed the caravan of trucks in which Johnny was traveling. One boy got hit in the face with a grenade. "It took off his face," Johnny said. "He had his head buried in his hands, trying to pull off the rest of his skin. The doctor said, 'Don't touch yourself.' He didn't. He just lay down, whimpering quietly, and ten minutes later he died." For the first time Johnny became conscious of his mortality.

A short time later an even worse realization set in: There were no good guys. His company took a prisoner, a wounded contra. Johnny's captain shot the contra in the head. "It made me see the war was a war," Johnny said. He had personally shot a lot of prisoners, he said. "You couldn't tie your men down guarding prisoners in a battle. I didn't think it was wrong or right. I just did it."

But, he said, his company never abused civilians. "Sometimes we'd reach a village and ask campesinos how many contras had come through and when, and one man would give us one figure, and another would give us a different one. Or they'd say, 'They left three days ago,' when we knew they left yesterday. But we knew these campesinos were just victims. The contras weren't mercenaries, like the propaganda said. They were just campesinos. A lot of them didn't know where the U.S. was. A lot of them weren't making a cent. I didn't believe they hated me, and I didn't hate them. I captured them and I thought, *This guy is not the enemy.* The war made no sense."

The first time he was wounded doctors told him he would never walk again. He did, and returned to the front. He fought in the war for four years and was wounded five times before leaving the army for good. What drove him out, in the end, had nothing to do with bullets. In April 1987 he was a second lieutenant, traveling in a helicopter with the lieutenant of his battalion, a few more Sandinista soldiers, and a contra prisoner named Douglas, who was tied up on the floor of the chopper. Douglas was twenty-five, Johnny said, the intelligence officer for a contra regional command, defiant, a real believer. The Sandinista commanding officer was muttering at Douglas. Something was going on; the other soldiers began to get jumpy. The CO started yelling at Douglas, "Do you want me to throw you out?" He lifted Douglas off the floor and threw him out the door. Johnny watched through the window of the chopper as Douglas, still tied up, fell to the tree line. *That motherfucker's crazy,* he was thinking of his CO. "You might shoot a prisoner if you can't guard him, although we weren't even doing that anymore," he said. "But you don't go throwing people out of helicopters." He left the army.

When he got back to civilian Nicaragua, the revolution had changed. "The corruption was the biggest difference," he said. "I started meeting people who were real opportunists. People would say anything to get power and benefits. There was no *mística.* People become Sandinistas just to get a good position. I know that if a minister in Venezuela gives his girl friend a car, it's not really even considered corruption. Here it's judged that way because the economy is so much harder and because they are calling themselves revolutionaries."

Johnny joined the *frente,* but he hated going to meetings. Any detour from the *frente* line was considered an ideological weakness to be cured by self-criticism. One night during the meeting one of the men ran outside to buy a pastry and a soda. "The compañero is hungry," said Johnny loudly. "He suffers from petty bourgeois weaknesses." His little joke was met by silence, and then someone suggested that maybe Compañero Johnny had some problems of his own.

"I still have a lot of respect for the party," he told me. "But being a member isn't for me." He respected Daniel Ortega, he said. "He's not corrupt and still has *mística*. I'll vote for him. I'll fight if there's an invasion. I'll never leave." But it wasn't as it had been.

He was working as a tour guide, making about sixty dollars a month, bored silly and feeling useless. "Tours come in, gringos who tell me, 'Oh, things are so screwed up in the States. You're so lucky to be living in a workers' state.' I just say, 'Thank you.' " He laughed.

He still kept up with the States. Johnny's bookshelves were filled with new books from the United States, and he lent me *The Color Purple*, signed by Alice Walker, whom he had met. He had cassettes of rap and go-go and Tracy Chapman. But the United States was not his country anymore. "What did the States want?" he said. "They wanted to tear the country down, and they did. They wanted to destroy the economy and make Nicaragua negotiate, and they did. They wanted to change our political ideals. They did. After our revolution, the guerrillas in Guatemala, Salvador, Colombia, all thought they could win. Now they see again what the U.S. can do. I am still a socialist, and I know revolution is necessary. We have to think historically and sacrifice ourselves for succeeding generations. But for right now, we're living a nightmare in this hour of chaos, as Public Enemy put it in a good rap song."

THE SANDINISTAS HAD MANAGED TO PREVENT A U.S. MILITARY occupation of Nicaragua, but the battle against U.S. cultural imperialism was lost before it began. On billboards, in TV commercials, in newspaper articles, the Sandinistas constantly exhorted their countrymen to become New Nicaraguans, to adopt the values of solidarity and cooperation, to work to build Nicaragua, and, of course, to reject wasteful, consumerist, individualist U.S. culture.

They failed. A psychiatrist would have seen Nicaragua's relationship with the United States as the international equivalent not of Jungian individuation but of sadomasochism. It was not uncommon to see joggers in Managua wearing "U.S. Embassy" T-shirts. The U.S. embassies in the rest of Central America were fortresses, but any thirteen-year-old could have lobbed a grenade into the U.S. Embassy in Managua and been quite satisfied with the results. The only people who would have stopped him were the Sandinista police. The Sandinistas, terrified that any damage to the U.S. Embassy would provoke a visit by the Marines, protected the building and its staff as if they were all comandantes. The day after the United States bombed Tripoli, 250 Sandinista police roped off the street in front of the U.S. Embassy, turning away thousands of angry demonstrators.

At times it seemed as if the only people in Nicaragua really outside the grasp of gringo values were the foreigners—just how far outside I learned one night in a salsa bar. I had gone out with friends and found myself across a table and a bottle of Flor de Caña rum from a Nicaraguan woman, Elizabeth, and Hans, her German husband. Elizabeth said she was a Buddhist, one of four hundred in the country. Her husband, she said, was keeping the official records of Nicaraguan Buddhism. "Are you a Buddhist, too?" I asked him.

"A Marxist," Hans replied.

He said he had come from West Germany in 1979 to fight in the revolution. I asked him if he had been back since.

"No," he said.

"Not even to visit?" I said. "Don't you miss it?"

"I can't go back," he said. "I've been sentenced to twenty-five years in prison in absentia."

I asked him politely what his crime had been. "Terrorism," he said. He had been a member of the Red Army Faction, the group famous for killing captains of industry, kneecapping German judges, and bombing U.S. military installations. He said he had been fighting in wars of liberation for fifteen years before coming to Nicaragua—in Lebanon, Northern Ireland, and Africa and also in France, Germany, and Italy, countries in which I was unaware wars of liberation existed. But he had retired after the Nicaraguan Revolution, he said. He was now a family man with two children and a Buddhist wife. He and his wife had installed an aquarium in their home and made a living selling tropical fish.

There were many earnest revolutionaries in Nicaragua, and many did not speak Spanish. The Eastern bloc visitors, older and usually here on official missions, kept to themselves. But I met dozens of young Brazilians, Western Europeans, Australians, and North Americans: French café socialists with their Gauloises cigarettes and Lenin buttons, earnest young Canadian women working in nutrition or soil preparation, North Americans with beards and peace sign pendants who demonstrated outside the U.S. Embassy every Thursday morning at seven-thirty, their guilt as citizens of Reagan's America compelling them to reject anything American.

The Nicaraguans, however, even those who hated U.S. policies, adored *yanqui* movies, books, and clothes. At first the Sandinistas permitted only movies that underlined the worst of U.S. culture: *The Godfather* to show corruption or *Norma Rae* about the repression of leftists and workers. But after a few years even this criterion was abandoned. By 1989 most of the films in Managua's theaters featured breakdancing, Jason the slasher, or Chuck Norris. Johnny's army company loved to watch Rambo on the unit's VCR. Dubbed versions of U.S. programs from *Land of the Giants* through *Dallas* were on TV. Radio Sandino, the armed forces' station, featured the ballads of the Beach Boys and Don Johnson.

The Managua Rotary Club continued to meet every Wednesday at seven-thirty in the Inter-Continental Hotel. The night I attended, twenty-four men looking exactly like Rotarians from Amarillo, Texas, saluted long-deceased Rotary founder Paul Harris on his birthday and discussed their project to set up a dental clinic in a poor barrio. Their printed program contained homilies about "giving without the hope of getting." One of the members was the military attaché at the U.S. Embassy. Although members said that the exodus of the middle class after the revolution had depleted their ranks, Nicaragua still boasted nine Rotary clubs.

The shrine of U.S.-style consumerism was the dollar store, a monument to the energy and vision of Herty Lewites, the minister of tourism, also known informally as Nicaragua's Donald Trump. The dollar store was designed to bring the government hard currency and make life easier for resident diplomats, journalists, and development workers—and, not incidentally, *frente* members. It had begun as one small building. By 1989 there were three huge buildings, the largest a supermarket with a photo processing shop, a wine and liquor store, and a huge selection of products— Kellogg's Sugar Frosted Flakes, stuffed olives, twenty-four kinds of hair spray, not counting mousses and gels—imported from Canada or from the United States via Panama to get around the trade embargo. There were usually no coins, so shoppers took their change in Hershey bars and bouillon cubes. Any Nicaraguan who could afford the twenty-dollar membership fee could now shop there with dollars sent from relatives in the United States.

If it was capitalism, it was capitalism socialist-style. The dollar store was as close to a perfect monopoly as existed anywhere, a fact that hadn't escaped Lewites, who charged about 50 percent more than the products would have cost in the United States or Canada.

Around the corner the building that used to house the entire dollar store was now filled with washing machines, refrigerators, calculators, and other appliances. The third building was a lush, carpeted department store, with racks of fashionable clothes and bathing suits, Reeboks, sheet sets, and Junior Wheel of Fortune board games.

On the street outside this fantasyland, women in rubber thongs with babies in their arms sold cigarettes one at a time or begged. Naked children played in the dust. The nine dollars I had spent on groceries one day—for a small jar of instant coffee, a box of cornflakes, a box of oatmeal, and a small jar of spaghetti sauce —was well over half a Nicaraguan worker's monthly salary. It was becoming increasingly rare to hear Spanish spoken in res- taurants; one had a billboard announcing "Bring your family and eat like a king"—in English. The dual economy was not reserved for party officials, as in other socialist nations. The criterion was simple ability to pay. Lewites's revolutionary capitalism looked suspiciously like capitalist bourgeois exploitation—except that now it was serving the revolution.

Just how comfortably the culture of revolution coexisted with bourgeois commercialism became clear one Friday night in 1989, when Managua hosted two long-awaited social events. The first was held in the lush garden of the Sandinista Association of

Cultural Workers; Tomás Borge was to read from his new autobiography, *The Impatient Patient*. The comandante-author was now a cliché in this revolution of poets: The president was a poet, the first lady a better poet (and a literary critic, too), the vice president a world-class novelist and short story writer. Omar Cabezas, a second-rank comandante, had enjoyed great commercial success with his autobiography, *Fire from the Mountain*. When Borge announced that he was writing a book, many of Managua's literati winced. Who could give the interior minister a bad review? But Borge's book was terrific. I had hardly expected an account of torture to be funny and picaresque, but Borge's was.

He read while sitting at a table in his uniform, flanked by the vice president and the first lady in her uniform of boots, leopard skin pants, dozens of bracelets, and a newly colored and permed mane of curls. The minister of culture, poet-priest Ernesto Cardenal, sat in the audience, wearing his signature beret and fisherman's sweater. Cabezas sat on the ground hugging his knees. The garden glowed with revolutionary hipness and sensitivity; I felt as if I had walked onto a movie set.

There was another cultural attraction in Managua that evening. At the Inter-Continental, the Miss Verano ("Miss Summer") pageant was beginning. A bridge studded with Christmas lights stretched across the waist of the hotel's kidney-shaped pool. A big band played salsa while a tuxedoed, unctuous emcee told terrible jokes and girls modeled dresses and bathing suits. The room was so crowded that when I arrived, the soldiers on guard duty were not even letting the models in.

I went back to the hotel lobby just in time to see Borge walk in with some Interior Ministry officials and a few other people who had been at his reading. He went upstairs for an interview, but a few hours later he came down to watch the pageant, drinking at a front table with an entourage from the reading.

The six finalists posed in bathing suit and evening gown. They were competing for trips to Colombia, Panama, and Guatemala; the fourth-place finisher received free use of the hotel pool. Some of the girls were fifteen. The winner, Elizabeth Guerrero, a student at the American School, was only fourteen.

The pageant prompted a series of newspaper articles and letters to the editor about the role of women in the revolution. *Barricada* attacked the pageant on its editorial pages but gushed about it in news stories. "Any one of the girls could have been the muse to awaken a poet's dream," one story said.

A few days before the pageant *Barricada* carried the following note:

> In yesterday's edition of *Barricada*, an error was involuntarily made due to a proofreader's mistake. In the information about the Miss Verano contest, *Barricada* published: "The businesses backing the event will use the girls for commercial purposes."
>
> The correct text should have said, "The business backing the event will NOT use the girls for commercial purposes because their principal interest is that the girls show, in addition to their beauty, poise, and modeling ability, their cultural values with respect to peace, friendship, and solidarity."

The pro-Sandinista paper *El Nuevo Diario* printed a letter suggesting that the girls could properly represent the revolution by promoting vaccination campaigns. It was a minority view. The day after the pageant I heard a *Nuevo Diario* vendor hawking the paper yelling, "*Vean a las muchachitas casi desnuditas,*" "see the almost naked girls" being the literal translation; "to hell with the New Nicaragua," the figurative one.

The Sandinistas' one lasting achievement in turning cultural imperialism to party advantage could be seen in the most beloved hangover from the days of U.S. domination: baseball. Even years after the Triumph, walking into a baseball stadium in Nicaragua was like taking a trip back in time to a Middle America ball park in the years before exploding scoreboards, electronic light shows, and Deodorant Days. Huge signs advertised Pepsi, Coke, and beer. Vendors sold hot dogs and ice cream. Drowsy fans lounged shirtless in the sun or cheered and started food fights. The announcers hawked local products, restaurants, and nightclubs. Managua's thirty-thousand-seat stadium had lights for night play; so did some of the stadiums in smaller cities.

The Nicaraguan baseball league has nine teams, each playing a seventy-two-game season from November to February, the summer season, and a seven-game championship series in April. The newspaper sports pages are filled with news of the U.S. major leagues—I once startled myself by opening *Barricada* to read "Yankees victorious!" before realizing the headline referred to the American League—endless analysis of trades, slumps, and especially the fortunes of Nicaraguan players in the majors. Soccer is practically unknown in Nicaragua.

It is no coincidence that Cuba and Nicaragua are obsessed with baseball. Baseball was a spin-off of U.S. intervention. Nicaragua's first team, the Boers, was founded by U.S. Consul Carter Donaldson in 1905. Impressed by the players' ferocity, Donaldson named the team for the South African fighters in the Boer War.

After the Triumph the Sandinistas toyed with the notion of banning baseball, but instead, they made it a Sandinista game. The league was named for a martyr of the revolution. The stadium in León, Nicaragua's second-largest city, was called Heroes and Martyrs of September. Managua's stadium, which had been named for Anastasio Somoza García, was renamed for the man who shot him. One team bore a martyr's nickname, and another the name of an important battleground. Opening day was usually filled with patriotic, anti-imperialist speeches and dedicated to the returning army veterans. Next to León's scoreboard, which used English terms such as "strikes" and "outs," was a sign that read LEÓN, FIRST CAPITAL OF THE REVOLUTION. WE FIGHT TO WIN. THEY SHALL NOT PASS! Before each game the crowd rose for the Sandinista hymn, singing, "We fight against the *yanqui*, enemy of humanity."

Baseball was more than a way to tell off the gringos in their own language. It was a way to mold the New Man, men like Julio Medina. In the early 1980s Medina was the biggest star in Nicaraguan baseball: second baseman for León and captain of the national All-Star team, an excellent fielder, and the only player to win two batting titles since the Triumph. Off the field he was a diligent science student and member of the Young Sandinistas.

Medina grew up watching U.S. baseball on television and cheering for the Reds. In 1984 Bill Clark, a talent scout for the Cincinnati Reds, came through León and tried to sign Medina. He walked up to Medina after a game, contract in hand, and started to talk. We want you to be a Cincinnati Red, he said. Here's a telex number. Here's a list of things you'll need to bring for the big leagues. Here's a promise of five thousand dollars for signing, more later.

And Medina said no.

I went to watch him play. He stood stiffly at attention during the Sandinista hymn, legs locked together, cap over his heart. León was playing at home against the Atlantic Coast team. When he stepped up to the plate in the first inning, he shook the catcher's hand. Later in the game, after drawing a walk, he shook hands with the first baseman. In the top of the third, with Medina in the field, an Atlantic Coast player tried to steal second. Medina snagged the catcher's throw and tagged the runner out. As the runner dusted off his pants and walked away, Medina shook his hand.

In November 1985 *El Nuevo Diario* ran a full-page article with four photos headlined THE EXAMPLE OF MEDINA. The article detailed Medina's careers: biology student, member of the Young Sandinistas, champion baseball player, and keeper of team discipline. It wound up with his heroic rejection of U.S. dollars. "He prefers to investigate the origins of cells and learn about bacteria in the morning and play ball with León at night than to gamble his future on a professional team," the article crowed.

Medina even sat up straight while he talked. Yes, he did have one complaint about the system, he said after an hour's conversation in a classroom in his university in León: "We get too many perks." After Nicaragua won a silver medal in the Pan Am Games, the government gave star pitcher Julio Moya a house. Medina asked for a room fan.

As the years went by, there were fewer and fewer Julio Medinas. Medina was the prototype of el Hombre Nuevo ("the new man"). The New Man was not nervous about the coming invasion, for he had calmly prepared for it by joining a militia, being a watchman for the revolution, picking more coffee, working Saturdays, working Sundays, working nights, always vigilant, always producing, always conscientious, clean, brave, thrifty, cheerful, and kind to animals, with boundless confidence in the revolution and its National Directorate.

The New Man was, in part, designed to inspire Nicaraguans to cure themselves of bad habits acquired in the past. The New Man was not macho. He was not corrupt or lazy; he denounced corruption, greed, and sloth. But the New Man was also an economic necessity. The revolution needed people to work harder than ever, and it could not pay them what they were worth. Not being Stalinists, the Sandinistas would not force Nicaraguans to work. They were left with exhortation.

In the early years there were many New Men. But as people began to realize that the benefits of the New Nicaragua would be a long time in coming, that they would have to go on being New Men forever, the appeal began to wane. Corruption eroded it especially fast even though Sandinista corruption was nowhere near as widespread or as gluttonous as Somoza's.

Under the Sandinistas, transactions with the government no longer had to be greased with money; I actually saw Sandinista policemen in the street refuse tips, and once in a customs line at the airport, the agent got so angry when the man in front of me offered him a bribe that he nearly had the man arrested. Sandinista corruption meant using a favorable exchange rate to import a Russian Lada auto. But in its way the Lada seemed worse than Somoza's greed. Nicaragua was poorer, the Sandinistas were demanding sacrifices of their countrymen, and after all, they had claimed to be the good guys.

Soon the New Man barely existed outside party speeches. Ten years after the revolution *Barricada* still carried the exhortations of party militants inspiring their compañeros to work a voluntary Sunday to construct a new health post. A few years earlier the whole effort would have been serious, and perhaps some people would have actually tried to construct a health post. But by 1989 the party official, the neighborhood residents, and the *Barricada* reporter all were going through the motions.

The old slogans now often took on an ironic subtext; they were spoken in quotation marks. At the time of the Triumph they had seemed natural, but when things started to sour, they turned on the Sandinistas, and I would wince at hearing them. Sandinista opponents loved to call their country *Nicaragua libre* ("free Nicaragua"). They loved the phrases the "workers' state" and the "Triumph." Even many of the compañeros smiled slightly when they used the word "compañero" or "compa." Calling someone a compa had lost its old meaning of "We're in this together." Now it often meant "I play by the rules, fella. And you?" It had become a wink.

The Sandinistas' warnings about the coming *yanqui* invasion also began to be met with cynicism. Not that Nicaraguans doubted the war—that was real enough. But each new incident of U.S. aggression or violence was such an important public relations tool for the Sandinistas that many Nicaraguans began to suspect that the Sandinistas either were exaggerating or had staged the incident themselves. The Reagan administration clearly used this tactic. A CIA training manual exhorted contras to kill innocent contra supporters so the Sandinistas would get the blame. In a Costa Rican jail I interviewed Stephen Carr and Peter Gibbery, two mercenaries who said they had been recruited by John Hull, who they said was a CIA agent, to blow up the U.S. Embassy in neighboring San José, Costa Rica. The idea was to blame the Sandinistas, prove they were exporting revolution, and thus provide a pretext for the invasion. (Carr later died in mysterious circumstances in Los Angeles.)

Each side in the war took charge of the other's public relations. The Sandinistas broadcast Reagan's contra aid speeches on Sandinista TV without comment, evidently believing that their eloquence spoke for itself. The U.S. State Department gave reporters copies of Bayardo Arce and Tomás Borge's speeches. Both sides needed to make villains of the opposition. The Reagan administration needed U.S. public support to keep contra aid flowing; the Sandinistas needed to mobilize their own society for the war. "While *yanqui* imperialism exists, Nicaragua will live under a constant threat," Luis Carrión said in a speech to *frente* cadres in 1984. "The danger of imperialist aggression will always be present until the United States ceases to be imperialist. . . . Military preparation and strength can't be seen as tasks of today. They are permanent tasks. . . . Every able citizen should sign up—and not just for a short time, but for the duration."

Carrión was right and could cite the entire history of Nicaragua as proof. But both sides seemed determined to compel history to repeat itself. In April 1985, just days before the U.S. Congress was to vote on a package of contra aid, Daniel Ortega made a famous trip to Moscow. "The U.S. congressional debate on contra aid is illegitimate," Ortega said, trying to explain the timing of his trip. Nicaragua would not snub its friends simply to please the United States. The cost, however, was twenty-seven million dollars in aid to the contras from a Congress that had voted it down only seven weeks before, thus prolonging the war, further destroying the economy, and, in effect, killing thousands of Nicaraguans.

Each side seemed to be itching to provoke the other into making its worst nightmares come true. Had the Sandinistas really blown up the U.S. Embassy in Costa Rica, the Reagan administration would have been delirious with joy. And nothing would have made the Sandinistas feel more heroic than a U.S. invasion.

The war had real effects and produced real damage, but it was not a real war. The Nicaraguans were not fighting the contras or even the United States; they were fighting the Goliath of imperialism. The United States was fighting not Nicaragua but the red stain of communism. The level of destruction and number of casualties hardly seemed to matter. Even winning the war, in a perverse way, didn't seem to matter. What mattered was being proven right. Each side was fighting for history.

THE WAR, THE GROWING DISENCHANTMENT, THE CYNICISM, AND the siege mentality of the government corroded the revolution. As the *mística* rusted away, the Sandinistas turned more and more to repression. Their image of themselves as a vanguard party hardened, producing a *frente* that was by definition always correct. If salaries dropped or bus prices rose or there was no rice, either it was for the greater good of the revolution, or it was one more consequence of imperialism, and improvement would require Nicaraguans to redouble their revolutionary commitment. When the party recognized a past error, it was always a well-intentioned mistake caused by revolutionary inexperience and required patience, not protest. The party was the revolution, which was the people, which was Nicaragua.

If the Sandinistas were, by definition, the people, then logic decreed that those who opposed the Sandinistas were enemies of the people. The abuses of the Sandinistas were well known. Marchers were beaten. Block committee officials spied on their neighbors and denied government services to those whose revolutionary commitment was considered insufficient. Independent unions were harassed, and their leaders jailed. Mobs known as *turbas* attacked government opponents and destroyed their houses and property; the opposition press, including Catholic Church media, was censored. Political opponents were arrested and held without charges for months; political prisoners were often held incommunicado, and habeas corpus was denied. Many prisoners were subjected to mock executions and other forms of psychological torture to extract confessions. Prisoners were tried in ersatz courts with few of the guarantees of due process.

The list of Sandinista human rights violations was quite impressive—most striking, perhaps, because it was not more extensive still. The repression relaxed considerably as the war wound down. By 1989 a new policy about block committees turned them from quasi-spy organizations—people used to break off their conversations when they heard footsteps outside the door—into true neighborhood councils that organized vaccination campaigns and food cooperatives. Censorship stopped. Thousands of political prisoners were freed. Even during the war, the Sandinistas' human rights record was far better than that of the contras, who regularly carried out terrorism against innocent civilians, killing children, teachers, relief workers, nurses, and, in one particularly gruesome incident, seventeen mothers who were traveling in civilian trucks to visit their sons in the Sandinista army. The Sandinista record was also better than most of its neighbors, including those which the United States was trying to promote as models of real democracy.

Very few prisoners reported having been tortured physically by the Sandinistas. Isolated cases of soldiers murdering and raping civilians did occur. But in several of them the government investigated, tried, and punished the guilty; one second lieutenant was sentenced to nineteen years for the rape of a Miskito Indian woman. In 1981 and 1982 Sandinista soldiers detained about seventy Miskito Indians on the Atlantic coast, who were not seen again. The Sandinistas later apologized for their abuses of the Miskitos, quietly paid retributions, and changed their policies. The next wave of Central America–style killings came in 1987 to 1989, when Sandinista soldiers and State Security police killed seventy-four people and disappeared fourteen others suspected of collaborating with the contras in the war zones, according to Americas Watch. That was the extent of death-squad activity in Nicaragua. Normally, when the antigovernment Permanent Commission on Human Rights in Nicaragua used the term "disappeared," it meant actual disappearance—a prisoner held incommunicado without the family's notification. But then the prisoner would reappear. "Disappearance" was not a euphemism in Nicaragua.

And few other countries would have permitted the public bouts of self-criticism called *Face the People* that the Sandinistas held every two or three weeks and televised nationally. The Managua school auditorium that held the meeting I attended was packed. The entire Cabinet sat on the stage in rows of school chairs, and a few hundred poor people sat in the audience. Daniel Ortega, dressed in jeans and a black T-shirt, was the emcee, directing questions from the audience to his ministers, marching up and down the aisle with a microphone, the Sandinista Oprah.

The women wagged their fingers at Ortega and lectured him on the price of milk or the garbage piling up in their neighborhood. After four hours of questions in sweltering heat—Vice-President Ramírez was by now snoring, his head down on the table—Ortega asked how many people still had something to say. About half the people in the audience raised their hands. "What's your question about?" asked Ortega, pointing to one woman.

"We want electricity," she said.

Ortega pointed to the director of the National Electricity Institute on the platform. "Go up and talk to him," he said. Within a few minutes he had a dozen women running to the stage and the ministers looking worried.

It was, admittedly, feedback held firmly within the limits of the system, a public version of party self-criticism. No one would have gotten up to accuse Ortega of being a Marxist-Leninist dictator. But it was, at least, bitching on national television, not normally a feature of repressive governments.

"Our record, in terms of human rights, is very good," Luis Carrión told me in 1989. "Not perfect but very good. Even better if you take into account that we were involved in a very intense war that caused thousands of deaths and that everyone in the security business had friends who died in combat. This is a country with no legal tradition. People didn't have a legal mentality, didn't try to get relief from problems through the courts. They just asked someone to resolve their problem for them. There is a low cultural level. Those are the conditions for a real display of cruelty, and that didn't happen." Throughout our conversation he continually compared his government's record with that of the governments of El Salvador and Guatemala and with that of the contras.

That the Sandinistas had good historical reasons to have committed abuses or that they were not as bad as their opponents or their neighbors, some of whom were very bad indeed, was a justification Carrión applied to his own government, but he had not applied it to Somoza. Nicaragua under Somoza featured the same lack of legal culture, a guerrilla insurgency—the Sandinistas—and a leader who was less brutal than his neighbors. But Carrión would hardly have characterized Somoza's as a very good—not perfect but very good—record.

Indeed, Carrión had even protested against Somoza's abuses. Those he had found particularly offensive were the repression of unions, the censorship of newspapers, the jailing and mistreatment of political prisoners, and the lack of due process that stripped people of their rights. But when the Sandinistas came to power, the Interior Ministry began to take on imperfections of its own.

While Carrión was not intimately involved with censorship or the repression of unions, he made numerous enthusiastic speeches about both policies. But he directly oversaw matters relating to the political security of the revolution: the arrest, detention, interrogation, and trial of political prisoners. And in imitating Somoza's abuses, he did a not perfect but very good job.

Enrique Sotelo Borgen was intimately acquainted with Carrión's jails. In the panorama of the "enemies of the revolution," Sotelo Borgen, an elderly lawyer with a heart condition, a lisp, and thick glasses, did not loom very large. The Sandinistas regarded him as a pest, not a threat. His distinguishing characteristic was his dogged persistence in taking cases that were bound to fail and leave him broke and in trouble. He had been jailed six times under Somoza. Under the Sandinistas he was one of the few lawyers who worked for the government's opponents. He enjoyed a brief moment of international fame as the lawyer for Eugene Hasenfus, the hapless, impassive gringo whose plane was shot down in the course of a contra resupply mission, breaking open the Iran-contra scandal. Hasenfus got a show trial and thirty years. (The Sandinistas later pardoned him to show revolutionary generosity.) But Sotelo Borgen was used to losing.

His office, a small, run-down house in a poor neighborhood, looks like a relic of the 1930s, with an ancient brass telephone, an iron crucifix with a brass Jesus, and densely flocked gold, red, and green wallpaper. The air conditioner emits considerable noise but little cold air. In the waiting room Sotelo's secretary, an old man with splitting pants, sat at a desk, fanning himself and occasionally pecking away at an ancient Remington typewriter.

In June 1984 Sotelo was arrested on charges of violating the laws maintaining order and public security. The Sandinistas said he was part of a complicated scheme involving then-U.S. Ambassador Anthony Quainton to transport all the opposition politicians to Costa Rica and declare the *frente* illegal—one of the Sandinistas' more peculiar charges. The knock on the door came at night. Armed men blindfolded Sotelo and drove him to El Chipote, the state security jail. He was fingerprinted, photographed, and put in a dim cell, and his captors confiscated his clothes and glasses. "The cell was as small as a grave, always dark," he said. "There was a hole in one corner to do your necessities and a tap for water. I had no idea how much time passed. I didn't know if it was morning or night. I heard voices from time to time, and the guards gave me rice and beans." He thought he was held that way for a month. It was thirteen days.

After that came questioning. His first interrogator was a Cuban, Sotelo said. His interrogators threatened him with torture. They showed him a newspaper with a report that his father had died of a heart attack brought on by the shock of Sotelo's treason. "I believed them until they said my mother went crazy," he said. "I knew she was tougher than that." They told him that mobs had attacked his house. All the stories turned out to be false. After twenty days of interrogation he was released.

On December 19, 1984, a few months after Sotelo was released, Cecilio Rivas Urbina, the manager of Sotelo's family's coffee farm in Boaco, failed to show up for work. Rivas was the father of Juan Ramón Rivas, a contra commander. Sotelo went to El Chipote. "Maybe the contras kidnapped him," the guard told him. "He's certainly not in here."

Sotelo then sent a telegram to each of the nine comandantes asking about Rivas. To his astonishment, he received one in return. "Cecilio Rivas Urbina is a prisoner in El Chipote being investigated for counterrevolutionary activity," it said. It was signed by Luis Carrión. "He was always a man one could at least talk to," Sotelo told me of Carrión. It seemed that the acknowledgment that a prisoner was held incommunicado was as close to a conversation between political antagonists as existed in Nicaragua.

Rivas was held in El Chipote for two years. In late 1986 he was tried in the special courts reserved for accused contra collaborators, the People's Anti-Somocista Tribunals (TPAs). The TPAs were similar to the special tribunals established after the Triumph to try Somoza's *guardia* and collaborators. One of the judges on each three-judge panel had to be a lawyer; two were chosen for their party activism. The TPAs were not part of the judiciary system. They answered to the presidency; the normal channels of appeal did not apply.

Sotelo was attorney for the defense in 230 of the TPA trials. "They begin in secret," he said of the trials. "The prisoner is brought in, and the charges read. Then the prisoner is allowed to call a lawyer. I get the call, go to the court, and then I can read a transcript of the charges. Each trial lasts six days, so I have six days to prepare my own evidence for the defense—while the trial is going on. The prosecutor presents the confession and any other proof he has—an eyewitness, for example. By law this proof must be automatically accepted by the judge; no arguments challenging the prosecution's evidence are permitted. I had illiterate clients in Estelí who were told to put their thumbprint on a letter freeing them, then afterward were informed that it was a confession. But I couldn't bring that up in court. The judge can see only the results of the confession. Meanwhile, I am trying to gather evidence. I go to the site and investigate and try to persuade witnesses to testify. Sometimes this means a long trip, and there is no money to bring them back to court. Often the witnesses are too scared to testify."

In 1984 and 1985, the first two full years of their existence, the TPAs had a conviction rate of 99 percent. Of 291 defendants in 1985, 1 was acquitted. In the next two years the conviction rate slipped—to 97 percent. Of the 230 cases Sotelo himself handled, he won 3.

One of them was Rivas's. "I nearly fainted from shock when I heard 'not guilty,' " he said. "I said, 'Now I can die happy.' " He won, Sotelo said, because he had made Rivas a celebrity by starting a debate about the case on the radio. In mid-1987 Rivas was freed.

"I cannot question the need to interrogate prisoners," Father Molina, Carrión's former spiritual mentor, told me. "As for whether any excesses were committed, I have no evidence of that."

Carrión himself was less squeamish. "Sometimes we were just unable to notify the families," he said when I asked him about incommunicado detention. "But sometimes we held prisoners incommunicado deliberately. You have to understand the conditions of the country. To make an arrest public right away was to lose the possibility of a quick raid to recover arms or bombs. It was not ideal, but it was the lesser evil under the circumstances."

It was hard to believe that a secret police renowned for its efficiency could track down a clandestine rebel but could not manage to find his family after the arrest, the idiosyncrasy of Nicaraguan street addresses notwithstanding. As for his argument about incommunicado detention, I had heard a version of it before—from the naval officer Jorge in Argentina. Jorge, of course, had carried it farther. He was explaining why he was required to torture and kill. Carrión did not torture and kill. But both men would have been horrified by the similarities in their thinking.

"The people will not stand seeing their heroes and martyrs degraded" was standard government-issue response to questions about its mistreatment of its opponents. Such mistreatment was useful to the government in three ways. The first was as intimidation. The thought of a month in El Chipote probably discouraged a few Nicaraguans who might otherwise have joined teachers' strikes or opposition political parties.

The second use was as propaganda. The parade of arrests and confessions, true or false, was "proof" for the country that the enemy was everywhere and that constant vigilance was required. The siege mentality of wartime Nicaragua gave rise to the need for such propaganda; the confessions, in turn, reinforced the siege mentality.

The third use was to placate the government's supporters. The Sandinista cadres and mass organizations—the women's groups, soldiers, unions—were constantly pressuring the government to

get tough on the opposition. And just as Colonel Arévalo of the
Colombian defense ministry "understood" when death squads
killed Unión Patriótica members, the Nicaraguan government
understood when mobs of Sandinista supporters attacked opposition presidential candidates. The police always arrived too late.
"They had more important things to do," Carrión told me. "Excesses will always occur."

Why do they always occur? One reason is that they were a
necessary component of Sandinista democracy, which had little
in common with democracy as practiced in the United States.
To the Sandinistas, Reagan's election in 1980 was proof that the
United States was no model of democracy and had no business
telling Nicaragua how to be one. They dismissed the United
States as a "bourgeois democracy," a society that had all the
trappings of democracy, but in which the same elites always held
power. Almost daily *Barricada* argued that in the United States
voter apathy was high, especially among the poor, that money
played a dominant role in elections, that the American people
had been mesmerized by demagoguery, and that the Democrats
were becoming copies of the Republicans. Most important, the
Sandinistas saw Reagan's election as concentrating power in the
hands of the wealthy, and this, they believed, was inherently
antidemocratic. In addition, the bourgeois democracies the
United States promoted in neighboring Honduras, Guatemala,
and El Salvador were even more repressive and unequal than the
one the Sandinistas had overthrown.

To the Sandinistas, democracy occurred when the people had
power. It was teaching Somoza's oxen to read. It was raising the
consciousness of the poor and creating mass organizations that
would let them participate in running their neighborhoods, cities,
and country. Until the revolution Nicaragua's poor, like Gladys
Meneses, believed that the only prudent attitude toward authority
was silence. The vast majority of Nicaraguans, if anyone had
bothered to ask, would have happily called the revolution a success if it had brought them a few chickens and a television set.
The Sandinistas set out to change that attitude and to teach the
people to demand power.

Democracy, to them, was not the process of choosing which
party would have power, or bourgeois democracy. Since the oligarchy enjoyed the electoral advantages of money and an easily

duped public, bourgeois democracy could have ended up putting the rich back in power. (Somoza had held regular elections; it had not made Nicaragua a democracy.) Democracy was not the process; it was the outcome. It meant maintaining the people's representatives in power. It meant having those representatives reveal to poor Nicaraguans where their self-interest really lay.

This system goes by another name: Leninism. The Sandinistas were scandalously relaxed by Leninist standards, permitting levels of dissent and opposition unheard of in Cuba or the Eastern bloc. But as in other Leninist countries, the identification of the party's interests with the people's interests meant that anyone who disagreed with a Sandinista was by definition a counterrevolutionary. This view, combined with the cultural heritage of deference to authority, had the effect of partially replacing the old patrón of wealth with a new one, the party.

Leninism is repressive by its very nature. But the Sandinistas' repression seemed to me less an outgrowth of Leninism than an outgrowth of Nicaragua, with its political culture shaped by authoritarianism and violent transitions. Nicaragua had no tradition of democracy under any definition; it was highly unlikely that an armed group, some of whose members had spent twenty-five years in the mountains, would suddenly surface to embrace League of Women Voters-style tea party democracy. There was probably no one in Nicaragua who would have governed in the U.S. mold because democracy as understood in the United States implies a social contract and a basic agreement on the values of society, neither of which exists in polarized Nicaragua.

Carrión was right, up to a point; excesses always occur. The U.S. government, for example, has practiced genocide against the Indians, slavery, de jure segregation, police brutality, censorship, state executions, and a host of other phenomena that in other countries the United States would be quick to label as violations of human rights. But excesses occur more in Nicaragua and in other countries that history has not blessed with the rule of law.

The Sandinistas' rhetoric introduced the poor to the novel concept that the people have power. This is important, but it is not the same as the concept of rights. For six years Nicaraguans had no right to habeas corpus. For seven years workers had no right to strike. At the end of the war there was still no right to public assembly, and although the press was not censored, the government could legally close any communications medium without a trial. The TPAs meted out revenge, not justice. Interior Minister Borge loved to put on a show for visiting reporters and human rights monitors by freeing small groups of prisoners, showing "revolutionary generosity." He would not, of course, have been able to open the jails at whim had Nicaragua been a society of law. But those prisoners might not have needed his generosity to begin with.

There was no reason to expect things to have turned out differently. The Sandinistas had more than just the war and Nicaragua's traditional authoritarianism and disregard for law driving them toward the use of repression. Many of the Sandinistas had spent years in the mountains or in jail. Especially in polarized, authoritarian societies, people who come to power in violent uprisings—in which the adversaries see each other not as political opponents but as mortal enemies—tend not to make fine distinctions about who is and is not an appropriate target. The Sandinista excesses were milder than most. But that excesses will always occur is as good an argument as any against armed revolution.

LUIS CARRIÓN MONTOYA, LIKE MANY OF NICARAGUA'S WEALTHY, lost his mansion and his four-thousand-acre farm when his children came to power. He lost his savings and loan network and his construction business. His financial empire was reduced to a gas station and 20 percent of Los Ranchos restaurant. He spent the first years of the revolution yelling at his children. "I thought this people's power stuff would destroy everything we had built," he said. But in 1990 Luis Carrión Montoya was elected to the Nicaraguan Assembly—as a Sandinista congressman.

"My children were right, and I was wrong," he told me as he, his wife, and I sipped Flor de Caña rum and Coke, ate salami, and looked through photo albums in the couple's large but not ostentatious house.

"For the first four years my father was pure bourgeois," said Carlos. "He kept saying that it was ridiculous to try to challenge Reagan. But with each day he began to see some good things along with the bad. Finally he said, 'I can live with the revolution.' He told me he realized that the only people more stubborn than Reagan were his own children.

"Now he calls me two or three times a week to tell me what I need to do about traffic or some other problem. He always wanted to be mayor himself. He doesn't think I listen to his advice, but I do. How much time does it take to run a gas station and a fifth of a restaurant? He has a lot of time to think."

It wasn't total surrender on Carrión Montoya's part; the revolution had met him more than halfway. In neighborhoods such as Santo Domingo or Las Colinas, where Carrión lives, a reasonable confusion could exist about whether there had been a revolution at all. The rich still dwelt in huge houses full of servants. On the two days a week when there was no water, a simple flick of a switch connected the pipes of the rich to a tank that their servants had filled the day before. Some houses featured their own generators. The rich—even some in the middle class—had microwave ovens, VCRs, dishwashers, and maybe a satellite dish to pull down HBO and big-league sports. The women spent their days in exercise classes or having teas. At night they attended embassy parties. They spent months in Europe or Miami.

This bubble would have quickly burst if Nicaragua's rich had depended on the income generated by their farms or businesses. But they remained rich precisely because they did not. They keep their money in dollars in Miami or Panama. As little as a hundred thousand dollars in a Miami bank can provide a Nicaraguan family with enough interest to maintain a comfortable house and several servants.

At the time of the revolution there were about two thousand families in the Nicaraguan elite. By the estimates of both government and business leaders, about half left the country under the Sandinistas. Those who stayed found that the ravages of war and economic crisis and the Sandinistas' economic reforms crippled their businesses—in most cases farms or basic factories that produced vital goods for Nicaragua—while their mansions and Mercedeses remained untouched. Living a life of wild extravagance was fine, the Sandinistas seemed to be saying. Just don't try to produce anything.

But in 1989 the fortunes of the rich took an unexpected turn as the Sandinistas moved the economy further, till it bore a suspicious resemblance to capitalism. It was born of desperation. People had begun to compare Nicaragua's 30,000 percent-a-year hyperinflation with that of Weimar Germany. Exports had dropped to the level of the 1930s—one half that of imports. The end of the war now allowed the Sandinistas to take politically unpopular steps to rescue the economy, and in a speech at the beginning of 1989 to the National Assembly, Daniel Ortega announced drastic measures.

The plan removed government subsidies on food and gasoline and reduced those on transportation. It lifted subsidies on interest rates. It consolidated the multiple rates of exchange into one. It drastically cut government spending, eliminating or combining ministries. It allowed private producers to sell their products at world market prices to private retailers. It opened lines of communication between the government and representatives of trade and industry. And it did all that, Ortega said, to protect socialism.

"The fact that we use the mechanisms of the market, that we use financial incentives, is not to consolidate or develop a capitalist regime, but to develop a regime where roles are distributed more equally," Ortega declared. "If there's one voice we must hear first in this country, it's the voice of the worker.

"We are not giving up our socialist orientation. We believe this is the way to build socialism. We are Sandinistas, Marxist-Leninists, and everything you want to add to that."

Three months later the plan was showing mixed results, according to the economy minister, Luis Carrión, who had been brought over from the Interior Ministry to run the program. Inflation had dropped. In March 1989 inflation was 20 percent, and by July it was 6 percent—not ideal, but down from 126 percent four months before. Interest rates dropped from 60 percent in January 1989 to 22 percent in March.

"The results, in spite of all the terrible predictions, are good. We have reduced government spending, but we have to reduce it more," said Carrión at a press breakfast, sounding like his own worst nightmare. "There is a general change in the political situation. We are creating the sociopolitical climate for people to invest resources, to stimulate the return of investment and production. We need a lot of new capital to reactivate the economy without falling into hyperinflation."

The new plan paid sugarcane producers world market prices —fifteen times the price the government had paid them the year before. They could plant as much as the mill could process, without waiting for government permission. Anyone could buy the dollars to import machinery without government approval. "I'm doing super," Roberto Callejas, a wealthy farmer in the northwestern town of Chinandega, told me. I had been visiting the family for years, always marveling at their block-square mansion with statues of saints from the conquest, mahogany doors, silk couches, and an arboretum. Before the new economic policy, Callejas and his wife had been talking about leaving. But now his sons were thinking of coming back from Miami. "I couldn't live this well anywhere else," he said.

Callejas's sons were planning to return, but his servants only wanted to talk to me about getting out. In this revolution of workers and peasants, life for the workers and peasants got harder with each passing day. I could measure the decline by my trips to see the Callejas family. On my first trip in 1986, I took the bus that left at 6:00 A.M. from a Managua market. Riding the bus in Nicaragua is always an adventure. There are so few buses that people sit on the roof or ride on the bumpers, and the intercity buses are more crowded still. The bus that morning was packed with women carrying small animals or baskets of vegetables, so crowded that not only did I stand the whole way, but there was room on the floor for only one of my feet. At times I could remain upright without touching the floor at all. Incoming passengers climbed in through the driver's window.

I didn't think things could have gotten worse when I went back three years later. But this time, instead of a bus, I could board only a truck. I paid just over a dollar—twice the price of my first trip—and sat down in the open back. Half the passengers were standing, clutching a rope that tied the two sides together. The sides swayed so far out as the truck bounced along that one of them was almost parallel to the ground. Half an hour outside Chinandega the truck's engine started to smoke, and it rumbled to a halt. The owner gave us each back about twenty cents. There was nothing around but field and a few scraggly trees. It was the hottest month in the hottest part of the country, and the sun was fierce. One truck came along, and about half the passengers climbed in. I started walking toward Chinandega with a group of seven women, one with her three-year-old daughter. We proceeded on foot a few kilometers to a big tree in the road where at least we could wait in the shade for a ride. Some of us tried to hitchhike, with the rest of the group hidden in a ditch; drivers were more likely to stop if they thought we were a small group. Half an hour later a truck stopped. Ten minutes later it turned off the road, and we got out and hitched again. Finally another truck stopped, and we climbed in back to sit on sacks of coffee. Half an hour later we pulled into Chinandega. We each gave the driver a few cents.

None of the women had complained or even been surprised at the difficulty of the trip. It was just daily life. The revolution had reduced the indignities of the poor in some ways, but in other ways it had just traded them for new ones. Until the new economic plan, the theme was *no hay* ("there isn't any"), and the poor could comfort themselves with knowing that the middle class suffered as well. At La Colonia supermarket near my house there was practically never any rice, oil, milk, butter, or beans. The meat case offered only testicles and lungs. On one visit the supermarket held only Russian canned sardines, plastic buckets, vinegar, pine-scented floor cleaner, rum, Bible coloring books, small balls of brown lettuce, and four-inch-long black bananas. In the bakery case sat two lonely decorated cakes.

The new economic plan changed all that. Now La Colonia was filled with beautiful vegetables, three kinds of milk, meats, cheeses, cans of Campbell's tomato soup, even chopped fish spread. What it didn't have was shoppers. The outdoor markets were the same: laden with products and deserted. Prices were slightly less than in the United States; wages were slightly less than in Mexico. In April 1989 a worker in Nicaragua made eighty thousand cordobas a month—about fifteen dollars, barely enough to buy beans and rice for one person. Cooking oil had become a luxury.

In the early 1980s advances in health care had been among the revolution's proudest achievements. But by 1989 polio had reappeared, malaria was at epidemic levels, and twice as many diarrhea patients were coming into Managua's children's hospital as the year before. The health budget, on paper, had dropped 30 percent from the year before; in practice the cut was deeper because the ministry received only half its allotted funds. The

Health Ministry was exhorting the use of herbal medicines from wild plants. Health care was still free in the state clinics and hospitals, but increasingly Nicaraguans got what they paid for.

The beds had no sheets in the Manolo Morales hospital, a 287-bed general hospital in Managua. Many men wore towels around their bodies as hospital gowns. There was a little shrine in the hallway with a statue of the Virgin and a collection box. "We have no plasma, no adhesive tape, no syringes," said Esperanza Borgen, a nurse's aide. "We have to call over a supervisor and get her signature to use surgical gloves." Other nurses agreed that while conditions had never been ideal, the serious deterioration was recent, dating back only to the new economic plan. Borgen led me over to the communal bathroom. It stank. "The toilets don't always work," she said. "The cleaning staff has to scoop out the dirty water with buckets." I asked her what she would do first if she had money. "What a beautiful question," she said. "Penicillin first." She tilted back her head, closed her eyes and rattled off a string of drugs.

Another nurse told me that the hospital did not have the medicine for an illness she suffered and that to buy it in a pharmacy would cost more than she earned in a month. "The new economic plan . . ." she said, her voice trailing off.

THE MAN IN CHARGE OF THE NEW ECONOMIC PLAN HUNCHED OVER in his chair. "I didn't invent this policy," Luis Carrión said, fiddling with his cigar. "And I didn't volunteer for this job." It was just after the revolution's tenth birthday, and I had come to see him one last time to get his thoughts on where the revolution had gone. He would have been content to stay in the Interior Ministry, he said. "But they wanted someone with political clout. I had some training in economics. And it was easiest to move me.

"As a revolutionary I have a lot of problems with the policy," he said. "I didn't want more unemployment, more poverty, a deterioration of the education and health we are fighting for. But I can't be emotional. We avoided a disaster. Hyperinflation was going to destroy us. We considered running a war economy, with rationing, but we threw that idea out. Politically it was impossible, and besides, it wouldn't have solved the problem. This was the only choice."

Are you saying, I asked, that after a clearheaded evaluation of the economy, the comandantes decided that socialism had failed and Nicaragua needed capitalism?

"It's not capitalism and not socialism. It's just necessary and the only alternative," he said. He looked even more uncomfortable than usual. "And if a revolutionary government takes these measures in defense of a revolutionary economy, it's different from a Pinochet doing it."

I doubted that the hunger felt by people in Managua was biologically different than that in Chile. If there was any difference that mattered, it was that since the United States had blocked IMF loans to Nicaragua, the Sandinistas had not adopted the plan as the price of fresh loans. They had imposed austerity not to get immediate rewards but for its own sake—because they believed it worked.

"It's true that the Soviet Union, in passing through a crisis, put in capitalist reforms," said Carrión. "But when the United States was passing through the Depression, Roosevelt instituted socialist reforms. It's not completely fair to compare the two. Especially when socialism is represented by the Soviet Union, a country that was destroyed in World War II and had no Marshall Plan. Socialism is historically very young. The competition is still unresolved. Many capitalist countries lag behind socialist countries in solving their economic problems. The economic crisis is not particular to Nicaragua. Latin America has not grown in this decade. And here we have been severely affected by the war. Our crisis is not just material; it's psychological and political. The migration from the countryside to Managua and to foreign countries left productive zones without people. We have had the embargo, the brain drain. It was never possible to get new credits from the banks."

Here we were back at those harsh realities, which to Carrión meant the United States. "The Sandinistas have known all along how the United States would react," he said. "It will be this way as long as the United States is an imperialist power."

"So why bother?" I said. He looked startled. "If the United States is always going to bring so many troubles to a revolution," I said, "isn't it irresponsible to have a revolution in the first place?

Why not just give in? Forget about revolution and work for incremental change?"

There's something to that, Carrión said, to my surprise. "In many countries," he said, "there are many advances that can be made to widen the spaces of sovereignty, open up political participation, democratize, work together to overcome economic blackmail and political pressure without a revolution. You have to support those democratic advances. Maybe you can postpone the moment of revolution.

"But you have to see it in the context of history," he continued. "In some places conditions make revolution inevitable. Who could have thought that the French bourgeoisie would revolt against a monarch who was supposed to have divine backing? Or look at Peru. It's unbelievable that Sendero Luminoso, which does the opposite of everything a guerrilla group is supposed to do, has so much force. People, in many cases, have no alternative."

There was another reason: Revolutions bring their own mirages. No matter what Luis Carrión had known all along about how the United States would react, it would have been impossible, in the revolution's bright morning, for him to imagine that he would one day be administering such an economic plan. Or that he would have been jailing protesters and breaking strikes. "I never imagined we would have an Interior Ministry," he told me. "Much less that I would have the talent or desire to become a policeman." It would have been impossible to imagine that the revolutionaries would grow weary and cynical, that the war would bring such intense misery—or what he himself would become.

Six months later Carrión was gone (in the fall of 1991 he began his studies in economics at Harvard's Kennedy School of Government). Daniel Ortega lost a landslide election to Violeta Barrios de Chamorro, publisher of *La Prensa* and favorite of the U.S. Embassy. Under tremendous pressure, not only from the United States but now also from its traditional friends in the Soviet bloc and the international community, the Sandinista Revolution dissolved itself.

In doing so, the Sandinistas accomplished their most revolutionary feat. By turning power over to the oligarchy, they brought to Nicaragua the bourgeois democracy they had so scorned. The revolution had been necessary because change through elections was impossible, and now it was the revolution that honored Nicaragua's political will for the first time. Ortega's last act as president was the first step in the real revolution Nicaragua needed: It moved his country toward replacing the rule of power with the rule of law.

It was a small step, but perhaps the best the Sandinistas could do. Establishing the rule of law in societies that have never known it may be too much to ask of those who take power through arms. The cause of the harsh realities—imperialism, the polarization that grows from violence, economic mismanagement—is in the end irrelevant. What matters is they exist.

The question is, then, can anyone accomplish this job, for it also seems to be beyond the grasp of governments that reach office through the ballot. The presidencies of José Napoleón Duarte in El Salvador, Alan García in Peru, and Virgilio Barco in Colombia were works of Greek tragedy. Determined to break their countries' traditions and impose the rule of law, they ended up presiding over some of the most violent and repressive periods in their nations' histories.

If those who remember the past are also condemned to repeat it, then maybe revolution is no worse than peaceful transition. Few revolutions create the just and free societies they seek to create. But at least they produce a few fleeting hours of hope. At least they bring about one glorious moment when a people can rise up and say: We can change our destiny. We are more than history's damned.

SIX

THE PIG'S TAIL

I N A CREAKY LOFT OVERLOOKING HEAPS OF TENNIS SHOES AND two-dollar sweaters on a noisy market street in Santiago, Jaime Pérez waited for the police. Pérez was thirty-six, a small, elfin man with a pointed beard, the owner of four clothing stores and the head of the Santiago Retail Business Association. It was July 1986. Pérez was the association's representative on the board of the Civic Assembly, a group of professional organizations that had just paralyzed Chile with a two-day national strike against General Augusto Pinochet. Pérez had stood in his suit and tie in the Plaza de Armas in the center of Santiago, singing the national anthem, when the sirens started and the green tanks with water cannons came clattering down the street. Then Pérez was caught in a crowd of people running back and forth like stampeding cattle, trying to escape the tear gas, gunshots, and torrents of water mixed with stinging acid. It was the way all demonstrations ended in Chile. "But you never really get accustomed to it," Pérez told me. It had taken him a few days to recover, to feel normal again.

Now he was waiting. One by one the demonstration's leaders were being imprisoned. As each man went to jail, another joined the board to take his place and be led off, a circle that might only end, the Assembly's fourth president speculated, when every civilian in Chile was behind bars and there was no one left for Pinochet to govern.

This was not Jaime Pérez's first foray into politics. In college in the early 1970s he was a Socialist party student leader and a supporter of Salvador Allende, Chile's Socialist president. For weeks after the coup that brought Pinochet to power Pérez lived underground. Friends were tortured—some forced to lie on the ground while their torturers drove trucks back and forth over their heads—shot, disappeared. To save his own life, Pérez changed his appearance and lived in hiding, shifting from house to house.

Gradually, as it became safe, he resumed normal life. He went into the family business, selling imported clothing. He spent time with his wife and children. Chile enjoyed a wild economic boom. Life was better than he had ever dreamed it could be. In 1979, when he was twenty-nine, he bought his first color television set. Over the next three years he bought his family three more TVs, three videocassette recorders, and a movie camera. He traded in his car for a new one every year. He thought of Pinochet with fondness when he thought of him at all. Politically he slept. He slept for nine years, until the economy crashed in 1982.

The crash brought about an abrupt flowering of Chile's social conscience. There had been no public protests in 1973, when Pinochet overthrew an elected government, and none in 1976, by which time the regime had killed and tortured thousands. The significant protests began in 1983, after the economic collapse. For one year there was a large protest every month, and then, as the economy improved, the protests died out. The national protest from which Pérez was recovering was the last of its kind in Chile.

In 1986, when I came to Chile for the first time, my first reaction upon seeing Santiago was one of surprise: But where are the soldiers? The images of Pinochet's Chile that reached the outside world were largely of students, bandannas covering their faces, fists in the air, beside a burning barricade, or of jackbooted policemen scattering demonstrators with water cannons and tear gas. Those living in exile could comfort themselves by turning on the radio every morning and thinking: *It's today. He will fall today.*

"You hear the news of protests, strikes, deaths," said a Chilean who spent eleven years exiled in Holland, "but not of daily things. I came back with the image that Chile was all protests, that more people were participating, and that the regime was more fragile. Instead, you see people in the center of the city sitting and reading the paper, eating ice cream, getting their shoes shined."

"Looking back on my years of silence, I feel like an accomplice," Jaime Pérez said. He quoted Pastor Martín Niemöller's dark parable about World War II: "When they came to look for my neighbor, I was silent. When they came to take my son, I became uneasy. Now they have come for me, and it is too late; there is no one left to speak out."

Many Chileans told me the same parable about themselves. Chile, ruled in 1989 by the only remaining right-wing military dictatorship in Latin America, used to be the only country where a military dictatorship was never thought possible. Chile had never contracted the afflictions of much of the rest of Latin America: the violence and breakdown of institutions, the passivity of the poor, or the absolute domination of the rich. In 1968 a prisoner's ears were boxed in the public jail. It created such a scandal that the president of the Senate, Salvador Allende, came to investigate. That was what passed for torture in Chile. The second-oldest democracy in the hemisphere after the United States, Chile had always solved its problems through politics, not violence. "We were wearing ties when you were shooting Indians," a radio station director told me. "We had streetlights before New York; we had opera before the United States." That a Pinochet could exist, could kill thousands of people, and could last for sixteen years was impossible. And that Chile would not struggle against him was too terrible even to contemplate.

Why this happened, why Chileans, even militant student leaders like Pérez slept for nine years, was in large part the result of the tremendous risks of speaking out. But it was also because Chile, a country with a lawyer's soul, waited for a legal, political end to the dictatorship. It was because Chileans, exhausted from the chaos of the Allende years, hesitated to jump back into political activism. Finally, it was because Pinochet offered his people a Faustian bargain. For many years Chile accepted.

The idea of a dictatorship imposed on a heroic people who, though initially crushed, struggle heroically until the tyrant is swept out on a tidal wave of protest, is a romantic myth. A shrewd dictator does not crush everyone. How much better simply to seduce: provide people with quiet streets, imported autos, or the luxury of having someone else do their thinking for them, in exchange for their silence and subservience. Dictatorship did not just coerce Chileans; it also corrupted them. A civilized people in a civilized country stripped themselves of their civilization for the opportunity to buy a TV set on credit.

"People see what they want to see and remember what they want to remember," said Orlando Sáenz, a businessman who had been an adviser to Pinochet in the year after the coup but had resigned from the government in 1974. Sáenz was working in the anti-Pinochet protests in 1986 when he told me of an old friend of his, a woman who worked for Pinochet at the United Nations in New York and returned to Chile to visit. She mentioned to Sáenz that she had read a magazine article in which he was quoted criticizing the government's human rights violations. "Orlando, I know you don't much care for this government," she told him. "But you were always a balanced, reasonable person. How can you believe all that about human rights violations? Don't you know that the left has made that up? I don't know anyone who's been a victim."

"I do," Sáenz told her. When he was in the government in 1974, he said to her, he had a journalist friend whose sister-in-law was arrested. The journalist asked Sáenz for help in finding the sister-in-law. After a long search Sáenz learned that she was being held in a secret police prison. She had been beaten and tortured. He managed to arrange for his friend to visit, and later he obtained her release.

As Sáenz recounted the story to the woman, she turned pale and began to cry softly. She was the journalist. It was her sister-in-law who had been imprisoned and tortured. For months she had been in a state of panic and despair. But thirteen years later she had forgotten. "She said that she had done well under Pinochet, these years had been good for her, and that made her forget," Sáenz said. "She asked me if I believed her that she had just forgotten. I believed her. After a while you no longer know what is nightmare and what is real."

IT IS HISTORY'S CRUEL JOKE THAT LATIN AMERICA'S LAST RIGHT-wing dictatorship in 1989 was also its oldest democracy. One of the most complete country-by-country comparisons of democracy ever attempted, by political scientist Kenneth Bollen, ranked Chile in 1965 as more democratic than the United States, France,

Italy, or West Germany, taking into account such factors as political competition, freedom of expression, and voter turnout. Constitutional succession was interrupted only twice in Chilean history, once during a civil war in the 1890s and again during a political and economic crisis coinciding with the Great Depression. Even those short-lived military governments, however, allowed Congress, political parties, and the press to function freely; generally respected human rights; and held prompt elections.

Chile escaped the typical troubles of Latin America largely because during its conquest and colonization, Providence blessed the land with isolation and poverty. Chile was practically an island, with the world's driest desert forming its northern frontier, the ridge of the Andes cutting it off to the east, the Pacific Ocean providing its western border, and Antarctica to its south. The few native Indian tribes did not go gently into slavery; the Araucanos were so fierce that they surrendered formally to the government only in the twentieth century. The Spanish could not, therefore, count on a ready labor force for their exploitation of Chile's land or minerals.

In addition, there was little for the Spanish to pillage. Chile's first conquistador was Diego de Almagro, who had participated in the conquest of Peru. Almagro followed the coast down from Peru to central Chile and, finding nothing of interest, promptly turned around and went back. The land was relatively ill suited for plantation agriculture. The Spanish monarchs and adventurers could not be bothered with Chile's nitrates and copper when Peru, Colombia, and Argentina were bursting with gold and silver. Of all Spain's colonies, only Chile consistently operated at a loss. The difficulty of reaching Chile and its meager financial rewards meant that instead of looting the land and returning to Europe, many Spanish settled in and so began to think about decent government.

Chile was also fortunate in its choice of leaders. Diego Portales came to power in 1830. He fired half the army and subordinated the other half to civilian rule. He constructed a state based on a concept novel to Latin America, that the government was there to serve the country as a whole, and he left office so poor that at times he borrowed money from friends to buy cigarettes. Portales instilled in Chileans loyalty to their government rather than to any one politician. His legacy was the rule of law.

In 1841 General Manuel Bulnes, hero of an 1839 war against Peru and Bolivia—Chileans still boast of when their flag flew in Lima—was elected president. The general, like Dwight Eisenhower, ruled as a civilian. He filled his Cabinet with representatives of Chile's various political parties, strengthened the Congress and courts at the expense of the executive branch, and replaced much of the armed forces with a small civilian militia. When he left office, his cousin tried to stage a coup against Bulnes's newly elected successor, Manuel Montt. Bulnes fought his cousin to ensure that Montt took office.

The Chilean military's training was similar to that of Argentina, but in a more democratic context it produced very different results. In 1880 a German lieutenant colonel came to teach in the Chilean military schools. More Germans followed, and they stayed until World War I, producing a legacy of German-style combat helmets and a tradition of authority and discipline. The Chileans, like the Argentines, absorbed the Teutonic idea that the armed forces were a species of unsullied nobility, above petty partisanship, that defended the nation as a whole. In Argentina the military's heroic self-concept merged with a national tradition of caudillos and personality cults to produce messianic military leaders who stepped in whenever they viewed the civilians as inept. Chile had no such tradition; its military leaders—before Pinochet—avoided politics or, like Bulnes, behaved like civilians. Chileans I met spoke with pride and nostalgia of their military before Pinochet: how the soldiers guarded the constitution and won all their wars. There were no coups in Chile.

In 1973 Allende's most trusted general threatened to sue *Tribuna*, a right-wing newspaper, for suggesting that the military stage a coup. "Such things are not done here," the general said. The general was Augusto Pinochet. When he broke with this tradition, the military's impulse to "save" Chile from Allende's chaos combined with its historic discipline to ensure that the troops blindly followed their commander in chief into another war, this time against the Chilean people.

As did the military, Chile's elites accepted the rules of democracy early. Chile enjoyed mass suffrage before France or Italy. But one reason Chile's upper class permitted widespread voting was that it resulted in governments they liked. Before Allende, the government of turn always took a solicitous interest in the welfare of Chile's businessmen and landowners. Women were enfranchised only in 1949, and illiterates could not vote until the mid-1960s.

But Chile's leaders, although relatively conservative, did not create the feudal excesses seen in other Latin American countries. While economically, Chile ranks near the middle in Latin America, its political profile—before Pinochet—was closer to that of a developed country. Chile had the largest middle class and the highest levels of education and literacy in Latin America. Democracy was not just an empty exercise in voting; people used democratic channels such as the courts and political parties to solve their everyday problems. They believed in the government and believed in politics. Chileans did not just inhabit their country. They were its citizens.

"There is a political consciousness here handed down from generation to generation," said Jaime Pérez. "Parents who have civic spirit pass it on to their children. Back when people could afford newspapers, you'd get on the bus and the workers would all be reading the newspaper. In other countries people drive on whatever side of the street they want. Here if you see a sign that says DO NOT ENTER, you don't enter." Chileans joke that theirs is the only country where tanks stop at traffic lights during a military coup.

Chileans pay taxes. While in 1989 in Argentina only thirty thousand people paid income taxes, in Chile, a country with two fifths the population, four hundred thousand did. For crimes without political connotations, even under Pinochet the Chilean courts were still the fairest and most efficient in Latin America, and Chileans had the sense that even the powerful submit to the rule of law. (In 1983 Rolf Lüders held the double portfolio of minister of economics and treasury; in January 1984 he was in jail awaiting trial for his involvement in shady business transactions.) For political crimes, justice did not exist under Pinochet, but this did not stop Chileans from filing thousands of habeas corpus petitions. Chile also never fell into the habit of corruption, even during Pinochet's years. Some government officials, military officers, and well-connected businessmen enriched themselves, but corruption was not endemic.

Before Pinochet, dissent was a part of Chilean culture. Students read books and wrote essays. The University of Chile attracted students and scholars from all over Latin America. Pinochet never managed to erase the remnants of democracy visible in how ordinary people relate to each other. People in Chile talk back to their bosses. Machismo exists, but less flagrantly than in the rest of Latin America. It is rare to hear men whisper at women on the street. Chileans seem more serious and less sensual than other Latins; the bright colors of the tropics give way in Chile to dark blues and grays. Taxi drivers wear suits, and women wear sensible shoes. Instead of going dancing, Chileans out for a good time are likely to uncork a bottle of wine and a political argument.

Politics has always been the national sport. A political scientist mapped out Chile's political parties from 1964 to 1987, coming up with 117 different parties or factions of parties; his design looked like a photo of an ant colony. "The first thing you do if you form a soccer team is elect officers and write up pages of bylaws and rules," Pérez told me. Even the Accountants Association and the Teachers Federation choose their officers in party elections.

Their respect for law meant that Chileans rarely turned to violence. Before 1973 the police were forbidden to raise their nightsticks over shoulder level. In 1969, under the government of Christian Democrat Eduardo Frei, the police shot eight people to death during an attempt by slum dwellers to take over unused land in Chile's south. The government apologized, the Cabinet resigned, the Christian Democrats called national emergency sessions, and the party's youth section condemned the president. The left always worked within the political system. There were no guerrilla movements in Chile—until Pinochet.

It was only fitting that in this land of politics a Marxist came to power through the ballot for the first time anywhere in the world. Salvador Allende narrowly lost to Frei in the 1964 presidential elections. Six years later he led the voting with 36.3 percent in a three-way race. Since no candidate had a majority, the decision went to Congress. The Christian Democrats threw their support to Allende, and on November 4, 1970, he became president.

Allende's years were a time of passion and *mística* for Jaime

Pérez, the oldest of six brothers and sisters growing up in Santiago's working-class neighborhood of San Miguel. His father
owned several shops selling cheap clothing. Pérez enrolled in the
University of Chile in 1969 to study political science. He became
an officer of the Student Federation and a cell chief for Allende's
Socialist party, during the Allende years a more hard-line party
than the Communists.

He lived at home with his family. His father hated Allende,
but Pérez wasn't around much to argue. "We spent our time
working for social causes, worrying about the world around us,"
he said. There were walls to paint, marches to join, neighborhoods to organize. Days often wound down at four in the morning
with guitars and a bonfire in a slum neighborhood. Pérez never
knew where he would end up at night; he went to class in the
morning with a sleeping bag. In the summer he traveled south
to the fruit orchards to teach farm workers to read.

"The university was for everyone," said Pérez. "It was free,
and there were night classes for people who worked. I went to
school with construction workers, campesinos, police, people
from the poorest sectors. There were workers studying medicine.
If you couldn't pay for food, there were free breakfasts for students.
Allende was the last democrat."

Allende provided a half liter of milk a day to each slum child
in Chile. Poor children got free notebooks. He built low-rent
housing, some of it in wealthy neighborhoods. He set up state
outlets for distributing food cheaply. He expropriated large, un-
derused farms and turned them into worker cooperatives. His
proposal to complete Frei's nationalization of the copper industry
won unanimous approval in both houses of Congress.

But just as in Nicaragua, Allende's policies brought shortages
and inflation; in his last year in office, inflation rose to over 1,000
percent, the highest ever seen in Latin America up to that time.
The economic chaos provoked a campaign of sabotage by Chile's
powerful, which in turn brought more chaos. Among Allende's
most vehement opponents was the organization Pérez now directed. "The retail businessmen were the rabid bourgeois, always
in the street screaming against communism," he told me. "They
said they were fighting only for their commercial interests, nothing to do with politics, but their activism was very political. We
called it the fascistization of the petty bourgeois." He smiled as

he slipped back into the old rhetoric, Pérez the businessman quoting Pérez the student, talking about what Pérez the businessman had become.

But the New Pérez had some ideas about the Old Pérez as well. He was still a member of the Socialist party, but the party's old dogma was gone. "Our party slogan was 'Advance without compromise,' " he said. "It would have been much better to compromise, negotiate. All that talk about the dictatorship of the proletariat now seems so ideological and closed. There is no proletariat. We should have grown closer to the Christian Democrats. We talked so much about 'power to the people.' Well, what for?"

What he hadn't seen about the Retail Business Association, explained Pérez, was that its members never were part of Chile's elite. The association is the largest professional organization in Chile, and its typical member owns one dry cleaning shop or corner grocery, employs only his family, and earns less than a textile worker. Life was never easy for such businessmen, and under Allende it became impossible. Everything was scarce; to stock his shop with noodles or tea, a storekeeper had to join government boards and sell his products at a very thin profit. Larger businesses had the constant worry of government expropriation. "First they expropriated big haciendas and factories," said Pérez, "then any farm or business. They even took over a Popsicle factory."

In October 1972 the retail businessmen went on strike. Hundreds of thousands of shops all over the country closed their doors. At the same time doctors struck as well as truckers, halting the movement of goods from top to bottom of the twenty-six-hundred-mile-long ribbon of a country. By that time almost every sector of society that could create chaos in Chile was doing its utmost. Some factory owners slowed production or hoarded products. Others burned their factories to the ground, sold their inventories on the black market, and took their money out of the country.

A second wave of strikes began in July 1973, creating still more chaos and shortages. Inflation was close to 1,000 percent a year. Families left their homes in the morning to stand in line—the husband for cooking oil, the wife for bread, the maid for meat. Society turned upside down. Elementary school students took over their schools. Men came home at night to find strange families living in their houses whom they were powerless to evict. Nothing worked—not the schools, the buses, the hospitals, the stores. The strikes ended with Pinochet's coup.

"People were sick of bad management, permanent strikes, no transportation, food shortages," said Pérez. "But the CIA gave the extra shove that precipitated the coup." Allende had always scared the United States, so much so that the Johnson administration had financed Frei's campaign in 1964. Two days before the Chilean congressional vote confirming Allende's electoral victory in 1970, the CIA sponsored the murder of the armed forces chief of staff René Schneider, who had sworn to uphold Allende's election. The purpose was to spark a coup by blaming leftist forces for the assassination.

The attempt failed, but it was a portent of things to come. President Nixon told CIA Director Richard Helms that the economy should be "squeezed until it screamed." The administration cut off U.S. Export-Import Bank credits to Chile, which had been $234 million in 1967. Short-term commercial credits from the United States, $300 million a year under Frei, dropped to $30 million.

Two years after the coup a U.S. Senate investigating committee found that the CIA had given eight million dollars to Allende's opposition. The money subsidized the anti-Allende press, financed strikes, and supported right-wing political groups such as the profascist Patria y Libertad, which ran death squads after the coup.

Had Allende been less of a democrat, perhaps, he might have found it easier to stave off the coup. But when his militant supporters pressed him to arm "people's militias," he refused. Allende's government had no political prisoners. He did not censor the press, even when the rabid right-wing newspaper *Tribuna* filled its headlines with spurious tales of Allende's plans to burn nuns and assassinate priests or when *El Mercurio*, Chile's most influential paper, exaggerated the meat shortage with fictitious stories about the sale of sausages made of human flesh.

In a perverse way, Chile's meticulous legal mentality paved the way for the coup. Allende did not take seriously the possibility of a coup until it was too late. And the Chileans who supported Allende's overthrow never foresaw the hell that was to come. "The great majority of our members were satisfied with the coup," said Eduardo Garín, the head of the retail businessmen. His own Christian Democratic party, with Patricio Aylwin as the president of the Senate, was calling for a coup as well. Roman Catholic Raúl Cardinal Silva Henríquez offered his services to the Pinochet government, as he put it, to "give the good news to the bishops of the world about what had happened in Chile, to say that this wasn't the putsch of some soldier."

"It gives me a stomachache to admit it, but the majority of Chileans were in favor of the coup," an Allende agrarian reform official told me. The army was to stay for six months, straighten up, and leave, people thought: a little light housecleaning.

For Jaime Pérez, the day of the coup began with the usual rumors that had been swirling for weeks. He woke early and listened to the radio while making breakfast. There was a lot of army movement, the radio said, but that was nothing new. He went to the university. "Don't come in here," the guard told him at the gate. "It's full of police; they're arresting everyone." In the case of a coup his instructions from the Socialist party were to meet at the Pedagógico, the teachers' college. Along the way he tore up his identity papers. At the Pedagógico his compañeros were waiting. They could see the planes circling over the center of the city, dropping bombs on La Moneda, the presidential palace. They were in shock. They had no plan, no arms. Pérez didn't have the faintest idea how to use a gun. He climbed to the rooftops and escaped over a back wall of the university.

He went to a friend's house near the National Stadium. He shaved his beard and put away his glasses. About an hour later, when he peered out the window, he saw a man standing in the street in front of the house. Pérez slipped out the back door and hid. Ten minutes later soldiers raided the house. It was one in the afternoon. Pérez went to another house in the center of town, two blocks from La Moneda. "We could see planes dropping bombs and feel the ground rocking," he said. "The first night we heard machine-gun fire all night long. It never let up." When the curfew lifted, on the afternoon of the third day, he made his way back to his parents' house. Along the way he saw people dancing in the streets.

The day after the coup, my friend who was exiled in Holland told me, soldiers took her to the Chile Stadium. "The soldiers broke all my teeth," she said. "They tied the men's hands behind their backs and put them in the front of the stadium. We women sat in the back. The lights were so bright I couldn't tell if it was day or night. They told us repeatedly over the loudspeaker that if anyone stood up, they would kill us. The soldiers took groups of forty people below; then we'd hear gunfire.

"We went for two days just sitting there, bent over with our hands behind our heads, without eating or sleeping. They let us go once to the bathroom. There was so much blood on the floor that I got sick and couldn't go. When I got back to my seat, I went to the bathroom on my seat. I was going crazy. I had a vision of my mother when I was five, passing me a piece of watermelon. It was so real that I opened my mouth to eat."

After two days she was released. "There were people walking around, kids eating ice cream. It looked so normal. Even right outside the stadium, no one knew about the hell inside."

GENERAL AUGUSTO PINOCHET, ONCE ALLENDE'S FAVORITE GEN-eral, now leader of the coup in which Allende died, set out to dismantle Chile's political culture. This was necessary, as he saw it, because Allende had demonstrated that democracy invariably leads to Marxism. That Chile's Marxists had always abided by democratic rules was further evidence that democracy was an intrinsic part of the inexorable march to communism. Communism, said Pinochet in a speech to a commission considering a new constitution, "is an enemy that did not exist before but today infiltrates, divides, and corrodes the government and has brought about violence and terrorism. If democracy was an instrument that fitted its times, today it is not adequate to survive in such a world. Traditional democracy is no longer able to face an adversary that has destroyed the state."

Pinochet's solution was an elegant system he called protected democracy. In order to prevent a return to communism, Pinochet proposed a withering away of the state. Protected democracy abolished the Congress and political parties, which Pinochet described as "Trojan horses" used by Marxists to "infiltrate themselves into the daily workings of the country." Protected democracy controlled the press and the judiciary and allowed the state to exile dissidents, hold prisoners incommunicado, and ban public figures. In this way Pinochet defended Chile against terrorism, "terrorism" being not the disappearances, kidnappings, bombings, torture, rape, threats, and murders committed by the state, but all forms of opposition to Pinochet, who, after all, was only trying to protect democracy.

The second purpose of outlawing political life was to pave the way for a free-market economic plan that sought to open Chile to world markets and reduce government interference in the economy. In the first years the plan brought about a recession. Its immediate effect was to close Chile's local industry, lower workers' salaries, and allow foreign financiers to operate practically without restriction. At the same time the government sharply cut public spending in health, child nutrition, and education. Serious objections to this plan could have been expected from Chile's unions, peasant organizations, professional organizations, and political parties. They were, therefore, closed.

Carrying aloft the double banner of protected democracy and economic progress, Pinochet set out to abolish community and intellectual life. The government dissolved university sociology and political science departments and cut back on the humanities. The spirit of argument and discussion vanished from the universities. Most social organizations were dismantled, and the few whose existence was condoned, such as soccer clubs, were taken over by the government. People were no longer allowed to hold meetings. Soup kitchens, block committees, football clubs, even senior citizens' centers were dissolved. Permission from the national police, or carabineros, was necessary to invite a group of people over for a birthday party.

Gradually most people got used to this new atomized style of life. Chileans had never been submissive and sycophantic, but it was not hard to learn. If a man lost his job for refusing to attend a Pinochet rally, the next month his neighbor went to the rally and even brought along a banner to wave. If silence was required to keep a job, to stay out of jail and maybe receive a bag of toys at Christmas, Chileans were silent.

But there were in Chile, as there are everywhere, always, people who were not so easily silenced. For such people, other means of intimidation were employed: torture or death. Pinochet used fear surgically, applying it in just the degree required for the task at hand, taking care not to rouse from their sleep those Chileans who preferred not to know what was going on.

In the first few days Pinochet's objective was a military victory. Bombing La Moneda, Chile's White House, was an act of almost inconceivable audacity; the man meant business. On the day after the coup the new government declared a state of siege and imposed martial law. Chileans were now citizens of an occupied territory. Hundreds of Allende supporters and some centrist union leaders were killed, tortured, or disappeared. In the provinces the deaths were especially numerous, as people reported to army headquarters as directed, believing that soldiers they had known for years would not harm them. Then they were shot. Some local military commanders and landowners summarily executed labor organizers and others who had gained a reputation as trouble-makers. In the first few years perhaps two thousand people were killed, and close to a thousand more disappeared. Thousands were tortured.

On June 17, 1974, the methodology of repression changed with the creation of the DINA, the National Intelligence Directorate, the secret police. Repression became more selective. People were arrested not in full view of their neighbors but at night, to be interrogated in secret camps. The purpose was to give the appearance of normality and reduce opposition by leaving alone those who renounced political work. A former Allende supporter who became a "good citizen"—who went to work, went home, and kept silent, a citizen like Pérez—was rewarded.

Then, in 1977, the method changed again. The regime stopped trying to wipe out the opposition forces and instead tried to contain them. Prohibitions on organizations and public meetings were slightly relaxed. The DINA was dissolved and replaced by another organization, the National Information Center (CNI). Political killings became even more selective—reduced to two killings a year in 1977 and 1978. While torture was still used, its purpose now was to extract information and send the victim back to his comrades changed, broken—a living testimonial to the dangers of political work.

In 1980 Pinochet offered Chile a new constitution, which gave repression a "legal" dressing. Pinochet was now trying to regain some international legitimacy while still stifling dissent. He liberalized some forms of expression, yet Article 24, for example, gave the government power to censor, exile, or ban opponents, sometimes without having to state its reasons. What the constitution couldn't legalize, for example, the murder of dissidents, had to be masked; this was now, after all, a constitutional government. Between 1980 and 1984 the army, carabineros, and secret police killed seventy people. Many were activists of the political left, but the great majority, curiously enough, died in "armed conflicts," according to the newspapers, with police and soldiers. In 1973 the army numbered thirty-two thousand men. By 1982 it had nearly doubled in size, although no external enemy threatened Chile.

When the economy collapsed in 1983, the protests began, at first timidly, gingerly, but then swelling in size and audacity, becoming a wave. Repression returned to its initial massive scale. While those who had suffered most in the past were dissident leaders, now the victims were largely the opposition's masses. Protesters were savagely beaten. The poor, suspect for simply being poor, got the worst of it. Masked men drove through the streets, shooting indiscriminately. Soldiers raided the slums at night, kicking open doors, beating up entire families, sometimes tossing tear gas canisters inside houses as they left. Secret police squads drove through the slums with portable electric shock machines to torture people in front of their families. Police carried out mass arrests in which they descended from the glare of helicopter searchlights to take all of a neighborhood's men—still in pajamas or underwear—to the soccer stadiums. In one two-week period in April 1986, fifteen thousand men were arrested, held briefly, and released.

As the protests died away in the mid-1980s, a victim of many things, including their own failure to accomplish their goal, the abuses changed again. Massive killings would have been counterproductive, and besides, they were no longer needed. ("If I put my knife to your throat once," said Gonzalo Taborga, an officer of the Chilean Human Rights Commission, "the next time I just have to take it out of my coat and show it to you.")

Repression became subtle, even elegant. Chile had always been one of the few Latin American countries where Gabriel García Márquez could not have found his muse, but in the mid-1980s events in Santiago seemed ripped from the pages of *One Hundred Years of Solitude*. To keep the funeral of two protesters from turning into a political march, police stole the bodies, laced the coffins to the top of a waiting car, and sped away. An activist's daughter received a phone call: Her father has been blown up, she was told, with a stick of dynamite in his mouth. It was a lie, her father was well, but the call served its purpose. A college student, the treasurer of the anti-Pinochet Students' Federation, was found drowned on a Pacific beach—with fresh water in his lungs. Two years later a lien was put on his parents' house for their failure to continue to pay off his student loan. A priest who mediated the successful release of an army colonel kidnapped by the guerrillas was detained by the government and investigated —for the crime of talking to the guerrillas. A Christian Democrat politician gave an unflattering description of Pinochet to a reporter. The politician was left alone, the reporter arrested for the crime of asking, "What do you think of Pinochet?" While the pope gave a homily of peace and reconciliation in a Santiago park, twenty feet below the podium tanks shot tear gas bombs and jets of stinging water into the terrified crowd. A doctor was imprisoned for treating a patient who later was found to have been fleeing an act of terrorism. A year later police encircled the hospital where the doctor worked and searched all the patients. The prosecutor subpoenaed their X rays. A human rights lawyer's office was broken into. The office was locked, but the lock was not touched. The only thing taken was a photo of the lawyer's children.

What these cases have in common is their precision, the way they make their point without resorting to the crude violence used in the first years after the coup. By the mid-1980s Pinochet was not interested in creating martyrs and their attendant newspaper headlines, demonstrations, and strikes. He wanted to speak quietly to a few people without the rest of Chile eavesdropping.

DURING THE FIRST DECADE OF THE DICTATORSHIP THE LONE VOICE against government repression could be found in a shabby, dimly lit office next to the cathedral on the Plaza de Armas in Santiago's downtown, the office of what was called first the Committee for

Peace and then the Vicariate of Solidarity. Up until the last days of the dictatorship people came to sit and wait hours for attention on the wooden benches, rearranging their sweaters and scarves against the dank cold and huddling around the paraffin heaters. From that undistinguished office the Vicariate saved thousands of lives.

That the church was permitted to run the Vicariate of Solidarity at all was a peculiarly Chilean miracle. The Vicariate was the successor to the Committee for Peace, which began in the first days after the coup. The committee was the creation of Catholic, Protestant, and Jewish leaders, who worked with the United Nations High Commission on Refugees and the World Council of Churches to help evacuate from Chile thousands of foreigners —leftists from all over Latin America who had come to study or work in Allende's time. Pinochet was only too grateful to be rid of the "armed infiltrators," as the regime called them, and he allowed the committee to go about its work. Then it struck some of the activists that the same organization could be used to help Chileans.

"The churches were the only institutions left," said José Zalequett, a lawyer who was one of the committee's organizers. Zalequett had been an agrarian reform official under Allende and at the time of the coup was the vice-rector of the Catholic University. "There were no unions, newspapers, Congress, or political parties, so people came knocking on the doors of their church." By July 1974 the committee had 150 staff members in Santiago and offices all over Chile. It began running an underground railroad, moving thousands of foreigners and Chileans into embassies and out of the country. Soon after the coup Cardinal Silva Henríquez realized that his assertion that this "wasn't just the putsch of some soldier" had been borne out in a way he had never imagined. "They can sleep under my bed if they have to," he said of the endangered, and the church became a firm supporter of the committee.

The committee staff members were extremely careful to limit their work to what had always been acceptable in Chile: the law. Their lawyers met with Pinochet's interior minister and assured him that the group had no political objectives. It was merely doing "humanitarian" work. "We confined ourselves to the most basic, most legitimate questions," said Zalequett, who during his subsequent exile became head of Amnesty International. "Pinochet's victory was so total that any opposition meant death. The only 'legitimate' issues were torture and killing. You had to say, 'We're not against the government; we're just against torture and killing.' And you say it with respect: 'I courteously submit to His Excellency that human rights be respected.' "

Immediately after the coup the committee filed a habeas corpus petition asking the court to find and produce seven of Allende's ministers. In March 1974 the committee filed 131 more petitions.

On the face of it, there was little to be gained by sending habeas corpus petitions to a government whose views about Chilean law had left little to the imagination. "We lost all the cases," said Zalequett. "But even so, we were achieving something intangible but clear." In the first place, there was no other recourse; the committee was responding to the pleas of the victim's family to try something, anything. In the process the committee was creating an archive that would later be used to document the dictatorship's abuses. Also, the government's response to the petitions gave the family some hint of what was going on. If the government acknowledged an arrest, that was good news. More often, however, the response was that since the regime did not commit illegal acts and since there was no arrest order for the person in question, the individual had obviously not been arrested. "Then we'd get alarmed," said Zalequett.

By 1975 Pinochet's patience with the committee was wearing thin. Twenty-five staff members were under arrest, and others were exiled, followed, or threatened. Zalequett was arrested in late 1975, released, rearrested, and exiled the following year. Two years after the coup Pinochet dissolved the Committee for Peace.

A few months later Cardinal Silva Henríquez created the Vicariate of Solidarity, and the committee was reborn under the protection of the only organization in Chile that could offer protection. But the church held little sway, even over a Catholic regime in a Catholic country. The cardinal later recounted that the head of the secret police, Colonel Manuel Contreras, came to see him. "Sure are a lot of crazy people running loose out there," said Contreras, who over the course of the dictatorship proved to be one of the craziest. "It would be a real shame if something were to happen to you."

Over the next thirteen years, until the end of the dictatorship, the Vicariate gave legal advice to an average of eleven thousand people each year. The petitions and lawsuits had a cumulative effect on the judges. "Some of the judges who later became known as models of courage were not so courageous in the beginning," said Zalequett. "The moral weight of the persistent petitions helped them overcome their natural fear." In some cases the courts acknowledged an arrest, thereby blocking the government from evading responsibility for a prisoner's death or disappearance. Some judges began to file dissenting opinions supporting the prisoners' rights. Between 1973 and 1988 the committee and then the Vicariate filed 8,706 habeas corpus petitions. But the Chilean instinct to file petitions could not compel Augusto Pinochet to abide by the rule of law. Exactly 23 were accepted. In the last years the Vicariate even won an occasional case, although the verdict was generally overturned immediately after.

In the courts of the dissident judges, Chile's legal mentality was stretched to surreal lengths. Judge René García had jurisdiction over a section of Santiago that happened to include the CNI's main torture center, a house at 1470 Borgoño Street, behind Santiago's central market. García so persistently investigated complaints of torture that the CNI began to torture its victims in vans specially equipped with electric shock machines, driving around Santiago simply to avoid bringing prisoners to Borgoño Street. The Supreme Court removed García from the bench in January 1990 for his activity against torture, finding, in an unintended comment on the Chilean court system, such activity "unjudicial."

PINOCHET'S USE OF REPRESSION OVER THE YEARS OF THE DICTA-torship is one reason why there were not more like García and the Vicariate lawyers. But the way in which the repression evolved gives rise to another question, that of why subtlety became necessary only after years of massive violence. In a country that had never known summary executions, torture, and disappearances, why had it been so easy for the government in the early years to execute, torture, and disappear?

My first clue to this mystery came while listening to people in the late 1980s talk about Allende. Fifteen years after the coup people still talked about him as if his overthrow had come fifteen days before. It was curious that waiting in line for cooking oil seemed to affect people more deeply than the sight of bodies in the street that came after the coup. But while at most one in a thousand Chileans had a close relative who was killed, the shortages touched almost everyone personally. Many Chileans believed they could not adjust to the constant uncertainty of whether tomorrow there would be food to buy, whether the schools would be open, whether the factories would be running. Adjusting to what came later was easier. Under Pinochet, if you kept your head down, worked hard, and never talked about politics, you could be safe. Life was hard. But it was predictable.

At first after the coup there was a recession, and the government called on Chileans to sacrifice. No one argued. Chile became a country of silence. In the street people avoided the eyes of their closest friends. People hurried home from work to be with their families. If a man was arrested one day and returned to his home three months later, bruised, hobbling, with dead eyes, no one asked him where he had been.

This was, of course, partly due to fear. But there was more at work. "The politicization was so exaggerated under Allende that people got tired," said Eduardo Garín of the retail businessmen. "People wanted to move away from politics, devote their attention to their personal lives, things that they had neglected. They retreated into their houses, to tend their gardens and be with their families. They thought the government would be in the hands of the military. Let the military solve their problems. The military would fix everything. It was a kind of dream."

Pinochet closed the pro-Allende papers and redesigned the TV news. *El Mercurio* ran stories with large headlines about economic disaster and violence in the Soviet Union, in the Middle East, in Peru, in Argentina, but not in Chile. In *El Mercurio*'s Chile the swimming pools opened for the summer, the Red Cross carried out its annual fund-raising drive, Susana Feick of Valparaíso was named Secretary of the Year, Bob Hope became a grandfather, and letters to the editor complained of too many TV commercials. The paper published a daily series on its second page of the history of the chaos during the Allende government. About the Pinochet government there was little: the pronouncements of the junta and praise from the regime's supporters for its "democratic and authentically Chilean spirit." And there were endless stories about "extremists" put down while attacking military posts and arsenals. A curious feature of these attacks was that although great cunning was attributed to the extremists, they always seemed to attack with large numbers of soldiers present.

"What would have happened," I asked Tamara Avetikian, an editor of *El Mercurio*, "if someone had come to *El Mercurio* in the early days and said, 'I've been tortured'?"

"No one would have believed it," she answered quickly. "If people started talking like that, we would just brush them off— 'Oh, come on.' We didn't believe that kind of thing went on."

Spared the necessity of confronting the torture over their morning coffee, many Chileans decided not to know. Orlando Sáenz, who had been an important opponent of Allende and an adviser to Pinochet, told me that people were shocked when he quit his job in 1974 over the issue of human rights. "People thought it was something the government staged to show some type of criticism," he said. "No one believed I left because I was against what was happening. It is very hard to convince human beings of a truth they do not like."

It was harder still because there was no advantage to recognizing reality. An individual could do nothing. "To speak out against the regime at a social gathering was unthinkable," said Ricardo Vacarreza. Vacarreza had been a leader of the Medical Association that had gone on strike against Allende; in 1986 he was to serve, with Jaime Pérez, on the Civic Assembly board that went on strike against Pinochet. But in the early years he was silent. "Even among family you couldn't talk. People just didn't believe there was anything wrong going on. Some doctors realized it; we had more contact with the suffering. But if you started to talk about it, people would say it wasn't true, or they decided that the victim deserved it in some form, perhaps because he was a terrorist. People simply trusted the government."

In 1975 the government turned the economy over to a group of economists, many of them trained by University of Chicago professor Milton Friedman, that came to be known as *los Chicago Boys*. They dropped tariffs to 10 percent. Imports flooded Chile. The policy had a twofold effect. Much of Chile's industry was forced to shut down because it could not compete with the new imported products. But for consumers, importers, and the financial sector, the policy marked the beginnings of a great boom.

The retail businessmen, many of whom went into bankruptcy, asked for meetings with the economic officials to discuss the free-market policy. The meetings were private, low-key, gentlemanly, but even so, they carried risks. The government closed down Eduardo Garín's lottery ticket store—"something that had never happened under Allende," he said. But the group raised no public outcry. "I think we could have done much more," said Garín, looking back. "But our members felt that the government would fix things."

Over the next few years it began to seem as though the government had fixed things. With the peso grossly overvalued at thirty-nine to the dollar, imports were cheap and credit was abundant. Based mainly on credit, the economy grew at 8.5 percent a year between 1977 and 1980. Santiago's streets looked like the Hong Kong airport duty-free zone. Even the middle class could buy cars with no money down and five years' credit. A Fiat was cheaper in Chile than in Italy, a Ford cheaper than in the United States.

Six months after the coup Jaime Pérez had reenrolled in college. The University of Chile was now a completely different place. There were no student organizations, no politics, only classes. Early-morning and night classes for working students had been phased out. Universities were now supposed to finance themselves, and the government gradually raised tuition; monthly tuition at the University of Chile eventually rose to more than the monthly minimum wage. The universities were soon left to the children of the wealthy or upper middle class.

Pérez was supporting himself. After the coup his parents had asked him not to return home for the safety of his family. Pérez was furious; relations with his parents were strained. In 1975 he got married and began to work in an uncle's clothing store. By that time there were no more night classes and he could no longer afford tuition. He dropped out one semester short of graduating. Then he left his uncle's business to start his own small shop selling shirts and focused his attention on his business, his wife, and, soon, his son.

"I was involved in my personal life, very isolated from what was going on," he said. "I was trying to earn money to live." For a few years he worried and struggled. But around 1978, as *los Chicago Boys'* boom got under way, Perez began to earn money, more than he had ever thought possible. Imports were so cheap that imported clothing, his sector, was growing 12 percent a year. From his own tiny shirt business he expanded into shoes and other clothes. Soon he owned four stores in the bazaar district of Franklin Street.

"We had what we wanted in my house," he said. At twenty-nine he was a financial success. "Everyone went into debt to grow and expand. Today was good, and tomorrow would be better; that was the government's theme. We trusted the government. Our values were very confused. We valued material things over humanity. All we knew was that we were going crazy with electronic goods and every brand of imported scotch.

"If one other person had caught my eye," he said, "had indicated in some way, 'This is wrong,' things would have been different. But there was no one. All you heard was how marvelous things were. I couldn't even talk to my friends, not even what I can say to you now. It may take a day, or it may take five years; but if you hear the same opinion every day, after a while you start to think, *Well, I must be wrong.*"

IN 1978 PINOCHET TOOK ADVANTAGE OF HIS POPULAR SUPPORT TO hold a vote—a "consultation"—to allow Chileans to express their feelings about a United Nations resolution denouncing Chile for violating human rights. If more proof that Chile was violating human rights was needed, the consultation itself provided it: The opposition to Pinochet had no access to the media and was not permitted to organize. There were no poll watchers. The vote counters were chosen by the government. Each ballot was transparent and carried the voter's ID number and thumbprint. The proposal went as follows: "In view of the international aggression directed against the government of our fatherland, I support President Pinochet in his defense of the dignity of Chile and reaffirm the legitimacy of the government of the republic to lead the institution-building process of the country in a sovereign manner." The *No* symbol was a black rectangle. The *Sí* symbol was a Chilean flag. The *Sí* won.

Two years later Pinochet held another exercise in democracy, this time with more serious consequences: a plebiscite to approve or reject his new constitution. It was not as ambitiously fraudulent as the 1978 consultation, but it was fraudulent nonetheless. The opposition was permitted one rally. Observers were allowed; they reported seeing fraud at 40 percent of the voting tables they monitored. Blank votes were counted as *sí*, and it was easy to vote several times because there were no voter registration rolls and there was no indelible ink for marking the thumbs of those who had voted. In some villages 110 percent of the eligible inhabitants cast ballots. Pinochet's constitution was approved with 67 percent of the vote. But it was possible that Chileans, distracted by their new television sets and refrigerators, would have approved the constitution in any case; in 1980 Pinochet was a popular man.

The constitution was a singular document, an epic paean to Chile's fascination with the law. Most Latin American constitutions are like Peru's, splendid expositions of rights that might form the basis for model societies if only people paid attention to them. Chile's situation was exactly the reverse. In one of the few Latin American countries whose citizens followed such documents to the letter, Chile's constitution would have been better ignored. Among the actions "legalized" were the banning of those who advocated antifamily doctrine or promoted violence, the exile or confinement to small villages of those Chileans the president deemed to be a threat to the security of the state, the holding of prisoners incommunicado for twenty days after arrest without habeas corpus, censorship of the press, and prohibitions on public gatherings. The constitution removed judicial review of many executive branch actions. It allowed the military to keep extraordinary powers even after a proposed plebiscite in 1988, creating a military-dominated National Security Council that could countermand presidential or congressional actions if it believed the actions threatened the security of Chile. It provided for a constitutional tribunal, nominated indirectly by Pinochet, that could declare any act of Congress unconstitutional and fire the responsible congressmen. It allowed Pinochet to appoint nine of forty-five senators.

But no matter. "Once something is legal, no one cares if it's ethical or not," Pérez told me. The constitution was down on paper and duly approved.

The constitution provided for a plebiscite in 1988, a *sí* or *no* vote on eight more years for the junta's candidate. No doubt Pinochet believed that this plebiscite would be as easy to rig as the 1978 and 1980 votes. It was an act of political genius, assuring Chileans that Pinochet would not be president for life. Even though the institutional, "legal" end to Pinochet's presidency was eight years away—sixteen years away if the *sí* won—it existed, and that was good enough for many Chileans.

Pinochet's timing was perfect. Two years after the approval of the constitution the economy crashed, contracting 14 percent in 1982. The crash was the result of several events: a fall in the price of copper, Chile's main export; a rise in the price of oil; but mostly the accumulation of too much debt. The boom had never been real. It had been based on cheap foreign credit, helped along by the overvalued peso, still fixed at thirty-nine to the dollar. With the shifts in commodity prices of 1982, Chile could no longer roll over its debts. Rumors began circulating that the peso was about to fall.

On June 6, 1982, Pérez, now a local officer in the Retail Business Association, went with thirty colleagues to La Moneda to meet with Pinochet on National Commerce Day. "The peso will remain firm," Pinochet promised. "I'll cut off my arm before devaluing the peso." Eight days later Pinochet devalued the peso to forty-six to the dollar. Over the next few months the peso fell by 75 percent, quadrupling all debts held in dollars. "Ninety percent of the debtors in Chile were our members," said Pérez. His own debts were small because they were in pesos; he had bought his stock from other importers rather than import it directly himself. The debts of the small businessmen, while personally overwhelming, added up to only 15 percent of the country's total. The other 10 percent of the debtors—a few large conglomerates and banks—owed the remaining 85 percent of the debt. These conglomerates, and not the small businessmen, had the clout to secure a government bailout, while the small businessmen were left to fend for themselves.

On January 14, 1983, Rolf Lüders, the double minister of economics and treasury, went on national television to announce that two important banks and a savings and loan had gone bankrupt. The government was taking over five other banks that carried dangerous levels of debt. Bad times had officially arrived. "A spiral began of falling personal income, higher interest rates, more bankruptcies, more unemployment, fewer sales, and around and around again," said Pérez. His customers, working-class Chileans, suddenly found themselves without money to buy goods. "It was like the movies we'd see about the Depression in the United States in the 1930s," said Pérez. "If you advertised for a job, the line would wind around the block. The government kept saying, 'It won't be long before we recover,' but we weren't recovering."

The people who believed Pinochet could do no wrong suddenly found everything wrong. "The reports of the human rights violations began to come out," said Pérez. "The United Nations began to talk about it." In truth, the United Nations had been talking about Chile's dismal human rights situation for years; it was a United Nations report that provoked the 1978 consultation. So had international human rights groups and the foreign press. The people who had not talked about it were the Chileans.

On February 22, 1983, Rodolfo Seguel, a twenty-nine-year-old cashier's assistant, was elected president of the Copper Workers Union, the most important union in Chile. No one could have dreamed that this little-noticed event would eventually lead Chileans to find their voice against the dictatorship and occupy the streets in protest. The regime had recently permitted union elections after purging the most traditional unionists: Five hundred labor activists had been exiled, and Chile's leading trade unionist, Manuel Bustos, had been sent to jail so often that guards said they kept a bed open for him. On December 3, 1982, the day after Bustos attempted to stage a public meeting for the first time since the coup, he was arrested, issued a passport, and put on a plane to Rio de Janeiro in his shirt sleeves and without a cent.

Seguel was considered a compromise candidate, a caretaker to mark time until the traditional union leaders could once again take over. He had been a local union official for exactly a month. He was not of the left, but a Christian Democrat. He was not even a miner. *Hoy*, a magazine associated with the Christian Democrats, noted the caution of the new leader. "The labor movement has been sleeping for nine years," Seguel told the magazine. "I think the awakening will be slow but sure: we won't eat the whole artichoke in one swallow but leaf by leaf, and the heart when we feel the time is right." Yet after only two months in office this most unexpected revolutionary did what no one had dared do since the coup: He called a national strike.

The call was like a bolt of lightning. "I had one objective: to bring an end to the Pinochet government through peaceful protest," Seguel told me six years later. "The country was sleeping, and the unions were repressed. If I'd had a more traditional career, I might not have done it. Everyone told me I was crazy, but for the first time we *felt* courageous. For the first time people began to say 'dictatorship' in public."

"The government did the opposition a huge favor," said Pérez. "It threw all the cautious union leaders out of the country. The leaders with experience knew that a strike would lead to more arrests, more firings. Seguel had no experience; he hadn't been mellowed by repeated failure. The risks hadn't really sunk in."

The copper workers began to sound out other unions and federations. At the Retail Business Association Pérez received the call: Will your members go on strike? "God knows," he replied. He was shocked. Who was this guy Seguel? "My reaction was that this was like a soccer game," he said. "People love to watch soccer, they love to yell at the other team, but when your team says, 'Come out onto the field and join us,' that's a different story. Especially if you know you'll be jailed." Meanwhile, the government threatened to send the army into the mines if the copper workers struck.

Seguel backed off. Instead of a strike, he, Pérez, and leaders of other unions and professional organizations planned a protest for May 11, 1983, with a *cacerola*—a pot banging, the form of demonstration the right had chosen to use against Allende to protest food shortages—scheduled for nine o'clock. That day most city buses stayed in the garages, the school absentee rate rose, and stores did scant business. Pérez went out to dinner that evening in Providencia, an upper-middle-class neighborhood, with two other Retail Business Association directors. At nine they left the restaurant and stood outside, holding their breaths. The racket was tremendous. "One of my companions said it was bigger than anything he had heard during Allende," said Pérez. "I felt terrific; it wasn't just in the poor neighborhoods."

Since the crash Chileans had turned against the dictatorship, but only in the privacy of their own homes. Now, for the first time, they could hear from the din of the pots that they were not alone.

That protest started the momentum rolling. The country's labor leaders quickly grouped almost all the country's unions into a new National Workers Command, with Seguel as its president. On June 14, 1983, he called a second, more daring protest. Slum dwellers set barricades on fire. Mysterious civilians, wearing the same short haircuts and dark glasses as the secret police, drove through the slums, shooting into crowds, killing two people and wounding seventeen others. Five men in civilian clothes broke down the door of the house in which Seguel was hiding and arrested him on charges of subversion. Seven other labor leaders were also detained. The copper workers had decided to strike if Seguel was arrested, and two days later workers struck in two of Chile's largest mines, El Salvador and El Teniente. The government sent troops to take over the mines and fired two thousand workers.

The first national strike came the next month, on July 12. This time the retail businessmen were not just onlookers. "We called on all our members to close their doors for the afternoon," Pérez said. "Almost everyone did." In the July strike 4 people were killed and 1,200 were arrested. Another strike was called for August. Pinochet sent 18,000 soldiers into the streets. Santiago was under occupation, with a soldier in the street for every 238 residents. In that strike 26 people died, most of them shot by unidentified civilians, some wearing face masks. The secret police, using portable electric shock machines, tortured people in public for the first time. That month 2,600 people were arrested, half again as many as had been arrested in all 1982. In the next month's demonstration, on September 8, police brutally beat the demonstrators, dragging several Christian Democratic politicians, including Frei's foreign minister, from the Plaza de Armas by their hair. At least 9 persons were killed. The slums became war zones, filled with tear gas and bullets; in La Victoria slum one man received eighty buckshot holes in his back. Seguel went to jail again the next day. He was released twelve days later after a hunger strike, leaving prison on his thirtieth birthday.

For a few brief months, life imitated journalistic cliché: Chileans became the heroic people of the TV news, fists in the air, barricades in flames, braving tear gas and bullets to raise their voices against the dictator. There were layers upon layers of protests: demonstrations to protest arrests from past demonstrations; strikes to protest the violent repression of past strikes. Funerals became political events, which were then dispersed with gunfire, creating more funerals.

Seguel became an international celebrity. He went to the Vatican to meet the pope. When the Polish government refused to let Lech Walesa go to Norway to pick up his Nobel Peace Prize in 1983, he sent his wife, Danuta—and Rodolfo Seguel. But on the night of November 6, 1984, as election returns in the United States were awarding Ronald Reagan four more years, Pinochet declared another state of siege, a "second September 11," he liked to call it, commemorating the day of the coup. He put Chile under curfew, closed the opposition media, banned public gatherings—including protests—and arrested dozens of opposition leaders. The police began to raid the slums at night, arresting hundreds of men at a time. Political arrests—fewer than a thousand in 1981—rose to forty thousand in 1984.

I had been in Chile for two days when I attended my first protest. At precisely noon on Wednesday, July 2, 1986, a column of well-dressed Chileans marched into the central Plaza de Armas in the sunny cold, singing the national anthem. Suddenly the ritual began: the trucks; the sirens; the tear gas; the water cannons. The trucks drove right into the crowd. We scattered, hiding behind posts or around corners; I was soaked with water mixed with acid. Police on foot with squirt guns filled with a liquid form of tear gas chased us through the streets, and the protesters congregated in store doorways to chant, "*Y va a caer*" ("He will fall"), the opposition anthem, in a game of hide-and-seek that occupied the whole center of the city. The typical downtown congestion was the protesters' ally; the carabineros' trucks sat stuck in traffic, while all around them horns bleated out *Y va a caer*.

The protest was part of a two-day national strike called by the

Civic Assembly, the confederation of professional organizations
—doctors, truckers, retail storekeepers—that had learned how to
strike in 1972, crippling the Allende government. It was a success;
it looked like a Sunday in Santiago that afternoon: stores shuttered, empty streets. Crowds watched as police led Juan Luis
González, the Assembly's president, and sixteen other board
members to jail. Pérez, who represented the retail businessmen
on the board, was not arrested. The government was maintaining
the fiction that the strike had not enjoyed business support, and
if this was the case, then Pérez, as the head of Santiago's small
business federation, had committed no crime. "If not this week,
then next week," Pérez told me a few days later in his store.
"There will be plenty more opportunities."

I went back to my hotel and changed out of the skirt and blouse
I had worn to the protest. They were covered with mud and
reeked of tear gas. I was still trembling. All I wanted to do was
go to bed for a week. There had been a pastry vendor in the
plaza during the demonstration. Every time the water cannons
came by, he rolled down the metal top of his cart to protect his
merchandise and stood behind it. When the truck passed, he
rolled it up again; one of the people running from the police
might want to buy a pastry.

I marveled at his ability to carry on business as usual under
unusual circumstances. Or maybe it was that these circumstances, to him, had simply become usual. At dawn that morning
I had gone to La Victoria, Santiago's most politicized slum, with
four other journalists. As we approached the slum, we could see
a truckful of soldiers, their faces painted green, their machine
guns at the ready, and we could hear shots and bombs exploding.
We turned the car around and left. How could people endure
this month after month?

"Shortly after I came back, I began to realize how controlled
I was by fear," said Sergio Bitar. It was two hours after the protest
in the Plaza de Armas, in which Bitar had been among those
tear-gassed. Now, dressed in a suit and tie, he was sitting in his
elegant sculpture-filled house. "It's very hard to fight the tendency
to passivity. It's unconscious. You know the march is at noon,
but you go at twelve-fifteen. Then you say, 'What if I don't go
at all? No one will know.' "

Bitar had been, at thirty-two, Allende's minister of mines. After the coup he was arrested, sent to a concentration camp near Antarctica, and finally exiled. He went to the United States. In 1984 he was allowed to return to Chile. "I started to understand the mechanism of fear and how the regime has adopted it. It's a combination of fear and impotence. People say, 'We've tried that. It doesn't work. The risk isn't worth it.' Pinochet has reduced the space of what is possible. After so many years you think that almost everything is impossible."

He got up to make a phone call. When he returned, he explained that just minutes before I arrived, he had learned that the son of one of his best friends had been stopped in a slum by soldiers pursuing protesters and apparently set on fire. The young man, Rodrigo Rojas, nineteen, was the son of Veronica de Negri, a Chilean exile living in Washington, a woman who had herself been arrested after the coup, tortured—rats inserted in her vagina—and exiled. Rodrigo, a U.S. citizen, had come back to Chile after ten years in exile to find his roots. He was working as a photographer. Bitar broke off our interview several times, trying unsuccessfully to get through to Veronica, to tell her about her son.

Veronica de Negri eventually found out. The government lifted her exile order temporarily so she could come to Chile three days later. She arrived in time to see her son wiggle his toes, the only part of his body he could move. He died the next day.

Carmen Gloria Quintana, eighteen, a student at the University of Santiago, was burned along with Rodrigo. I met her for the first time eight months after her burning, during the pope's visit in 1987, when she returned to Chile from the hospital in Montreal where she was being treated. She spoke at a student rally in the University of Chile's engineering building. She could not walk well and had to be helped onto the stage, and her hands, wrapped in long white gloves, hung uselessly in front of her. She wore a blue sweater adorned by a button with Rodrigo's face. Her aunt, Ana María, stood behind her on the platform. Carmen Gloria told the hushed students that she had just met Rodrigo at dawn on the morning of the burning. They had exchanged a few words—he told her that he was happy to be back in Chile—and they had walked out to join the protests. At seven-thirty in the morning the soldiers arrived. They ran, but she and Rodrigo didn't run fast enough. The soldiers doused them with gasoline and set them on fire. She felt like a human torch. They rolled on the ground to put out the flames and then struggled to their feet. They walked and walked, looking for help. She couldn't breathe. Finally a bus of carabineros arrived. Carmen Gloria asked them to shoot her, then lost consciousness.

As Carmen Gloria talked, Ana María held her hand over her mouth, as if hearing the story for the first time. Ana María was beautiful, with long dark hair and huge eyes. I had seen pictures of Carmen Gloria before the burning. She had looked like that. Now she was a walking ghost, her face a frozen mask of scar. The students stood and clapped for her. She tried to smile but could not.

Military officials put forth several inventive explanations for the burning before the lieutenant in charge of the patrol was tried. He was sentenced to three hundred days in jail for the "quasi crime" of negligence, for not having helped the students.

After the rally the students spilled out of the building and set the barricades in the street on fire. Then, instead of standing and chanting, they inexplicably, spontaneously, began to run. I ran with them. Two students grabbed my hands and pulled me along. We ran hard through a residential neighborhood toward the center of the city, a group of about five hundred people, and as we reached the end of each block, the streetlights turned off behind us—I never could find out if it was the police or students shutting off the electricity—giving the impression that the world was dropping away as we passed, that we were fleeing something sinister. We ran for about twenty minutes, and as we approached the center, for the first time we heard the sirens of the carabineros. It was almost a relief to hear the familiar wail and to begin the ritual, by now almost comforting, of facing the police. And within ten minutes the whole thing was over, and we were soaked and gasping for breath, from the tear gas and water cannons and also from the run. Why had we started to run? No one was chasing us. It was simply a release. To run was to feel the exhilaration of diving headlong into the dark.

But something new was going on. The protests were becoming predictable. During the pope's visit I was tear-gassed at least twice a day for a week, and I began to comprehend the blithe persistence of the pastry vendor who covered and uncovered his cart as the tear gas trucks passed by. When I left my house in the morning,

I would bring a bandanna and maybe some salt—a tear gas antidote—in a small plastic bag; preparing for the twice-daily dose of tear gas seemed no more out of the ordinary than bringing a sweater.

"When the protests started, there were no rules," Pérez had told me. "They could have been the spark drawing millions into the street, provoking the government's resignation. Or we could have all been shot. Or we could have been completely ignored. Then a pattern developed. People learned the routine." I found encouragement in the general impression that the police were restraining themselves during the pope's visit. The government wanted no deaths that week.

While the assurance of police restraint greatly boosted my enthusiasm for attending protests, it seemed to have the opposite effect on the student demonstrators. The protests had initially made them feel like heroes. For the first years they had lived for the sensation of pushing the dictatorship to see how far it could go, of the adrenaline high of not knowing whether the carabinero would raise his rifle and shoot. During the protests they felt alive and powerful. Protesting was better than sex, one student told me. They were on a roller coaster climbing and climbing, and they could see the top. But once the regime had drawn the line—we are not going to shoot—the high was over. Everyone was aware that the police were not shooting because it was not necessary to shoot; these kids were not such a threat after all.

The truth was that, for the moment, the regime had won. In August 1983, after the protests started, the government had begun negotiations with the moderate opposition, mediated by the church. The groups involved withdrew from the protests while the negotiations were going on. The negotiators demanded Pinochet's resignation, but they lacked the power to make him listen; Pinochet just laughed and waited. "It was not realistic," said Pérez. "It bought time for Pinochet and knocked the wind out of the protests." Isolated demonstrations went on. But the protests had fallen to the left-wing parties, and so became smaller, more militant, and more violent. By the time the negotiations collapsed, the protests, as well, ran out of momentum.

The last successful strike under Pinochet was the one marked by Rodrigo Rojas's burning in July 1986. The next month the secret police uncovered an arsenal loaded with sophisticated weaponry belonging to the most important guerrilla movement, the Manuel Rodríguez Patriotic Front. Then in September members of the front fired on Pinochet's car as he was being driven from his country house, wounding him in the hand and killing five bodyguards. The government cracked down with another state of siege that stopped all political activity, and Pinochet regained some of the international sympathy that Rojas's burning had cost him.

Pinochet outlasted the protests, but they accomplished some smaller goals. They woke up some Chileans to the abuses of the dictatorship. They created political pressures that allowed some exiles to return and gave other anti-Pinochet organizations more space in which to maneuver. One protest, in the University of Chile in August 1987, even accomplished its purpose: to remove a new university president who had gutted the school's budget and closed its doors. Students, professors, and deans worked together, planning daily sit-ins and events that gradually escalated the pressure. Ten weeks later Pinochet fired the president and reopened the university.

It was the protests' only clear victory. It succeeded because it was highly coordinated, because there was no other way to save the university, and, most important, because it had a realistic goal. The fight against Pinochet enjoyed none of those advantages.

Many Chileans stayed away from the protests because they were looking forward to the "legal" exit of the plebiscite in 1988. In addition, the economy was improving. But most important, the protests died because Chileans began to lose faith in their ability to bring down Pinochet. He was too strong at home—the protesters were no match for the Chilean armed forces—and still enjoyed the support of the United States and of international lending organizations. In February 1985 Langhorne Motley, the U.S. assistant secretary of state for inter-American affairs, praised Pinochet, saying, "The democracies of the Western World owe a debt of gratitude for what the people of Chile did in 1973." Later that year the chairman of the Inter-American Development Bank, an important source of loans, presented Pinochet with a sword and congratulated him for liberating Chile "from the twin scourges of terrorism and communism."

As cathartic as they were, the protests had no formula for turning their energy into matter. Shouting, "Down with Pinochet" was exhilarating, but after the twentieth time the exhilaration grew hollow. They were only words, and they were not bringing him down. Even the students, the people on the front lines, began to complain that the protests only produced frustration. "How many Chileans does it take to change a light bulb?" joked Humberto Burotto, who was president of the Student Federation. "It doesn't matter. It will never light."

It was impossible to pinpoint the precise moment in which the protests failed, the instant in which the roller coaster reached the top of the hill, when one more barricade burned, one more fist in the air might have pushed the car over the top and sent it flying downward with unstoppable force. All Chileans knew was that the momentum stopped, and Chile fell back into silence.

As the protests ground to a close, Chileans began to despair of a peaceful end to Pinochet's rule. The democratic opposition splintered, as if eager to render itself more meaningless. In August 1985 the opposition think tank Sur asked slum dwellers to grade the actions of different groups in Chile. Professors ranked highest, followed by students, vendors, and police. Politicians ranked second to last, followed closely by drug addicts. In a public opinion survey of dozens of political leaders published in the magazine *Qué Pasa* in April 1986, only Rodolfo Seguel received a favorable rating.

The opposition was trying to function in a vacuum. Political parties could not talk to Chileans, and Chileans could not talk to them. A political group had no way of measuring its support; new leaders could not emerge, and nothing was lost in resolving every dispute by forming yet another party. There were six socialist parties. The Christian Democrats were split about whether to talk with the Communists or the military. The Communists were split about whether to support the use of violence. Even the guerrilla groups were split. The parties could do nothing but talk, mostly bickering at one another, like twenty telephones ringing at once. "In Nicaragua they say, 'A free country or death,'" joked a photographer. "In Chile the opposition says, 'A free country or let's talk about it.' "

The opposition leaders had learned to live within Pinochet's limits. They never ceased to oppose the regime, but opposition life settled into a predictable and comfortable routine. The people arrested, tortured, or shot in the 1980s were largely protesters, guerrillas, slum activists, or those suspected of being protesters, guerrillas, or slum activists. Life as an opposition intellectual was not a bad deal. There were good jobs as economists or sociologists in opposition think tanks financed by the Ford Foundation or the Dutch government. There were opposition coffeehouses, poetry readings, and plays. There were opposition magazines, underwritten by the Italian Christian Democrats or French Socialists, filled with brilliant, ironic essays, scathing in their analysis of the dictatorship and what it had done to Chile. The magazines and playhouses were a bargain for Pinochet, speaking only to the faithful, convincing no one. They provided a way for the opposition to let off steam without threatening the dictatorship. And in the summers all political activity stopped. "We can have a revolution in Chile, but it has to be eight hours a day with weekends and summers off," Luis Moya, a lawyer at the Chilean Human Rights Commission, told me. "No one yells, 'Okay, compañeros, now we're going on vacation for three months.' But that's how it works."

BEGINNING AROUND 1987, CHILEANS FOUND THEMSELVES ENgaged in a debate that would have seemed surreal only five years before. The debate, which spread well beyond Chile's borders, concerned the "Chilean economic miracle," a phoenix that arose from the crash of 1982. Talk of the Chilean economic miracle appeared in magazine and newspaper articles, in the pronouncements of the U.S. secretary of state, and especially in the conversations in the more exclusive neighborhoods of Chile. While in 1982 it had seemed that a dictatorship was incapable of creating a healthy economy, five years later the Chilean elite was coming to a radically different conclusion: The new Chile was modern, vibrant, in the process of leaving Latin America behind. Over long seafood lunches in the Union Club, at the gatherings of exporters and financiers at the Sheraton Hotel, men in Italian suits told each other that perhaps *only* dictatorship could create a healthy economy. Perhaps only by restricting political freedoms could economic freedoms be guaranteed. It would be indeed a shame if dictatorship were the price of the economic miracle, the conversation went. But if such sacrifices were required for the good of the country . . .

In fact, viewed in the context of the nation's past, the economic miracle was not so miraculous. Pinochet's regime had been a time of wild swings: at first a mild recession; in the late 1970s an immense, credit-led boom; the crash of 1982; and then a steady recovery. During his tenure the country's average annual rate of growth was 2.6 percent—slightly more than half the annual rate of growth during the 1960s. And this figure mainly reflected the growth of the country's "paper" companies—the financial sector. During the 1960s per capita investment had been 25 percent higher than during the dictatorship.

Still, compared with its democratic neighbors, Chile looked pretty good. In 1988 its inflation rate was 10.9 percent. In Argentina that year inflation was 370 percent, and in Peru, over 1,000 percent. Chile was growing at 5 percent a year, and the economy was diversifying.

The Chilean "miracle" was the product of an antipopulist set of policies that was certainly facilitated by dictatorship. One of Pinochet's memorable phrases summed up his social philosophy: "The rich must be treated well so they'll give more money." The idea was to encourage investment by giving business everything it asked for. At a time when many Latin American countries had not paid interest on their debts in years, Chile's technocrats were prepaying the country's debt service to increase investor confidence. The lower the wages, the fewer the number of unionized workers, the less attention paid to laws protecting workers or the environment, the better. Chile's attraction for foreign business was based in part on the misery of its people.

The economic miracle was evident in Chile's wealthy neighborhoods, with their manicured parks, new boutiques, chic hairdressing salons, European cars, and few beggars to spoil the scenery. I lived in Providencia, a neighborhood of California-style houses on quiet, clean, tree-lined streets. I could do my banking by automatic teller machine; spend Sunday afternoons lounging poolside on top of the mountain behind my house with a 360-degree view of the city; and shop at the Almac, which was as luxurious as the Safeway in Washington's Georgetown, featuring a deli counter, natural foods section, video rental club, and a photocopy machine. I could buy everything I had ever eaten in the United States—from fresh spinach fettucine to Kraft creamy cucumber salad dressing—and some things I could not find in the United States, such as milk in boxes that stayed fresh for months. The malls offered labels such as Fiorucci, Calvin Klein, and Bally. To go downtown, I could take the futuristic, hermetically clean subway, where, during the 85-degree Chilean Christmas, piped-in Muzak played "Frosty the Snowman."

But the miracle looked less miraculous to others in Chile. Every Chilean, of course, was free to come to the swimming pool on top of my mountain. It was simply a matter of paying the admission fee of two dollars, more than the daily minimum wage. Everyone was free to choose from thousands of products in my Almac. But the average housewife would buy only six: bread, tea, noodles, rice, cooking oil, and potatoes. And she would shop not in the Almac but in the corner store in her slum, which sold cooking oil on credit so she could pay a few pesos at a time.

The rich had in their grasp the silliest excesses of development: banks that reported account balances over the phone; supermarkets with photocopy machines. The notion that the fax machines, automatic tellers, and skyscrapers meant that Chile was modern, or had left the rest of Latin America behind, was the modern-day equivalent of Louis XIV's belief that his peasants were happy because Versailles was large. But Pinochet's peasants were not happy. Bank machines did not make them proud; they made them angry at the contrasts between modern Chile and the Chile in which the vast majority lived. During the first thirteen years of Pinochet's regime, consumption of the poorest 10 percent of Santiago's population dropped 30 percent, and that of the wealthiest 10 percent increased 15 percent. From 1979 to 1989, according to the Pinochet government's own statistics, the proportion of national wealth owned by the top 20 percent of the population rose from 51 to 60 percent. Chileans coming back from exile repeatedly mentioned their shock at the evaporation of the middle class and the new contrasts between rich and poor. Private hospitals boasted of their CAT scan machines while at public hospitals women with sick babies were told to wait two months for medical attention.

But in comfortable neighborhoods like mine, the wealthy did

not hear such voices. Whereas the rich of Peru and Salvador see the poor as vaguely human creatures carrying water through their streets or begging with children on their backs, in Pinochet's Chile the rich did not see the poor at all. Taking the bus to and from work each day cost a third of the minimum daily wage. Those with no jobs could not afford fifty-five cents a day to take the bus to come downtown to look for work or beg for money. They stayed in the slums.

To be born in the slums meant to live in the slums and die in the slums, giant settlements of wasted talent where nothing grew and life revolved around scraping together a few pesos to get through the day. The government spent fourteen times as much for education on each child in Providencia, my neighborhood, as on students in the slums. Of every 1,000 school-age children in Chile, only 290 began high school and 49 finished, 12 went to college and 6 finished. During Allende's years hundreds of students in the La Pincoya slum had gone to college. People could think of only one person in that neighborhood who had attended college since the coup.

A once-middle-class country was now full of teenagers who had never been to a movie or eaten a meal outside their houses. In 1988 the buying power of a worker making the minimum wage was 25 percent less than that in 1970, when Allende became president. From 1969 to 1984 the number of people in Chile who could not satisfy their basic needs doubled. The number of people whose incomes did not even cover food tripled. Not only were the poor making less, but they had fewer social programs, such as subsidized medical care, education, and housing, to soften their fall; real social spending in 1987 was 15 percent lower than in 1970.

Alcides Barros, who ate lunch each day in a soup kitchen financed by the Vicariate of Solidarity in the neighborhood of La Pincoya, was the translation into flesh and blood of all these facts and figures. The neighborhood, named for a mythological mermaid, sat at the dusty top of Santiago, at the end of Recoleta, a long road leading north from the center of the city up into the mountains. I started going to the soup kitchen to peel potatoes and talk to the members about politics and the price of cooking oil in March 1988 and went almost weekly for the next year and a half. The streets of La Pincoya in the summer were filled with yellow dust, skinny dogs, and young people hanging out on the corners. In the winter people in home-knit sweaters—the wool often obtained by unraveling an old sweater that had stretched out—went to bed early to escape the hunger and cold that penetrated the wooden walls and dirt floors of the houses they had built themselves.

Barros was fifty-five, a small, courteous man who always wore the same clean shirt and trousers and was always well shaved and groomed. He lived alone, sat by himself at lunch, and rarely spoke during the soup kitchen's organizational meetings. He had worked as a night guard in a textile factory that closed down during the recession and was now receiving a 5,000-peso-a-month pension—about $20. He spent 2,000 pesos a month on rent, 750 pesos for electricity, and 500 pesos on water. That totaled about $12.50. With the remaining 1,750 pesos—about $7.50— he bought bread and tea bags. He said that without the soup kitchen, which fed him lunch six days a week—sometimes a stew with bits of meat or chicken soup but sometimes just beans or noodles—he would eat only bread and drink tea.

THE SOUP KITCHEN WHERE I FIRST MET BARROS WAS THE ONLY organized entity in the whole of the Ultima Hora part of La Pincoya, a district renowned for its politicization under Allende and combativeness in the protests against Pinochet. But by 1987 political activity had died away in Ultima Hora.

"When we took part in the protests, we hoped that things would get better here, but nothing happened," said Julia Miranda, a resident. "Now there is nothing going on. Some things are organized, but people don't want to participate. We lack leaders and organization, and people have lost interest."

The lack of interest was obvious in my weekly visits to the soup kitchen. The Vicariate had set up its soup kitchens not only to help slum dwellers feed themselves but also to encourage neighbors to organize and perhaps to begin workshops or neighborhood committees. But this soup kitchen, at least, was a disaster. The members could hardly prepare meals without fighting. At the urging of the Vicariate's social worker, the women agreed to hold a knitting workshop; no one showed up. They had no energy for politics at all. At times Barros and the rest reminded me of Gladys Meneses. Despite the unemployment, the poverty, the hopelessness, the humiliation—or maybe because of these things— La Pincoya was quiet.

I had first become acquainted with La Pincoya on a hot Sunday in February 1988, during an afternoon of what was optimistically called a voter registration drive. The volunteers arrived two hours late. They had been waiting, said Cristóbal Durán, an earnest twenty-seven-year-old Christian Democrat, for the stacks of the comic books they would give out explaining why people should register to vote. The other two volunteers were Marcelino Colio, a Socialist, and a Communist named Ricardo Ramírez.

On the street dogs lay stretched out in the dust, people sat on the curb, and a horse-drawn cart bearing vegetables rumbled by. A radio played "Bye Bye, Love," and a small girl in a sparkling white communion dress ran past. Durán knocked at the first house. A woman answered.

"Good afternoon," he said, "we're from the Committee for Free Elections. Have you registered to vote?"

"No," she said.

"What are you waiting for?" asked Durán.

"For him to leave," she said. She did not need to say who "him" was. Durán explained that registering was a way to get him to leave. The woman shrugged. "I don't have the money for an ID card."

The government could have declared that the national ID card that all Chileans carried meant they were automatically registered to vote. Instead, it chose to start the process from scratch. Each person who wanted to vote had to first get a new ID card, which cost 390 pesos, more than a day's minimum wage, plus bus fare for two trips downtown.

We went to another house. "I don't mix in politics," said the woman who answered. "Is it true you can be arrested for registering?"

A man in jeans and an orange T-shirt said there was no point to registering because the vote was going to be a fraud, just as in 1980, when Pinochet won approval for his constitution.

A young man and woman were sitting on the curb under a tree. They said they lived in the street and had no work. "Are you interested in changing your situation?" asked Ramírez.

"Getting rid of Pinochet won't change anything," the man said. "They're all the same."

A man came out of his house in blue sweat pants. He was the first one on the block who seemed eager to talk about politics. He said he was afraid that if Pinochet lost, there would be a return to the Allende years, which he remembered as chaotic. Ramírez bit his tongue but didn't argue. The man said he had heard rumors that Pinochet's party, Avanzada Nacional, was helping people get houses if they registered to vote and signed up as party members. He was thinking about it. I met one person in the whole afternoon who had registered to vote.

At the top of La Pincoya in the foothills of the mountains was a cluster of small wooden box houses that used to be known as the Oscar Romero Camp, after the martyred archbishop of El Salvador. The Romero residents were among the poorest in the slum. They had organized a communal soup kitchen but closed it in November 1988, when Avanzada Nacional activists told residents that the party would take care of them if they signed up as members. About half the families in the camp, which then became known as Augusto Pinochet Camp, had signed up with Avanzada. Irene Pérez's family was one. "They offered us a house—not free, but they offered to help us get the paperwork going so we could get the process started in only two weeks, not three or four months," she said. I asked what she thought of Pinochet. "We don't think about Pinochet," she said. "We're not against or in favor. We just wanted a better house."

This was politics at its most basic, and it was working. One day I went with a friend to what seemed to be La Pincoya's only restaurant. The proprietress, Mercedes Hernández, was seventy-five, with a leg wrapped in bandages. She invited us into her house, sat us in her dining room, which was also her living room and kitchen and featured a large shrine to the Virgin in one corner, and served us the soup she had made for her family. "What brings you here?" she said. When I told her, she beamed. "I'm the local head of Avanzada Nacional," she said. "Is there anything you need to know?" She sat down at the table.

"We know people register for their own interest," she said. "Most people are most enthusiastic about getting their own house. So we help people with houses, and we help people get food or clothing. And of course, we provide their ID card free."

"Isn't that the government's job?" I asked.

"To tell the truth, the government doesn't work very well here. Avanzada helps by telling the government what people need." After that she showed us pictures of her son, who lived in Chicago. The system she described—government services in exchange for political loyalty—sounded like the Chicago machine. Opposing the government in Chile, of course, meant more than the risk that your garbage would be left on the sidewalk. But it didn't seem to matter to her.

SOCIAL PSYCHOLOGISTS BELIEVE THAT EVEN IN A WELL-MAINtained building, if a single window is broken and left unrepaired, people will soon break the rest of the building's windows. Philip Zimbardo, a Stanford University psychologist, conducted an experiment in which he left a car on a street in a good neighborhood in Palo Alto, California. He returned after a week; the car was intact. Then Zimbardo took a sledgehammer and smashed part of the car. When he returned a few hours later, the car had been completely looted and destroyed.

It seemed in early 1988 to be an apt metaphor for Chile. A year before the plebiscite three opposition think tanks gathered 150 poor Chileans together to hear what they thought about life under Pinochet. The young people talked about feelings of fear, frustration, and humiliation stirred up by the arbitrary raids, unemployment, and starvation wages. They felt impotence and skepticism about politics and the chance for change and had retreated to an internal, apolitical life. A country's agreement to live in democracy is a precarious contract; once broken, it is easily broken again.

A country that had once been so proud of its political culture now declined to register to vote a dictator out of office. A country that had escaped the state terror of most of the rest of Latin America was now governed by a man who had become a worldwide symbol of state terror. Yet what most citizens wanted from Pinochet was a shortcut through the housing bureacracy and a bowl of potato soup. Chile, once the symbol of law in Latin America, had learned to live as a symbol of state violence. The ease with which its citizens made this adjustment is not just a paradox. It is also a warning.

The crudest justification I heard in Chile was known as the omelet rationale after the saying "If you want to make an omelet, you have to break some eggs." This was Roger Beltrán's reasoning and that of the Argentine military. The greatest threat to human rights, it maintained, was communism. To save the country from it, drastic measures were required. If in the course of this effort the soldiers of truth were called on to commit certain indelicacies, well, freedom had its price. This was war. In a war people die.

"You've heard the joke about the vultures," said Hermógenes Pérez de Arce. "After the coup the junta's biggest supporters were the vultures because there were so many cadavers in the street." Pérez de Arce, a lawyer in his early fifties, was not an officer of the Human Rights Commission. He did not tell me the vulture joke to illustrate his rejection of the regime's brutality. In fact, he was not much bothered by the deaths or by torture. He was an adviser to the regime, a member of its Legislative Commission—what passed for Congress—and its untiring defender on the editorial page of *El Mercurio*.

"Torture is not something new to Chile," he said. "You see it more because people are looking harder. But it's also true that people on the left invent torture for political purposes. They may say, 'I was tortured,' but they don't let a doctor examine them. And people are so sensitive about the subject that any claim makes it to the papers. Our adversaries are not the same as in Europe. They are less civilized. You've always had torture when you've had subversion. It's a shame, but that's the way it is."

The government was fond of the omelet rationale. In 1985 the Inter-American Commission on Human Rights issued a report charging the Pinochet regime with grave violations. The government replied: "It is essentially the persistent and serious nature of terrorist activity that constitutes the greatest obstacle to the restoration of democracy in Chile. . . . It is precisely for this reason that exceptional measures must be applied, so that the Executive Power may have the legal tools necessary to combat this aggression and to carry out its essential duty to maintain public order and security. . . . The commission of some excesses on the part of the security forces is a regrettable, but inevitable, consequence of this situation."

"Oh, those were sad days, black days," Pinochet said, reminiscing about the Allende years in a speech in 1981. "But it was necessary to draw on all the reserves of patriotism and the intervention of the armed forces to stop the fall into the abyss."

But the omelet rationale was not convincing enough in a country with Chile's civic history. Chileans needed another idea. The disappeared were not disappeared, said government officials; they had merely left the country or joined the guerrillas. Never mind that the bodies of some who had supposedly left the country later turned up in mass graves. Never mind that former torturers had confessed, that solid evidence existed that the security forces tortured and kept torturing right up to the end of the dictatorship.

In 1988 María Paz Santibáñez, a piano student taking part in a peaceful march—she was one of the students who had pulled me by the hand as we ran mindlessly through the night—was shot in the head by a carabinero at a distance of two meters. The event was captured on video. Interior Minister Sergio Fernández offered the following version to the press: "A small number of people trying to cause agitation and disorder destroyed public and private property, and the most unfortunate part is that they provoked a traffic policeman, forcing him to use his weapon, accidentally wounding a demonstrator." Santibáñez was charged with aggression against a carabinero, and police were placed by her hospital bed to ensure she could not escape.

This was not just official-speak from official spokesmen. Over and over I heard the firm conviction from Pinochet's supporters that the government—obviously a civilized government, since they supported it—was incapable of committing uncivilized crimes. If Chileans had been more like Roger Beltrán, more people would have seen the human rights violations as a necessary price for clean streets and cheap television sets. But many Chileans, too cultured, too refined to confront the issue, were left only with denial.

Even as the protests had brought the human rights violations into plain view, I still met Chileans who maintained that torture and political murder did not happen. "The human rights problem in this country has been greatly exaggerated," said Patricia Matte, a social worker in charge of the government's Extreme Poverty programs. A member of one of Chile's wealthiest families, she has a graduate degree from the University of Chicago. Referring to Rojas and Quintana, the burned students, she said, "I know both young people belonged to extremist movements, we have proof. I think the burning is as strategic as the killing of Benigno Aquino: Isn't it suspicious that his wife is president two years later, and we still don't know who killed him?"

"It's unbelievable that men would cut people's throats," said Fernando Léniz, when I talked to him in his office in 1986. Léniz was a former chairman of the board of *El Mercurio* and served as Pinochet's economics minister. He was referring to a famous case of three Communist leaders found with their throats slit in 1985, and he was using "unbelievable" literally; he didn't believe it. "It's so foreign to our habits. You see these things in other areas of the world where violence is common, but it was never common here. The kids who were burned— were they burned by soldiers? How do we know that they weren't burned by people disguised as soldiers? The Leftist Revolutionary Movement openly confesses that it uses violence as an instrument. But the government is responsible for law and order. The government does not kill innocent people on purpose. I must believe that.

"I must believe that," he repeated. Léniz was a thoughtful man. By the mid-eighties he had begun to think that Pinochet had stayed in office too long, and he had helped form the National Accord, a group of centrist anti-Pinochet parties. Was he telling me what he believed or what he wanted to believe? He was watching me very intensely as he talked. There was something in his gaze that said, "I am not as convinced as I once was." But I blinked, and it was gone.

The day after my first tear gassing I went to see Miguel Schweitzer, a jovial and likable lawyer who had been Pinochet's foreign minister. "The demonstrators were only singing the national anthem," I said. "Why did the police have to tear-gas them?"

"It was a preventive move," he replied. We were sitting in Schweitzer's office, on the eighth floor of a downtown building, and even with the windows closed I could hear the sirens as the police carried out yet another preventive move. I tilted my head to indicate the sirens, and Schweitzer laughed. "I don't even hear it anymore," he said.

"Some excesses might occur, but what you have been told about human rights is exaggerated and doesn't happen in Chile," he said. "Normal life goes on here under the standards of any civilized society."

Schweitzer himself seemed very civilized. He spoke perfect English with a British accent and had lived abroad for many years. He loved the opera and skiing. Miguel Schweitzer, Patricia Matte, and Fernando Léniz and their like-minded upper-class friends were at home in Paris or San Francisco, charming, educated, refined. It startled me how comfortable I felt with these people, how much they reminded me of well-bred people back in the States.

I had come to Chile thinking that if only Chileans could become more like North Americans or Europeans—in a culturally sensitive way, of course—future Pinochets could be prevented. I was wrong. Sophistication was not the solution; it was the problem. The more cultured the Chileans were, the more willing they appeared to be to blind themselves to what was going on around them.

Many Chileans were exasperated by what they saw as foreign visitors' unreasonable fixation on human rights. "Most people in the United States are obsessed with it," Sergio Reiss, a wealthy lawyer, told me in 1987. "Well, people here don't really care. They care about the economy. When things are good, they like Pinochet. When they are bad, they don't. I've seen surveys that show that people's first concern is a job, next is a good salary, and then, third, human rights."

Reiss was, if anything, too generous. A poll by the research group FLACSO in 1985 asked Chileans to rank their country's problems in terms of their importance. "Economic problems" came first, of course, then "Lack of work." "Human rights, torture" was not third, but eleventh of the twelve possible responses, cited by a mere 2 percent of those polled. It came well after "Terrorism," and even after "Lack of communication" and "Moral crisis."

The results of the FLACSO poll were repeated time and again. In 1984, when Pinochet imposed the state of siege in response to the protests, Radio Cooperativa, the most important voice of the opposition, conducted a poll. "The pollster called me afterward and said, 'You're not going to believe this. Sixty percent of

the people were in favor of Pinochet's move,' " Guillermo Mu-
ñoz, Cooperativa's director, told me. "I didn't believe it. We
redid the poll twice, and it came out the same. People said that
during the state of siege there aren't any protests, and when there's
a protest, it's like being in a war, and my grandmother nearly
choked on tear gas, and you can't sleep at night there's so much
noise."

During the strike of 1986 complete reports of the protests and
the deaths came out in *El Mercurio* and on the television news.
At first I wondered why the progovernment media chose to pub-
licize the fact that troops had killed seven unarmed demonstrators.
The answer lay in Radio Cooperativa's poll. To many Chileans
it was of secondary importance that the demonstrators did not
merely die, but were killed by soldiers. If there had been no
protest, the thinking went, they would not have died. It was the
opposition's fault. It was a form of the collective amnesia that
affected Medellín: Violence simply occurs. When Pinochet imposed a state of siege that ended the protests, he was saving lives.
When he overthrew an elected president and bombed La Moneda, he was saving Chilean democracy. Chile had come full
circle; Pinochet had become the solution to Chile's poverty, not
its cause, the guarantor of Chileans' security, not the reason for
their terror. It was the relationship of the jailer and the prisoner,
so grateful to the jailer for a kind word or a piece of bread thrown
into the cell.

In *One Hundred Years of Solitude* García Márquez writes of
the Buendía family's tendency to fall in love with brothers and
cousins, producing children born with the tail of a pig. The fable's
horror goes deeper than the tragedy of a deformed child. It is
more primordial: the shock to the parents of realizing that they
themselves are less than human, realizing the horror of what
their own bodies could produce. Chile, once so proud, the country of afternoon tea and habeas corpus, had produced a Pinochet.
The Chilean body politic had given birth to a child with a pig's
tail.

BEFORE THE 1988 PLEBISCITE, IN WHICH CHILEANS WOULD SAY *sí*
or *no* to the idea of free elections, Pinochet went to Valparaíso

to campaign. Valparaíso is Chile's second-largest city, a haunt-ingly beautiful port of blue Pacific, fishing boats, gulls, and wooden houses once brightly colored but now faded and peeling, nestled precariously into hills so steep that wooden trains creak up the sides to carry people home. Valparaíso suffered from high unemployment, and Pinochet, as part of his campaign, had decided to construct a new Congress Building there, three times the size of the existing one in Santiago, at a cost of forty million dollars. Other countries as well had experimented with decentralization—the Brazilians moving their capital to Brasília, for example—but to move only those parts that challenged pres-idential power was an inspired variation. Today Congress in Val-paraíso; tomorrow the Supreme Court in Tierra del Fuego.

It was a sunny noon when Pinochet arrived at the main plaza to sign the law making the move official. About two thousand people had gathered for the occasion. I asked one woman who had been bussed in from one of Mrs. Pinochet's mothers' centers why the president was here today. "I don't know," she said. She was wearing a sticker that said "FNI." She didn't know what it stood for. "I wonder if I can take it off," she said anxiously. "I'm a mother of four children. . . ."

A man giving out the stickers came over. "It's the National Independent Front," he said. "It means we're independent, but we support President Pinochet because he's freed us from com-munism."

It was a cheerful event. Taped songs such as "Let's Go Forward, Pinochet" alternated with numbers played by a marching band. A huge red, white, and blue plastic Sí perched on the top of the platform's backdrop, just in case anyone forgot. Pinochet, in a white military uniform, sat with his ever-smiling wife, Lucía, who gave queenly waves to people in the crowd. They looked alike, the Pinochets, the twinkling grandparents, both grown a little round with the years. Pinochet read his speech in a high, nasal whine. He ran quickly through the historic aspect of moving the Congress, a potentially awkward subject because there was no Congress; he had abolished it in 1973. The larger theme was that Valparaíso could enjoy another advance from the govern-ment that cared. "We don't sell false promises and illusions," he said. "We continue to progress. . . . We don't fool people with politicking and demagoguery." Me or chaos.

Promising Valparaíso a new Congress was something different; the usual currency of Pinochet's campaign was more tangible goods. In 1987 Pinochet and his ministers cut ribbons on thirty thousand homes, most of them in the four-story square apartment buildings that dotted Chile's neighborhoods—modest, small apartments but with electricity and plumbing. A poll showed that "housing construction" was the only department where Chileans gave Pinochet high marks, testimony not to the government's dedication to housing—new housing construction was lower per capita under Pinochet than under Frei or Allende—but to the government's dedication to publicizing each new house. Pinochet flew around the country, giving out bicycles, forgiving mortgage debts, raising pensions, and, to make sure Chileans could be informed of his magnanimity, lowering the tariffs on imported television sets. "The opposition makes these grand speeches about democracy, but people don't really care about politics," said Andrés Sáiz, a young press adviser to Pinochet. "They want a nice house, nice things, a quiet life."

In associating the opposition with chaos, the regime's most important allies were the Leftist Revolutionary Movement and the Manuel Rodríguez Patriotic Front, which continued to bomb banks and kidnap military officials. The political opposition to Pinochet—with the important exception of the Communists, who continued to hold that "all forms of struggle" were legitimate against a dictatorship—condemned the violence, but Pinochet employed it to tar the whole opposition. The guerrillas' actions seemed so pointless and were so useful to Pinochet—killing a carabinero who played the flute in the carabinero orchestra, for example—that many Chileans believed that some of the smaller fringe groups had been created or were run by agents of the government—or at the least that many of the bombs that blew up had not been planted by the guerrillas at all. A friend of mine, driving by the headquarters of the secret police on the day of a protest, watched as young people wearing bandannas around their faces that said "Socialist Youth" or "Christian Democrats" spilled out of the building and began to destroy cars parked nearby.

In La Reina, a wealthy neighborhood, people traveling in a truck that had been seen the day before at the Sí campaign headquarters knocked on doors and introduced themselves as members of the Communist party. They informed startled residents that if the No won, their houses would be expropriated, wished them good afternoon, and left. In the small town of Rengo, the central plaza one morning was carpeted with pamphlets that read: "We are the Christian Democrats and the Communists. We want to go back to the supply and price boards, bread lines, shortages, and agrarian reform, and we will abolish all private schools. We want foreign intervention to continue and to keep receiving money and orders from the Department of State and the KGB, and arms from Comrade Fidel. Join the crusade to destroy the country and return to the beautiful and unforgettable days of the Allende government." The pamphlet was comical in its crudity; the thought crossed my mind that it had perhaps been written by the opposition after all.

Subtle it was not, but at least the *Sí* campaign was an honest representation of the Pinochet government. It was the perfect reflection of the regime it sought to perpetuate. It was the continuation of an enormously successful fifteen-year effort that first terrorized Chileans, next bought their favor, then traded on the very Chilean need for stability and order. And it won the support of more than two in five voters.

In the end, however, Pinochet could not overcome four centuries of history. The only country in the world to come to Marxism through elections became the only country in the world to vote a dictator out of office without his permission. After having used Chile's love of the institutional solution to keep himself in power for so long, Pinochet seemed unable to conceive of the possibility that if he gave Chile a "legal" way to end his rule, Chile might actually use it.

In the months before the plebiscite the opposition—for once —did everything right. The parties suddenly forgot their differences, and the party leaders curbed their egos to create a single organization for the No. Its head was Patricio Aylwin, a seventy-year-old Christian Democrat who had been Senate president during the coup. Opposition technicians, advised by international experts, built fraudproof computer networks to track the vote count. For fifteen years the anti-Pinochet television producers had been shut out of the TV channels and exiled to the world of commercial advertising, and as they applied their skills to politics for the first time, they proved to be masterful. The ads, with their attractive young Chileans running through fields, had the slickness, catchy songs, and upbeat feel of yogurt commercials, but they hit Pinochet hard on issues that mattered to Chile: public health; salaries; education. And they countered Pinochet's charges of chaos not with countercharges but by presenting a positive vision of a united Chile with room for all.

The apathy I had witnessed dissolved as rapidly as it had when the protests first started in 1983. People began to see that they would not be punished for registering, that millions of Chileans were doing the same, and that this time politics could make a difference. A week before the plebiscite 1.2 million people—a tenth of the population of Chile—gathered on the Pan-American Highway outside Santiago for a No rally, the largest political rally in the country's history.

Pinochet seemed not to notice. He had commissioned polls, of course, and being a dictator, he was brought the results he wanted. His pollsters may or may not have believed them; but Pinochet apparently did, and so he let the electoral process continue. And on the day of the plebiscite 92 percent of those eligible voted, waiting in long lines in the broiling heat.

As the votes were being counted, the official newspaper, La Nación, was printing a hundred thousand copies with headlines awarding the Sí 51.3 percent of the vote. It quoted Mrs. Pinochet: "We showed the world that we are a democratic country and that only we decide our future." As the night wore on, the mood in the opposition headquarters was a mix of euphoria, as spokesmen announced growing vote totals confirming an opposition victory, and anxiety. Hour after hour went by, and still the government press spokesman insisted the votes were not yet counted. What was going on? Pinochet called his supporters into the street to "celebrate." The TV channels broadcast interview after interview with confident government officials. Only at one-thirty in the morning, when one of the junta's own generals paused while entering La Moneda to tell the assembled TV cameras that it was clear to him that the No had won, did the government acknowledge that Pinochet had lost. His bid for eight more years in office was endorsed by 44 percent of the voters, while 56 percent voted to hold free elections in 1989. Mrs. Pinochet had turned out to be a prophet.

The general who had ruled his country for fifteen years with an iron fist had called the election and designed the rules. He was the only candidate. He enjoyed the resources of the national treasury, the television channels, the military, and the secret police. He had changed his image, handing out bicycles and patting babies and smiling like Grandpa at Christmas. And he lost. He tried to stage a self-coup and was blocked by one of his own generals.

A year later Pinochet was still in office, presiding over his own demise, a lame-duck dictator. He made threatening noises and nobody listened; even his own partisans treated him like a drunken uncle. He had become a disgrace to dictators everywhere.

As the free elections of 1989 approached, Chile was back to its hyperpolitical self. The television channels showed little else but political talk shows, with endless permutations of presidential and congressional candidates. On weekends the streets were filled with caravans, cars with horns blaring and young people spilling out, waving banners and balloons and throwing flyers. Children went to kindergarten wearing the T-shirts and visors of their candidate.

Pinochet's candidate, the forty-year old *Chicago Boy* and Finance Minister Hernán Büchi, lost to Aylwin. Aylwin was the very essence of the traditional Chilean politician, a sober, rather gray man of the center. Using the slogan "No more enemies," he won the support of parties from the old right to the Leftist Revolutionary Movement. Even the advertising of the Communist congressional candidates carried the line "Aylwin for president."

Politics was back, and Jaime Pérez was a happy man. On the day of the plebiscite he had set out early to drive around the city, sleeping bag in the car, just like old times. In his new office in the back of his store, pictures of his four children shared wall space with photos of Pérez with Aylwin. He was now the organizational secretary of the national Retail Business Association and still active in the Socialist party.

Compromise and negotiation were his new style. "If only Allende had negotiated with the right and the United States, the problems could have been avoided. You have to have everyone at the table. It's better to have a conversation than a demonstration." One reason he was working for Aylwin, he said, was that Aylwin knew the importance of compromise. "There won't be chaos," he said. "We'll be working together. Democracy is more than just having congressmen. It means a responsibility to reach agreements and hold to them. In the past I was a purist. But now I think politics is the art of the possible."

Some people in his party, he said, had talked to him about running for Congress. He had decided not to, but politics still occupied most of his spare time. He would be attending a Socialist party dinner that night, he said, and the next day a meeting between Retail Business Association officials and Communist leaders. All the candidates were coming to speak to the association. As we talked, his phone rang with more invitations to political events.

During the course of the campaign I saw Jaime Pérez from time to time at speeches or political meetings, sitting on the podium or in the first rows of the public with other dignitaries. Once I saw him walking into a packed hall with Aylwin, buried in the crush of people pressing in to shake hands with the candidate, Pérez blinking in the glare of the TV lights, just one more face in the crowd.

SELECTED BIBLIOGRAPHY

GENERAL

ARRIAGADA HERRERA, GENARO. *El Pensamiento Político de los Militares (Estudios Sobre Chile, Argentina, Brasil y Uruguay)*. Santiago: Centro de Investigaciones Socioeconomicas (CISEC), no date.

BARRY, TOM, and DEB PREUSCH. *The Central American Fact Book*. New York: Grove Press, Inc., 1986.

BERTRAND, LOUIS, and SIR CHARLES PETRIE. *The History of Spain: From the Musulmans to Franco*. New York: Collier Books, 1971.

DECKER, CARLOS G. *La Iglesia: Una Mirada a Su Historia*. Santiago: Instituto Catequisis, 1984.

DIAMOND, LARRY; JUAN J. LINZ; and SEYMOUR MARTIN LIPSET, eds. *Democracy in Developing Countries, Vol. IV, Latin America*. Boulder, Colo.: Lynne Rienner Publishers, 1989.

DUNKERLEY, JAMES. *Power in the Isthmus: A Political History of Modern Central America*. London: Verso, 1988.

HARRISON, LAWRENCE E. *Underdevelopment Is a State of Mind: The Latin American Case*. Cambridge, Mass.: Madison Books, Center for International Affairs, Harvard University, 1985.

LAFEBER, WALTER. *Inevitable Revolutions: The United States in Central America*. New York: W. W. Norton & Co., 1984.

LINZ, JUAN J., and ALFRED STEPAN, eds. *The Breakdown of Democratic Regimes: Latin America*. Baltimore: Johns Hopkins University Press, 1978.

NOVAK, MICHAEL, and MICHAEL P. JACKSON, eds. *Latin America: Dependency or Interdependence?* Washington, D.C.: American Enterprise Institute for Public Policy Research, 1985.

SECCO ELLAURI, OSCAR, and PEDRO DANIEL BARIDÓN. *Historia Universal: Epoca Moderna*. Buenos Aires: Editorial Kapelusz, 1972.

U.S. Department of State. *Country Reports on Human Rights Practices for 1983*. Report Submitted to the Committee on Foreign Relations, U.S. Senate, and Committee on Foreign Affairs, U.S. House of Representatives. Washington, D.C.: U.S. Government Printing Office, 1984.

———. *Country Reports on Human Rights Practices for 1984*. Report Submitted to the Committee on Foreign Relations, U.S. Senate, and Committee on Foreign Affairs, U.S. House of Representatives. Washington, D.C.: U.S. Government Printing Office, 1985.

———. *Country Reports on Human Rights Practices for 1985*. Report Submitted to the Committee on Foreign Relations, U.S. Senate, and Committee on Foreign Affairs, U.S. House of Representatives. Washington, D.C.: U.S. Government Printing Office, 1986.

COLOMBIA

Americas Watch Committee. *The Killings in Colombia*. New York, 1989.

COLLAZOS, OSCAR. *Tal Como el Fuego Fatuo*. Barcelona: Plaza & Janes Editores, S.A., 1986.

DONADIO, ALBERTO. *Banqueros en el Banquillo*. Bogotá: El Ancora Editores, 1983.

EDDY, PAUL; HUGO SABOGAL; and SARA WALDEN. *The Cocaine Wars: Murder, Money, Corruption and the World's Most Valuable Commodity*. New York; W. W. Norton & Co., 1988.

GUGLIOTTA, GUY, and JEFF LEEN. *Kings of Cocaine: Inside the Medellín Cartel*. New York: Simon & Schuster, 1989.

GUZMÁN CAMPOS, HERMÁN; ORLANDO FALS BORDA; and EDUARDO UMAÑA LUNA. *La Violencia en Colombia*. Bogotá: Carlos Valencia Editores, 1986.

OQUIST, PAUL. *Violencia, Conflicto y Política en Colombia*. Bogotá: Instituto de Estudios Colombianos, 1978.

SÁNCHEZ, GONZALO, ed. *Once Ensayos Sobre la Violencia*. Bogotá: Centro Gaitán, Centro Editorial CEREC, 1985.

Universidad Nacional de Colombia. *Colombia: Violencia y Democracia*. Bogotá: Colciencias, 1988.

ARGENTINA

Americas Watch Committee. *Truth and Partial Justice in Argentina*. New York: 1987.

Argentine National Commission on the Disappeared. *Nunca Más*. New York: Farrar, Straus & Giroux, 1986.

Asamblea Permanente por los Derechos Humanos. *Las Cifras de la Guerra Sucia*. Buenos Aires: 1988.

Asociación Patriótica Argentina. *La Argentina y Sus Derechos Humanos*. Buenos Aires: Asociacíon Patriótica Argentina, no date.

BONAFINI, HEBE DE. *Historias de Vida*. Buenos Aires: Fraterna/Del Nuevo Extremo, 1985.

BONASSO, MIGUEL. *Recuerdo de la Muerte*. Mexico City: Ediciones Era, 1984.

DÍAZ BESSONE, RAMÓN GENARO. *Guerra Revolucionaria en la Argentina (1959–1978)*. Buenos Aires: Circulo Militar, 1988.

FONTANA, ANDRÉS. *Fuerzas Armadas, Partidos Políticos y Transicíon a la Democracia en Argentina*. Buenos Aires: El Centro de Estudios de Estado y Sociedad (Cedes), 1984.

GASPARINI, JUAN. *La Pista Suiza*. Buenos Aires: Editorial Legasa, 1986.

GILLESPIE, RICHARD. *Soldados de Perón: Los Montoneros*. Buenos Aires: Grijalbo, 1987.

GÓMEZ, OSCAR, ed. *El Libro del Diario del Juicio*. Buenos Aires: Editorial Perfil, 1985.

GUEST, IAIN. *Behind the Disappearances: Argentina's Dirty War Against Human Rights and the United Nations*. Philadelphia: University of Pennsylvania Press, 1990.

GUISSANI, PABLO. *Montoneros: La Soberbia Armada*. Buenos Aires: Editorial Sudamericana Planeta, 1984.

LANGGUTH, A. J. *Hidden Terrors*. New York: Pantheon Books, 1978.

LÓPEZ, ERNESTO. *El Ultimo Levantamiento*. Buenos Aires: Editorial Legasa, no date.

MIGNONE, EMILO F. *Witness to the Truth: The Complicity of Church and Dictatorship in Argentina, 1976–1983*. New York: Orbis Books, 1988.

MIGUENS, JOSÉ ENRIQUE. *Honor Militar, Violencia Terrorista y Conciencia Moral*. Buenos Aires: Editorial Sudamericana/ Planeta, 1986.

PAOLETTI, ALIPIO. *Como los Nazis, Como en Vietnam*. Buenos Aires: Editorial Contrapunto, 1987.

PIÑERO, MARÍA TERESA, ed. *Culpables para la Sociedad: Impunes por la Ley*. Buenos Aires: Abuelas de la Plaza de Mayo et al., 1988.

TAYLOR, J. M. *Eva Perón: The Myths of a Woman*. Chicago: University of Chicago Press, 1979.

TIMERMAN, JACOBO. *Prisoner Without a Name, Cell Without a Number*. New York: Alfred A. Knopf, Inc., 1981.

WASMAN, CARLOS H. *Reversal of Development in Argentina: Postwar*

Counterrevolutionary Policies and Their Structural Consequences.
Princeton, N.J.: Princeton University Press, 1987.

PERU

Americas Watch Committee. *In Desperate Straits: Human Rights in Peru After a Decade of Democracy and Insurgency.* New York: 1990.

Comisión Especial del Senado Sobre las Causas de la Violencia y Alternativas de Pacificacion en el Peru. *Violencia y Pacificacion.* Lima: Desco/Comisión Andina de Juristas, 1989.

Comisión Investigadora del Congreso. *Informe al Congreso sobre los Sucesos de los Penales.* Lima: 1988.

Comite Central del Partido Comunista del Peru. *Entrevista al Presidente Gonzalo.* Ediciones Bandera Roja, 1989.

DEGREGORI, CARLOS IVÁN. *Ayacucho 1969–1979: El Surgimiento de Sendero Luminoso; Del Movimiento por la Gratuidad de la Enseñanza al Inicio de la Lucha Armada.* Lima: Instituto de Estudios Peruanos, 1990.

———. *Sendero Luminoso,* Vol. I, *Los Hondos y Mortales Desencuentros,* Vol. II, *Lucha Armada y Utopia Autoritaria.* Lima: Instituto de Estudios Peruanos, 1989.

FAVRE, HENRI. *Peru: Sendero Luminoso y Horizontes Ocultos.* México City: Universidad Nacional Autonoma de Mexico, 1987.

GARCÍA-SAYÁN, DIEGO, ed. *Coca, Cocaína y Narcotráfico: Laberinto en los Andes.* Lima: Comisión Andina de Juristas, 1989.

MAO TSE-TUNG. *Quotations from Chairman Mao Tse-tung.* Peking: Foreign Language Press, 1977.

McCORMICK, GORDON H. *The Shining Path and the Future of Peru.* Santa Monica, Calif.: Rand Corporation, 1990.

SIMÓN MUNARO, YEHUDE. *Estado y Guerrillas en el Peru de los '80.* Lima: Asociación Instituto de Estudios Estrategicos y Sociales, 1988.

WIENER, RAUL F., ed. *Guerra e Ideología: Debate Entre el Pum y Sendero.* Lima: Ediciones Amauta, 1989.

EL SALVADOR

ARIAS PEÑATE, SALVADOR. *Los Subsistemas de Agroexportación en El Salvador: El Café, el Algodón, y el Azúcar.* San Salvador: UCA-Editores, 1988.

BARRY, TOM, and DEB PREUSCH. *The Soft War: The Uses and Abuses of U.S. Economic Aid in Central America.* New York: Grove Press, Inc., 1988.

BONNER, RAYMOND. *Weakness and Deceit: U.S. Policy and El Salvador.* New York: Times Books, 1984.

DURHAM, WILLIAM H. *Scarcity and Survival in Central America: Ecological Origins of the Soccer War.* Stanford, Calif.: Stanford University Press, 1979.

Lawyers Committee for International Human Rights. *El Salvador: Human Rights Dismissed—a Report on 16 Unresolved Cases.* New York: 1986.

———. *Underwriting Injustice: A.I.D. and El Salvador's Judicial Reform Program.* New York: 1989.

McCLINTOCK, MICHAEL. *The American Connection,* Vol. I, *State Terror and Popular Resistance in El Salvador.* London: Zed Books, Ltd., 1985.

MONTES, SEGUNDO. *El Agro Salvadoreño (1973–1980).* San Salvador: UCA-Editores, 1986.

———. *El Salvador: Las Fuerzas Sociales en la Presente Coyuntura (Enero 1980 a diciembre 1983).* San Salvador: Universidad Centroamericano José Simeon Cañas, 1984.

NICARAGUA

Americas Watch Committee. *Human Rights in Nicaragua: August 1987–August 1988.* New York, 1988.

BOOTH, JOHN A. *The End and the Beginning: The Nicaraguan Revolution.* Boulder, Colo.: Westview Press, 1985.

CARRIÓN MONTOYA, LUIS. *Memoria de Chiltepe.* Managua: Editorial Nueva Nicaragua-Midinra, 1987.

CLOSE, DAVID. *Nicaragua: Politics, Economics and Society.* London: Pinter Publishers, Ltd., 1988.

COLBURN, FORREST D. *Post-Revolutionary Nicaragua: State, Class, and the Dilemmas of Agrarian Policy.* Berkeley: University of California Press, 1986.

CRAWLEY, EDUARDO. *Dictators Never Die: A Portrait of Nicaragua and the Somoza Dynasty.* New York: St. Martin's Press, 1979.

Lawyers Committee for International Human Rights. *Nicaragua: Revolutionary Justice—A Report on Human Rights and the Judicial System.* New York: 1985.

MILLET, RICHARD. *Guardians of the Dynasty.* New York: Orbis Books, 1977.

Nicaraguan Permanent Commission on Human Rights. *A Second Look at the Electoral Process in Nicaragua.* Managua: 1990.

PAYNE, DOUGLAS W. *The Democratic Mask: The Consolidation of the Sandinista Revolution.* New York: Freedom House, 1985.

RUDOLPH, JAMES D., ed. *Nicaragua: A Country Study.* U.S. Government as Represented by the Secretary of the Army. Washington, D.C.: 1982. (The American University Foreign Area Studies Program. Area Handbook Series.)

STAHLER-SHOLK, RICHARD, and others. *La Política Económica en Nicaragua 1979–88.* Managua: Coordinadora Regional de Investigaciones Economicas y Sociales, 1989.

WALKER, THOMAS W. *Nicaragua: The Land of Sandino.* Boulder, Colo.: Westview Press, 1981.

CHILE

CHAVKIN, SAMUEL. *Storm over Chile: The Junta Under Siege.* Westport, Conn.: Lawrence Hill & Co., 1985.

EDWARDS, ALBERTO. *La Fronda Aristocrática en Chile.* Santiago: Editorial Universitária, 1982.

PINOCHET, AUGUSTO. *Pinochet: Patria y Democracia.* Santiago: Editorial Andrés Bello 1983.

POLITZER, PATRICIA. *Fear in Chile: Lives Under Pinochet.* New York: Pantheon Books, 1989.

VERDUGO, PATRICIA. *Los Zarpazos del Puma.* Santiago: CESOC Ediciones ChileAmérica, 1982.